LESS COMPETITIVE COLLEGE GRANTS & LOANS

UPDATED & EXPANDED 2ND EDITION

STUDENT COLLEGE AID PUBLISHING DIVISION
7950 N. STADIUM DRIVE # 229
HOUSTON, TEXAS 77030

Editorial, Mail Order, Book Club correspondence to:
Student College Aid
7950 N. Stadium Drive #229
Houston, TX 77030
800-245-5137

Bookstore inquiries to:
Login Publications Consortium
Ben Woodworth
312-939-0959

FORWARD

In searching for awards the idea is to find those awards that are less competitive. Your odds for getting money from these awards are therefore greater. The title of the book comes about because less people know of these awards and still less qualify. Still fewer students are eligible to apply for these awards, since the student must normally be a resident of the respective area or have a particular college major. Students in a particular state do not have to compete with all of the USA for these awards. So if you qualify, apply.

Most students are overlooking these preferential sources of college grants, money that does not have to be repaid. These sources are not found in usual source books and private foundations don't publicize. You should not expect someone else to tell you about these awards. Be your own advocate. There is no one as interested in your education as you are. Find your appropriate awards in this book. The most important step in securing a college award is to apply, apply, apply.

In the main you will qualify to apply for these awards by your place of residence or your anticipated college major(s). This makes finding your sources easy. But don't forget, if you get turned down, apply again the next application period. Persistence pays off.

What's in the book? Inside are private foundations we found that give money to college students or college bound high school graduates. Some awards are for a few hundred dollars; others are for thousands. The student should take their time, look through the entire book at first, making notes as you go.

This book gives the name of the award, what is required to qualify, how and when to apply, and name and address of your contact.

What's the most important step in getting a college award? You must apply! But where to apply? Apply where there is less competition and more favoritism. On many of these awards only residents of specific states will be awarded!

The updating of our books are done by phone or fax in order to get to print as soon as possible and not allow information to become outdated. The listings that have no electronic contact and carry the caution of not being extant can be written, but wait no longer than 3 weeks for a reply. In all inquiries include SASE (self addressed stamped envelope).

TABLE OF CONTENTS

"HOW TO OBTAIN MAXIMUM COLLEGE FINANCIAL AID"
NEW UPDATED 4TH EDITION
for 95-96 school year

You may think everyone in the financial aid loop is working for you to receive your maximum awards. Such Is not the case! The financial aid counselor's job is to make sure you don't get too much money. Your job is to make sure you get the maximum amount due you. To do this you must know how the answers to the questions on the Financial Aid Form impact your awards. This information is in readable form in this book.

* college financial aid is an involved process. This book makes the steps clear and understandable.
* the book clarifies the questions on the financial aid form.
* the book shows with sample situations how the answers to the questions on the form impact the amount of your award. This understanding allows the student and/or family to arrange their assets and income in such a way as to maximize their awards.
* the book introduces the reader to different categories of governmental awards.
* see how to finance correspondence courses * remedial courses * foreign study
* if this book doesn't answer your questions, it tells you where to get the answers.
* you can substitute state grants for some federal loans.
* use the new loan repayment plans to avoid defaulting.
* choose a trade school properly.
* have maximally assured employment after graduation.
* locate non-governmental loaning sources
* see how institutions prevent sexual assault

ORDER FROM YOUR BOOKSTORE or

Student College Aid, 7950 N. Stadium Dr. #229 · Houston, TX 77030
(800) 245-5137 * (713) 796-2209 · FAX (713) 796-9963

ISBN 0-932495-09-5   5 1/2 X 8 1/2 PAPERBACK 200 PAGES $12.95

ALASKA

FOUNDATION: Alaska Commission on Post-Secondary Education
REQUISITE: Scholarships granted to residents of Alaska. Scholarships awarded to encourage outstanding high school seniors & undergraduate students to pursue teaching careers at the elementary or secondary levels. USA citizen or legal resident.
APPLICATION: Write for info. Application deadline is May 30th.
CONTACT: POBOX FP, 400 Willoughby, Juneau, AK 99811. (907)465-2854

FOUNDATION: Goldstein Scottish Rite Trust
REQUISITE: Scholarships to needy high school graduates of Juneau, AK.
APPLICATION: Write for info. Application deadline is May 1st.
CONTACT: James H. Taylor, 4365 N. Douglass Rd., Juneau, AK 99801.
TEL: (907)586-2849

FOUNDATION: Arctic Education Foundation
REQUISITE: Scholarships for shareholder and children of shareholders of Arctic Slope Regional Corporation. These scholarships are for use in obtaining a two or four year degree. You must have already been accepted to an institution before you apply.
APPLICATION: Applications are accepted throughout the year.
CONTACT: Flossie Andersen, POB 129, Barrow 99723. (907)852-8633

FOUNDATION: Alaska State Council on the Arts
REQUISITE: Scholarships granted to experienced professional artists to assist them in creating new work.
APPLICATION: Write for info. Application deadlines is 10/16.
CONTACT: 619 Warehouse Ave., #220, Anchorage, AK 99501.
Tel: (907)269-6610

ALABAMA

FOUNDATION: James M. Hoffman Scholarship Trust
REQUISITE: Scholarships awarded to high school or preparatory school graduates in Calhoun County, AL.
APPLICATION: Write for info. Deadline March.
CONTACT: c/o S. Trust Bank of Calhoun County, N.A., POB 1000, Anniston, AL 36202. (205)238-1000

FOUNDATION: E.L. Gibson Foundation
REQUISITE: Scholarships for residents of Coffee County, AL, & bordering counties. Studies must be health-related.
APPLICATION: Write for info. No deadline listed.
CONTACT: J. B. Brunson, Manager, 201 S. Edwards, Enterprise, AL 36330. TEL: (205)393-4553

FOUNDATION: The Simpson Foundation
REQUISITE: Scholarships for residents in Wilcox County, AL.
APPLICATION: Can be sent January 1-March 31. With application send school transcripts, photograph, & letters of recommendation.
CONTACT: c/o First Alabama, POB 511, Montgomery, AL 36101-0511. TEL: (205)832-8011

FOUNDATION: Tommy C. Turner Memorial Foundation
REQUISITE: Must be a student of Wetumpka High School, AL & will attend University of AL.
APPLICATION: Write for info. Deadline April 30.
CONTACT: POB 89, Wetumpka, AL 36092. TEL: (205)567-5141

FOUNDATION: Pickett & Hatcher Educational Fund, Inc.
REQUISITE: Undergraduate student loans to residents of AL, FL, GA, KY, MS, NC, SC, TN, & VA. No loans granted for individuals entering medicine, law, or the ministry.
APPLICATION: Write for info. Deadline May 15. Requests for applications may be made after 10/1.
CONTACT: Robert E. Bennett, Exec. VP, 1800 Buena Vista Rd., POB 8169, Columbus, GA 31908. TEL: (706)327-6586

FOUNDATION: The Daniel Ashley & Irene Houston Mmrl Fndtn
REQUISITE: Must be a child of an employee of Crystal Springs Printwork, Inc., Chickamagua, GA, or high schl senior residing in the area of Dade, Catoosa, or Walker county, GA. You must also be planning to attend an accredited college in GA, AL, or TN.
APPLICATION: Write for info. No deadline listed.
CONTACT: Paul Chambers, Superintendent, Chickamango City School, Lee Circle, Atlanta, GA 30707. TEL: (615)757-3306

FOUNDATION: Cooper Industries Foundation
REQUISITE: Scholarships for children of employees of Cooper Industries, Inc. in AL, CA, CT, GA, IL, IN, ME, MI, MO, MS, NJ, NY, NC, OH, OK, PA,

SC, TN, TX, and VA.
APPLICATION: Applications are accepted throughout the year.
CONTACT: First City Tower, Suite 4000, 1001 Fannin, POB 4446, Houston, TX 77210. Patricia B. Meinecke, Secretary. (713)739-5632

FOUNDATION: Sonat Foundation, Inc.
REQUISITE: Scholarships for children of employees of Sonat, Inc.
APPLICATION: Write for details. Application deadline is not specified.
CONTACT: Sonat Foundation, Lera Jordan, POB 2563, Birmingham, AL 35203. (205)325-7456

FOUNDATION: Tractor & Equipment Company Foundation
REQUISITE: Scholarships for children of employees of Tractor & Equipment Company, Inc.
APPLICATION: Write for details. Application deadline is not specified.
CONTACT: 5336 Airport Highway, POB 12326, Birmingham, AL 35201-2326. James A. Waitzman, Sr., President, c/o Tractor & Equipment Company, Inc. TEL: (205)591-2131

ARKANSAS

FOUNDATION: Wal-Mart Foundation
REQUISITE: Must be a graduating high school senior in an area where Wal-Mart Stores, Inc. or Sam's Wholesale Warehouse are located or must be a dependent or close relative of a Wal-Mart employee.
APPLICATION: Interviews required for finalists. Applction deadline is 2/20.
CONTACT: High school counselor or area Wal-Mart or Sam's Whlsl Wrhs stores for info. (501)273-8509

FOUNDATION: The Murphy Foundation
REQUISITE: Must be a student from southern AR.
APPLICATION: Write for info. Application deadline August 1.
CONTACT: 200 N. Jefferson #400, El Dorado, AR 71730. (501)862-2884

FOUNDATION: Lyon Foundation, Inc.
REQUISITE: Must be a resident of AR.
APPLICATION: Write for info. & give all pertinent info. Application deadline is not specified.
CONTACT: Ralph Cotham, Secty.-Treasurer, POB 4408, Little Rock, AR 72214 (We were not able to verify this listing; it may not be extant.)

FOUNDATION: Trinity Foundation
REQUISITE: Must be a resident of AR.
APPLICATION: Application information available only at high school guidance office. Deadline April 10 of senior year in high school.
CONTACT: POB 7008, Pine Bluff, AR 71611 TEL: (501)534-7120

FOUNDATION: Ed E. & Gladys Hurley Foundation
REQUISITE: Scholarships to any student who is attending Scarritt College for Christian Workers, TN; educational loans to any resident of AR, LA, or TX who will attend any institution of their choice.
APPLICATION: Write for info. Application deadline May 31.
CONTACT: c/o The First National Bank of Shreveport, POB 2116, Shreveport, LA 71154. (318)226-2110

FOUNDATION: The Harvey & Berniece Jones Foundation
REQUISITE: Must be a needy student whose principal place of residence is Springdale, AR, & who is pursuing further education in the fields of health care, i.e. medicine, nursing, & religion.
APPLICATION: Write for info. Application deadline listed.
CONTACT: Berniece Jones, Co-Chairman, POB 233, Springdale, AR 72765. TEL: (501)756-0611

FOUNDATION: Tyson Foundation, Inc.
REQUISITE: Must be a student who is attending an accredited college or university within a reasonable distance of factory.
APPLICATION: Write for info. Application deadline is not specified.
CONTACT: Cleta Selman, PO Drawer E, Springdale, AR 72764.

FOUNDATION: Potlatch Foundation for Higher Education
REQUISITE: Must be an undergraduate who resides in an area where the Potlatch Corp. operates.
APPLICATION: Submit letter requesting application no later
than October 15 preceding the year for which the scholarship is sought.
Deadline 2/1 for new applications & July 1 for renewals.
CONTACT: George C. Check, Pres., POB 3591, San Francisco, CA 94119.
TEL: (415)576-8800

FOUNDATION: Levi Strauss Foundation
REQUISITE: Business Opportunity Scholarships to any disadvantaged high school senior in any U.S. community where Levi Strauss & Co. has production or distribution facilities including AR, CA, GA, NV, NM, TX, &

VA. Foundation also awards international scholarships.
APPLICATION: Write for info. Application deadline is not specified.
CONTACT: Martha M Brown, Dir. of U.S. Contributions, 1155 Battery St., POB 7215, San Francisco, CA 94106. TEL: (415)544-6577

FOUNDATION: Ed E. & Gladys Hurley Foundation
REQUISITE: Scholarships to any theological student who is a resident of AR, LA, or TX & will attend any institution in U.S.
APPLICATION: Write for info. Application deadline April 15.
CONTACT: Alice Gayle, c/o Premier Bank, POB 83776, Dallas, TX 45283. TEL: (318)226-2345 or (318)221-5231

ARIZONA

FOUNDATION: B F Foundation
REQUISITE: Scholarships & student loans to any undergraduate who is attending a college or a university in AZ & CA.
APPLICATION: Letter requesting application between February 1 & May 1. Submit copy of official grade transcript. Application deadlines May 31 for 1st time applicants & March 31 for continuations.
CONTACT: David Chase, Secty.-Treasurer, 114 N. San Francisco St., Ste. 100, Flagstaff, AZ 86001. TEL: (602)774-2547

FOUNDATION: Dougherty Foundation, Inc.
REQUISITE: Scholarships & loans based on financial need only to any AZ resident who is a U.S. citizen & is enrolled in an accredited college-degree program.
APPLICATION: Call or write for info. Applctn deadline January-April.
CONTACT: Mary J. Maffeo, Secty., 3336 N. 32nd St., Ste. 115, Phoenix, AZ 85018. TEL: (602)264-7478

CALIFORNIA

FOUNDATION: Marin Educational Foundation
REQUISITE: Scholarships granted to continuous residents of Marin county for at least three years prior to application who are currently unemployed or under-employed or changing occupations.
Vocational training program must be 18 weeks or less in duration.
APPLICATION: Write for info. Application deadline is monthly
CONTACT: 1010 B Street, Suite 300, San Rafael, CA 94901 415-459-4240

California

FOUNDATION: Hilgenfeld Foundation for Mortuary Education
REQUISITE: Scholarships granted to qualified individuals and organizations with interest in Funeral Service. Preference given to Southern California residents.
APPLICATION: Write for info. Application deadline is not specified.
CONTACT: POBOX 6272, Anaheim, CA 92806.

FOUNDATION: California Student Aid Commission
REQUISITE: Scholarships granted CA residents enrolled in a vocational -technical program for 4-months to 2-years in CA. Must be US citizen.
APPLICATION: Write for info. Application deadline is March 2nd.
CONTACT: POBOX 942845, Sacramento, Ca 94245 916-445-0880

FOUNDATION: Sourisseau Academy for State and Local History
REQUISITE: Scholarships granted to undergraduate and graduate students to support research on California History. Preference to research on Santa Clara County History.
APPLICATION: Write for info. Application deadline is 4/1 & 11/1.
CONTACT: C/O San Jose State University, San Jose, CA 95192.
Tel: 408-277-2421 or 227-2657

FOUNDATION: California Chicano New Media Association
REQUISITE: Scholarships granted to all Latino undergraduate students interested in pursuing a career in Journalism or Communications. This does not have to be a school major. Must be attending an accredited institution in California. Must be US citizen.
APPLICATION: Write for info. Application deadline is March 30th.
CONTACT: C/O USC School of Journalism (GFS 315), Los Angeles, CA 90089. Tel: 213-743-7158

FOUNDATION: Golden Gate Restaurant Association
REQUISITE: Scholarships granted to residents of Northern California. High school seniors with minimum of 2.75 GPA who plan to enroll full-time in the Hotel and Restaurant Management or Food Science field at an accredited institution in the USA.
APPLICATION: Write for info. Application deadline is March 31st.
CONTACT: 291 Geary Street, Suite 600, San Francisco, CA 94102   415-781-5348

FOUNDATION: California Congress of Parents and Teachers, Inc.
REQUISITE: Scholarships granted to California residents enrolled in an

6

accredited institution full-time in California. Student must be US citizen & preparing to become a teacher in the field of Nursing.
APPLICATION: Write for info. Application deadline is not specified.
CONTACT: 930 Georgia St., Los Angeles, CA 90015 213-620-1100

FOUNDATION: American Legion Auxiliary-California Auxiliary
REQUISITE: Scholarships granted to women veterans or wives, widows; children; or grandchildren of veterans that are California residents studying Nursing in California Nursing Schools.
APPLICATION: Write for info. Application deadline is May.
CONTACT: 113 War Memorial Building, San Francisco, CA 94102.

FOUNDATION: California Congress of Parents and Teachers, Inc.
REQUISITE: Scholarships granted to California residents attending a California Community College full-time studying health services. Must have completed first year of the associate degree program.
APPLICATION: Write for info. Application deadline is not specified.
CONTACT: 930 Georgia St., Los Angeles, CA 90015 213-620-1100

FOUNDATION: Well Fargo Bank
REQUISITE: Scholarships granted to California high school seniors who are 4-H/FFA members who participate in the grand national and is planning to enroll in any accredited institution with a two or four year agriculture program in the USA.
APPLICATION: Write for info. Application deadline is April 10th.
CONTACT: Cow Palace, POBOX 34206, San Francisco, CA 94134 (415)477-1000

FOUNDATION: Theresa Corti Family Agricultural Trust
REQUISITE: Scholarships granted to students who are graduates of Kern County High Schools to be used for undergraduate study at an accredited institution.
APPLICATION: Write for info. Application deadline is February 28th.
CONTACT: Wells Fargo Bank, Trust Dept, 2222 Shaw Ave, Ste 22, Fresno, CA 93711. (209)442-6231

FOUNDATION: Safeway Stores Inc.
REQUISITE: Scholarships granted to California high school seniors who are 4-H/FFA members who participate in the grand national and plan to enroll in any accredited institution that has a two or four year Agricultural program in the US.

APPLICATION: Write for info. Application deadline is April 10th.
CONTACT: Cow Palace, POBOX 34206, San Francisco, CA 94134
(415)469-6000

FOUNDATION: San Mateo County Farm Bureau
REQUISITE: Scholarships granted to students interested in pursuing a
career in agriculture. Students may be entering freshman and continuing
college students. Must be a member of San Mateo Farm Bureau or
dependent child of a member.
APPLICATION: Write for info. Application deadline is April 1st.
CONTACT: 765 Main Street, Half Moon Bay, CA 94019. (415)726-4485

FOUNDATION: California Farm Bureau Scholarship Foundation
REQUISITE: Scholarships granted to students entering or attending an
accredited four year college or university in California and is majoring in
an agriculture related field.
APPLICATION: Write for info. Application deadline is March 1st.
CONTACT: 1601 Exposition Blvd., Sacramento, CA 95815. (916)924-4047

FOUNDATION: Santa Barbara Foundation
REQUISITE: Scholarships granted to talented music students who are
Santa Barbara country residents or have strong Santa Barbara ties.
Applicants may be any age and awards may be used for music lessons;
camps or college tuition. Must be US citizen.
APPLICATION: Write for info. Application deadline is April and May.
CONTACT: 15 E. Carrillo St., Santa Barbara, CA 93101. (805)963-1873

FOUNDATION: Etude Music Club of Santa Rosa
REQUISITE: Competition is open to any high school student who is a
resident of Sonoma, Napa or Mendocino counties and is studying music
with a private teacher of music or is recommended by his/her school's
music department.
APPLICATION: Write for info. Application deadline is December 25th.
CONTACT: POBOX 823, Santa Rosa, CA 95402.
(We were not able to verify this listing; it may not be extant.)

FOUNDATION: Luso-American Education Foundation
REQUISITE: Scholarships granted to California residents under the age
of 21. High school seniors who are enrolled full-time in a 4 year program
and will take Portuguese language classes/or is of Portuguese descent,
member of organization whose scholarships are administered by Luso-

America foundation. Must have 3.0 GPA.
APPLICATION: Write for info. Application deadline is March 1st.
CONTACT: POBOX 1768, Oakland, CA 94604.
(We were not able to verify this listing; it may not be extant.)

FOUNDATION: Native Sons of the Golden West
REQUISITE: Contest is open to California high school students under the age of 20. Speeches must be 7-9 minutes in length and may be made on any subject related to past or present California.
APPLICATION: Write for info. Application deadline is January.
CONTACT: 414 Mason St., Suite 300, San Francisco, CA 94102 (415)392-1223

FOUNDATION: San Francisco Foundation
REQUISITE: Scholarships granted to California Born artists in the areas of print making, photography and film and video. Must be USA citizen.
APPLICATION: Write for info. Application deadline is early fall.
CONTACT: 685 Market St., Suite 910, San Francisco, CA 94105 (415)563-3366

FOUNDATION: Delta Kappa Gamma
REQUISITE: Scholarships granted to residents living in Humboldt or Del Norte counties or attend Humboldt State University in Arcata or College of Redwood in Eureka. Scholarships granted on the basis of GPA, school activities and need.
APPLICATION: Write for info. Application deadline is May 1st.
CONTACT: C/O Maureen Johannsen, 1566 1 Street, Arcata, CA 95521.
(We were not able to verify this listing; it may not be extant.)

FOUNDATION: California Congress of Parents and Teachers Inc.
REQUISITE: Scholarships granted to upper-level undergraduates or graduates pursuing a career in teaching in early childhood education in California public schools. Must be a student at an accredited college or university. Must be a US citizen and a resident of California.
APPLICATION: Write for info. Application deadline is not specified.
CONTACT: 930 Georgia St., Los Angeles, CA 90015

FOUNDATION: California Student Aid Commission
REQUISITE: Scholarships granted to California resident that is a top high school senior or college freshmen who is pursuing a career in teaching. Scholarships awarded only at eligible California school. Must be US

citizen or legal resident.
APPLICATION: Write for info. Application deadline is July 1st.
CONTACT: Your high school counselor or POBOX 942845, Sacramento, CA 94245. (916)445-0880

FOUNDATION: Charles A. Winans Memorial Trust
REQUISITE: Must be a graduating student from Beaumont High School, Beaumont, California.
APPLICATION: Write for info. Application deadline January 15th.
CONTACT: Beaumont High School, 1591 Cherry Avenue, Beaumont, CA 92223. TEL: (909)845-3171

FOUNDATION: Caldwell-Pitts Scholarship Fund
REQUISITE: Must be graduate of Biggs High School, Biggs, CA.
APPLICATION: Write for info. Deadline April 1 to file completed application with high school principal.
CONTACT: Biggs Unified Schl District, POB 379, Biggs, CA 95917 (916)868-1281

FOUNDATION: Borrego Springs Educational Schlrshp Committee
REQUISITE: Must be a graduating senior of Borrego Springs High School in Borrego Springs, CA.
APPLICATION: Contact scholarship committee for current deadline.
CONTACT: POB 59, Borrego Springs, CA 92004. TEL: (619)767-5314

FOUNDATION: Julius Rudel Award Trust Fund
REQUISITE: Must study opera.
APPLICATION: Write for info. to General Dir., New York City Opera, State Theater, Lincoln Ctr., New York, NY 10023. Application deadline is not specified.
CONTACT: 1800 W. Magnolia Blvd., Burbank, CA 91506
(We were not able to verify this listing; it may not be extant.)

FOUNDATION: California Teachers Association
REQUISITE: Must be a member or a dependent of a member of CA Teachers Association.
APPLICATION: Write for info. Application deadline is January 15.
CONTACT: Manager, Human Rights Dept., CA Teachers Association Schlrshps, 1705 Murchison Dr, Burlingame, CA 94010. (415)697-1400

FOUNDATION: Peninsula Community Foundation

REQUISITE: Must be a resident of San Mateo County or northern Santa Clara County, CA.
APPLICATION: Write for info. No deadline listed.
CONTACT: Bill Somerville, Exec. Dir., 1204 Burlingame Ave., POB 627, Burlingame, CA 94011-0627. TEL: (415)342-2477

FOUNDATION: Almanor Scholarship Fund
REQUISITE: Must be graduate student from Chester High School.
APPLICATION: Deadline August of each year.
CONTACT: Charles M. Karns, Secty., POB 796, Chester, CA 96020. TEL: (916)258-2111

FOUNDATION: American Association of Physics Teachers
REQUISITE: Must be either a CA or WY high school student currently enrolled as an undergraduate or as a graduate of the mid-year high school class who is not currently taking college physics. Any student who has taken a college physics course as part of an accelerated program may participate in the examination & be listed in the winner's rankings but will not be eligible for the college scholarship awards.
APPLICATION: Application with $1.00 registration fee should be received no later than April 15. Write for further info.
CONTACT: Walter T. Ogier, Dept. of Physics, Pomona College, Clarement, CA 91711. (909)621-8000

FOUNDATION: Landscape Architecture Foundation
REQUISITE: Scholarships granted to students at California Polytechnic Institute and those enrolled in the extension programs
at UCLA and UC Irvine. Students must have need and commitment to Landscape Architecture as a profession.
APPLICATION: Write for info. Application deadline is 4/15 - 5/15.
CONTACT: 1733 Connecticut Ave. SW, Washington, D.C. 20009 (202)686-2752

FOUNDATION: The Humboldt Area Foundation
REQUISITE: Must be a resident of Humboldt County, CA.
APPLICATION: Write for info. No deadline listed.
CONTACT: The Foundation, POB 99, Bayside, CA 95524. (707)442-2993

FOUNDATION: Charles E. Saak Trust
REQUISITE: Must be an underprivileged student under 21 years of age residing in Porterville/Poplar area of Tulare County, CA.

California

APPLICATION: Submit letter requesting application. Applications must be submitted with educational statement, financial statements of student & parents, latest income tax return, & transcripts of high school & (if applicable) college grades. Deadline March 31.
CONTACT: Fndtion c/o Wells Fargo Bank-Trust Dept., 618 E. Shaw Ave., Fresno, CA 93710. (209)442-6232

FOUNDATION: Whittier College
REQUISITE: Scholarships granted to Eagle Scouts planning a career in youth leadership. Fields could vary from Professional Scouting, Teaching, Missionary work or Ministry.
APPLICATION: Write for info. Application deadline is not specified.
CONTACT: Admissions Office, Whittier, CA 90605. (310)907-4200

FOUNDATION: Corti Family Agricultural Fund
REQUISITE: Must be a graduate of a Kern County hgh schl & pursuing agricultural education in a college or university.
APPLICATION: Reference letters (1 from academic source, 1 from personal source), financial statement, transcript of grades, & letter stating goals & plans required. Write for info. Deadline February 28.
CONTACT: William F. Richey, Assistant VP-Trust, Wells Fargo Bank, 618 E. Shaw Ave., Fresno, CA 93710. TEL: (209)442-6232

FOUNDATION: Fresno-Madera Medical Society Schlrshp Fndtn
REQUISITE: Must have been a resident of Fresno County or Madera County for at least 1 year & your application for matriculation at either a medical school, dental school, school of pharmacy or school of nursing must have been approved.
APPLICATION: Write for info. Deadline May 15.
CONTACT: Ellen, POB 31, Fresno, CA 93707. TEL: (209)224-4224

FOUNDATION: Boys Club of San Diego
REQUISITE: Scholarships granted to male USA high school seniors pursuing a career in Medicine, Law, Engineering, and Political Science. Special preference to students living within a 250 mile radius of San Diego. Granted on the basis of academic performance, need and potential leadership.
APPLICATION: Write for info. Must enclose a self-addressed stamped envelope to receive application. Application deadline is May 15th.
CONTACT: 3760 Fourth Ave., #1 Admin Office, San Diego, CA 92103. (619)442-0371

California

FOUNDATION: Richard & Jessie Barrington Educational Fund
REQUISITE: Must be an enrolled member of the Washoe Tribe & use schlrshp at college (undergraduate or graduate) or a vocational schl.
APPLICATION: Write for info. No deadline listed.
CONTACT: Washoe Tribe of NV & CA Education Dept., 919 Highway 395 S., Gardnerville, NV 89410. TEL: (702)265-4191

FOUNDATION: San Mateo County Farm Scholarship Bureau
REQUISITE: Member or dependent of San Mateo CA Farm Bureau.
APPLICATION: Write for info. Deadline April 1.
CONTACT: Jack Olson, 765 Main St., Half Moon Bay, CA 94019. TEL: (415)726-4485

FOUNDATION: Charles Lee Powell Foundation
REQUISITE: Must major in engineering science, computer science, or applied mathematics.
APPLICATION: Write for info. No deadline listed.
CONTACT: Charles Rees, Pres., 7742 Herschel Ave., Ste. K, La Jolia, CA 92037. TEL: (619)459-3699

FOUNDATION: Fannie & John Hertz Foundation
REQUISITE: Reside in US & be in doctoral work at selected college
APPLICATION: Write for info. Deadline November 1.
CONTACT: Kathryn Smith, POB 2230, Livermore, CA 94550 (510)449-0855

FOUNDATION: Arthur C. Boehmer & Florence Schubert Boehmer Scholarship Fund
REQUISITE: Must be a graduate of a high school in the Lodi Unified School District, Lodi, CA (including Lodi High School, Tokay High School, Liberty High School, & Lodi Academy) & plan to attend a CA institution.
APPLICATION: Write for info. Deadline June 15.
CONTACT: Robert K. Elliott, Co-Trustee, POB 1827, Lodi, CA 95241. TEL: (209)369-2781

FOUNDATION: California Congress of Parents & Teachers, Inc.
REQUISITE: Must be high school senior preparing to teach or a degreed teacher returning to school for further education.
APPLICATION: Write for info. No deadline listed.
CONTACT: Lilly, 930 Georgia St., Los Angeles, CA 90015 (213)620-1100

FOUNDATION: CA Congress of Parents, Teachers, & Students Inc.
REQUISITE: US citizen, CA resident for one year, & attending or accepted by an accredited CA institution.
APPLICATION: Submit letter requesting application & indicate college choice, course of study, grade level & school period for which the loan is desired. Interviews required. Deadline 5/15 to be considered in July & 11/15 to be considered in January.
CONTACT: Student Loan Program, 930 Georgia St, Los Angeles, CA 90015. TEL: (213)620-1100

FOUNDATION: Nestle Foundation
REQUISITE: Must be child of employee or employee of a Nestle Co. only.
APPLICATION: Write for info. No deadline listed.
CONTACT: Anna Gonzalez, 800 N. Brand Blvd., Glendale, CA 91203. TEL: (818)549-6109

FOUNDATION: Joseph Drown Foundation
REQUISITE: Emphasis given to residents of CA.
APPLICATION: Write for info. No deadline listed.
CONTACT: Your local university or college financial aid office.
TEL: (310)277-4488

FOUNDATION: Ebell of Los Angeles Scholarship Endowment & Mr. & Mrs. N. Flint Endowment Fund
REQUISITE: Sophomore in college or university & from LA Cnty.
APPLICATION: Contact Financial Aid Office. No deadline.
CONTACT: Mrs. Daniel Bloxsom, Jr., Scholar, Chairman, 743 S. Lucerne Blvd., Los Angeles, CA 90004. TEL: (213)931-1277

FOUNDATION: The May Centers Corporation
REQUISITE: Must be a CA or NV student.
APPLICATION: Write for info. No deadline listed.
CONTACT: 10738 W. Pico Blvd., Los Angeles, CA 90064. (310)446-3446

FOUNDATION: Mexican-American Business & Professional Scholarship Association
REQUISITE: Must be a Mexican-American undergraduate student from Los Angeles County.
APPLICATION: Write for info. Deadline May.
CONTACT: Roberto Zuniga, Scholarship Program, POB 22292, Los Angeles, CA 90022. TEL: (213)265-8764

FOUNDATION: Spence Reese Foundation
REQUISITE: Must be a male CA student of medicine, law, engineering, or political science.
APPLICATION: Write for info. No deadline listed.
CONTACT: c/o Security Pacific National Bank, POB 3189 Terminal Annex, Los Angeles, CA 90051. TEL: (213)622-9484

FOUNDATION: Youth Opportunities Foundation
REQUISITE: Must be a CA student with a Spanish surname.
APPLICATION: Write for info. Deadline March 1.
CONTACT: Awards for Spanish Surnamed Californians, 8820 Sepulveda Blvd., Ste. 208, Los Angeles, CA 90045. TEL: (213)670-7664

FOUNDATION: Raychem Corp. & Foundation
REQUISITE: Raychem scholarship limited to students in Sequoia Union High School District.
APPLICATION: Write for info. No deadline listed.
CONTACT: Scott Wylie, 300 Constitution Dr., Menlo Park, CA 94025. TEL: (415)361-4554

FOUNDATION: Community Foundation for Monterey County
REQUISITE: Must be a resident of Monterey County, CA.
APPLICATION: Write or call for info. No deadline listed.
CONTACT: Local university or college financial aid office.(408)375-9712

FOUNDATION: Avon Products, Inc.
REQUISITE: Must be an employee or relative of employee of Avon.
APPLICATION: Write for info. Deadline November 1.
CONTACT: Scholarship Program, 2940 E. Foothill Blvd., Pasadena, CA 91121. TEL: (818)578-8000

FOUNDATION: James Grubb Schlrshp Fndtn
REQUISITE: African or American student who is a graduate student at a college or university situated between Bakersfield in the central part of CA & the northern part of the state. Must be able to provide proof of graduate student status.
APPLICATION: Interview required. Request info. Deadline 3/31.
CONTACT: James Bishop, 1547 Lakeside Drive, Oakland, CA 94612. TEL: (510)895-8494

FOUNDATION: Vincent A. Davi Memorial

REQUISITE: Student of the Pittsburg Unified School District, CA.
APPLICATION: Must take a school district administered test. Write for info. Deadline beginning of semester.
CONTACT: Pittsburg Unified School District, 2000 Railroad Ave., Pittsburg, CA 94565. TEL: (510)473-4251

FOUNDATION: Perry S. & Stella H. Tracy Scholarship
REQUISITE: Must be a graduate of an El Dorado County high school or have resided in the county for at least 2 years.
APPLICATION: Applications available at Counseling Office of El Dorado High School. Application deadline is April.
CONTACT: Bart Tamblyn or Paula Sanderson, Counselors, El Dorado Hgh Schl, 561 Canal St., Placerville, CA 95667. TEL: (916)622-3634

FOUNDATION: W.P. Bartlett Trust Fund
REQUISITE: Must be a current student of the Porterville, CA, High School District or the Porterville College District desiring to attend a CA college or university.
APPLICATION: Submit a letter stating residence, schools attended, present school status, & the name of your prospective school. Deadline February of each school year.
CONTACT: William B. Richardson, Secty., 27349 Ave. 138, Porterville, CA 93257. TEL: (209)784-6642

FOUNDATION: Riverside County Physicians Memorial Fndtn
REQUISITE: Must be a resident of Riverside County, CA, & studying medical education.
APPLICATION: Submit letter for application. No deadline listed.
CONTACT: C. P. Rowlands, Exec. Dir., 3993 Jurupa Ave., Riverside, CA 92506. TEL: (714)686-3342

FOUNDATION: Switzer Foundation
REQUISITE: Graduate student in the environmental sciences in CA.
APPLICATION: Submit letter. No deadline listed.
CONTACT: A Swander, Trustee, Box 1697, Ross CA 94957 (415)459-5812

FOUNDATION: Boye Scholarship Trust
REQUISITE: Must be a resident of Sacramento County, CA. Preference to those pursuing studies in agriculture related fields.
APPLICATION: Write for info. No deadline listed.
CONTACT: Wells Fargo Bank, 400 Capitol Mall, Sacramento, CA 95814.

FOUNDATION: California Farm Bureau Federation
REQUISITE: Must be a CA resident who meets admission requirements of a 4-year college or university in CA.
APPLICATION: Write for info. Deadline March 1.
CONTACT: CFB Scholarship Foundation, Nina Danner, 1601 Exposition Blvd., Sacramento, CA 95815. TEL: (916)924-4047

FOUNDATION: California Student Aid Commission
REQUISITE: Must be a CA undergraduate or graduate with secondary language competence.
APPLICATION: Write for info. Deadline February 1.
CONTACT: Customer Service, POB 510845, Sacramento, CA 94245-0845. TEL: (916)322-2807

FOUNDATION: California Student Aid Commission
REQUISITE: Must be a resident of CA who is in graduate study & attends a school accredited by the CA Student Aid Cmmssn.
APPLICATION: Write for info. Deadline February 9.
CONTACT: Customer Service, POB 5110845, Sacramento, CA 94245-0845. TEL: (916)322-2807

FOUNDATION: California Student Aid Commission
REQUISITE: Must be a CA nursing student.
APPLICATION: Write for info. Deadline February 1.
CONTACT: Customer Service, POB 510845, Sacramento, CA 94245-0845. TEL: (916)322-2807

FOUNDATION: Delta Kappa Gamma, Chi State (CA)
REQUISITE: Must be a female who is in graduate study & has been a member in good standing of Delta Kappa Gamma in CA for 2 years prior to January 5 of year of application.
APPLICATION: Write for info. Deadline January 5.
CONTACT: Chi State Graduate Study Awards, 2530 J St., Ste. 301 or POB 160363, Sacramento, CA 95816. TEL: (916)444-9752

FOUNDATION: George Grotefend Scholarship Foundation
REQUISITE: For children of Wells Fargo employees.
APPLICATION: Write for info. Deadline May 1.
CONTACT: Trust Officer, Wells Fargo Bank Trust Dept., 400 Capital Mall, Main Floor, Sacramento, CA 95814. TEL: (916)920-2507

California

FOUNDATION: Annie Swift Pratt Memorial Foundation
REQUISITE: Must be a resident of the Sacramento, CA, area.
APPLICATION: Submit letter requesting application. Interviews required. No deadline listed.
CONTACT: Herschel Beauchamp, Trustee, 820 Senior Way, Sacramento, CA 95831. TEL: (916)488-5544

FOUNDATION: Fed-Mart Foundation
REQUISITE: Graduating high school senior from San Diego City or Cnty.
APPLICATION: Applications sent to students in San Diego City & County. Application deadline March 15.
CONTACT: Ralph S. Colonell, Chairman, POB 81667, San Diego, CA 92138. (Note: We think it's still in existence but not for sure.)

FOUNDATION: Ruth Jenkins Scholarship Fund
REQUISITE: Must be a black student from San Diego, CA, area.
APPLICATION: Submit letter requesting application. Interviews required. Deadline May 31.
CONTACT: Doris Towne, Wells Fargo Bank, N.A., San Diego, CA 91103. TEL: (619)230-5871

FOUNDATION: American Legion Auxiliary-California Auxiliary
REQUISITE: Veteran, wife, widow, child, or grandchild of a male veteran.
APPLICATION: Write for info. Deadline May.
CONTACT: Nurses Scholarships, 401 Van Ness Ave., Room 113, 113 War Memorial Bldg, San Francisco, CA 94102. TEL: (415)861-5092

FOUNDATION: Bank of America-Giannini Foundation
REQUISITE: In postdoctoral research in a medical school in CA.
APPLICATION: Write or call for info. Deadline December 1.
CONTACT: Caroline O. Boitano, Administrator, Bank of America Ctr., Dept. 3246, Box 37000, San Fran, CA 94137. TEL: (415)953-0932

FOUNDATION: Bank of America, Grand National Jr Livestock Exposition
REQUISITE: Must be a student who is attending a 4-year agricultural college in CA, & is a member of FFA & 4-H.
APPLICATION: Write for info. Deadline April 2.
CONTACT: Gailen P. Marten, VP, POB 37000, San Francisco, CA 94137. (We think it's still in existence but not for sure.)

FOUNDATION: Bankamerica Foundation

California

REQUISITE: Must be high school junior with a GPA 3.25 for academic competition for award for freshman year of college.
APPLICATION: Write for info. Deadline February 24.
CONTACT: POB 37000, San Francisco, CA 94137. TEL: (415)953-3175

FOUNDATION: California Masonic Foundation
REQUISITE: Undergraduate, U.S. citizen, & a resident of CA or HI.
APPLICATION: Request application. No deadline listed.
CONTACT: Judy Liang, Trustee, 1111 California St., San Francisco, CA 94108. TEL: (415)776-7000

FOUNDATION: Italian Catholic Federation, Inc.
REQUISITE: Must be a California or Nevada graduating senior of Italian ancestry & Catholic faith.
APPLICATION: Write for info. No deadline listed.
CONTACT: 1801 Van Ness Ave., Ste. 330, San Francisco, CA 94109. TEL: (415)673-8240

FOUNDATION: Japanese American Citizens League
REQUISITE: Must be citizen or legal resident US of Japanese ancestry.
APPLICATION: Write for info. Deadline April.
CONTACT: Henry & Chiyo Kuvahara Scholarships, 1765 Sutter St., San Francisco, CA 94115. TEL: (415)921-5225

FOUNDATION: Mate Foundation
REQUISITE: For present/former I. Magnin employees.
APPLICATION: Write for info. No deadline listed.
CONTACT: William Curley, Pres., c/o I. Magnin Administration, POB 7651, San Francisco, CA 94120. TEL: (415)362-2100

FOUNDATION: George Henry Mayr Trust
REQUISITE: None listed.
APPLICATION: No unsolicited applications accepted. Write for info. No deadline listed.
CONTACT: Brian D. Crahan, Advisor, c/o Wells Fargo Trust Tax, POB 44002, San Francisco, CA 94144. (We think it's still in existence but not for sure.)

FOUNDATION: Order of Eastern Star
REQUISITE: Must be a CA resident, a high school senior or college student in CA or a member of The Order of Eastern Star.

APPLICATION: Write for info. Deadline May 1.
CONTACT: Miss Diane Dixon, Grand Secty., 870 Market St., Ste. 722, San Francisco, CA 94102.

FOUNDATION: Pacific Gas & Electric Co.
REQUISITE: Minority high school senior who has advanced despite disadvantages. Nominated & recommended by principal or guidance counselor. Awards given in service areas of Pacific Gas & Electric.
APPLICATION: Write for info. Deadline is Mid-November.
CONTACT: Pacific Gas & Electric Special Recognition Scholarships, 215 Market St., San Francisco, CA 94106. TEL: (415)973-5195 Ext. 1

FOUNDATION: Potlach Foundation for Higher Education
REQUISITE: Applicant's permanent residence or high school must be located within 30 miles of a Potlatch corporate facility.
APPLICATION: Write for info. No deadline listed.
CONTACT: George C. Cheek, Pres., POB 3591, San Francisco, CA 94119. (We think it's still in existence but not for sure.)

FOUNDATION: David Rubenstein Memorial Scholarship Foundation
REQUISITE: Must have a recommendation & be a northern CA student graduating from hotel & restaurant high school or junior college programs & planning to continue training full-time on the college level.
APPLICATION: Interviews required. Applications must be submitted by teachers & administrators of high school & junior college food preparation & service programs on behalf of qualified students. Deadline 4/30.
CONTACT: Cecilia Metz, c/o Golden Gate Restaurant Association, 720 Market #200, San Francisco, CA 94102. TEL: (415)781-5348

FOUNDATION: The San Francisco Foundation
REQUISITE: Must have been born in CA, be between 20 & 35 years of age on the closing date of the competition, & also be able to provide proof of birth date & birthplace. You must be the author of an unpublished, incomplete work of fiction or non-fictional prose & short story, poetry, or drama.
APPLICATION: Deadline for application & supporting materials 1/15. Recipients announced about 6/15.
CONTACT: 685 Market, Suite 910, San Francisco 94105. (415)495-3100

FOUNDATION: Swiss Benevolence Foundation
REQUISITE: Swiss national or descendent living within a 150 mile radius

of San Francisco City for 4 years prior to application.
APPLICATION: Write for info. Deadline May 15.
CONTACT: Caroline, 456 Montgomery, Suite 1500, San Francisco, CA 94104. TEL: (415)929-8429

FOUNDATION: Trust Funds Inc.
REQUISITE: Must be resident of San Francisco Bay Area, CA.
APPLICATION: Write for info. No deadline listed.
CONTACT: Mr. Heely, 100 Broadway, 3rd Fl., San Francisco, CA 94115. TEL: (415)434-3323

FOUNDATION: Harkham Foundation
REQUISITE: Israeli student pursuing higher edctn in US or abroad
APPLICATION: Write for info. No deadline listed.
CONTACT: 857 S. San Pedro St., Los Angeles, CA 90014. (213)765-5100

FOUNDATION: Marin Educational Foundation
REQUISITE: Must be a Marin County undergraduate who is currently enrolled or accepted for enrollment on at least a half-time basis at an eligible post-secondary institution. Additionally, you must be a student who has applied for the Marin Educational Grant but your financial circumstances have since worsened; or who was declared ineligible for various reasons; or who because of previous better financial circumstances did not apply for the Educational Grant; or who because of an exceptional reason could not meet the application deadline.
APPLICATION: You must file an Exceptional Circumstances Fact Sheet, a school verification form, a Marin Educational Grant Application & a Student Aid Application for CA. Write for further info. Deadline from August-April.
CONTACT: Exceptional Circumstances Grant, 1010 B St., Ste. 300, San Rafael, CA 94901. TEL: (415)459-4240

FOUNDATION: Marin Educational Foundation
REQUISITE: Must be a resident of Marin County, CA.
APPLICATION: Write for info. Deadline April 15.
CONTACT: Marin Educational Grant, 1010 B St., Ste. 312 (Albert Bldg.), San Rafael, CA 94901. TEL: (415)459-4240

FOUNDATION: Marin Educational Foundation
REQUISITE: If you are independent applicant you must be a continuous Marin County resident for at least 3 years before application. If you are

dependent applicant, ward of the court &/or residing in a foster home in Marin County you must be graduate of a County hgh schl &/or resident for at least 1 year prior to application. U.S. citizenship or eligible non-citizen status is required. You must be currently unemployed, under-employed, or changing occupations. You must be accepted by a vocational training program of 18 weeks or less duration & you must demonstrate high employment potential or promise of a job after training. Ability to maintain living expenses during the training period & financial need for educational aid are also required.

APPLICATION: Apply for all other sources of direct aid for which you are eligible. This may include Federal, State &/or school edctnl grnts & Fdrl, State &/or cnty general assistance. An original & 1 copy of student application, student budget worksheet, & school verification form must be submitted to the Fndtn. No deadline listed

CONTACT: Marin Educational Grant for Short-Term Occupational Study, 1010 B St., Ste. 300, San Rafael, CA 94901. TEL: (415)459-4240

FOUNDATION: Marin Educational Foundation

REQUISITE: Complete high school education in Marin County in the year in which you are nominated for the award. Have attended public or private Marin County high school for at least 2 years & be a resident of Marin County. You may be recommended for outstanding achievement in 1 of 2 categories: specific achievement or personal achievement. Any specific achievement student may be recommended for his/her accomplishments in any academic subject, business, home & industrial arts, or community service. You must show exceptional achievement, self-motivation, dedication, & outstanding potential for further development & intent to pursue further educational goals. Any personal achievement candidate may be recommended for having evidenced outstanding personal achievement despite adversity. You must show exceptional perseverance, courage, commitment, significant potential & intent to pursue further achievement & education.

APPLICATION: Any person, other than the student or family members, who has a personal knowledge of the candidate may make a recommendation. Nominators have to respond to 10 statements appropriate to the category under which the student is being recommended. The nominee must prepare a folder that includes written evidence of his/her achievements & a 500-word written essay or oral tape supporting his/her claims. Awards are based on demonstrated achievement without regard to financial need. Deadline for recommendations is early February to the Student Award Nominating

Committee of the school the nominee attends. Awards are announced in early May.
CONTACT: Outstanding Student Achievement Award, 1010 B St., Ste. 300, San Rafael, CA 94901. TEL: (415)459-4240

FOUNDATION: Anna H. & Albert W. Bee Scholarship Fund
REQUISITE: Must be long-term resident of Santa Barbara Cnty.
APPLICATION: Letters of reference & official school transcript required. Applications accepted 1/1-6/1.
CONTACT: Foundation, c/o Crocker National Bank-Trust Dept., PO Drawer H-H, Santa Barbara, CA 93102. (805)963-0811 (We think it's still in existence but not for sure.)

FOUNDATION: Mary K. & Edith Pillsbury Foundation
REQUISITE: Must be a U.S. citizen & reside or have resided in Santa Barbara County, CA, & pursuing an education in music.
APPLICATION: Interviews & auditions required. Write for info. No deadline listed.
CONTACT: Isabel H. Bartolome, Student Aid Dir., c/o Santa Barbara Foundation, 15 E. Carrillo St., Santa Barbara, CA 93101. (805)963-1873

FOUNDATION: Santa Barbara Foundation
REQUISITE: Must be a resident who is also a graduate of a Santa Barbara County, CA, high school, have attended that school for 3 years & pursuing undergraduate study. Loans for graduate study are available only in the fields of family practice or internal medicine.
APPLICATION: Write or call for info. Deadline mid-February. Applications accepted 10/1 - 2/14.
CONTACT: Edward R. Spaulding, Exec. Dir., 15 E. Carrillo St., Santa Barbara, CA 93101. TEL: (805)963-1873

FOUNDATION: Florence B Graham & Clemma B Fancher Scholarship Foundation
REQUISITE: Must be from Northern Santa Cruz County.
APPLICATION: Distributed to high schools. Deadline May 31.
CONTACT: Robert Darrow, 149 Josephine St., Santa Cruz, CA 95060. TEL: (408)423-3640

FOUNDATION: The Getty Grants Program
REQUISITE: Must be in a postdoctoral fellowship in the history of art & the humanities, & senior research grants.

APPLICATION: Submit 2 page preliminary letter & general financial requirements. No deadline listed except for publication grants (6 months before book goes into production).
CONTACT: Harold M. Williams, Pres., 401 Wilshire Blvd., Ste. 1000, Santa Monica, CA 90401. TEL: (310)393-4244

FOUNDATION: Mabelle McLeod Lewis Memorial Fund
REQUISITE: Must be an advanced doctoral candidate affiliated with Northern CA unvrsties & colleges & be from Northern CA.
APPLICATION: Submit letter or request. Deadline January 15.
CONTACT: Shirleyann Shyne, Exec. Secty., POB 3730, Stanford, CA 94305. (415)399-7921 (We think it's still in existence but not for sure.)

FOUNDATION: Isabelle G. Showler Scholarship Fund
REQUISITE: Graduate of Torrance High School, Torrance, CA.
APPLICATION: Write for info. & include name of college you plan to attend, need for scholarship, transcript of grades, & a letter of recommendation. Deadline May 15.
CONTACT: Mrs. E. Kenny de Groot, c/o Torrance Teachers Assctn, 1619 Cravens Ave., Torrance, CA 90501. TEL: (310)320-8200

FOUNDATION: Stephenson Scholarship Foundation
REQUISITE: Must be a graduating senior in the Vacaville, CA, Unified School District or a college undergraduate who resided in the school district at the time you graduated from a public high school & was involved in athletics.
APPLICATION: Interviews required. Write for info. No deadline.
CONTACT: Helen E. Stephenson, 5 Hillside Ln., Vacaville, CA 95688 (707) 448-2128 or Donald Stephenson, 500 Main St., Vacaville, CA 95688 (707) 448-6894

FOUNDATION: A. B. Guslander-Masonic Lodge Scholarship Fund
REQUISITE: Must be a graduate of Willits High School, Willits, CA, in your junior or senior year of college or in graduate school.
APPLICATION: Submit letter which includes education completed, where you are enrolled for ensuing year & references. Deadline 5/1
CONTACT: Secty., Masonic Lodge, POB 67, Willits, CA 95490. (707)459-2307

FOUNDATION: Mary M. Aaron Memorial Trust & Schlrshp Fnd
REQUISITE: Must be student from Marysville or Yuba Hgh Schls, Yuba

Cllg, or an institution for higher learning within CA.
APPLICATION: Write for info. Deadline 3/15 of following school year.
CONTACT: W.D.Chipman, POB 241, Yuba Cty, CA 95991. (916)741-5200

FOUNDATION: Fieldcrest Foundation
REQUISITE: Must be a NC, CA, GA, IL, NJ, or VA resident.
APPLICATION: Write for info. No deadline listed.
CONTACT: c/o Fieldcrest Mills, Stadium Rd., Eden, NC 27288 (910)627-3000

FOUNDATION: The S.S. Johnson Foundation
REQUISITE: Must be a student residing in OR or northern CA studying health or related areas.
APPLICATION: Submit letter requesting application. No deadline listed.
CONTACT: POB 356, Redmond, OR 97756. TEL: (503)548-8104

FOUNDATION: Cooper Industries Foundation
REQUISITE: Scholarships only to children of employees of Cooper Industries, Inc. in AL, CA, CT, GA, IL, IN, ME, MI, MO, MS, NJ, NY, NC, OH, OK, PA, SC, TN, TX and VA.
APPLICATION: Accepted throughout the year. Write letter.
CONTACT: First City Tower, Ste. 400, POB 4446, Houston, TX 77210.
TEL: (713)739-5632

FOUNDATION: Levi Strauss Foundation
REQUISITE: Business Opportunity Scholarships to disadvantaged high school seniors in U.S. communities where Levi Strauss & Co. has production or distribution facilities including AR, CA, GA, NV, NM, TX, & VA. Foundation also awards international scholarships.
APPLICATION: Accepted throughout the year. Initial approach by letter requesting application. Completion of formal application required.
CONTACT: Contact Martha Montag Brown, Dir. of U.S. Contributions, 1155 Battery St., POB 7215, San Francisco, CA 94106 (415)544-6577

FOUNDATION: Golden Gate Restaurant Association
REQUISITE: Scholarships granted to Northern California residents. Open to high school students with minimum GPA of 2.75 who plan to enroll full-time in fields of hotel & restaurant management/food service at an accredited college or university in the USA.
APPLICATION: Write for info. Application deadline is March 31st.
CONTACT: 291 Geary St., Suite 600, San Francisco, CA 94102

(415)781-5348

FOUNDATION: San Francisco Bay Area Chapter-National Defense Transportation Association
REQUISITE: Scholarships granted to students studying in the field of transportation; physical distribution or business logistics in preparation for pursuit of a career in transportation. Student must be studying at a San Francisco Bay area school only. Must be US citizen. Undergraduate students only.
APPLICATION: Write for info. Application deadline is May 1st.
CONTACT: POBOX 24676, Oakland, CA 94623.
(We were not able to verify this listing; it may not be extant.)

FOUNDATION: Golden State Minority Foundation
REQUISITE: Scholarships granted to minority California residents who attend California colleges & universities. Must be studying at the undergraduate junior/senior or graduate levels and maintaining a GPA of 3.0 or better. USA citizen or legal resident.
APPLICATION: Write for info. Application deadline is quarterly.
CONTACT: 1999 W. Adams Blvd., Los Angeles CA 90018 (213)482-6300

FOUNDATION: Empire College
REQUISITE: Scholarships to high school seniors or other applicants who meet admission requirements for study at Empire College only.
APPLICATION: Write for info. Application deadline is April 1st.
CONTACT: Ms. Roni Carr, 3033 Cleveland, Santa Rosa CA 95401. (707)546-4000

FOUNDATION: National FFA Center
REQUISITE: Scholarships granted to FFA member planning to enroll as a freshman in a 4-year undergraduate program at an accredited university or college in USA. Must be a USA citizen or legal resident. Must be a resident of CA;FL;SC;TN; or TX.
APPLICATION: Write for info. Application deadline is April 1st.
CONTACT: Scholarship Office, POBOX 15160, Alexandria, VA 22309. (703)360-3600

COLORADO

FOUNDATION: Colorado Society of CPA's
REQUISITE: Scholarships granted to Colorado residents. Open to high

school seniors with at least 3.75 GPA who intend on majoring in accounting at one of the 11 Colorado colleges & universities.
APPLICATION: Write for info. Application deadline is March 1st.
CONTACT: 7720 E. Belleview Ave; Bldg 46B, Englewood, CO 80111. (303)773-2877

FOUNDATION: Colorado Society of CPA's
REQUISITE: Scholarships granted to Colorado residents. Must have completed their first year of college with at least a 3.0 GPA or better & must be majoring in accounting at a college or university in Colorado.
APPLICATION: Write for info. Application deadline is 6/1 & 11/31.
CONTACT: 7720 E. Belleview Ave, Bldg 46B, Englewood, CO 80111 (303)773-2877

FOUNDATION: Otis A. Barnes and Margaret T. Barnes Trust
REQUISITE: Must be a student planning to major in chemistry at Colorado College, Colorado Springs, CO.
APPLICATION: Initial approach by submitting admission application w/a letter requesting consideration to Colorado College, Chemistry Department, Colorado Spring, Colorado 80903. Deadline Spring semester prior to matriculation.
CONTACT: First National Bank-Trust Departmentr , P.O. Box 1699, Colorado & Connecticut
Colorado Springs, CO 80942.

FOUNDATION: Lucille R. Brown Foundation, Inc.
REQUISITE: Must be a Colorado resident who is doing undergraduate work at a Colorado school.
APPLICATION: By letter, giving name, address, telephone number, and brief description of purpose for which grant will be used. No deadline.
CONTACT: Cecilia A. Well, Secretary-Treasurer, 5770 West Milan Place, Denver, CO 80235. TEL: (303)986-3797

FOUNDATION: Colorado Masons Benevolent Fund Association
REQUISITE: Must be a graduate of a high school in Colorado who is planning to attend an institution of higher learning in Colorado. Educational loans only to any child of a Master Mason of Colorado Lodge, who is either a junior or senior in college.
APPLICATION: Must complete a formal application
CONTACT: 1770 Sherman St., Denver, CO 80203. (303)837-0367

CONNECTICUT

FOUNDATION: Connecticut League for Nursing
REQUISITE: Scholarships granted to undergraduates enrolled in Connecticut Schools of Nursing. Students must have financial need and good academic record. Must be agency member of the Connecticut League for Nursing.
APPLICATION: Write for info. Application deadline is October 30th.
CONTACT: POBOX 365, Wallingford, CT 06492 203-265-4248

FOUNDATION: Woman's Seaman's Friend Society of Connecticut Inc.
REQUISITE: Scholarships granted to students who are residents of Connecticut and majoring in Marine Science at any college. Students must have need for financial aid.
APPLICATION: Write for info. Application deadline is April 1st.
CONTACT: 74 Forbes Ave., New Haven, CT 06512. (203)467-3887

FOUNDATION: Barnum Festival and People's Savings Bank
REQUISITE: Competition in open to women between the ages of 18-25 who has had formal voice training in operatic or concert singing and not have reached professional status. Applicants must be accepted from residents and students from the state of Connecticut.
APPLICATION: Write for info. Application deadline is May 30th.
CONTACT: 1070 Main St., Bridgeport, CT 06604. (203)367-8495

FOUNDATION: University of Connecticut-Department of Dramatic Arts
REQUISITE: Scholarships granted to undergraduate and graduate students in dramatic arts at the University of Connecticut.
APPLICATION: Write for info. Application deadline is not specified.
CONTACT: U-127, 2 Bolton Road, Storrs, CT 06268. (203)486-4025

FOUNDATION: Connecticut Department of Higher Education
REQUISITE: Scholarships granted to student attending a Connecticut college and plans to teach in designated teacher shortage area in Ct. Public School. Scholarships granted based on academic and financial need. Must be a US citizen or legal resident.
APPLICATION: Write for info. Application deadline is not specified.
CONTACT: 61 Woodland Street, Hartford, CT 06105. (203)566-2618

FOUNDATION: Young Printing Executives Club
REQUISITE: Scholarships granted to residents of New York, New Jersey,

and Connecticut who are enrolled at the Rochester Institute of Technology. Students should have at least a 3.0 GPA and be committed to a career in the Tri-State area.
APPLICATION: Write for info. Application deadline is 5/15 - 6/1.
CONTACT: 5 Penn Plaza, New York, NY 10001. (212)318-9608

FOUNDATION: Vitramon Foundation, Inc.
REQUISITE: High school student in any 1 of these 5 communities: Newtown, Monroe, Trumbull, Shelton, or Easton-Redding.
APPLICATION: Write for info. Deadline 11/1 for project proposal for Barton L. Weller Scholarship Award.
CONTACT: Robert Swart, Trustee, POB 544, Bridgeport, CT 06601. TEL: (203)268-6261

FOUNDATION: The Balso Foundation
REQUISITE: Must be a senior in Cheshire High School or a college undergraduate in a town which surrounds Cheshire, CT.
APPLICATION: Contact principal of Cheshire High School, S. Main St., Cheshire, CT 06410 (203) 272-5361, for application info. Deadline 4/10.
CONTACT: Neil Longobardi, Trustee, c/o Ball & Socket Mnfctrng Co., 493 W. Main St., Cheshire, CT 06410. TEL: (203)272-5361

FOUNDATION: Frank H. Scheehl Trust
REQUISITE: Senior of Conard High School, West Hartford, CT.
APPLICATION: Write for info. No deadline listed.
CONTACT: Robert Satter, Trustee, c/o CT Bank & Trust Co., POB 3334, Hartford, CT 06103.

FOUNDATION: The Society for the Increase of the Ministry
REQUISITE: Must be preparing for ordination in Episcopal Church & studying in accredited Episcopal theological seminary.
APPLICATION: Write for info. Contact foundation for current application deadline. Deadline March 1.
CONTACT: Rev. Canon J.S. Zimmerman, Exec. Dir., 120 Sigourney St., Hartford, CT 06105. TEL: (203)724-0053

FOUNDATION: The Vera H. & William R. Todd Foundation
REQUISITE: Must be student of Derby-Shelton Schl System, CT.
APPLICATION: Must submit 2 letters of recommendation: for high school seniors, 1 letter must be from a high school teacher or administrative personnel; for college students, 1 letter must be from current college,

preferably an assistant to or a dept. head (neither letter can be from high school personnel). Write for application info. Deadline March 15.
CONTACT: Sandra Porr, CT National Bank, 777 Main St., Hartford, CT 06115. TEL: (203)579-3534

FOUNDATION: Maud Glover Folsom Foundation, Inc.
REQUISITE: Must be a male of American ancestry & of Anglo-Saxon or German descent up to the age of 35. Initial grants limited to males between the ages of 14 & 20.
APPLICATION: Interviews required in CT at applicant's expense. Write for info. No deadline listed.
CONTACT: Leon A. Francisco, Pres., POB 151, Harwinton, CT 06791. TEL: (203)485-0405

FOUNDATION: Mary B. & William Rubinow Schlrshp Fnd Trst
REQUISITE: Interest-free loans to any resident of Manchester, CT, for undergraduate or graduate education.
APPLICATION: Applications available only through the guidance office of Manchester High School, 134 Middle Turnpike E., Manchester, CT 06040. No deadline listed.
CONTACT: Secty., 49 Pitkin St., Manchester, CT 06040. (203)643-5632

FOUNDATION: The Meriden Foundation
REQUISITE: Must reside in the Meriden-Wallingford, CT, area.
APPLICATION: Write for info. No deadline listed.
CONTACT: Jeffrey F. Otis, Secty., Distribution Committee, Meriden Trust & Safe Deposit Co., POB 951, Meriden, CT 06450. (203)235-4456

FOUNDATION: Elisha Leavenworth Foundation, Inc.
REQUISITE: Must be a college woman who is a resident of the Waterbury, CT, area.
APPLICATION: Write for info. Include copy of trnscrpt, personal info., & explanation of why help is needed. No deadline listed.
CONTACT: Mrs. E. Donald Rogers, 3 Mile Hill, Middlebury, CT 06702. TEL: (203)758-1042

FOUNDATION: Charles B. Allyn Foundation, Inc.
REQUISITE: Must be a resident of New London County, CT.
APPLICATION: Submit letter requesting application & include grades. No deadline listed.
CONTACT: Alfred J. Goodman, Pres., POB 214, Mystic, CT 06355

Connecticut

FOUNDATION: Herbert L. Batt Memorial Foundation, Inc.
REQUISITE: Grants are for advancement of Hebrew education for any resident of CT or MA.
APPLICATION: Write for info. & include name of school to be entered & planned course of study. No deadline listed.
CONTACT: Irving Kroopnick, Pres., 27 Vista Terrace, New Haven, CT 06515. TEL: (203)389-0213

FOUNDATION: Woman's Seamen's Friend Society of CT
REQUISITE: Scholarships for the study of marine sciences in CT or by any CT resident in schools out-of-state, & for any dependent of a CT merchant marine seaman who is pursuing any course of study.
APPLICATION: Write for info. Interviews granted upon request. Deadline April 1 for summer programs & May 15 for academic yr.
CONTACT: Capt. Jack M. Seymour, USN (Ret), Exec. Dir., 74 Forbes Ave., New Haven, CT 06512. TEL: (203)467-3887

FOUNDATION: Trustees of The Bulkeley School
REQUISITE: Must reside in New London, CT.
APPLICATION: Write for info. by March 15. Interviews & a copy of financial aid statement required. Additional application address: POB 1426, New London, CT 06320. Deadline April 1.
CONTACT: Rchrd Woodworth, Crocker St, New London, CT 06320 (203)447-1461

FOUNDATION: William H. Chapman Foundation
REQUISITE: Must reside in New London County, CT, & plan to study at an accredited institution.
APPLICATION: Interviews required. Write for info. before 3/20. Deadline April 1.
CONTACT: Caroline Driscoll, POB 1321, New London, CT 063205 (203)443-8010

FOUNDATION: Ray H. & Pauline Sullivan Foundation
REQUISITE: Must be a graduate of St. Bernard's Hgh Schl, CT
APPLICATION: Write for info. Deadline May 1.
CONTACT: John J. Curtin, c/o CT National Bank, 250 Captain's Walk, New London, CT 06320. TEL: (203)447-6132

FOUNDATION: The MacCurdy-Salisbury Edctnl Fndtn, Inc.
REQUISITE: Must reside in Lyme or Old Lyme, CT.

APPLICATION: Write for info. Deadlines April 30 for 1st semester & November 15 for 2nd semester.
CONTACT: Willis H. Umberger, Secty.-Treasurer, Old Lyme, CT 06371.
TEL: (203)434-7983

FOUNDATION: Adelphic Educational Fund, Inc.
REQUISITE: Schlrshps & honorariums to any undergraduate student at Wesleyan University, CT.
APPLICATION: Request application. Deadline October 1.
CONTACT: Herbert A. Arnold, One Edwards Rd., Portland, CT 06480.
TEL: (203)342-2607

FOUNDATION: Cntss Frances Thorley Palen-Klar Schlrshp Fnd
REQUISITE: Student attending a college or university in New England.
APPLICATION: Write for info. No deadline listed.
CONTACT: Dianne L. Nason, c/o Casco Northern Bank, N.A.;
Trust Dept., POB 678, Portland, ME 04104. TEL: (207)774-8221

FOUNDATION: James Z. Naurison Scholarship Fund
REQUISITE: Scholarships to any college-bound student who is a resident of Hampden, Hampshire, Franklin or Berkshire cnties, MA, or a resident of Enfield or Suffield counties, CT, for at least 1 year.
APPLICATION: Write for info. No interviews. Deadline May 1. Applications accepted between Dec & April.
CONTACT: Phyllis J. Farrell, Administrator, c/o Bank of New Englnd-West, POB 9006, Springfield, MA 01102-9006. TEL: (413)787-8745

FOUNDATION: Arthur H. Carter Scholarship Fund
REQUISITE: Student who has completed 2 years of accounting courses & wishes to pursue the accounting field in college or graduate school.
APPLICATION: Letters of recommendation & school transcript required. Write for info. Deadline 4/1.
CONTACT: Cummings & Lockwood, POB 120, Stamford, CT 06904. TEL: (203)327-1700

FOUNDATION: Marjorie Sells Carter Boy Scout Schlrshp Fnd
REQUISITE: Former Boy Scout who resides in New England area
APPLICATION: Letter requesting application. Deadline 4/1.
CONTACT: Joan Shaffer, POB 527, West Chatham, MA 02669.

FOUNDATION: The Westport-Weston Foundation

REQUISITE: For needy resident of Westport or Weston, CT.
APPLICATION: Write for info. Interviews sometimes required. No deadline listed.
CONTACT: Sue M. Allen, Trust Officer, c/o The Westport Bank & Trust Co., POB 5177, Westport, CT 06881. TEL: (203)222-6938

FOUNDATION: The William T. Morris Foundation, Inc.
REQUISITE: Undergraduate student loans for any child of an employee of American Chain & Cable Co., Inc. or its subsidiaries; in addition, the Thomas J. Morris Scholarship is awarded each year to a resident of West Pittston, PA.
APPLICATION: Send application to Oak Hill Rd., RD 4, Box 500 Dallas, PA 18612 (717)639-5629. Write for info. Deadline 7/31.
CONTACT: Bruce August, Assistant Secty., POB 5786, New York, NY 10163. TEL: (212)986-8036

FOUNDATION: Emery Air Freight Educational Foundation, Inc.
REQUISITE: Scholarships for children of employees of Emery Air Freight Corporation.
APPLICATION: Application deadline is in January by testing date of SAT. Parents will have to apply to their Regional Manager or Department Head.
CONTACT: Old Danbury Road, Wilton, CT 06897. John C. Emery, Prsdnt, c/o Coleman Association, POB 1283, New Canaan, CT 06840.

FOUNDATION: Amax Foundation, Inc.
REQUISITE: Schlrshps for children of employees of AMAX Inc.
APPLICATION: Write for more details.
CONTACT: Amax Center, Greenwich, CT 06836. Sonja B. Michaud, President. (203)629-6901

FOUNDATION: Eder (The Sidney & Arthur) Foundation
REQUISITE: Scholarships for children of employees of Eder Brothers, Inc.
APPLICATION: Write for current applctn deadlines and info.
CONTACT: Awards Cmmttee, POB 949, New Haven, CT 06504.

FOUNDATION: Ensign-Bickford Foundation
REQUISITE: Scholarships for children of employees of Ensign-Bickford Industries, Inc.
APPLICATION: Applications are accepted throughout the year.
CONTACT: 660 Hopmeadow Street, Simsbury, CT 06070. Linda M. Walsh

Secretary. TEL: (203)658-4411

FOUNDATION: Cooper Industries Foundation
REQUISITE: Scholarships for children of employees of Cooper Industr Inc. in AL, CA, CT, GA, IL, IN, ME, MI, MO, MS, NJ, NY, NC, OH, OK, PA, SC, TN, TX, and VA.
APPLICATION: Applications are accepted throughout the year.
CONTACT: First City Tower, Suite 4000, POB 4446, Houston, TX 77210. Patricia B. Meinecke, Secretary. TEL: (713)739-5632

FOUNDATION: Allyn (Charles B.) Foundation, Inc
REQUISITE: Educational loans for residents of New London County, CT. Funds are very limited.
APPLICATION: Write for more information.
CONTACT: POB 214, Mystic, CT 06355. Alfred Goodman, President.

FOUNDATION: Rubinow (Mary B. & William) Schlrshp Fnd Trst
REQUISITE: Interest-free loans for residents Manchester, CT
APPLICATION: Applications are accepted throughout the year.
CONTACT: 49 Pikin Street, Manchester, CT 06040, Jay Rubinow, Secretary. TEL: (203)643-5632

FOUNDATION: Charles H. Hood Fund
REQUISITE: Must be a CT, MA, ME, NH, RI, or VT resident.
APPLICATION: Write for info. No deadline listed.
CONTACT: 500 Rutherford Ave., Boston, MA 02129.

FOUNDATION: New England Regional Student Program
REQUISITE: Must reside in 1 of the New England States: CT, ME, MA, NH, RI, or VT. You may attend a public college or university within the region at a reduced tuition rate for certain degree programs that are not offered by their own state's public institutions.
APPLICATION: Write for info. No deadline listed.
CONTACT: Office of the Regional Student Program, New England Board of Higher Education, 45 Temple Place, Boston, MA 02111. (617)357-9620

FOUNDATION: Fred Forsyth Educational Trust Fund
REQUISITE: Must be a CT, MA, ME, NH, RI, or VT student.
APPLICATION: Write for info. No deadline listed.
CONTACT: Rose Marie Bates, c/o Fleet Bank, Fleet Investment Services, POB 923, Bangor, ME 04402-0923. TEL: (207)941-6000

FOUNDATION: The Horbach Fund
REQUISITE: Must be needy, gifted, young person under the age of 20 residing in CT, MA, NJ, NY, or RI.
APPLICATION: Write for info. Deadline August 1.
CONTACT: c/o National Community Bank of NJ, 113 W. Essex St., Maywood, NJ 07607 (We were not able to verify this listing; it may not be extant.)

DISTRICT OF COLUMBIA

FOUNDATION: District of Columbia Commission of the Arts and Humanities
REQUISITE: Schlrshps granted to artists and residents of Washington, DC
APPLICATION: Write for info. Application deadline is not specified.
CONTACT: 1111 E St NW #B500 Washington DC 20004 (202)724-5613

FOUNDATION: James A. Suffridge UFCW Scholarship Fund
REQUISITE: Scholarships are divided equally among six states and Canada. Write for more information.
APPLICATION: Application deadline is March 15th.
CONTACT: 1775 K St., N.W., Washington, D.C. 20006. Jerry Menapace, Trustee.

FOUNDATION: Jerusalem Fund for Education and Community Development
REQUISITE: Scholarships, fellowships, and travel and research grants for residents of Palestinian communities in Israel.
APPLICATION: Application deadlines are August 31st and December 15th. Write for more information.
CONTACT: 2435 Virginia Avenue, N.W., Washington, D.C. 20037 (202)338-1958

DELAWARE

FOUNDATION: H. Fletcher Brown Fund
REQUISITE: Scholarship granted to students born in Delaware; who graduated from a Delaware High School and is still a resident of Delaware. Must be pursuing a career in Law and have good academic record, need and good moral character. For undergraduate and graduate study. Must be US citizen.
APPLICATION: Write for info. Application deadline is April 15th.

CONTACT: C/O Bank of Delaware, Trust Department, Wilmington, De 19899. Tel: 302-429-1109

FOUNDATION: H. Fletcher Brown Fund
REQUISITE: Scholarships granted to students born in Delaware who graduated for a Delaware high school and is still a resident there. Students must be attending school majoring in Medicine; Dentistry; Law; Engineering or Chemistry. Students must have good academic record, need and good moral character in order to receive award. This is for both undergraduate and graduate study. Must be US citizen.
APPLICATION: Write for info. Application deadline is April 15th.
CONTACT: C/O Bank of Delaware, Trust Department; Wilmington, DE 19899. (302)429-1011

FOUNDATION: Society for Computer Applications in Engineering; Planning & Architecture
REQUISITE: Scholarships granted to undergraduate juniors and snrs at the University of Delaware. Must have good academic record and need.
APPLICATION: Write for info. Application deadline is not specified.
CONTACT: The Director of Scholarships & Student Financial Aid.
(We were not able to verify this listing; it may not be extant.)

FOUNDATION: Kutz (Milton and Hattie) Foundation
REQUISITE: Scholarships only to Delaware residents.
APPLICATION: First time applications for freshmen only. Deadline 3/15. A formal application must be completed first.
CONTACT: 101 Garden of Eden Road, Wilmington, DE 19803. Robert N. Kerbel, Executive Secretary TEL: (302)764-7000 Ext. 25

FOUNDATION: Lynch (John B.) Scholarship Foundation
REQUISITE: Scholarships to residents of the Wilmington, DE, area, Must not be more than 30 years of age. Deadline 3/15.
APPLICATION: Completing a formal application required, must include a transcript, three references, and handwritten letter describing academic goals, summer employment, and other efforts to finance education, and some autobiographical info.
CONTACT: POB 4248, Wilmington, DE 19807-0248. Miss Eleanor L. Clemo, Secretary. (302)654-3444

FOUNDATION: Avon Products Foundation, Inc.
REQUISITE: Scholarships for children of current Avon Products, Inc.

employees and for high school seniors who reside in proximity to an Avon location.
APPLICATION: Deadline 11/2 Apply with letter & formal application
CONTACT: Nine West 57th Street, New York, NY 10019. Glenn S. Clarke, President. (212)546-6015

FOUNDATION: Beneficial Foundation, Inc.
REQUISITE: Scholarships for children of employees of affiliated corporations of Beneficial Corp or of the Beneficial Financial System.
APPLICATION: Application deadline is December 1st.
CONTACT: 1100 Carr Road, POB 911, Wilmington, DE 19899. John O. Williams, Vice-President. TEL: (302)425-2500

FOUNDATION: Presto Foundation
REQUISITE: Scholarships for children of employees of National Presto Industries, Inc.
APPLICATION: Accepted throughout the year.. Write for information.
CONTACT: POB 2105, Wilmington, DE 19899. Harriet Rose, 3925 North Hastings Way, Eau Claire, WI 54703. TEL: (715)839-2121

FOUNDATION: Raskob (The Bill) Foundation, Inc.
REQUISITE: Student loans to American citizens who are full-time, upper-class students and are attending accredited institutions.
APPLICATION: Application deadline is May 1st.
CONTACT: P.O. Box 4019, Wilmington, DE 19807. Patricia Garey, 1st Vice-President. (302)655-4440

FOUNDATION: H. Fletcher Brown Fund
REQUISITE: Scholarships granted to students born in Delaware, graduated for a Delaware school and is still a resident of Delaware. Must be pursuing a career in the field of Medicine, Dentistry, Law, Engineering or Chemistry. Must have good academic standing, need and good moral character. Undergraduate or graduate students. Must be USA citizen.
APPLICATION: Write for info. Application deadline is April 15th.
CONTACT: C/O Bank of Delaware, Trust Dept., Wilmington, DE 19899 (302)429-1109

FLORIDA

FOUNDATION: Florida Department of Education
REQUISITE: Scholarships granted to Florida resident for at least two

years.   Florida high school seniors enrolling as first time in college students studying Liberal Arts or Education.
APPLICATION: Write for info. Application deadline is March 1st.
CONTACT: Office of Student Financial Assistance, Knott Bldg., Tallahassee, FL 32399   Tel 904-488-4095

FOUNDATION: J. Hugh and Earle W. Fellows Memorial Fund
REQUISITE: Scholarship loans granted to bonafide residents of Escambia; Santa Rosa; Oklahoma; or Walton counties who are admitted to or currently enrolled in an accredited institution studying Medicine; Nursing; Medical Technology or Theology. Must have a minimum 2.5 GPA and be a US citizen.
APPLICATION: Write for info. Application deadline is not specified.
CONTACT: C/O Pensacola Junior College, 1000 College Blvd., Academic Affairs, Pensacola, FL 32504. Tel: 904-476-5410 ext. 1706

FOUNDATION: Florida Dental Association
REQUISITE: Scholarships granted to residents of Florida accepted to an accredited Dental Hygiene School in Florida.
APPLICATION: Write for info. Application deadline is July, Dec and 4/1.
CONTACT: 3021 Swann Ave., Tampa, FL 33609 Tel: 813-877-7597

FOUNDATION: J. Hugh and Earle W. Fellows Memorial Fund
REQUISITE: Scholarships granted to bonafide residents of Escambia, Santa Rosa, Okaloosa or Walton counties who are admitted to or currently attending an accredited institution. Must maintain at least a 2.5 GPA. Must be US citizen.
APPLICATION: Write for info. Application deadline is not specified.
CONTACT: C/O Pensacola Junior College, 1000 College Blvd., Academic Affairs, Pensacola, FL 32504. (904)484-2120

FOUNDATION: Cape Canaceral Chapter Retired Officers Association
REQUISITE: Scholarships granted to Brevard County Florida residents who are undergraduate juniors or seniors at any four year college in the USA and is the son or daughter of an active duty or retired military personnel. Must be US citizen.
APPLICATION: Write for info. Application deadline is June 30th.
CONTACT: POBOX 4186, Patrick AFB, FL 32925.
(We were not able to verify this listing; it may not be extant.)

FOUNDATION: Florida Department of Education

REQUISITE: Scholarships granted to Florida resident high school students enrolling in an accredited institution as a first-time college student pursuing a liberal arts or teaching degree.
APPLICATION: Write for info. Application deadline is March 1st.
CONTACT: Office of Student Financial Assistance, Knott Bldg., Tallahassee, FL 32399. (904)488-4095

FOUNDATION: Florida Department of Education
REQUISITE: Scholarships granted to certified Florida Public School Teachers. Scholarships provide repayment of education loans in return for teaching in department of education designated critical teacher shortage areas in Florida Public Schools.
APPLICATION: Write for info. Application deadline is March 1st.
CONTACT: Office of Student Financial Assistance, Knott Bldg., Tallahassee, FL 32399. (904)488-4095

FOUNDATION: Florida Department of Education
REQUISITE: Loans granted to full-time undergrad junior/senior or graduate student enrolled in a state approved teacher education program in a Florida college or university pursuing a career in education-designated critical teacher shortage field.
APPLICATION: Write for info. Application deadline is April 1st.
CONTACT: Office of Student Financial Assistance, Knott Bldg., Tallahassee, FL 32399. (904)488-4095

FOUNDATION: National FFA Center
REQUISITE: Scholarships granted to FFA member planning to enroll as a freshman in a 4-year undergraduate program at an accredited university or college in USA. Must be a USA citizen or legal resident. Must be a resident of CA;FL;SC;TN; or TX.
APPLICATION: Write for info. Application deadline is April 1st.
CONTACT: Scholarship Office, POBOX 15160, Alexandria, VA 22309. (703)360-3600

FOUNDATION: Abernathy (Sally) Charitable Education Fund
REQUISITE: Grants for individuals with preference given to students who live in the Winter Haven, FL area, and residents of Florida, attending schools in Florida.
APPLICATION: Write for more information.
CONTACT: c/o NationsBank, POB 1469, Tampa, Fl 33601. (813)224-5805

Florida

FOUNDATION: Children's Foundation of Lake Wales, Florida, Inc.
REQUISITE: Scholarships for students of the Lake Wales, FL, high school district.
APPLICATION: Deadline is May 15th. Write for more information.
CONTACT: c/o Albert E. McCormick, 1175 Yarnell Ave.,Lake Wales, FL 33853. Or David Rockness, Chairman, Organization Committee, 16 North Third Street, Lake Wales, FL 33853. TEL: (813)996-3600

FOUNDATION: Eagles Memorial Foundation
REQUISITE: Scholarships for the children of deceased Eagle servicemen and women, law officers, or fire fighters.
APPLICATION: Write for more information.
CONTACT: 4710 14th Street West, Bradenton, FL 33507. (813)391-2323

FOUNDATION: Ft Pierce Memorial Hospital Scholarship Fndtn
REQUISITE: Scholarships are limited to unmarried residents of St. Lucie County, FL, who will be studying in the health field.
APPLICATION: Application deadline is April 15th. Write for info.
CONTACT: c/o Lawnwood Medical Center, POB 188, 1700 South 23rd Street, Fort Pierce, FL 33450. Written inquiry only. (305)461-4000

FOUNDATION: Gore Family Memorial Foundation
REQUISITE: Scholarships for graduate and undergraduates who are handicapped. Scholarships for undergraduate residents of Broward County, FL, also.
APPLICATION: Applications are accepted throughout the year.
CONTACT: c/o Sun Bank, POB 14728, Ft Lauderdale, FL 33302 (305)781-8634

FOUNDATION: Heath Educational Fund
REQUISITE: Scholarships for male high school graduates who live in southeastern U.S. and wish to study for the ministry, missionary activities, or social work.
APPLICATION: Applications are accepted throughout the year.
CONTACT: c/o First Florida Bank, N.A., POB 11311, St. Petersburg, FL 33713. TEL: (813)892-1721 or 1(800)562-5725

FOUNDATION: Olliff (Matred Carlton) Foundation
REQUISITE: Scholarships for students primarily in Florida.
APPLICATION: Application deadline is July 1st.
CONTACT: POB 385, Wauchula, FL 33873. Mr. Doyle E. Carlton, Jr.,

Trustee. TEL: (813)773-4478

FOUNDATION: Palm Beach County Community Foundation
REQUISITE: Scholarships for residents Palm Beach Cnty, FL area
APPLICATION: Write for more information.
CONTACT: 324 Datura Street, Suite 340, West Palm Beach, FL 33401-9938. TEL: (407)992-9500

FOUNDATION: Pinellas County Community Foundation
REQUISITE: Schlrshps only for residents of Pinellas Cnty, FL.
APPLICATION: Write for more information.
CONTACT: 1253 Park Street, Clearwater, FL 33516. Thomas R. Bruckman, Executive Dir. (813)464-4851

FOUNDATION: Poynter Fund
REQUISITE: Undergraduate scholarships and graduate fellowships for students studying in journalism.
APPLICATION: Write foundation for application information.
CONTACT: 490 First Avenue South, POB 1121, St. Petersburg, FL 33731. TEL: (813)893-8650 ask for Mike Foley

FOUNDATION: Rinker Companies Foundation, Inc.
REQUISITE: Scholarships for Florida residents with business or construction industry-related majors.
APPLICATION: Application deadline is April.
CONTACT: 1501 Belvedere Road, West Palm Beach, FL 33406. Jack L. Osteen, Assistant Secretary. TEL: (407)835-5200

FOUNDATION: Robertson (Lois & Edward) Foundation
REQUISITE: Scholarships for graduates of Winter Park High School, Winter Park, FL.
APPLICATION: Write for more information.
CONTACT: 691 Lake Sue Ave., Winter Park, FL 32789. Edward H. Robertson, Vice-President. TEL: (407)644-6921

FOUNDATION: Sample (Adrian M.) Trust No. 2
REQUISITE: Scholarships for Protestant residents of St. Lucie or Okeechobee counties, FL.
APPLICATION: Deadline is April 15th and forms are available only through churches in those counties.
CONTACT: c/o Sun Bank/Treasure Coast, N.A., POB 8, Fort Pierce, FL

41

34954. Tel.:(305)461-6300. Or Charles W. Sample, 5311 Burningtree Drive, Orlando, FL 32811. TEL: (307)877-9901

FOUNDATION: Sorey (Vincent) Music Foundation, Inc.
REQUISITE: Grant for needy students for music education
APPLICATION: Write for more information.
CONTACT: 1039 18th Street, Miami Beach, FL 33139. (305)757-5073

FOUNDATION: Southwest Florida Community Foundation, Inc.
REQUISITE: Scholarships only to students from Lee County High School who have a B average or better.
APPLICATION: Application deadlines are February 1st and May 1st. Write for more information.
CONTACT: Drawer LL, Fort Meyers, FL 33902. Christine M. Roberts, Executive Director. TEL: (813)334-0377

FOUNDATION: Cape Canaveral Chapter Retired Officers Assoc
REQUISITE: Scholarships granted to Brevard County Florida residents who are undergraduate juniors or seniors at any 4-year college in the USA and is the so or daughter of an Active Duty or Retired Military Personnel. Must be USA citizen.
APPLICATION: Write for info. Application deadline is June 30th.
CONTACT: POBOX 4186, Patrick AFB, FL 32925.
(We were not able to verify this listing; it may not be extant.)

FOUNDATION: Stark (Donald A. & Jane C.) Charitable Trust
REQUISITE: Scholarships for student
APPLICATION: Write for more information
CONTACT: c/o B. Wade White, Trustee, 5036 Willow Leaf Way, Sarasota, FL 33583. TEL: (813)755-5165

FOUNDATION: Watterson (Grace Margaret) Trust
REQUISITE: Scholarships for graduating seniors of the Datona Beach area and certain areas of Canada.
APPLICATION: Application deadline is December 31st.
CONTACT: Frst Unn Ntnl Bnk of FL, 444 Seabreeze Blvd, Daytona Beach, FL 32018. June Phelps, Trust Officer. TEL: (904)252-5591

FOUNDATION: Inland Steel-Ryerson Foundation
REQUISITE: Scholarships for children of employees of Inland Steel Company and its subsidiaries.

APPLICATION: Applications accepted throughout the year.
CONTACT: Inland Steel Indstrs, 30 W Monroe St, Chicago, IL 60603. Earl Thompson, Drctr, State & Regnl Affairs. TEL: (312)899-3421

FOUNDATION: Florida Department of Education
REQUISITE: Scholarships granted to Florida residents for at least two years. Florida public high school seniors enrolling as first-time students at a state university or community college in Florida. Students must be pursuing a career in Liberal Arts or Teaching.
APPLICATION: Write for info. Application deadline is March 1st.
CONTACT: Office of Student Financial Assistance, Knott Bldg., Tallahassee, FL 32399. (904)488-4095

FOUNDATION: Florida Arts Council
REQUISITE: Fellowships granted to individual artists who must be residents of Florida and over the age of 18. Must be USA citizen.
APPLICATION: Write for info. Application deadline is February 9th.
CONTACT: FL Dept of State/Divn of Cultural Affairs/ The Capitol, Tallahassee, FL 32301. (904)487-2980

FOUNDATION: Kelly Foundation, Inc.
REQUISITE: Scholarships for children of employees of Kelly Tractor Company and also for residents FL.
APPLICATION: Applications accepted throughout the year.
CONTACT: 800 East Sugarland Highway, Clewiston, FL 33440. Robert Kelly, President. (813)983-8177

FOUNDATION: Pantry Pride Foundation
REQUISITE: Schlrshps for children of employees of Food Fair Stores, Inc., Pantry Pride, Inc. and others.
APPLICATION: Application deadline is March 1st.
CONTACT: 555 Southwest 12th Avenue, Pompano Beach, FL 33069. TEL: (305)785-4334 or leave a message on voice mail.

FOUNDATION: Fellows (J. Hugh & Earl W.) Memorial Fndtn
REQUISITE: Low-interest loans for students of nursing, medicine, medical technology, and theology. These students must live in Escambia, Santa Rosa, Okaloosa, or Walton counties, FL. These students must also agree to pursue their professions in this area for five years.
APPLICATION: Applications are accepted throughout the year.
CONTACT: Beggs and Lane, POB 12950, Pensacola, FL 32576-2950.

FOUNDATION: Phillips (The Dr. P.) Foundation
REQUISITE: Student loans for residents of Orange County, FL, for studying medicine, engineering, or accounting.
APPLICATION: Write for more information.
CONTACT: 60 West Robinson Street, P.O. Box 3753, Orlando, FL 32802. J. A. Hinson, President. TEL: (305)422-6105

FOUNDATION: Pickett & Hatcher Educational Fund, Inc.
REQUISITE: Undergraduate student loans for those who live in AL, FL, GA, KY, MS, NC, SC, TN, and VA. There is no support for those planning to study medicine, law, or ministry.
APPLICATION: Application deadline is May 15th. First-time applicants may request their application after October 1st.
CONTACT: 1800 Buena Vista Rd, P.O. Box 8169, Columbus, GA 31908. Robert Bennett, Executive VP. TEL: (404)327-6586

FOUNDATION: Scadron (Irene Haas) Memorial Edctnl Fndtn
REQUISITE: Educational loans for young white needy students who graduated from Florida high schools, preference given to those in Gadsden County.
APPLICATION: Applications are accepted throughout the year.
CONTACT: c/o Quincy State Bank, Trust Department, P.O. Box 898, Quincy, FL 32351.

FOUNDATION: The ITT Rayonier Foundation
REQUISITE: Must be a student graduating from a high school or residing in an area of company operations in Nassau County, FL, Wayne Cnty, Georgia, or Clallem, Mason, & Grays Harbor counties, WA.
APPLICATION: Applications available from principals of high school in areas of company operations. No deadline listed.
CONTACT: Corporate Relations, 1177 Summer St., Stamford, CT 06904. TEL: (203)348-7000

GEORGIA

FOUNDATION: Georgia Council for the Arts
REQUISITE: Scholarships granted to support professional artists. Awards given on the basis of projects artistic merit and potential for career development. It must be sponsored by nonprofit organization in GA.
APPLICATION: Write for info. Application deadline is April 20th.
CONTACT: 2082 E. Exchange Pl., Suite 100, Tucker, GA 30084

(404)651-7920

FOUNDATION: Baker (Clark and Ruby) Foundation
REQUISITE: Scholarships based on financial need to Georgia residents for study at a college or university operated by or affiliated with the Methodist church.
APPLICATION: Applications must be in letter form, telling your educational plans and anticipated expenses. Interviews required.
CONTACT: c/o Bank South, Personal Trust Department, POB 4956, Atlanta, GA 30302. Odette Capell, Scrtry, or Tom Murphy.

FOUNDATION: Brightwell (A.T.)School, Inc.
REQUISITE: Scholarships awarded to unmarried or divorced (proof necessary) students under the age of 30. They must have lived in Maxey, GA, area for six months prior to the date of the scholarship. Parents of students must live in and remain living in Maxey, GA for the lifetime of the award.
APPLICATION: Write for more info.
CONTACT: 254 Oakland Ave, Athens, GA 30606.   Harold Darden, Executive Secretary.

FOUNDATION: Callaway (Fuller E.)Foundation
REQUISITE: Schlrshps only to residents of Troup Cnty, GA.
APPLICATION: Deadlines February 15th for college scholarships, July 15th for law school scholarships. Must send a letter and complete a formal application.
CONTACT: 209 Broome Street, POB 790, La Grange, GA 30241. J.T. Gresham, General Manager.

FOUNDATION: Cape Foundation, Inc.
REQUISITE: Scholarship grants to undergraduate students attending colleges or universities in the Atlanta, GA, area.
APPLICATION: Applications are supplied between 3/1 and 9/10. Must submit financial aid papers from the financial aid office for the year that you wish to attend and are applying for.
CONTACT: 550 Pharr Road, N.E. Suite 605, Atlanta, GA 30305. S.G. Armstrong, Trustee.

FOUNDATION: Churches Home Foundation, Inc.
REQUISITE: Scholarships primarily to Georgia residents with evidence of financial need and good academic performance.

APPLICATION: Applications are accepted throughout the year. A letter must be submitted also.
CONTACT: Bank South, N.A.- Personal Trust Department, POB 4956 Atlanta, GA 30302. Duncan G. Peek, President, 1100 Spring St.,N.W., Suite 600, Atlanta, GA 30367 TEL: (404)872-8733.

FOUNDATION: Cobb (Ty) Educational Fund
REQUISITE: Schlrshps limited to needy GA residents who have completed one year at an accredited institution of higher learning. Graduate scholarships available for law, medical, or dental students.
APPLICATION: Deadlines July 15th for applications and July 1st for college transcripts for the most recent term of attendance.
CONTACT: POB 725, Forest Prk, GA 30051. Rosie Atkins, Secretary.

FOUNDATION: Georgia Student Finance Authority
REQUISITE: Scholarships granted to Georgia resident of 12 months or more. Undergraduate or graduate students at a Georgia institutions with a GPA of 3.25 or more planning to pursue a career in teaching on a elementary or secondary level only.
APPLICATION: Write for info. Application deadline is May 1st.
CONTACT: 2082 East Exchange Place, Suite 200, Tucker, GA 30084. (404)414-3200

FOUNDATION: Georgia Student Finance Authority
REQUISITE: Scholarships granted to high school seniors that have been residents of Georgia for at least 1 year. Undergraduate study must be at a Federally funded program in Georgia for students pursuing a career in teaching on a pre-school, elementary or secondary level. Must be a US citizen or legal resident.
APPLICATION: Write for info. Application deadline is May 1st.
CONTACT: 2082 East Exchange Plance, Ste 200, Tucker, GA 30084 (404)414-3200

FOUNDATION: Community Welfare Assctn of Colquitt Cnty
REQUISITE: Scholarships for higher education.
APPLICATION: Write for more information.
CONTACT: POB 460, Moultrie, GA 31776.

FOUNDATION: GFF Educational Foundation, Inc
REQUISITE: Scholarships primarily for residents of Georgia.
APPLICATION: Write for information.

CONTACT: POB 826, Norcross, GA 30091. F. Roy Nelson, Secretary TEL: (404)729-5700.

FOUNDATION: Sapelo Island Research Foundation, Inc.
REQUISITE: Scholarships only to Georgia residents for study in marine biology and marine research.
APPLICATION: Application deadlines are 3/15 and 9/15.
CONTACT: 1425 21st St, N.W., Washington, DC 20036. Margery Tabankin, Executive Dir. TEL: (202)822-9193

FOUNDATION: Wetherbee (Harold and Sara) Foundation
REQUISITE: Schlrshps for residents of Dougherty Cnty, GA.
APPLICATION: Submitted through the superintendent's office of the Dougherty County School System.
CONTACT: c/o First State Bank & Trust Company, POB 8, Albany, GA 31703. Joe Powell, Trust Officer.

FOUNDATION: Avon Products Foundation, Inc
REQUISITE: Schlrshps for children of current Avon Products, Inc. employees and for high school seniors that live close to Avon location.
APPLICATION: Deadline is 11/2. Formal letter is required.
CONTACT: Nine West 57th Street, New York, NY 10019. Glenn S. Clarke. TEL: (212)546-6731

FOUNDATION: Jewell (The Daniel Ashley and Irene Houston) Mmrl Fndtn
REQUISITE: Undergraduate scholarships for children of employees of Crystal Springs Printwork, Inc., Chickamauga, GA, and high school seniors that live in the areas of Dade, Catoosa, or Walker counties, to attend accredited college in Georgia, Alabama, or Tennessee.
APPLICATION: Accepted throughout the year. Letter is needed.
CONTACT: c/o American National Bank and Trust Company, POB 1638, Chattanooga, TN 37401. Peter Cooper, Treasurer. (615)757-3203

FOUNDATION: Levi Strauss Foundation
REQUISITE: Business Opportunity Schlrshps to disadvantaged hgh schl snrs in US communities where Levi Strauss & Co. has production or distribution facilities including AR, CA, GA, NV, NM, TX, & VA.
APPLICATION: Applications accepted throughout the year. Must send letter requesting an application.
CONTACT: 1155 Battery St, POB 7215, SF, CA 94106 Martha Brown, Drctr of U.S. Contributions. (415)544-6577

Georgia

FOUNDATION: Bibb Foundation, Inc.
REQUISITE: Scholarships for children of employees of The Bibb Co
APPLICATION: Application deadline is April 30th.
CONTACT: POB 4207, Macon, GA 31208. Allan V. Davis, President.
TEL: (912)741-0226

FOUNDATION: Evinrude (The Ole) Foundation
REQUISITE: Scholarships for children of employees of
Outboard Marine Crprtn in WI, IL, TN, MS, NC, GA, and NE.
APPLICATION: Application deadline is October 31st.
CONTACT: 100 Sea Horse Drive, Waukegan, IL 60085. F. James Short,
Vice-President. TEL: (312)689-5235

FOUNDATION: World Carpets Foundation, Inc.
REQUISITE: Schlrshps to kids of employees of World Carpets, Inc.
APPLICATION: Application deadline is March 15th.
CONTACT: One World Plaza, POB 1448, Dalton, GA 30722-1448. Jim
Carrier, Chairman, Scholarship Committee. TEL: (706)278-8460

FOUNDATION: Pickett & Hatcher Educational Fund, Inc.
REQUISITE: Undergraduate student loans for those who live in AL, FL,
GA, KY, MS, NC, SC, TN, and VA. There is no support for those planning
to study medicine, law, or ministry.
APPLICATION: Application deadline is May 15th. First-time applicants
may request their application after October 1st.
CONTACT: 1800 Buena Vista Rd, P.O. Box 8169, Columbus, GA 31908.
Robert Bennett, Executive VP. TEL: (706)327-6586

FOUNDATION: Student Aid Foundation
REQUISITE: Student loans for female legal residents of Georgia.
APPLICATION: Applications are accepted throughout the year.
CONTACT: c/o First National Bank of Atlanta, Trust Tax Dept., P.O. Box
4148, MC701, Atlanta, GA 30302. Or Marjorie Ware, Executive Secretary,
788 Reckle Drive, Decatur, GA. TEL: (404)332-5000

FOUNDATION: The ITT Rayonier Foundation
REQUISITE: Must be a student graduating from a high school or residing
in an area of co. operations in Nassau County, FL, Wayne County,
Georgia, or Clallem, Mason, & Grays Harbor counties, WA.
APPLICATION: Applications available from principals of high school in
areas of company operations. No deadline listed.

CONTACT: Jerome D. Gregoire, VP, 1177 Summer St., Stamford, CT 06904. TEL: (203)348-7000

HAWAII

FOUNDATION: Hawaiian Trust Company Limited
REQUISITE: Scholarships granted to graduates of Hawaii Public High Schools who attend an accredited Mainland College or University. Scholarships granted for all Social Sciences and various other majors.
APPLICATION: Write for info. Application deadline is March 1st.
CONTACT: POBOX 3170, Honolulu, HI 96802. Tel: 808-525-6512

FOUNDATION: Hawaiian Trust Company Limited
REQUISITE: Scholarships granted to residents of Leeward-Oaho-Hawaii who plan to pursue a career of study leading to a career in a health related profession at an accredited institution.
APPLICATION: Write for info. Application deadline is March 1st.
CONTACT: POBOX 3170, Honolulu, HI 96802. (808)538-4444

FOUNDATION: Women's Association for the Honolulu Symphony
REQUISITE: Scholarships granted to Hawaii residents undergraduates orchestra majors.
APPLICATION: Write for info. Application deadline is during Spring Break.
CONTACT: 1441 Kapiolani Blvd. Suite 1515, Honolulu, HI 96814 (808)942-2200

FOUNDATION: Atherton Family Foundation
REQUISITE: The Hawaii scholarships go to residents who are children of Protestant ministers, or graduate theological students at a Protestant seminary.
APPLICATION: Initial approach contact the foundation or the financial aid administrator as well as high school counselor. Deadline March 1st completion of formal application is required.
CONTACT: Jane R. Smith Secretary, c\o HI Trust Company, Ltd., P.O. Box 3170, Honolulu,HI 96802.

FOUNDATION: Bohnett Vi Memorial Foundation
REQUISITE: Scholarships to individuals,
APPLICATION: Initial approach by letter.
CONTACT: 315 Ulumiu St, Room 208A P.O. Box 1361 Kailua, HI 96734.

FOUNDATION: California Masonic Foundation
REQUISITE: The scholarships are for full-time freshman undergraduate students in California with residency of at least one year or Hawaii who are U.S. citizens.
APPLICATION: Accepting applications on Nov. 1 and the deadline is Feb. 28. The initial approach is by personal letter requesting a schlrshp. Completion of formal application is required, including transcripts, name of college where accepted, evidence of financial need, and information about other scholarships received, also letters of recommendations. Interviews not granted.
CONTACT: Judy Liang; 1111 California Street, San Francisco, CA 94108 (808)776-7000

FOUNDATION: Fukunaga Scholarship Foundation
REQUISITE: Scholarships are for residents of Hawaii for a minimum of one year to study business administration at the University of Hawaii or any other accredited university.
APPLICATION: The deadline is 3/15. Completion of formal application alone with school transcript, SAT scores, and at least two letters of reference (one) from high school principal, teacher, or counselor, and (one) from business or professional person in the community. Interviews are required for semi-finalists.
CONTACT: The Scholarship Selection Committee, P.O. Box 2788, Honolulu, HI 96803.

FOUNDATION: Hemenway (Charles R.) Scholarship Trust
REQUISITE: Scholarships are for residents of Hawaii who plan to or do attend the University of Hawaii. Deadline is April 1st.
APPLICATION: Applications can be obtained from the financial aid offices of the University of Hawaii campuses. Manoa Campus, 2442 Campus Road, Honolulu, HI; Tel.:(808)961-9311, and Hilo Campus, Box 1357, Hilo, HI; Tel.:(808)961-9323. Interviews are required.
CONTACT: c/o Hawaiian Trust Company, Ltd., Box 3170, Honolulu, HI 96802 TEL: (808)525-8511

FOUNDATION: Kaiulani Home for Girls Trust
REQUISITE: Undergraduates scholarships for girls that are legal residents of Hawaii. Preference given to those of Hawaiian ancestry.
APPLICATION: Application deadline is March 1st. Applicants must reapply each year.
CONTACT: c/o Hawaiian Trust Company, Ltd., POB 3170, Honolulu, HI

96802. TEL: (808)525-8511

FOUNDATION: Pope (Ida M.) Memorial Scholarship Fund
REQUISITE: Scholarships for female residents of Hawaii who are of Hawaiian ancestry.
APPLICATION: Application deadline is May 1st and a Financial Aid Form (FAF) is required.
CONTACT: c/o Hawaiian Trust Company, Ltd., POB 3170, Honolulu, HI 96802. Mrs. G. Johansen, c/o The Kamehameha Schools, Counseling Office, Kapalama Heights, Honolulu, HI 96817. TEL: (808)842-8612

FOUNDATION: Ross (John M.) Foundation
REQUISITE: Undergraduate scholarships only for residents of the Island of Hawaii (Big Island).
APPLICATION: Applications accepted throughout the year.
CONTACT: Bishop Trst Co, Ltd., Hilo Branch, Box 397, Hilo, HI 96720.

FOUNDATION: Straub (Gertrude S.) Trust Estate
REQUISITE: Scholarships for Hawaiian high school graduates who plan to attend mainland U.S. colleges or universities. Major must be relating international understanding and cooperation and world peace.
APPLICATION: The times for submitting applications are between 1/1 and 3/1 with 3/1 being the deadline.
CONTACT: c/o Hawaiian Trust Co, Ltd., POB 3170, Honolulu, HI 96802, Janis A. Reischman, Administrator. TEL: (808)525-6512

FOUNDATION: Zimmerman (Hans and Clara Davis) Foundation
REQUISITE: Scholarships for legal residents of Hawaii who are going to be full-time students at an accredited two or four-year college or university. Preference given to those majoring in medicine, nursing, or other related health fields.
APPLICATION: Application deadline is March 1st. Requests for applications must be made by 2/1.
CONTACT: Hawaiian Trust Company, Ltd., POB 3170, Honolulu, HI 96802. Janis A. Reischmann, Administrator. TEL: (808)525-6512

IOWA

FOUNDATION: Iowa College Aid Commission
REQUISITE: Scholarships granted to Iowa residents enrolled in or accepted for enrollment into a program of vocational-technical study at a

51

school in Iowa. Must be US citizen or legal resident.
APPLICATION: Write for info. Application deadline is March 2nd.
CONTACT: 201 Jewett Building, 9th and Grand Avenue, Des Moines, IA 50309. Tel: 515-281-3501

FOUNDATION: Easter Seal Society of Iowa
REQUISITE: Scholarships granted to Iowa residents who are full-time undergraduate sophomores, juniors, seniors or graduate students at an accredited institution pursuing a career in the field of rehabilitation. Applicants must be needy and in top 40% of their class.
APPLICATION: Write for info. Application deadline is April 15th.
CONTACT: POBOX 4002, Des Moines, IA 50333. (515)274-1529

FOUNDATION: Bradish (Norman C.) Trust
REQUISITE: Scholarship for a male graduate of Decorah High School, Decorah, IA, and a male graduate student at the University of Wisconsin who is majoring in the Department of Philosophy and selected by the Dean of the Graduate School and Chairman of the Dept of Philosophy.
APPLICATION: Write for an application.
CONTACT: Freedom Savings, POB 1420, Winter Park, FL 32790. Decorah High School, Decorah, IA; University of Wisconsin, Department of Philosophy.

FOUNDATION: Collins (Paul and Mary) Trust, No. 2
REQUISITE: 1st stipulation: last name has to be in the 1969 Manhattan, NY telephone book. Schlrshps for students pursuing a college education.
APPLICATION: Deadline is February 15th.
CONTACT: Lyons County State Bank, 203 S Second Ave., Rock Rapids, IA 51246 (712) 472-2581

FOUNDATION: Fahrney Education Foundation
REQUISITE: Scholarships only for residents Wapello Cnty, IA.
APPLICATION: Deadline is 2/15.
CONTACT: c/o Union Bank-Trust Department, 123 East Third St., Ottumwa, IA 52501. Scholarship Committee. TEL: (515))683-1641

FOUNDATION: Furnas Foundation, Inc.
REQUISITE: Schlrshps for undergraduates residing within 12 miles of Batavia Government Center, Batavia, IL, or in Clarke Cnty, IA
APPLICATION: Application deadline is 3/15. Can write a letter requesting an application from the Scholarship Committee.

CONTACT: 1000 McKee St, Batavia, IL 60510. Jo Ann Hogan. (312)879-6000

FOUNDATION: Lee Endowment Foundation
REQUISITE: Scholarships for residents of Mason City and Cerro Gordo County, IA.
APPLICATION: Application deadline is February 24th.
CONTACT: c/o First Trust Company of Montana, POB 30678, Billings, MT 59115. Dr. David L. Buettner, Chairman, Nominating Committee, North Iowa Area Community College, 500 College Drive, Mason City, IA 50401. TEL: (515)423-1264

FOUNDATION: Preston (Elmer O. & Ida) Educational Trust
REQUISITE: Scholarships and student loans for worthy and needy young Protestant men who live in IA and will be attending a university in IA.
APPLICATION: Application are accepted throughout the year.
CONTACT: Monica Morgan. Des Moines Building, 801 Grand, Suite 3700, Des Moines, IA 50309. TEL: (515)243-4191

FOUNDATION: Reifel-Ellwood Education Trust
REQUISITE: Scholarships for high school seniors who live in Montgomery County, IA.
APPLICATION: Application deadline is April 21st.
CONTACT: 323 Reed St., POB 378, Red Oak, IA 51566. Kenneth Rech, Trustee. TEL: (712)623-3218

FOUNDATION: Sinek (Joseph J.)Scholarship Trust
REQUISITE: Undergraduate scholarships for graduates of Pocahontas Community Schl, Pocahontas, IA. APPLICATION: Application deadline is March 31st.
CONTACT: Martin Jacobemier, Guidance Counselor, Pocahontas Community School, 201 1st Ave. Southwest, Pocahontas, IA 50574. (712)335-4848

FOUNDATION: Iowa College Aid Commission
REQUISITE: Scholarships granted to Iowa high school seniors who have applied to Iowa State Scholarship Program, are in the top 10% of their class and want to teach in specific areas of need on an elementary or secondary level. US citizen or legal resident.
APPLICATION: Write for info. Application deadline is December 1st and March 1st.

CONTACT: 201 Jewett Bldg, 9TH & Grand Ave., Des Moines, IA 50309 (We were not able to verify this listing; it may not be extant.)

FOUNDATION: Swiss Benevolent Society of Chicago.
REQUISITE: Scholarships for full-time, undergraduate students who are of Swiss decent & live in IA, IL, IN, MI, WI.
APPLICATION: Application deadline is March 1st.
CONTACT: Professor Jean Devaud, Chairman of S.B.S. Scholarship Committee, 629 South Humphrey Avenue, Oak Park, IL 60304.

FOUNDATION: Waverly Community Foundation
REQUISITE: Scholarships for students who live in Waverly, IA.
APPLICATION: Write for info.
CONTACT: State Bank of Waverly, Waverly, IA 50677. Arnold A. Frederick, Senior Trust Officer.

FOUNDATION: McElroy (R.J.) Trust
REQUISITE: Fellowships are granted by nomination only for graduate students of liberal arts colleges located in the KWWL viewing area in northeast Iowa.
APPLICATION: Nomination deadline is in Feb. Contact well before then
CONTACT: 500 E 4th St., KWWL Bldg, Waterloo, IA 50703. Linda L Klinger Executive Dir (319)291-1299

FOUNDATION: Maytag Company Foundation
REQUISITE: Scholarships for graduating seniors of Newton High School, IA, and also for children of employees of Maytag Company or the Maytag Corporation staff.
APPLICATION: Application deadlines vary, so contact the foundation for current application deadlines.
CONTACT: c/o Maytag Corporation, One Dependability Square, Newton, IA 50208. Chairman, Scholarship Committee or Chrmn, Career Education Awards Committee. TEL: (515)791-8216

FOUNDATION: Pella Rolscreen Foundation
REQUISITE: Scholarships for kids of employees of Pella Rolscreen Co.
APPLICATION: Applications are accepted throughout the year.
CONTACT: Rolscreen Company, 102 Main Street, Pella, IA 50219. Bill Anderson. TEL: (515)628-1000

FOUNDATION: Jay (George S. & Grace A.) Memorial Trust

REQUISITE: Student loans for graduates of high schools in the Shenandoah, Essex, or Farragut areas.
APPLICATION: Application deadline is May 31st.
CONTACT: Eileen Dinville, 612 1/2 Sheridan Ave., Shenandoah, IA 51601.
TEL: (712)246-3399

FOUNDATION: Pritchard Educational Fund
REQUISITE: Student loans for residents Cherokee Cnty, IA.
APPLICATION: Applications are accepted throughout the year.
CONTACT: James R. Mohn. Cherokee State Bank, 212 W Willow St, Cherokee, IA 51012. TEL: (712)225-3000

IDAHO

FOUNDATION: Idaho Society for Medical Technology
REQUISITE: Internships granted to Idaho residents who are fourth year undergraduates or graduates with a bachelor's degree for medical technology internship. Must be recommended by a teaching supervisor in the clinical area, by supervising pathologists and two professors in science courses at the undergraduate level.
APPLICATION: Write for info. Application deadline is not specified.
CONTACT: C/O Magic Valley Memorial Hospital, Twin Falls, ID 83301.
208-737-2000

FOUNDATION: Rouch (A.P. and Louise) Boys Foundation
REQUISITE: Scholarships for needy student attending college in the area of Magic Valley of ID.
APPLICATION: Write for info.
CONTACT: c/o Twin Falls Bank & Trust, Trust Department, POB 7, Twin Falls, ID 83303-0007. TEL: (208)736-1400

FOUNDATION: Foundation Northwest
REQUISITE: Schlrshps for students living in Bonner Cnty, ID.
APPLICATION: Deadline 4/1. Contact by letter for application.
CONTACT: Citizen Scholarship Fndtn of America, POB 297, St. Peter, MN 56082 (800)537-4180

FOUNDATION: Steele-Reese Foundation
REQUISITE: Schlrshps for residents of Lemhi and Custer cntys, ID.
APPLICATION: Applications accepted throughout the year. Can contact by letter for application. High school seniors apply through their schools.

CONTACT: c/o Messrs. Davidson, Dawson and Clark, 330 Madison Ave, New York, NY 10017. Lydia Schofield, Scholarship Director, Box 922, Salmon, ID 83467.

FOUNDATION: Treacy Company
REQUISITE: Scholarships for undergraduate study for residents of ID, MT, ND, SD or attending institutions in ID, MT, ND, SD.
APPLICATION: Application deadline is June 15th.
CONTACT: Box 1700, Helena, MT 59624 James O'Connell. (406)442-3632

FOUNDATION: Potlatch Foundation for Higher Education
REQUISITE: Scholarships for undergraduates who live in areas of Potlatch Corporation operations.
APPLICATION: Application deadline is February 1st for new applications and July 1st for renewals. Request for applications must be made by 10/15 preceding the year for which the scholarship is sought.
CONTACT: POB 3591, San Francisco, CA 94119. George C. Check, President. TEL: (415)576-8800

ILLINOIS

FOUNDATION: Peoria Journal Star
REQUISITE: Scholarships granted to high school seniors living in the "Journal Star" readership area. Student must appear for personal interview. Student must be studying Journalism-Newspaper.
APPLICATION: Write for info. Application deadline is May 1st.
CONTACT: 1 News Plaza, Peoria, IL 61643 Tel: 309-686-3027

FOUNDATION: Illinois Restaurant Association
REQUISITE: Scholarships granted to Illinois resident undergraduate students studying food service management; culinary arts; food processing or related areas at an accredited institution in the USA.
APPLICATION: Write for info. Application deadline is not specified.
CONTACT: 20 North Wacker Dr. Chicago, IL 60606 Tel: 312-372-6200

FOUNDATION: McFarland Charitable Foundation Trust
REQUISITE: Scholarships granted to Illinois resident undergraduate nursing degree candidates enrolled in an accredited institution who must agree to return to the Havana, IL area to work as a nurse for an agree upon number of years upon completion of education.
APPLICATION: Write for info. Application deadline is May 1st.

CONTACT: C/O Havana National Bank, 112 S. Orange; POBOX 489, Havana, IL 62644 309-543-3361

FOUNDATION: Dupage Medical Society Foundation
REQUISITE: Scholarships granted to residents of Depage county or requisite college degree with good academic record.
APPLICATION: Write for info. Applctn deadline is Dec. thru March.
CONTACT: 800 Roosevelt Bldg., B. #300, Glen Ellyn, IL 60137. (708)858-9603

FOUNDATION: University of Illinois at Urbana-Champaign
REQUISITE: Scholarships granted to undergraduates at the University of Illinois with a GPA of 3.85 or higher and is registered for at least 15 hours. Must be US citizen or legal resident.
APPLICATION: Write for info. Application deadline is not specified.
CONTACT: Student Services Bldg, 610 East John Street, Champaign, IL 61820. (217)333-0100

FOUNDATION: Illinois Arts Council
REQUISITE: Scholarships granted to complete or create new work in the various fields of the Arts.
APPLICATION: Write for info. Application deadline is November 1st.
CONTACT: 111 North Wabash Ave., Chicago, IL 60602.
(We were not able to verify this listing; it may not be extant.)

FOUNDATION: University of Illinois at Urbana-Champaign
REQUISITE: Scholarships granted for undergraduate study at the University of Illinois. Students must maintain a 3.85 GPA or better and carry 15 hour full-time study each semester. Must be US citizen or legal resident.
APPLICATION: Write for info. Application deadline is Mid-March.
CONTACT: Student Services Bldg., 610 East John ST., Champaign, IL 61820. (217)333-0100

FOUNDATION: Joseph Blazek Foundation
REQUISITE: Scholarships granted to residents of Cook county, Illinois high school seniors pursuing a career in Science, Chemistry, Engineering, Mathematics and Physics at an accredited 4-year institution.
APPLICATION: Write for info. Application deadline is February 1st.
CONTACT: 8 South Michigan Ave., Chicago, IL 60603.
(We were not able to verify this listing; it may not be extant.)

FOUNDATION: National FFA Center
REQUISITE: Scholarships granted to FFA member planning to enroll as a freshman in a 4-year undergraduate program at an accredited university or college in USA. Must be a USA citizen or legal resident. Must be a resident of Illinois and Missouri.
APPLICATION: Write for info. Application deadline is April 1st.
CONTACT: Scholarship Office, POBOX 15160, Alexandria, VA 22309. (703)360-3600

FOUNDATION: Furnas Foundation, Inc.
REQUISITE: Must be a student who resides within 12 miles of the Batavia Government Center, Batavia, IL, or in Clarke Cnty, IA.
APPLICATION: Submit letter requesting application from Scholarship Committee. Deadline March 1.
CONTACT: K. Nance, 1000 McKee St., Batavia, IL 60510. (708)879-2404

FOUNDATION: The Cultural Society, Inc.
REQUISITE: Must be a Muslim student.
APPLICATION: Write for info. No deadline listed.
CONTACT: Mohammed Nasr, M.D., Treasurer, POB 1374, Bridgeview, IL 60455. TEL: (312)371-6429

FOUNDATION: Joseph Blazek Foundation
REQUISITE: Must be a high school senior in public or private scndry school in Cook Cnty, IL, who is planning to major in engineering, mathematics, chemistry, physics, or related scientific fields.
APPLICATION: Write for info. Deadline 2/1 of high school senior year.
CONTACT: Samuel S. Brown, Exec. Dir., 8 S. Michigan Ave., No. 801, Chicago, IL 60603. (312)372-3888

FOUNDATION: Educational Foundation of the National Restaurant Association
REQUISITE: Scholarships & Fellowships to any individual studying in the food service area. Work-study grants are also available to teachers & administrators.
APPLICATION: Write for info. Deadlines April 1 for scholarships & fellowships & December 31 for work-study grants.
CONTACT: 250 S. Wacker Dr., Chicago, IL 60606. TEL: (312)715-1010

FOUNDATION: Marcus & Theresa Levie Educational Fund
REQUISITE: Must be a Jewish student who resides in Cook Cnty, IL, &

has demonstrated career promise & has financial need.
APPLICATION: Write or call for info. & application requests; preferably by phone. Interviews required. Deadline March 1; applications accepted between November & February.
CONTACT: Ruth Elbaum, Secty., Jewish Federation of Metropolitan Chicago, One S. Franklin St., Chicago, IL 60606 TEL: (312)346-6700

FOUNDATION: Robin Scholarship Foundation
REQUISITE: Must be an IL high school senior who is from a low income family & shows high promise.
APPLICATION: Applications available through high schls. Deadline 1/15.
CONTACT: 1333 N. Wells St., Chicago, IL 60610 (312)642-6301

FOUNDATION: The Schweppe Foundation
REQUISITE: Medical research fellowships for training at Chicago area medical schools or university-affiliated hospitals. All fellowships are granted to institutions on behalf of individuals.
APPLICATION: Write for info. Deadline September 1.
CONTACT: 845 N. Michigan Ave., Rm. 949 W, Chicago, IL 60611

FOUNDATION: Skidmore, Owings & Merrill Foundation
REQUISITE: Fellowships, scholarships & awards for research, education or publication relating to architecture &/or architectural engineering.
APPLICATION: Write for info. No deadline listed.
CONTACT: Sonia Cooke, Administrative Dir., 33 W. Monroe St., Chicago, IL 60603 TEL: (312)554-9090

FOUNDATION: Katherine Bogardus Trust
REQUISITE: Must be a graduate of high schools in DeWitt County, IL, or a descendant of the first cousins of the creator of this trust.
APPLICATION: Interviews required. Contact foundation for deadline.
CONTACT: Cecil L. Nunnery, Trust Officer, c/o The John Warner Bank, 301 S. Side Sq., Clinton, IL 61727 (217)935-3144

FOUNDATION: DeKalb County Producer's Supply & Farm Bureau Scholarship Trust Fund
REQUISITE: Must be an IL resident obtaining a medical education (including veterinary medicine, nursing, & pharmacology) whose parents have been members of the DeKalb County Farm Bureau in good standing for 2 years.
APPLICATION: Write for info. No deadline listed.

CONTACT: 315 N. 6th St., DeKalb, IL 60115 TEL: (815)756-6361

FOUNDATION: Karnes Memorial Fund
REQUISITE: Must be a college student who resides in Fairbury, Forrest or Chatsworth, IL.
APPLICATION: Write for info. Deadline March 1.
CONTACT: Board of Governors, POB 2, Fairbury, IL 61739

FOUNDATION: Charles M. Ross Trust
REQUISITE: Primarily graduate scholarships in the fields of religion, sociology, medicine & teaching.
APPLICATION: Write for info. by 01/02. Deadline January 22.
CONTACT: Paul G. Mason, Dir., 113 West Walnut, Fairbury, IL 61739
TEL: (815) 692-4336

FOUNDATION: Geneseo Foundation
REQUISITE: Must be a graduate of Geneseo High School, IL.
APPLICATION: Write for info. Deadline first week of the month.
CONTACT: John DuBois, c/o Central Trust & Savings Bank, 101-N. State St., Geneseo, IL 61254 TEL: (309)244-5601

FOUNDATION: McFarland Charitable Foundation
REQUISITE: Must be a student nurse from Mason County, IL.
APPLICATION: Interviews required. Write by 5/1 for info.
CONTACT: Kathy Tarvin, Dir. of Nursing Service, Mason District Hospital, 520 E. Franklin St., Havana, IL 62644 (309) 543-4431

FOUNDATION: Fred G. Harrison Foundation
REQUISITE: Must be a senior in Herrin High School, IL.
APPLICATION: Write for info. No deadline listed.
CONTACT: 101 S. Park Ave., Herrin, IL 62948

FOUNDATION: Educational Communications Scholarship Fndtn.
REQUISITE: Must be a high school student in the U.S.
APPLICATION: Write & request an application form. Applications may also be obtained from high school guidance offices. Deadline June 1.
CONTACT: Ms. J.E. McGuinn, 721 N. McKinley Rd., Lake Forest, IL 60045
TEL: (312)295-6650

FOUNDATION: Charles A. Beebe Scholarship Fund
REQUISITE: Graduate of Forman Community High School in Manito, IL.

APPLICATION: Available from Peoples State Bank. Deadline May 15.
CONTACT: William Heinhorst, Pres., Peoples State Bank, 105 South Adams St., Manito, IL 61546 TEL: (309)968-6689

FOUNDATION: The William, Agnes & Elizabeth Burgess Memorial Scholarship Fund
REQUISITE: Must be a graduating senior of Mattoon Community High School in Mattoon, IL.
APPLICATION: Applications available at Mattoon Community High School. No deadline listed.
CONTACT: Mike Hagan, First National Bank, POB 499, Mattoon, IL 61938. TEL: (217) 234-7454

FOUNDATION: Jacob Stump, Jr. & Clara Stump Memorl Schlrshp Fnd
REQUISITE: Must be a high school graduate from Coles, Cumberland, Douglas, or Moultrie county, IL who is planning to attend any state-supported college or university in IL.
APPLICATION: Applications available at high schools & at Central National Bank. No deadline listed.
CONTACT: c/o Central National Bank of Mattoon, POB 685, Mattoon, IL 61938 TEL: (217)234-6434

FOUNDATION: Swiss Benevolent Society of Chicago
REQUISITE: Must be a full-time undergraduate student of Swiss descent who resides in IL, IN, IA, MI, or WI.
APPLICATION: Write for info. Deadline March 1.
CONTACT: Professor Jean Devaud, Chairman of S.B.S. Schlrshp Committee, 629 S. Humphrey Ave., Oak Park, IL 60304

FOUNDATION: Ailees S. Andrew Foundation
REQUISITE: Must be a child of an Andrew Corp. employee or a graduate of a local high school in Orland Park, IL.
APPLICATION: Write for info. Deadline April 1.
CONTACT: Robert Horde, 14604 John Humphrey Dr., Orland Park, IL 60462 TEL: (708)349-4445

FOUNDATION: Father James M. Fitzgerald Scholarship Trust
REQUISITE: Priesthood student attending a Catholic university or college or the highest ranking boy or girl at St. Mark's Catholic School, Peoria, IL, enrolling in any Roman Catholic high school.
APPLICATION: Write for info. No deadline listed.

CONTACT: c/o Commercial National Bank of Peoria, 301 SW Adams St., Peoria, IL 61631 TEL: (309) 655-5322

FOUNDATION: Charles Foundation
REQUISITE: Must reside in Rockford, IL.
APPLICATION: Write for info. No deadline listed.
CONTACT: c/o Steven Charles, 1700 N. Alpine, Ste. 311, Rockford, IL 61107 TEL: (815) 394-1700

FOUNDATION: Anita H. Richards Trust
REQUISITE: Must reside in Carroll County, IL.
APPLICATION: Write for info. Deadline April 15.
CONTACT: Donald S. Wolf, Jr., 353 Chicago Ave., Savanna, IL 61074 TEL: (815) 273-2028

FOUNDATION: Boynton Gillespie Memorial Fund
REQUISITE: Must be a student in local area of foundation.
APPLICATION: Submit letter requesting applctn. Deadline 5/1.
CONTACT: John Clendenin, Trustee, Heritage Federal Bldg., Sparta, IL 62286 TEL: (618) 443-4430

FOUNDATION: Henry Bunn Memorial Fund
REQUISITE: Must be a graduating senior of Sangamon Cnty, IL.
APPLICATION: Applications accepted through local high school counselors. Write for info. Deadline 3/1.
CONTACT: Joanne Ley, c/o Bank One Springfield, One Old State Capitol Plaza East, Springfield, IL 62701 TEL: (217)525-9747

FOUNDATION: Susan Cook House Educational Trust
REQUISITE: Must reside in Sangamon County, IL.
APPLICATION: Write for info. No deadline listed.
CONTACT: Lynn Jones, Marine Bank of Springfield, One East Old State Capital Plaza, Springfield, IL 62794 TEL: (217) 525-9600

FOUNDATION: Nesbitt Medical Student Foundation
REQUISITE: Must be a student attending medical school who is in need of financial assistance.
APPLICATION: Letter requesting application. Forms available in appropriate office of medical college. If you are a previous recipient, submit a renewal application for each succeeding year. Deadline April 1 for application materials including letters of recommendation.

CONTACT: James M Kirby, Asst VP, The Ntnl Bnk & Trst Co of Sycamore, 230 W. State St., Sycamore, IL 60178 TEL: (815)895-2125

FOUNDATION: Ella G. McKee Foundation
REQUISITE: Must be a current resident of Fagette County, IL.
APPLICATION: Write for info. No deadline listed.
CONTACT: c/o First National Bank, First National Bank Bldg., Vandalia, IL 62471 TEL: (618) 283-1141

FOUNDATION: Villa Park Bank Foundation
REQUISITE: Must be a high school or preparatory school senior in foundation's immediate area.
APPLICATION: Applications available at Villa Park area high schools or at Villa Park Trust & Savings Bank. Deadline December 1; applications only accepted in September, October, & November of each year.
CONTACT: Carol Ruane, 10 S. Villa Ave., Villa Park, IL 60181 (708)834-0800

FOUNDATION: Benjamin Trust Fund
REQUISITE: Must be a graduate of West Chicago Community High School District No. 94, IL.
APPLICATION: Applications available from superintendent. Deadline 4/15 of year preceding graduation.
CONTACT: Suprntndnt of Schools, 326 Joliet St., West Chicago, IL 60185

FOUNDATION: Avon Products Foundation, Inc.
REQUISITE: Child of a current Avon Products, Inc. employee or a high school senior who resides in proximity to an Avon location.
APPLICATION: Write for info. Deadline November 2.
CONTACT: Glenn S. Clarke, Pres., Nine W. 57th St., New York, NY 10019 TEL: (212)546-6731

FOUNDATION: Abbott (The Clara) Foundation
REQUISITE: Scholarships and loans for employees or retirees of Abbott Laboratories or members of their family.
APPLICATION: Application deadline is 3/16 for schlrshps and 5/15 for student loans.
CONTACT: Debp. 579, 1 Abbott Park Rd., Abbott Park, IL 60064-3500. TEL: (708)937-1090

FOUNDATION: Belden (Joseph C.) Foundation

REQUISITE: Schlrshps for children of emplys of Belden Crprtn.
APPLICATION: Applications are accepted from 11/1 to 12/ 31.
CONTACT: c/o Belden Wire and Cable, Division of Cooper Industries, 2000 S Batavia Ave, Geneva, IL 60134. James Eaton. (312)232-8900

FOUNDATION: Cooper Industries Foundation
REQUISITE: Scholarships for children of employees of Cooper Indstrs, Inc. in AL, CA, CT, GA, IL, IN, ME, MI, MO, MS, NJ, NY, NC, OH, OK, PA, SC, TN, TX VA.
APPLICATION: Applications are accepted throughout the year.
CONTACT: First City Tower, Suite 4000, POB 4446, Houston, TX 77210. Patricia B. Meinecke, Secretary. TEL: (713)739-5632.

FOUNDATION: The OMC Foundation
REQUISITE: Scholarships for children of employees of Outboard Marine Crprtn in WI, IL, TN, MS, NC, GA, and NE.
APPLICATION: Application deadline is October 31st.
CONTACT: Denise Charts, 100 Sea Horse Drive, Waukegan, IL 60085. TEL: (708)689-6200

FOUNDATION: Fansteel Scholarship Foundation
REQUISITE: Scholarships for children (sometimes grandchildren) of current, deceased, or retired employees.
APPLICATION: Application deadline is April 8th.
CONTACT: One Tantalum Place, North Chicago, IL 60064. Maryann Maki TEL: (708)689-4900

FOUNDATION: Harris Bank Foundation
REQUISITE: Scholarships for children of employees of Harris Trust and Savings Bank.
APPLICATION: Write for more information.
CONTACT: 111 W Monroe Street, POB 755, Chicago, IL 60690. H. Kris Ronnew, Secretary-Treasurer. TEL: (312)461-6660

FOUNDATION: Inland Steel-Ryerson Foundation, Inc.
REQUISITE: Scholarships for children of employees of Inland Steel Company and its subsidiaries.
APPLICATION: Applications are accepted throughout the year.
CONTACT: c/o Inland Steel Industries, 30 West Monroe Street, Chicago, IL 60603. David Hawley, State and Regional Affairs, Inland Steel Industries. TEL: (312)899-3421

FOUNDATION: Midas International Corporation Scholarship
REQUISITE: Scholarships for dependents of employees of Midas International Corporation.
APPLICATION: Application deadline is March 1st.
CONTACT: 225 North Michigan Avenue, 11th Floor, Chicago, IL 60601
TEL: (312)565-7500

FOUNDATION: Stone Foundation, Inc.
REQUISITE: Scholarships for children of employees of who have two or more years at Stone Container Corporation.
APPLICATION: Application deadline is April 1st.
CONTACT: Betsy Stotter, 150 North Michigan Ave., Chicago, IL 60601.
TEL: (312)346-6600

FOUNDATION: Illinois Congress of Parents and Teachers
REQUISITE: Scholarships granted to resident of Illinois. Open to high school seniors who plan to major in Education at an accredited institution in the USA.
APPLICATION: Write for info. Application deadline is March 1st.
CONTACT: 901 S. Springs St., Springfield, IL 62704. (217)528-9617

INDIANA

FOUNDATION: Ball State University
REQUISITE: Scholarships granted to undergraduate juniors at Ball State University who have demonstrated reasonable expectations of becoming professionals in the telecommunications industry. Scholarships are based on creativity, grades are not considered.
APPLICATION: Write for info. Application deadline is April 1st.
CONTACT: Department of Telecommunications, Muncie, IN 47306. 317-285-1480

FOUNDATION: Heritage Fund of Bartholomew County, Inc.
REQUISITE: Must reside in Bartholomew County, IN.
APPLICATION: Write for info. No deadline listed.
CONTACT: Edward F. Sullivan, Exec. Dir., 430 Second St., Columbus, IN 47201. TEL: (812)376-7772

FOUNDATION: George W. Burkett Trust
REQUISITE: Must be a graduating senior from the following high schools in Starke County, IN: Culver Community High

APPLICATION: Submit letter for applctn. Deadline Spring. High School students, contact 1. William F. Mills, 222 N. Ohio St., Culver, IN 46511 (219)842-3364 2. For Knox Community High School students, contact Dr. Harold Huff, 306 S. Pearl St., Knox, IN 36534 (219) 772-3712 3. For Oregon-Davis High School students, contact John Slusher, POB 65, Hamlet, IN 46532 (219) 867-2111 4. For North Judson-San Pierre High School students, contact Dr. Steven Timler, Highway 10 West, N. Judson, IN 46366 (219) 896-2155
CONTACT: For Culver Community High School, Knox Community High School, North Judson-San Pierre High School, & Oregon-Davis Hgh Schl.

FOUNDATION: Miles Foundation
REQUISITE: Must be an employee of Miles Foundation.
APPLICATION: Submit letter requesting application. Interviews required by high school administrator. Contact Fndtn for deadline
CONTACT: 1127 Myrtle St., POB 40, Elkhart, IN 46515 (219) 264-8111

FOUNDATION: Olive B. Cole Foundation, Inc.
REQUISITE: Must be a graduate of hgh schl in Noble Cnty, IN.
APPLICATION: Submit letter for application. Deadline 3/15.
CONTACT: John E. Hogan, Jr., Exec. VP, 3242 Mallard Cove Ln., Fort Wayne, IN 46804 (219)436-2182

FOUNDATION: E. H. Kilbourne Residuary Charitable Trust
REQUISITE: Must be a graduating senior in Allen County, IN.
APPLICATION: Submit letter for application. Deadline 4/15.
CONTACT: Alice Kopfer, Asst. VP, c/o Norwest Bank, Trust Dept., 116 East Berry, Fort Wayne, IN 46802-6632 TEL: (219)461-6451

FOUNDATION: The Lincoln National Life Foundation, Inc.
(McAndless Scholarship)
REQUISITE: Must be from Ft. Wayne area; student of actuarial science or a minority student pursuing business-related studies. Scholarships bases year to year, actuarial science exam in sophomore year. Must be eligible for hire at Lincoln National upon graduation, and willing to work during summers.
APPLICATION: Submit letter requesting application. No deadline listed.
CONTACT: W. Smith or Melvin McFall, POB 1110, 1300 S. Clinton St., Ft Wayne, IN 46801 TEL: (219)427-2064, (219)427-3057

FOUNDATION: Marion D. & Eva S. Peeples Foundation

REQUISITE: Graduate of an IN high school who will pursue studies in nursing or dietetics, or will obtain training in teaching industrial arts.
APPLICATION: Interviews required. Submit completed application to Fndtn's Schlrshp Committee, Union Bank & Trust Co., 34 W. Jefferson St., Franklin, IN 46131. Write for application info. Deadline 3/20.
CONTACT: Michael Ramsey, Union Bank & Trust Co., 111 Monument Circle, Suite 1501, Franklin, IN 46277 TEL: (317)736-7191

FOUNDATION: Niccum Educational Trust Foundation
REQUISITE: Graduate of a public school in the Goshen, IN, area
APPLICATION: Must submit student transcripts, high school recommendation, & 3 references with application. Applications available from Midwest Commerce Bank. Deadline March 1.
CONTACT: Joyce Blachly or Sue Simmons, c/o NBD Bank, POB 27, Goshen, IN 46526 (219)533-2175

FOUNDATION: Charles C. & Elizabeth V. Babcock Memrl Schlrshp Fnd
REQUISITE: Be a graduate of Rochester High School, Rochester, IN.
APPLICATION: Submit letter requesting application. Interviews required. Deadlines May & November.
CONTACT: W. Francis Brezette, c/o Bank One of Indianapolis N.A., 101 Monument Cr., Indianapolis, IN 46277 TEL: (317)321-7544

FOUNDATION: William S. & Lillian R. Coleman Schlrshp Trst
REQUISITE: Must reside in Rush County, IN.
APPLICATION: Write for info. Deadline April 1 or 60 days prior to beginning of a school term.
CONTACT: Jackie Weitz, Asst. VP, Bank One IN, NA, 101 Monument Cr., Indianapolis, IN 46277 TEL: (317)639-7544

FOUNDATION: Delta Tau Delta Educational Fund
REQUISITE: Scholarships & student loans to any undergraduate member of Delta Tau Delta.
APPLICATION: Some grants are restricted to a specific chapter or curriculum. Write for info. No deadline listed.
CONTACT: Sonya Gill, 8250 Haverstick Rd., Ste. 155, Indianapolis, IN 46240 TEL: (317)259-1187

FOUNDATION: The Endowment Fund of Phi Kappa Psi Fraternity, Inc.
REQUISITE: Student loans, fellowships, grants, & awards to any student enrolled in a college or university in the U.S.

APPLICATION: Write for info. No deadline listed.
CONTACT: 510 Lockerbie St., Indnpls, IN 46202 TEL: (317)632-5647

FOUNDATION: James E. Hughes Scholarship Fund
REQUISITE: Resident of Marian Cnty, attending Butler University, University of Indianapolis, or Marian College in Indianapolis, IN.
APPLICATION: Applications made through the scholarship office of each school. Contact schools for current application deadlines.
CONTACT: Financial aid offices of schools listed above.

FOUNDATION: Arthur A. & Hazel S. Auer Scholarship Fund
REQUISITE: Must be a senior or graduate of East Noble High School, Kendallville, IN.
APPLICATION: Write for info. Deadline 1st Friday in February.
CONTACT: Peggy Donovan, East Noble School Corp., 901 S. Garden St., Kendallville, IN 46755 TEL: (219)347-2032

FOUNDATION: Peter G. Flinn Estate
REQUISITE: Scholarships by nomination only to any Grant County high school senior who has resided in Grant County, IN, at least 1 year & has maintained at least a "C" average in school.
APPLICATION: Applicants are selected by committees from Grant County, IN, high schools only. Winners are then selected from these applications only. Deadline 2nd week of April.
CONTACT: Bank One, 302 S. Washington St., Marion, IN 46952
TEL: (317)662-6611

FOUNDATION: Thomas, Myrtle, Arch, Eva Alexander Schlrshp Fndtn.
REQUISITE: Be graduating student of Posey Cnty, IN, high school.
APPLICATION: Applications available at Posey County, IN, area high schools. Submit application to respective high school by May 1.
CONTACT: K. Richard Hawley, c/o Citizen Bank, 112 E. 3rd St., Mt. Vernon, IN 47620 (812)838-4333

FOUNDATION: Swiss Benevolent Society of Chicago
REQUISITE: Must be a full-time undergraduate student of Swiss descent who resides in IL, IN, IA, MI, or WI.
APPLICATION: Write for info. Deadline March 1.
CONTACT: Professor Jean Devaud, Chairman of S.B.S.
Schlrshp Cmmtt, 629 S. Humphrey Ave, Oak Prk, IL 60304

FOUNDATION: Weisell Baber Foundation, Inc.
REQUISITE: Be a graduate of 1 of the high schools in Miami County.
APPLICATION: Must apply in person. Interviews required. No deadline
CONTACT: Roger D. Baber, Pres., 535 S. Broadway, Peru, IN 46970 TEL: (317)473-7526

FOUNDATION: Porter Art Foundation
REQUISITE: Must be a graduating senior in a Miami County, IN, high school for higher education in fine arts, music, & performing arts.
APPLICATION: Interviews required. Contact foundation for application info. & current deadline.
CONTACT: James O Cole, Bx 536, Peru, IN 46970 TEL: (317)472-2723

FOUNDATION: R.B. Charitable & Educational Foundation
REQUISITE: Student loans for undergraduate studies, primarily to any child of employee of the McMahan-O'Connor Cnstrctn Co.
APPLICATION: Write for info. No deadline listed.
CONTACT: Lall Heyde, Lucas & Wentzel Streets, Rochester, IN 46975 TEL: (219)223-2171

FOUNDATION: Nelson P. Bowsher Foundation
REQUISITE: Be a graduate of hgh schl in St. Joseph Cnty, IN.
APPLICATION: Submit a letter to your local high school principal requesting application. Interviews, 3 letters of character reference, & high school transcript required. Applicants must file a Financial Aid Form (FAF) prior to March 1. Deadline March 31.
CONTACT: Pam Henderson, c/o Norwest Bank, 112-114 W. Jefferson Blvd., South Bend, IN 46601 TEL: (219)237-3342

FOUNDATION: Fred A. Bryan Collegiate Students Fund, Inc.
REQUISITE: Be a male graduate of a high school in S. Bend, IN.
APPLICATION: Ask your high school counselor for application info. Interviews, 3 letters of reference, & high school transcript required. Applicant must file a Financial Aid Form (FAF) prior to 3/1 &, if Boy Scout, include copy of Scout Record. Deadline 3/31
CONTACT: Hgh schl counselors, First Interstate Bank of Northern IN, N.A., 112-114 W. Jefferson Blvd., South Bend, IN 46601 (219)237-3342

FOUNDATION: Grge & Marie G. Spencer Edctn Fndtn & Trst
REQUISITE: Must reside in Tipton County, IN.
APPLICATION: Interviews needed. Write for info. Deadline 9/1

CONTACT: Tipton Community High School, 619 S. Maine, Tipton, IN, 46072 or Tri-Central High School, R.R. No. 2, Sharpsville, IN 46072 (317)675-7431

FOUNDATION: Ruth M. Minear Educational Trust
REQUISITE: Graduate of Wabash Hgh Schl, Wabash, IN. Apply annually
APPLICATION: Submit State of IN financial aid form & certification of acceptance at accredited college with application. No deadline
CONTACT: Allen P Spring, Snr VP, POB 397, Wabash, IN 46992

FOUNDATION: Cecil Armstrong Foundation
REQUISITE: Must reside in Warsaw, IN.
APPLICATION: Must attend an interview. Applications available at local schools & Lake City Bank.
CONTACT: Trust Dept., c/o Lake City Bank, POB 1387, Warsaw, IN 46580 (219)267-9110

FOUNDATION: Valparaiso University
REQUISITE: Scholarships granted to outstanding students for their junior and senior year of undergraduate study. Must be enrolled full-time at Valparaiso University studying Mechanical Engineering to gain award.
APPLICATION: Write for info. Application deadline is April 1st.
CONTACT: Mechanical Engineering Department, Valparaiso, IN 46383 (219)464-5054

FOUNDATION: McDonald Memorial Fund Trust
REQUISITE: Limited to students who live in Kosciusko County.
APPLICATION: Contact the Superintendent of Warsaw Community Schools, Warsaw, IN 46580, for application info.
CONTACT: First Ntnl Bank of Warsaw, POB 1447, Warsaw, IN 46580

FOUNDATION: Murphy College Fund Trust
REQUISITE: Must reside in Kosciusko County, IN, or have graduated from Kosciusko County School.
APPLICATION: Write for info. Deadline April 15.
CONTACT: c/o First National Bank of Warsaw, Trust Dept., POB 1447, Warsaw, IN 46580 TEL: (219)267-3271

FOUNDATION: James Moorman Orphans Home
REQUISITE: Graduating senior of a high school in Randolph County
APPLICATION: Applications available through Randolph County, IN, high

schools. Deadline usually late April or early May; contact foundation for current application deadlines.
CONTACT: James M. Mock, Secty.-Treasurer, 526 West N. St., Winchester, IN 47394

FOUNDATION: The Winchester Foundation
REQUISITE: Must reside in Randolph County.
APPLICATION: Write for info. No deadline listed.
CONTACT: Don Welch, Chairman, c/o People Loan & Trust Bank, 100 Meridian St., POB 409, Winchester, IN 47394 TEL: (317) 584-3501

FOUNDATION: August Michael Rocco Scholarship Foundation
REQUISITE: Must be a graduate of Central Catholic High School or St. Thomas Aquinas in Stark County, OH, who plans to attend Notre Dame University in IN.
APPLICATION: Write for info. No deadline listed.
CONTACT: Christine E. Sutton-Kruman, AmeriTrust Co., 237 Tuscarawas St. W., Canton, OH 44702

FOUNDATION: Central Newspapers Foundation
REQUISITE: Scholarships for children of employees who have been in continuous employment for three years with newspapers affiliated with Central Newspapers, Inc.
APPLICATION: Application deadline is mid-February.
CONTACT: 307 N Pennsylvania St, Indianapolis, IN 46204.(317)231-9200

FOUNDATION: Cooper Industries Foundation
REQUISITE: Scholarships for children of employees of Cooper Industries, Inc. in AL, CA, CT, GA, IL, IN, ME, MI, MO, MS, NJ, NY, NC, OH, OK, PA, SC, TN, TX, and VA.
APPLICATION: Applications are accepted throughout the year.
CONTACT: First City Tower, Suite 4000, POB 4446, Houston, TX 77210. Patricia B. Meinecke, Secretary. TEL: (713)739-5632

FOUNDATION: Credithrift Financial- Richard E. Meier Foundation, Inc.
REQUISITE: Four scholarships are awarded to children of employees of Credithrift Financial and its subsidiaries.
APPLICATION: Applications are accepted throughout the year.
CONTACT: POB 59, Evansville, IN 47701. Norb Devine, Vice President TEL: (812)424-8031

FOUNDATION: CTS Foundation
REQUISITE: Interest-free student loans for children of employees of the CTS Corporation and its subsidiaries.
APPLICATION: Application deadline is prior to start of the school year
CONTACT: 905 North West Blvd, Elkhart, IN 46514. (219)293-7511

FOUNDATION: Cummins Engine Foundation
REQUISITE: Scholarships for children of employees of Cummins Engine Company, Inc.
APPLICATION: Applications are distributed internally.
CONTACT: MC 60814, 500 Jackson St, Columbus, IN 47201. Or Adele J. Vincent, Associate Director, Box 3005, MC 60029, Columbus, IN 47202-3005. TEL: (812)377-3114

FOUNDATION: Habig Foundation, Inc.
REQUISITE: Scholarships for children of employees of Kimball International, Inc.
APPLICATION: Application deadline is April 1st.
CONTACT: 1600 Royal St, Jasper, IN 47546 Douglas Habig, Trsrr (812)482-1600

FOUNDATION: Inland Container Corporation Foundation, Inc.
REQUISITE: Scholarships for children of employees of Inland Container Corporation.
APPLICATION: Application deadline is November 1st.
CONTACT: 151 Delaware Street, POB 925, Indianapolis, IN 46206. Frank Hirshman, President TEL: (317)262-0308

FOUNDATION: Mead Johnson & Company Foundation, Inc.
REQUISITE: Scholarships for children of employees of Mead Johnson & Company.
APPLICATION: Application deadline is February 15th.
CONTACT: 2404 West Pennsylvania Street, Evansville, IN 47721. Rolland Eckels, President. TEL: (812)429-5000

FOUNDATION: Meridian Mutual Foundation, Inc.
REQUISITE: Scholarships for children of employees of Meridian Mutual Insurance Company and it affiliates.
APPLICATION: Application deadline is April 15th.
CONTACT: 2955 North Meridian Street, Indianapolis, IN 46207. Gary McCloud, Secretary-Treasurer. TEL: (317)927-8266

FOUNDATION: R.B. Charitable and Educational Foundation
REQUISITE: Student loans for children of employees of
McMahan-O'Connor Construction Company.
APPLICATION: Applications are accepted throughout the year.
CONTACT: Lucas and Wentzel Streets, Rochester, IN 46975. Lalla Heyde.
TEL: (219)223-2171

FOUNDATION: Reilly Foundation
REQUISITE: Scholarships for children of employees of Reilly Tar &
Chemical Corporation.
APPLICATION: Applications are accepted throughout the year.
CONTACT: 1510 Market Square Center, 151 North Delaware Street,
Indianapolis, IN 46204. Lorraine Schroeder, Trustee. (317)638-7531

FOUNDATION: Baber (Weisell) Foundation, Inc,
REQUISITE: Loans for graduates of hgh schls in Miami Cnty area
APPLICATION: Applications are accepted throughout the year.
CONTACT: 535 South Broadway, Peru, IN 46970. Roger Baber, President.
(317)473-7526

FOUNDATION: McDonald Memorial Fund Trust
REQUISITE: Loans for college or professional studies.
APPLICATION: For application information, contact the Sprntndnt of
Warsaw Community Schools, Warsaw, IN 46580.
CONTACT: Nellie Robinson, Frst Ntnl Bnk of Warsaw, POB 1447, Warsaw,
IN 46581 TEL: (219)267-3271

KANSAS

FOUNDATION: Pentax Corporation
REQUISITE: Scholarships granted to undergraduate students at Kansas
State University Manhattan Kansas in its four year journalism and mass
communications program. Scholarships are granted on the basis of a
photography competition. Must be US citizen.
APPLICATION: Write for info. Application deadline is April 1st.
CONTACT: 35 Inverness Dr East, Englewood, CO 80112 303-799-8000

FOUNDATION: Borton-Ryder Memorial Trust
REQUISITE: Scholarships for residents in the Emporia, KS, area, who plan
to study medicine at the Newman Hospital.
APPLICATION: Applications are accepted throughout the year.

Kansas

CONTACT: Bnk IV Emporia, N.A., POB 1048, Emporia 66801-1048

FOUNDATION: Brey (Claude and Ina) Memorial Endwmnt Fund
REQUISITE: Scholarships are available for fourth degree Kansas Grange members only.
APPLICATION: Application deadline is July 1st. Formal application must be completed. Interviews are required. Contact a local Grange Chapter for application.
CONTACT: c/o The Merchants National Bank of Topeka, POB 178, Topeka, KS 666001. Marlene Bush, Box 186, Melvern, KS 66510 (913)549-3563

FOUNDATION: Cantrall (Ruth A.) Trust
REQUISITE: Assistance given only to needy students who are attending the Kansas State School for the Deaf.
APPLICATION: Applications are accepted throughout the year.
CONTACT: c/o Bank IV Olathe, POB 14040, Shawnee Mission, KS 66285-9989. TEL: (913)782-3010

FOUNDATION: Davis (James A. and Julie L.) Foundation, Inc.
REQUISITE: Scholarships for graduates of Hutchinson High School, KS who will attend college in Kansas and Missouri.
APPLICATION: Application deadline is March 15th.
CONTACT: 802 First National Center, POB 2027, Hutchinson, KS 67504-2027. William Y. Chalfant, Secretary. TEL: (316)663-5021

FOUNDATION: Hansen (Dane G.) Foundation
REQUISITE: Scholarships are available for high school graduates in central or northwest Kansas. Scholarships are also available for postgraduate students in fields of theology, medicine, and dental in all geographical areas.
APPLICATION: Deadlines are September and October.
CONTACT: POB 187, Logan, KS 67646. Dane G. Bales, Vice-President. TEL: (913)689-4832

FOUNDATION: Helvering (R.L. and Elsa) Trust
REQUISITE: Scholarships available only for high school seniors in Marshall County, KS.
APPLICATION: Application deadline is May 1st.
CONTACT: 307 South 13th Street, Marysville, KS 66508. Ira O. Shrock, Trustee. (913)562-3437

FOUNDATION: Jones (Walter S. and Evan C.) Foundation
REQUISITE: Scholarships available for residents of Lyon, Coffey or Osage counties for at least one year, and under the age of 21.
APPLICATION: Write for application. Application deadline: May.
CONTACT: Nancy Rhodes, 527 Commercial Street, Room 515, Emporia, KS 66801. TEL: (316)342-1714

FOUNDATION: Jordaan Foundation Trust
REQUISITE: Scholarships for high school graduates of Pawnee County seeking an undergraduate degree.
APPLICATION: Deadline is April 15th. Interviews are required.
CONTACT: c/o First State Bank and Trust Company, 111 East Eighth St, POB 360, Larned, KS 67550 Glee S. Smith, Chairman. (316)285-3127

FOUNDATION: Porter (Laura E.) Trust
REQUISITE: Educational loans and grants for men who will gradate from Pratt County Community College, KS who will be attending a university approved by the trustees.
APPLICATION: Accepted throughout year. Write for application.
CONTACT: Drawer H, Pratt, KS 67124. B.V. Hampton, Fill Hampton, Jr., E.M. Baker, Trustees. TEL: (316) 672-5533

FOUNDATION: Beech Aircraft Foundation
REQUISITE: Scholarships for children of employees of Beech Aircraft Corporation, in Kansas.
APPLICATION: Write for more details.
CONTACT: 9709 East Central Avenue, Wichita, KS 67201 Larry Lawrence, Secretary-Treasurer. TEL: (316)676-7111

FOUNDATION: Block (The H&R) Foundation
REQUISITE: Schlrshps for children of emplys H&R Block, Inc.
APPLICATION: Accepting date - Feb. 1, Deadline date April 1. Prefer new applications that were reprinted this year.
CONTACT: Citizen Scholarship Foundations of America, 1505 Riverview Rd., POB 297, St. Peter, MN 56082. TEL: 1(800)537-4180

FOUNDATION: Hall Family Foundations
REQUISITE: Scholarships for children of emplys of Hallmark.
APPLICATION: Are available to Hallmark employees only.
CONTACT: Charitable & Crown Investment - 323, POB 419580, Kansas City, MO 64141. Margaret Pence or Wendy Hockaday, Program Officers.

FOUNDATION: Koch (The Fred C.) Foundation, Inc.
REQUISITE: Schlrshps for kids of employees of Koch Indstrs
APPLICATION: Application deadline is in February.
CONTACT: POB 2256, Wichita, KS 67201. Public Affairs. (316)832-5404

FOUNDATION: Baker (J.H.) Trust
REQUISITE: Student loans for graduates of high schools in Rush, Barton, Ellis, Ness, and Pawnee counties, KS. They must be under the age of 25.
APPLICATION: Applications are accepted throughout the year.
CONTACT: c/o J.H. Becker Trust Scholarship, Box 280, 802 Main, La Crosse, KS 67548. Tom Dechant, Trustee. (913)222-2537

KENTUCKY

FOUNDATION: Midway College
REQUISITE: Scholarships granted to women who are accepted for enrollment at Midway College for undergraduate study in Paralegal studies.
APPLICATION: Write for info. Application deadline is March 15th.
CONTACT: Financial Aid Office, Midway, KY 40347   606-846-4421

FOUNDATION: Midway College
REQUISITE: Scholarships granted to women who are accepted for enrollment at Midway College studying in the Nursing; Paralegal; Bilingual Business; French, Spanish, or Equine studies.
APPLICATION: Write for info. Application deadline is March 15th.
CONTACT: Financial Aid Office, Midway, KY 40347. (606)846-4421

FOUNDATION: Hope (Blanche and Thomas) Memorial Fund
REQUISITE: Scholarships available for graduating high school students of Boyd and Greenup Cnts, KY & Lawrence Cnty, OH.
APPLICATION: Deadline is March 1st. Write for an application.
CONTACT: National City Bank, POB 1270, Ashland, KY 41105   (606)329-2900

FOUNDATION: Louisville Community Foundation, Inc.
REQUISITE: Schlrshps and loans are given in the greater Louisville, KY, area for professional development.
APPLICATION: Write for application and deadlines.
CONTACT: C. Dennis Riggs, The Waterfront Plaza, Suite 1110, 325 West Main St., Louisville, KY 40202. TEL: (502)585-4649

FOUNDATION: The Ogden College Fund
REQUISITE: Scholarships are awarded to high school graduates of public or private schools in Kentucky who have a grade average of 'B' or better and plan to pursue a major or minor in the Ogden College of Science, Technology and Health at Western Kentucky University. Scholarships are awarded on a first-come, first-served basis.
APPLICATION: Submission of applications is encouraged by 1/1
CONTACT: POB 930, Bowling Green, KY 42101. c/o Cooper R. Smith, Jr., 520 Hillwood Drive, Bowling Green, KY 42101. TEL: (502)745-4448

FOUNDATION: Young (John B. & Brownie) Memorial Fund
REQUISITE: Scholarships are awarded to students who live in school districts of Owensboro Daviess, and McClean counties, KY.
APPLICATION: Applications are accepted throughout the year. Write for an application.
CONTACT: c/o Owensboro National Bank, Trust Department, 230 Frederick Street, Owensboro, KY 42301. TEL: (502)926-3232

FOUNDATION: Pickett & Hatcher Educational Fund, Inc.
REQUISITE: Undergraduate student loans for those who live in AL, FL, GA, KY, MS, NC, SC, TN, and VA. There is no support for those planning to study medicine, law, or ministry.
APPLICATION: Application deadline is May 15th. First-time applicants may request their application after October 1st.
CONTACT: 1800 Buena Vista Rd, P.O. Box 8169, Columbus, GA 31908. Robert Bennett, Executive Vice-President. TEL: (404)327-6586

LOUISIANA

FOUNDATION: Louisiana Library Association
REQUISITE: Scholarships granted to Louisiana resident students who are accepted at Louisiana State University.
APPLICATION: Write for info. Application deadline is May 1st.
CONTACT: POBOX 3058, Baton Rouge, LA 70821. (504)342-4928

FOUNDATION: Burton (The William T. & Ethel Lewis) Fndtn
REQUISITE: Scholarships awarded to southwest LA high school seniors.
APPLICATION: Write for an application.
CONTACT: 1 Lake Shore Dr., Suite 1700, Sulphur, LA 70629 (318)433-0142

FOUNDATION: Hurley (Ed E. & Gladys) Foundation
REQUISITE: Educational loans for residents of Louisiana, AR, and TX.
APPLICATION: Application deadline is May 31st.
CONTACT: c/o Premier Bank, POB 2116, Shreveport, LA 71154. TEL: (318)226-2110

FOUNDATION: Hurley (Ed E. & Gladys) Foundation
REQUISITE: Scholarships awarded to students studying theology and are residents of Louisiana, Arkansas, and Texas.
APPLICATION: Application deadline is May 31st.
CONTACT: c/o InterFirst Bank Dallas, POB 83776, Dallas, TX 45283. Alice Gayle.

FOUNDATION: Masonic Educational Foundation, Inc.
REQUISITE: Scholarships awarded to residents of Louisiana.
APPLICATION: Formal completed application and family financial statement required.
CONTACT: 1300 Masonic Temple Building, 333 St. Charles St., New Orleans, LA 70130. Jack Crouch, Grand Secretary.

FOUNDATION: Pellerin (Willis & Mildred) Foundation
REQUISITE: Scholarships awarded to Louisiana residents who are attending a college or university in that state. One-half of the grant must be repaid by the recipient.
APPLICATION: Submission of applications must be six months prior to school term. Write for an application.
CONTACT: 6514 Pratt Drive, New Orleans, LA 70122. A.A. Harman and Co., 311 Baronne St., First Floor, New Orleans, LA 70122.

FOUNDATION: Texas Interscholastic League Foundation
REQUISITE: Scholarships awarded only to high school seniors who place 1st, 2nd, and 3rd in the State UIL contest.
APPLICATION: Accepted throughout the year. Write for application.
CONTACT: 602 West Main St., POB 909, Orange, TX 77631-0909. Clyde V. McKee, Jr., Secretary-Treasurer. TEL: (409)883-3513

FOUNDATION: Texas Industries Foundation
REQUISITE: Schlrshps for children of employees of TX Industries, Inc.
APPLICATION: Application deadline is January 15th.
CONTACT: 1341 West Mockingbird Ln., Suite 700W, Dallas, TX 75247. James R. McCraw, Controller. TEL: (214)647-6700

MASSACHUSETTS

FOUNDATION: Edward Bangs and Elza Kelley Foundation
REQUISITE: Scholarships granted to Barnstable County MA residents to undergraduate, graduate and professional institutions to supports their study in Medicine; Nursing; Health Sciences or related areas.
APPLICATION: Write for info. Application deadline is April 30th.
CONTACT: 243 South St., Hyannis, MA 02601.
(We were not able to verify this listing; it may not be extant.)

FOUNDATION: Amelia Greenbaum Scholarship Fund
REQUISITE: Female of Jewish faith who resides in & attends a degree granting college in or around Boston.
APPLICATION: Letter requesting application by 1/1 with transcript & recommendation from principal, guidance counselor or professor. Deadline 4/30. Interviews required. Recipients notified 6/30.
CONTACT: Administrative Dir., Ntnl Council of Jewish Women, Greater Boston Section, 75 Harvard Ave., Allston, MA 02134

FOUNDATION: The Bailey Foundation
REQUISITE: Must reside in Amesbury, MA.
APPLICATION: Write for info. Deadline April 15.
CONTACT: Edwin Bailey, 414 Main St., Amesbury, MA 01913

FOUNDATION: Arlington Catholic High School Scholarship Fund
REQUISITE: Must be a graduating student of Arlington Catholic High School, MA.
APPLICATION: Write for info. No deadline listed.
CONTACT: Sister Katherine Clifford, C.S.F., Principal, Arlington Catholic High School, 16 Medford St., Arlington, MA 02174 TEL: (617)646-7770

FOUNDATION: Terri Ann Holovak & Joseph P. Logan Memorial Scholarship Fund
REQUISITE: Freshman student commuting from eastern MA.
APPLICATION: Write for info. Deadline June 1.
CONTACT: POB 201, Arlington, MA 02174

FOUNDATION: Warren Benevolent Fund, Inc.
REQUISITE: Must graduate from Ashland High School, Ashland, MA.
APPLICATION: Write for info. No deadline listed.
CONTACT: POB 46, Ashland, MA 01721

Massachusetts

FOUNDATION: William A. Lynch Trust
REQUISITE: Must be a deserving Catholic graduate of a public high school in Beverly, MA, or any nearby Catholic school.
APPLICATION: Write for info. Deadline on or about June 1.
CONTACT: Principal, Beverly High School, Beverly, MA 01915

FOUNDATION: Charles H. Kohlraush Trust Fund
REQUISITE: Must be a Billerica, MA resident who has successfully completed 1 year of college.
APPLICATION: Write for info. Deadline July 15.
CONTACT: POB 341, Billerica, MA 01821
(We were not able to verify this listing; it may not be extant.)

FOUNDATION: Albert B. & Evelyn H. Black Scholarship Fund
REQUISITE: Must attend or have attended a Concord, MA, public school.
APPLICATION: Must submit a letter establishing your academic standing. Deadline April 1.
CONTACT: Patricia Tomsyck, c/o Fleet Bank, 75 State St., Boston, MA 02109 TEL: (317)346-2484

FOUNDATION: The Blanchard Foundation & The Luke & Jerusha Blanchard Scholarship Fund
REQUISITE: Must reside in Boxborough, MA, & have graduated from Blanchard Memorial High School.
APPLICATION: Contact principal of Blanchard Memorial High School for all application inquiries & submissions. Applications available only from Blanchard Memorial Hgh Schl. Deadline 4/1
CONTACT: Judith Casey, c/o Boston Safe Deposit & Trst Co., One Boston Place, Boston, MA 02108 TEL: (617)722-7340

FOUNDATION: The Boston Globe Foundation
REQUISITE: Must be an employee of Affiliated Publications, Inc. or its subsidiaries, their families, or a resident in the area of co-operations of metropolitan Boston, MA.
APPLICATION: Write for info. No deadline listed.
CONTACT: George M. Collins, Jr., Exec. Dir., The Boston Globe Building, Boston, MA 02107 TEL: (617)929-2895

FOUNDATION: Florence Evans Bushee Foundation, Inc.
REQUISITE: Must be a student residing in Newburyport, MA.
APPLICATION: Write or call for info. Deadline May 1.

CONTACT: Ann Reidy, Secty., Palmeer & Dodge, One Beacon St., Rm. 2000, Boston, MA 02108

FOUNDATION: Charles W. Caldwell Scholarship Fund
REQUISITE: Must be a male senior from Princeton.
APPLICATION: Write for info. No deadline listed.
CONTACT: State St. Bnk & Trst Co., POB 351, Boston, 02101 (317)786-3000

FOUNDATION: Elaine R. Croston Scholarship Fund
REQUISITE: Be graduate of Haverhill Hgh Schl, Haverhill, MA.
APPLICATION: Write for info. No deadline listed.
CONTACT: c/o Bank of Boston, POB 1891, Boston, MA 02105 (617)434-4016

FOUNDATION: The Deloura Family Trust
REQUISITE: Must be a Martha's Vineyard, MA resident.
APPLICATION: Write for info. No deadline listed.
CONTACT: Shawmut Bnk of Boston, POB 4276, Boston, 02106

FOUNDATION: Duxbury Yacht Club Charitable Foundation
REQUISITE: Must be a graduate of a Duxbury, MA, high school.
APPLICATION: Write for info. No deadline listed.
CONTACT: Mr. Powell Robinson Jr., 19 Depot St., POB 2804, Duxbury, MA 02331 (617)786-3000

FOUNDATION: Edwards Scholarship Fund
REQUISITE: Under age of 25 & have family who resides in Boston.
APPLICATION: Write for info. Deadline March 1.
CONTACT: One Federal St., Boston, MA 02110 TEL: (617)426-4434

FOUNDATION: Friendship Fund, Inc.
REQUISITE: Virtually all funds for scholarship grants are committed in advance by the trustees.
APPLICATION: Submit cover letter during May only. Additional info. will be requested if trustees' interest so warrants.
CONTACT: Boston Safe Deposit & Trst Co, One Boston Place, OBP-2, Boston, MA 02106 (617) 722-7538

FOUNDATION: George L. Gooding Trust
REQUISITE: Graduating senior Plymouth Rgnl High Schl, Plymth, MA.

APPLICATION: Write for info. No deadline listed.
CONTACT: State St. Bnk & Trst Co., POB 351, Boston, 02101 (617)786-3000

FOUNDATION: Cynthia E. & Clara H. Hollins Foundation
REQUISITE: Must be a graduate residing in Boston, MA & studying medicine, nursing, social work, psychology, etc.
APPLICATION: Write for info. Deadline April 1.
CONTACT: Ms. Alette E. Reed, Trustee, 140 Federal St., Rm. 1300, Boston, MA 02110 (617)426-5720

FOUNDATION: Charles H. Hood Fund
REQUISITE: Must be a CT, MA, ME, NH, RI, or VT resident.
APPLICATION: Write for info. No deadline listed.
CONTACT: 500 Rutherford Ave., Boston, MA 02129
(We were not able to verify this listing; it may not be extant.)

FOUNDATION: Humane Society of the Commonwealth of MA
REQUISITE: Reside in MA & be in medical edctn or research.
APPLICATION: Write for info. No deadline listed.
CONTACT: 177 Milk St., Boston, MA 02109

FOUNDATION: Charles A. King Trust
REQUISITE: Postdoctoral fellowships for research in medicine & surgery in institutions within the Commonwealth of MA.
APPLICATION: Write or call for info. Deadline October 15 for projects to start on or after February 1 of following year.
CONTACT: Kerry Sullivan, Fleet Bank, 75 State St., Boston, MA 02109
TEL: (617)346-4000

FOUNDATION: Lotta Agricultural Fund
REQUISITE: Farm loans to a student &/or graduate of the University of MA College of Natural Resources or of the Stockbridge School of Agriculture at the University.
APPLICATION: Send in a letter or resume. Interviews required. Write for info. No deadline listed.
CONTACT: Claire M. McCarthy, Trust Manager, c/o Estate of Lotta Crabtree, 11 Beacon St., Suite 1110, Boston, MA 02108 (617)742-5920

FOUNDATION: Massachusetts Board of Higher Education
REQUISITE: Must be a MA resident aged 16-24, of parents killed serving

in WWI, WWII, Vietnam or Korea.
APPLICATION: Write for info. No deadline listed.
CONTACT: Public Service Scholarship, Office of Student Financial Assistance, 330 Stuart St., Boston, MA 02116 TEL: (617)727-9420

FOUNDATION: Massachusetts Scholarships for Children of Deceased Members of Fire, Police, Corrections Dept., State Police, State Capitol Police or Metropolitan District Police
REQUISITE: Must be a MA high school graduate; child of fire, corrections, police Dept.; state police, capitol police, or metropolitan police dept. members killed in line of duty.
APPLICATION: Write for info. No deadline listed.
CONTACT: MA Board of Higher Education, Scholarship Office, 330 Stuart St., Boston, MA 02116 TEL: (617)727-9420

FOUNDATION: New England Education Society
REQUISITE: Loans to any graduate student for theological education in Christian ministry in New England theological schools or seminaries.
APPLICATION: Interviews required. Write for info. No deadline listed.
CONTACT: Rev. Earl Beane, Boston University School of Theology, 745 Commonwealth Ave., Boston, MA 02215. TEL: (317)353-3050

FOUNDATION: New England Regional Student Program
REQUISITE: Must reside in 1 of the New England States: CT, ME, MA, NH, RI, or VT. You may attend a public college or university within the region at a reduced tuition rate for certain degree programs that are not offered by their own state's public institutions.
APPLICATION: Write for info. No deadline listed.
CONTACT: Office of the Regional Student Program, New England Board of Higher Edctn, 45 Temple Place, Boston, 02111 TEL: (617)357-9620

FOUNDATION: Wilmot Evans Roby Corp.
REQUISITE: Be a student from the Newburyport, MA area.
APPLICATION: Write for info. Deadline April 1.
CONTACT: Mrs. Eleanor M. Goldthwait, 1 Beacon St., Rm. 2200, Boston, MA 02108 (We were not able to verify this listing; it may not be extant.)

FOUNDATION: William E. & Bertha E. Schrafft Chrtble Trst
REQUISITE: Must be a MA resident.
APPLICATION: Write for info. No deadline listed.
CONTACT: Hazen H. Ayer, Trustee, c/o Standish, Ayer & Wood, 1

Financial Center, Boston, MA 02111 TEL: (617)350-6100

FOUNDATION: Madeleine H. Soren Trust
REQUISITE: Scholarships by nomination only to any female resident of MA for studies in music & music education.
APPLICATION: Write for info. Applications are sent to participating schools in MA. The schools then recommend students who meet the noted limitations. Individual applications not accepted. Deadline 4/1
CONTACT: Sylvia Salas, Trust Officer, Boston Safe Deposit & Trust Co., One Boston Place, Boston, MA 02106 TEL: (617)722-7000

FOUNDATION: Jan Veen Educational Trust
REQUISITE: Must be studying the Laban Method in the dance dept. of the Boston Conservatory of Music.
APPLICATION: Write for info. No deadline listed.
CONTACT: Ruth S. Ambrose, Dir., Dept. of Dance, Boston Conservatory of Music, 8 The Fenway, Boston, MA 02110

FOUNDATION: The Pilgrim Foundation
REQUISITE: Must reside in Brockton, MA.
APPLICATION: Interviews required. Write for info. Deadline
4/1 for graduating hgh schl seniors & 5/1 for returning college students.
CONTACT: Sherry Yuskaitis, Exec. Dir., 478 Torrey St., Brockton, MA 02401-4654 TEL: (617)586-6100

FOUNDATION: Urann Foundation
REQUISITE: Must be a member of a family located in MA who are engaged in the production of cranberries.
APPLICATION: Applications available at guidance depts. of high schools. Write or call for info. Deadline April 15.
CONTACT: Rbrt LeBoeuf POB 1788 Brockton MA 02403 (508)588-7744

FOUNDATION: Microwave Associates Charitable Foundation
REQUISITE: Scholarships for children of employee of Microwave Assoc.
APPLICATION: Write for info. Deadline September 30.
CONTACT: 1011 Pawtucket Blvd., Lowell, MA 01853 (617)272-3000

FOUNDATION: Cambridge Martin Luther King Memorial Fund
REQUISITE: Must have attended school in Cambridge, MA.
APPLICATION: Write for info. Deadline last week in April.
CONTACT: Mr. Leslie Kimbrough, 6 Mead St., Cmbrdge, 02138

(We were not able to verify this listing; it may not be extant.)

FOUNDATION: Rotch Travelling Scholarship, Inc.
REQUISITE: Architect under age 35, with educational or professional experience from MA for foreign travel & study in architecture.
APPLICATION: Must submit a letter of request by 1/2. Deadline 1/22.
CONTACT: Norman C. Fletcher, Secty., 46 Brattle St., Cambridge, MA 02138 (We were not able to verify this listing; it may not be extant.)

FOUNDATION: Massachusetts/Rhode Island League for Nursing
REQUISITE: Member of the MA/RI League for Nursing for at least 1 year prior to applying; a resident of MA or RI; & a registered nurse who has been in full-time practice for at least 1 year immediately prior to acceptance into a graduate program. You must also be accepted into a National League for Nursing accredited graduate program for nursing or be already enrolled in such a program & be continuing for a 2nd year.
APPLICATION: References, written presentation of goals, & at the discretion of the scholarship committee a personal interview. Submit letter requesting application & include a self-addressed stamped business envelope. Deadline May 1.
CONTACT: Mary B. Conceison Scholarship Committee, One Thompson Square, Charlestown, MA 02129 TEL: (317)242-3009

FOUNDATION: Massachusetts/Rhode Island League for Nursing
REQUISITE: Must have resided in the MA/RI League for Nursing geographical area for the 4 years immediately prior to the receipt of the scholarship. You may also be either a registered nurse that is accepted into a program leading to a baccalaureate degree in nursing; a generic student who is entering the senior year in any undergraduate nursing program; or a student who has successfully completed 4 months of a practical nursing program.
APPLICATION: Submit letter requesting application along with a self-addressed stamped business size envelope. Deadline June 1. Recipients notified by August 15.
CONTACT: Scholarship Committee, Nursing Scholarship, One Thompson Square, Charlestown, MA 02129 TEL: (617)242-3009

FOUNDATION: Housen Foundation, Inc.
REQUISITE: Scholarships for study at U.S. colleges & universities only to any student who is a resident of MA & any child of an Erving Paper Mills employee.

Massachusetts

APPLICATION: Write for info. No deadline listed.
CONTACT: Ms. Dawn Williams, c/o Erving Paper Mills, 47 E. Main St., Erving, MA 01344 (617)544-2711

FOUNDATION: Henry E. Warren Scholarship Fund
REQUISITE: Must have a scouting background with the Algonquin Council, Boy Scouts of America. A Scout, Explorer or former member of the Algonquin Council who needs additional financial help for approved advanced educational institutions (not limited to colleges or universities) may apply. Must have good character, scholastic ability, no less than 3 years of Scouting, no less than 2 weeks of Scout camping at Resolute, or other approved activity, achieved 1st Class Rank & demonstrated worthiness as a Scout or Explorer. Payment is normally made in 2 installments directly to school upon presentation of bursar's bill. Payments not made to individuals.
APPLICATION: High school seniors should fill out a preliminary application & fill a completed application following graduation. Must furnish letters of reference from Scouting, religious, educational or other sources to the Council. Official transcript of high school grades required. No deadline listed.
CONTACT: Boy Scouts of American, Algonquin Council, POB 149, 34 DeLoss St., Framingham, MA 01701 TEL: (208)872-6551

FOUNDATION: Albert H. & Reuben S. Stone Fund
REQUISITE: Reside in Gardner, MA, & be full-time day student.
APPLICATION: Interviews required. Applications may be obtained personally through group appointments set with guidance dept. of high school. Write for further info. Deadline end of June.
CONTACT: Carlton E. Nichols or Carlton E. Nichols, Jr., Trustees, 232 Logan St., Gardner, MA 01440 (We were not able to verify this listing; it may not be extant.)

FOUNDATION: Fred W. Wells Trust Fund
REQUISITE: Must reside in Greenfield, Deerfield, Shelburne, Ashfield, Montague, Buckland, Charlemont, Heath, Leyden, Gill, Northfield, Conway, Bernardston, Hawley, Rowe, or Monroe, MA.
APPLICATION: Write for info. Deadline May 1.
CONTACT: Fleet Bank, POB 9006, Springfield, MA 01102-9006 (413)787-8700

FOUNDATION: Arthur Ashley Williams Foundation

REQUISITE: Generally locally oriented giving for undergraduate scholarships only. Funding is limited.
APPLICATION: Must complete a financial questionnaire. Write for info. No deadline listed.
CONTACT: Frederick Cole, Chairman, POB 397, Holliston, MA 01746 (We were not able to verify this listing; it may not be extant.)

FOUNDATION: The Hopedale Foundation
REQUISITE: Must be a local high school graduate.
APPLICATION: Write for info. No deadline listed.
CONTACT: Thad R. Jackson, Treasurer, 43 Hope St., Hopedale, MA 01747 (We were not able to verify this listing; it may not be extant.)

FOUNDATION: Edward Bangs Kelley & Elza Kelley Fndtn, Inc.
REQUISITE: Must reside in Barnstable County, MA. Preference given to those entering medical & paramedical fields.
APPLICATION: Write for info. Deadline April 30.
CONTACT: Henry L. Murphy, Jr., Admnstrtv Manager, 243 South St., PO Drawer M, Hyannis, MA 02601 (We were not able to verify this listing; it may not be extant.)

FOUNDATION: Joseph & Florence A. Price Scholarship Fund
REQUISITE: Must be a senior of Hyde Park High School, MA.
APPLICATION: Write for info. No deadline listed.
CONTACT: Michael Donato, Headmaster, Hyde Park High School, Hyde Park, MA 02126

FOUNDATION: Isaac Harris Cary Educational Fund
REQUISITE: Must be a male of New England parentage, with emphasis on a resident of the Lexington, MA, area.
APPLICATION: Contact foundation for info. & application deadline.
CONTACT: c/o Lexington Savings Bank, 1776 Massachusetts Ave., Lexington, MA 02173 (617)862-1775

FOUNDATION: Josiah Willard Hayden Recreation Center, Inc.
REQUISITE: Must be a Lexington, MA resident.
APPLICATION: Write for info. No deadline listed.
CONTACT: Joseph P. Crosby, Dir., 24 Lincoln St., Lexington, MA 02173
TEL: (617)852-8480

FOUNDATION: William E. Maloney Foundation

REQUISITE: Must reside in MA.
APPLICATION: Write for info. No deadline listed.
CONTACT: POB 515, Lexington, MA 02173 TEL: (617)860-7313

FOUNDATION: Mary T. & William A. Richardson Fund Corp.
REQUISITE: Must be a MA resident.
APPLICATION: Write for info. Deadline June 1.
CONTACT: Robert M. Wallask, Trust Officer, c/o Eastern Bank, 94 Pleasant St., Malden, MA 02148 TEL: (617)321-1111

FOUNDATION: Ladies Branch of The New Bedford Port Society
REQUISITE: Be needy student from the New Bedford, MA, area.
APPLICATION: Must submit a letter explaining educational plans & financial situation. Deadline May 1.
CONTACT: Chairperson, Educational Grants Committee, One Johnny Cake Hill, New Bedford, MA 02740
(We were not able to verify this listing; it may not be extant.)

FOUNDATION: The General Charitable Society of Newburyport
REQUISITE: Must be a Newburyport, MA resident.
APPLICATION: Write for info. No deadline listed.
CONTACT: 21 Collins St., Newburyport, 01950
(We were not able to verify this listing; it may not be extant.)

FOUNDATION: Wheelwright Scientific School
REQUISITE: Must be a Protestant young man who resides in Newburyport, MA, & is pursuing education in the sciences.
APPLICATION: Write for info. Deadline is published in the Newburyport Daily News in Feb. each year.
CONTACT: Josiah H. Welch, Pres., c/o Chase & Lunt, 47 State St., Newburyport, MA 01950 TEL: (508)462-4434

FOUNDATION: Orange Scholarship Foundation
REQUISITE: Graduate of Ralph C. Mahar Rgnl Hgh Schl, Orange, MA.
APPLICATION: Write for info. Deadline June 1.
CONTACT: Rbrt P. Collen, Chrmn, 25 Pleasant St, Orange 01364
(We were not able to verify this listing; it may not be extant.)

FOUNDATION: Adams Scholarship Fund
REQUISITE: Reside in Adams-Chesire, MA, Regional Schl Dstrct
APPLICATION: Write for info. No deadline listed.

CONTACT: Paula Hilchey, c/o The Bank of Boston, 99 W. St., Pittsfield, MA 01201 TEL: (413)499-3000

FOUNDATION: Clinton O. & Lura Curtis Jones Memorial Trust
REQUISITE: Scholarships for Mass. residents only.
APPLICATION: Write for info. & submit school transcripts.
CONTACT: F.M. Meyers, Trustee, 184 North St., Pittsfield, MA 01201
(We were not able to verify this listing; it may not be extant.)

FOUNDATION: Flynn Foundation
REQUISITE: Scholarships for undergraduate study, including grants to children & other relatives of any employee of John Flynn & Sons, Inc., & any child of any employee of Pownal Tanning Co., Inc.
APPLICATION: Write for info. No deadline listed.
CONTACT: 80 Boston St., Salem, MA 01970
(We were not able to verify this listing; it may not be extant.)

FOUNDATION: Mack Industrial School
REQUISITE: Must be a female resident of Salem, MA, & a student at a New England institution.
APPLICATION: Write for info. Deadline May 1.
CONTACT: Mrs. William F. Cass, 92 Columbus Ave., Salem, MA 01970 (617) 744-7640 or Mrs. Robert F. Prentiss, 24 Dearborn St., Salem, MA 01970 (We were not able to verify this listing; it may not be extant.)

FOUNDATION: Wilcox-Ware Scholarship Trust
REQUISITE: Must be a graduate of Mohawk Regional High School or reside in Buckland, Clorain, or Shelburne, MA.
APPLICATION: Write for info. No deadline listed.
CONTACT: Mohawk Rgnl Hgh School, Achfield Star Rte., Shelburne Falls MA 01370 (We were not able to verify this listing; it may not be extant.)

FOUNDATION: The James W. Colgan Fund
REQUISITE: Must reside in MA.
APPLICATION: Write or call for info. Deadline May 31.
CONTACT: Fleet Bank, Trust Dept., POB 9003, Springfield, MA 01101 (413)787-8700

FOUNDATION: James Z. Naurison Scholarship Fund
REQUISITE: Must be a college-bound student & a resident of Hampden, Hampshire, Franklin or Berkshire counties, MA, or a resident of Enfield or

Suffield counties, CT, for at least 1 year.
APPLICATION: Write for info. Deadline 5/1; accepted Dec to April.
CONTACT: Fleet Bank, POB 9006, Springfield, MA 01102-9006 (413)787-8700

FOUNDATION: Horace Smith Fund
REQUISITE: Must be a resident or secondary school graduate of Hampden County, MA.
APPLICATION: Applications available after April 1 for loans, after September 1 for fellowships. Scholarship applications available in the guidance offices of Hampden County, MA, high schools. Interviews required. Deadlines before June 15 for loan applications for college students & before July 1 for high school seniors; December 31 for scholarships; & February 1 for fellowships.
CONTACT: Philip T. Hart, Exec. Secty., 1441 Main St., Box 3034, Springfield, MA 01101 (413)739-4222

FOUNDATION: Massachusetts State Federation of Women's Clubs
REQUISITE: Scholarships granted to undergraduate students who are residents of Massachusetts only. A letter of endorsement from the local Federated Women's Club President must be submitted along with a transcript of grades.
APPLICATION: Write for info. Application deadline is February 15th.
CONTACT: 245 Dutton Rd., Sudbury, MA 01776. (617)443-4569

FOUNDATION: Permanent Endwmnt Fnd for Martha's Vineyard
REQUISITE: Be graduate of Martha's Vineyard Rgnl Hgh Schl
APPLICATION: Write for info. No deadline listed.
CONTACT: John H. Ware, Jr., Chairman, RFD Box 149, Vineyard Haven, MA 02568 TEL: (617)693-0721

FOUNDATION: Grover Cronin Memorial Foundation
REQUISITE: Must be a MA student.
APPLICATION: Write for info. No deadline listed.
CONTACT: Lawrence D. Chappell, Trustee, 223 Moody St., Waltham, MA 02154 (We were not able to verify this listing; it may not be extant.)

FOUNDATION: Marjorie Sells Carter Boy Scout Schlrshp Fnd
REQUISITE: Be former Boy Scout who resides in New England.
APPLICATION: Submit letter requesting application by 4/1.
CONTACT: Joan Shaffer, POB 527, West Chatham, MA 02669

(We were not able to verify this listing; it may not be extant.)

FOUNDATION: Greater Worcester Community Foundation, Inc.
REQUISITE: Must be a student who resides in Worcester County, MA, or a child of an employee of Guaranty Bank or Rothman's Furniture.
APPLICATION: Call or write to Scholarship Coordinator for info. Interviews required for finalists. Deadline March 15.
CONTACT: Cynthia Taylor, Scholarship Coordinator, 44 Front St., Ste. 530, Worcester, MA 01608 TEL: (508)755-0980

FOUNDATION: Sudbury Foundation
REQUISITE: Must reside in Sudbury, MA, or have matriculated from the Sudbury Rgnl School District.
APPLICATION: Write for info. Deadline April 1.
CONTACT: John E. Arsenault, VP & Trust Officer, Mechanics Bnk Trst Dpt., POB 15073, Worcester, MA 011615-0073 TEL: (508)798-6400

FOUNDATION: Herbert L. Batt Memorial Foundation, Inc.
REQUISITE: Grants are for advancement of Hebrew education. Must reside in CT or MA.
APPLICATION: Must submit a letter with name of school to be entered & planned course of study. No deadline listed.
CONTACT: Irving Kroopnick, Pres., 27 Vista Terrace, New Haven, CT 06515 (We were not able to verify this listing; it may not be extant.)

FOUNDATION: The Horbach Fund
REQUISITE: Must be a needy, gifted, young person under the age of 20 who resides in CT, MA, NJ, NY, or RI.
APPLICATION: Write for info. Deadline August 1.
CONTACT: Natnl Community Bank of NJ, 113 W. Essex St., Maywood, NJ 07607 (We were not able to verify this listing; it may not be extant.)

FOUNDATION: The Theodore H. Barth Foundation, Inc.
REQUISITE: Hgh school graduate of the Wareham, MA, Schl Dstrct
APPLICATION: Write for info. No deadline listed.
CONTACT: Irving P. Berelson, VP, 1211 Ave. of the Americas, NY, NY 10036 (We were not able to verify this listing; it may not be extant.)

FOUNDATION: The Vatra's Educational Foundation
REQUISITE: Must be a student of Albanian lineage or descent.
APPLICATION: Write for info. No deadline listed.

CONTACT: Peter D. Peterson, Chrmn, 517 East Ave., NY 10017
(We were not able to verify this listing; it may not be extant.)

FOUNDATION: The Golub Foundation
REQUISITE: Be a graduating hgh schl student in area served by
Price Chopper Supermarkets, including NY, MA, PA, & VT.
APPLICATION: Write for info. Deadline April 1.
CONTACT: Scholarship Committee, c/o Golub Corp., Deanes Burg Rd.,
Schenectady, NY 12306 TEL: (518)356-9390

FOUNDATION: William P. Anderson Foundation
REQUISITE: Must reside in Cincinnati, OH, or Boston, MA.
APPLICATION: Write for info. No deadline listed.
CONTACT: Paul D. Myers, Secty., 3552 Bayard Rd., Cincinnati, OH 45208
(We were not able to verify this listing; it may not be extant.)

FOUNDATION: Boston Area Black Alumni Association
REQUISITE: Must be black high school senior enrolling at a college in the
Boston, MA metropolitan area.
APPLICATION: Write for info. No deadline listed.
CONTACT: District of Columbia Public Schools, Division of Student
Services, 4501 Lee St., NE, Washington, DC 20019 TEL: (202)724-4934

FOUNDATION: American Optical Foundation
REQUISITE: Scholarships and student loans for children of AOC
APPLICATION: Application deadline is 4/25. Write for details.
CONTACT: American Optical Corporation, 14 Mechanic St., POB 1,
Southbridge, MA 01550 Ernie Duquette TEL: (508)765-9711

FOUNDATION: Cranston Foundation
REQUISITE: Schlrshps for 2 yrs study for children of emplys of Cranston
Print Works Company, its divisions or subsidiaries.
APPLICATION: Application deadline is April 15th.
CONTACT: c/o Administrator, 1381 Cranston ST., Cranston, RI 02920.
TEL: (401)943-4800

FOUNDATION: Hood (Charles H.) Fund
REQUISITE: Scholarships for children of employees of H.P. Hood Inc. and
Agri-Mark, Inc.
APPLICATION: Application deadline is January 15th.
CONTACT: 500 Rutherford Ave., Boston, MA 02129. Prudence M. Dame,

Executive Director and Secretary. TEL: (617)242-0600

FOUNDATION: Perini (Joseph) Memorial Foundation
REQUISITE: Scholarships for children of employees of Perini Corp., or its subsidiaries in Massachusetts.
APPLICATION: Application deadline is October 1st.
CONTACT: 73 Mt. Wayte Ave., Framingham, MA 01701. Joseph Perini, Jr., Secretary. (508)628-2000

FOUNDATION: Perini Memorial Foundation
REQUISITE: Schlrshps for chldrn of employees of Perini Corp.
APPLICATION: Write for more information.
CONTACT: 73 Mt. Wayte Ave., Framingham, MA 01701 or Elctn Committee, POB 31, Framingham, MA 01701. TEL: (508)628-2000

FOUNDATION: Stop & Shop Charitable Foundation
REQUISITE: Scholarships for children of employees of Stop & Shop Companies, Inc., including, Bradlees Department Stores, Medi Mart Drug Stores, Charles B. Perkins Tobacco Shops, Stop & Shop Supermarkets, and Stop & Shop Manufacturing Co.
APPLICATION: Application deadline is January 31st.
CONTACT: P.O. Box 369, Boston, MA 02101. Frank Ippolito, Corporate Employee Benefits, The Stop & Shop Companies, Inc. (617)380-8000

FOUNDATION: Colgan (The James W.) Fund
REQUISITE: Undergraduate loans for residents of MA
APPLICATION: Write a letter requesting an application and include a self-addressed stamp envelope.
CONTACT: Community Foundation of Western Massachusetts, POB 15769, Springfield, MA 01115 TEL: (413)732-2858

FOUNDATION: Edwards Scholarship Fund
REQUISITE: Scholarship loans for students under the age of 25, and whose parents reside in Boston.
APPLICATION: Application deadline is March 1st.
CONTACT: One Federal St., Boston, MA 02110. TEL: (617)426-4434

FOUNDATION: Baybank Norfolk
REQUISITE: Scholarships to female seniors at Brookline High School.
APPLICATION: Write for info. Application deadline is April thru May.
CONTACT: Bernadette Stephan, POBOX 422-TA 7 NE Executive Park,

Burlington, MA 01803. (617)273-1700 ext. 4583

FOUNDATION: Hopedale Foundation
REQUISITE: Student loans for local high school graduates.
APPLICATION: Write for application and more details.
CONTACT: 43 Hope Street, Hopedale, MA 01747. Thad Jackson, Treasurer. (We were not able to verify this listing; it may not be extant.)

FOUNDATION: Lotta Agricultural Fund
REQUISITE: Farm loans for students or graduates of University of Massachusetts College of Natural Resources or the Stockbridge School of Agriculture.
APPLICATION: Applications are accepted throughout the year.
CONTACT: c/o Trustees under the Will of Lotta M. Crabtree, 11 Beacon St., Suite 1110, Boston, MA 02108. TEL: (617)742-5920

MARYLAND

FOUNDATION: Maryland State Scholarship Board
REQUISITE: Scholarships granted to Maryland residents to support training at private vocational-technical schools in Maryland. Applicant must be nominated by their school.
APPLICATION: Write for info. Application deadline is March 2nd.
CONTACT: 2100 Guilford Avenue, Baltimore, MD 21218. 301-659-6420

FOUNDATION: University of Maryland
REQUISITE: Competition open to young performing pianists aged 18-33
APPLICATION: Write for info. Application deadline is April 1st.
CONTACT: Office of Summer and Special Programs, College Park, MD 20742. (301)405-1000

FOUNDATION: Maryland State Scholarship Board
REQUISITE: Scholarships to Maryland residents who agree to teach in critical shortage area in Maryland for 1 year. Full-time undergraduates and public school teachers doing part-time graduate study.
APPLICATION: Write for info. Application deadline is November.
CONTACT: 2100 Gulford Avenue, Baltimore, MD 21218. (410)974-5350

FOUNDATION: Knott (Marion Burk) Scholarship Fund
REQUISITE: Scholarships for Catholic students who live in the Archdiocese of Baltimore and will be attending Loyola College or College

of Notre Dame of Maryland or Mt St Mary's College, Emmittburg, MD. APPLICATION: Contact fund office for current applctn gdlnes. CONTACT: St. Mary's Seminary Bldg, 5400 Roland Ave, Bltmre, MD 21210. TEL: (410)323-3200

FOUNDATION: Loats Foundation, Inc.
REQUISITE: Scholarships awarded to residents of Frederick County, MD. For application deadlines contact Glenn e. Biehl, Treasurer, c/o Evangelical Lutheran Church, 35 East Church St., Frederick, MD 21701 Tel.:(301)663-6361.
APPLICATION: Can be picked up at Frederick County high schools.
CONTACT: POB 240, Frederick City, MD 21701 TEL: (301)662-2191

FOUNDATION: McKaig (Lalitta Nash) Foundation
REQUISITE: Scholarships to residents of Allegany and Garrett counties, MD for undergraduate, graduate, and professional education.
APPLICATION: Application deadline is May 31st. Applications are available from Cumberland, MD, area high school guidance offices. You must also submit Financial Aid Form (F.A.F.).
CONTACT: c/o PNC Bank, Trust Charitable Division, One Oliver Plaza, Pittsburgh, PA 15265. Henry C. Flood, Vice-President, Pittsburgh National Bank. TEL: (412)762-3441

FOUNDATION: Stewart (J.C.) Memorial Trust
REQUISITE: Schlrshps & loans awarded to Maryland residents and planning to attend college.
APPLICATION: Write a letter requesting an application and include a self-addressed stamp envelope.
CONTACT: 7718 Sinns Lane, Lanham MD 20706. Robert s. Hoyert, Trustee. TEL: (301)459-4200

FOUNDATION: Wyman (Mary Byrd) Memorial Assctn of Baltimore City
REQUISITE: Scholarships awarded for secondary education.
APPLICATION: Deadline is January 1st.
CONTACT: 3130 Golf Course Road West, Owings Mills, MD 21117. A. Rutherford Holmes, President.
(We were not able to verify this listing; it may not be extant.)

FOUNDATION: Gemco Charitable and Scholarship Fund
REQUISITE: Scholarships are available for high school seniors in communities where there is a Gemco Corporation.

APPLICATION: Schools will select scholarship entrants and send out applications.
CONTACT: 6565 Knott Avenue, Buena Park, CA 90620, Jim Barnett (714)739-6351

FOUNDATION: Knapp Educational Fund, Inc.
REQUISITE: Scholarships for children of employees of Macmillan, Inc.
APPLICATION: Applications are accepted throughout the year.
CONTACT: POB O, St. Michaels, MD 21663. Mrs. Antoinette Vojvoda, President. TEL: (301)745-5660

FOUNDATION: Martin Marietta Corporation Foundation
REQUISITE: Scholarships for children of employees of Martin Marietta Corporation.
APPLICATION: Applications are accepted throughout the year.
CONTACT: 6801 Rockledge Drive, Bethesda, MD 20817. Donna Price, Contributions Representative. TEL: (301)897-6863

FOUNDATION: Thorn(Columbus W.), Jr. Foundation
REQUISITE: Educational loans for worthy and needy graduates of Cecil County, MD, high schools.
APPLICATION: Applications are accepted throughout the year.
CONTACT: 109 E Main St., Elkton, MD 21921. TEL: (301)398-0611

MAINE

FOUNDATION: University of Maine Pulp & Paper Foundation
REQUISITE: Scholarships granted to students accepted into the University of Maine at Orono planning to pursue a career in a paper related career. Must be US citizen or Canadian citizen.
APPLICATION: Write for info. Application deadline is March 15th.
CONTACT: 217 Jenness Hall, Orono, ME 04469. Tel: (207)581-2296

FOUNDATION: Edith M. Daso Scholarship Trust
REQUISITE: Graduate Mt. Desert Island Regional High School
APPLICATION: Write for info. Deadlines April 15 & May 15.
CONTACT: Trust Dept., c/o Bar Harbor Banking & Trust Co., 82 Main St., Bar Harbor, ME 04609-0400 TEL: (207)288-3314

FOUNDATION: William Searls Scholarship Foundation
REQUISITE: Must reside in Southwest Harbor, ME.

APPLICATION: Write for info. No deadline listed.
CONTACT: Margo Stanley, Box 1105, Southwest Harbor, ME 04679.
TEL: (207)244-7011

FOUNDATION: George P. Davenport Trust Fund
REQUISITE: Must be a Bath, ME area high school graduate.
APPLICATION: Write for info. No deadline listed.
CONTACT: 55 Front St., Bath, ME 04530 TEL: (207)443-3431

FOUNDATION: Fred Forsyth Educational Trust Fund
REQUISITE: Must be a graduate of Bucksport High School, ME.
APPLICATION: Write for info. No deadline listed.
CONTACT: Bucksport High School, Bucksport, ME 04416 (207)469-6650

FOUNDATION: Tibbetts Industries Foundation
REQUISITE: Be a graduate of a specified high school or college in ME.
APPLICATION: Submit letter including written request detailing projected income for next school year, most recent transcript of grades, & any other scholastic info. Written requests should be submitted by mid-July for consideration for next school year. Write for application info.
CONTACT: W K Stanley, Bx 1096, Camden 04843 TEL: (207)236-3301

FOUNDATION: Gould Point Sebago Scholarship fund
REQUISITE: Scholarships to any employee or a child of an employee of Point Sebago in Casco, ME, a graduate of Lake Region High School, Naples, ME or a graduate of Windham High School, Windham, ME.
APPLICATION: Write for info. Deadline April 15.
CONTACT: Don Toms, Point Sebago, RR 1, Box 712, Casco, ME 04015 (207) 655-7948

FOUNDATION: Sumner O. Hancock Scholarship Fund
REQUISITE: Must be a student of the Casco, ME area.
APPLICATION: Write for info. Deadline May 15.
CONTACT: Elizabeth Hancock, Pres., Casco, ME 04015 (207)627-4354

FOUNDATION: The Maine Community Foundation, Inc.
REQUISITE: Must reside in ME.
APPLICATION: Write or call for info. Deadlines February 1, April 1, August 1, Oct. 1, & Dec. 1.
CONTACT: Patty D'Angelo, 210 Main St., POB 148, Ellsworth, ME 04605
TEL: (207)667-9735

FOUNDATION: John W. Robinson Welfare Trust
REQUISITE: Must be a resident of Gardiner, ME.
APPLICATION: Interviews required. Write for info. Deadline 6/15
CONTACT: Maxine Lamb,12 Spruce St, Gardiner, ME (207)582-2488

FOUNDATION: Phi Kappa Sigma Educational Fndtn of Orono
REQUISITE: Member of Alpha Delta Chapter of PKS
APPLICATION: Write for info. No deadline listed.
CONTACT: Peter Averill, Phi Kappa Sigma House, Orono, ME

FOUNDATION: Beulah Pack Scholarship Fund
REQUISITE: Must be a resident of Union, ME.
APPLICATION: Write for info. No deadline listed.
CONTACT: Deanne L. Nason, c/o Casco Northern Bank, N.A.; Trust Dept.,
POB 678, Portland, ME 04104 TEL: (207)774-8221

FOUNDATION: Marion W. Warman Irrevocable Schlrshp Fnd
REQUISITE: Graduate of a school in Aroostook County, ME
APPLICATION: Write for info. Deadline May 10.
CONTACT: c/o Gordon W.H. Buzza, Jr., POB 1029, Presque Isle, ME
04769 (207)769-2211

FOUNDATION: Marjorie Sells Carter Boy Scout Schlrshp Fndtn
REQUISITE: Former Boy Scout who resides in the New England
APPLICATION: Submit letter requesting application by 4/1
CONTACT: Joan Shaffer, POB 527, W. Chatham, MA 02669
(We were not able to verify this listing; it may not be extant.)

FOUNDATION: Charles H. Hood Fund
REQUISITE: Must be a CT, MA, ME, NH, RI, or VT resident.
APPLICATION: Write for info. No deadline listed.
CONTACT: 500 Rutherford Ave., Boston, MA 02129 (617)695-9439

FOUNDATION: Cooper Industries Foundation
REQUISITE: Scholarships for children of employees of Cooper Industries,
Inc. in AL, CA, CT, GA, IL, IN, ME, MI, MO, MS, NJ, NY, NC, OH, OK, PA,
SC, TN, TX, and VA.
APPLICATION: Applications are accepted throughout the year.
CONTACT: First City Tower, Suite 4000, POB 4446, Houston, TX 77210.
Patricia B. Meineckie, Secretary. TEL: (713)739-5632

FOUNDATION: New England Regional Student Program
REQUISITE: Must reside in 1 of the New England States: CT, ME, MA, NH, RI, or VT. You may attend a public college or university within the region at a reduced tuition rate for certain degree programs not offered by own state's public institutions.
APPLICATION: Write for info. No deadline listed.
CONTACT: Office of Regional Student Program, New England Board of Hghr Edctn, 45 Temple Place, Boston, MA 02111 TEL: (617)357-9620

FOUNDATION: Fred Forsyth Educational Trust Fund
REQUISITE: Must be a CT, MA, ME, NH, RI, or VT student.
APPLICATION: Write for info. No deadline listed.
CONTACT: Rose Marie Bates, c/o Fleet Bank, Fleet Investment Services, POB 923, Bangor, ME 04402-0923. TEL: (207)941-6000

MICHIGAN

FOUNDATION: Muskegon County Community Foundation
REQUISITE: Scholarships granted to Muskegon county residents ONLY for vocational-technical training. Must be US citizen.
APPLICATION: Write for info. Application deadline is April 16th.
CONTACT: 425 West Western Avenue, #304 Frauenthal Building, Muskegon, MI 49440 616-722-4538

FOUNDATION: Women in Communications
REQUISITE: Scholarships granted to Michigan resident undergraduate juniors or seniors or graduate students attending an accredited institution in Michigan studying Communications. Must have a 3.0 GPA.
APPLICATION: Write for info. Application deadline is April 7th.
CONTACT: 35918 Rewa, Detroit, MI 48043 Tel: 313-791-1277

FOUNDATION: Auxiliary to the Michigan Optometric Association
REQUISITE: Scholarships granted to Michigan residents who are student members of Michigan Optometric Association. Students must be in their third year of study at an accredited institution
maintaining a "B" average. Must be US citizen.
APPLICATION: Write for info. Application deadline is March 1st.
CONTACT: POBOX 352, Iron River, MI 49935.
(We were not able to verify this listing; it may not be extant.)

FOUNDATION: Michigan United Conservation Clubs

REQUISITE: Scholarships granted to Michigan resident high school juniors and seniors who are planning to study any of the many areas in the natural resource field in college.
APPLICATION: Write for info. Application deadline is March 11th.
CONTACT: POB 30235, 2101 Wood St, Lansing, MI 48912 (517)371-1041

FOUNDATION: SAE/Uniroyal
REQUISITE: Scholarships granted to seniors in a Michigan High School with at least a 3.0 GPA and in the 75th percentile in both math and verbal SAT intending to pursue an engineering program that is accredited by EAC/ABET.
APPLICATION: Write for info. Application deadline is December 15th.
CONTACT: 400 Commonwealth Dr, Warrendale, PA 15096 (412)776-4841

FOUNDATION: Transportation Clubs International
REQUISITE: Scholarships granted to students who have attended school in Michigan at any level and is now enrolled in an accredited college or university offering a degreed or vocational program related to Transportation or Traffic Management.
APPLICATION: Write for info. Application deadline is April 15th.
CONTACT: 203 E. Third Street, Suite 201, Sanford, FL 32771.
(We were not able to verify this listing; it may not be extant.)

FOUNDATION: AEI Scholarship Fund
REQUISITE: Must be a female student who has been accepted to or is attending an accredited medical school in the U.S.
APPLICATION: Write for info. Deadline May 1.
CONTACT: B. Todd Jones, Trust Officer, c/o Citizens Trust, POB 8612, Ann Arbor, MI 48104 TEL: (313)994-5555

FOUNDATION: Ann Arbor Area Foundation
REQUISITE: Must reside in the area of Ann Arbor, MI.
APPLICATION: Call for info. No deadline listed.
CONTACT: Joan U. Nagy, Exec. Dir., 125 W. Washington, Ste. 400, Ann Arbor, MI 48104 (313)663-0401

FOUNDATION: McCurdy Memorial Scholarship Foundation
REQUISITE: Undergraduate schlrshps to resident of Calhoun Cnty
APPLICATION: Interviews required. Write for info. Deadline 4/1
CONTACT: Michael C. Jordan, 142 W. Van Buren St., Battle Creek, MI 49017 (616)962-9591

FOUNDATION: Winship Memorial Scholarship Foundation
REQUISITE: Must be a graduate of a Battle Creek, MI, area public high school, including those in the school systems of Battle Creek/Springfield, Climax-Scotts, Galesburg-Augusta, Harper Creek, Lakeview, & Pennfield.
APPLICATION: Interviews required. Applications processed through local high schools. Write for info. Deadline March 1.
CONTACT: Marcia A. Owen, c/o Comerica Bank-Battle Creek, Trust Division, 25 W. Michigan Mall, Battle Creek, MI 49017 (616)966-6340

FOUNDATION: The Tiscornia Foundation, Inc.
REQUISITE: Must be a Northern Berrien County High School senior & a child of an employee of Auto Specialties Manufacturing Co.
APPLICATION: Write for info. Deadline April 1.
CONTACT: Laurianne T. Davis, Secty., POB 8787, 2303 Pipestone Rd., Benton Harbor, MI 49022-8787 TEL: (616)983-4711

FOUNDATION: Cora B. Parkhurst Scholarship Trust
REQUISITE: Must be a graduate of Berrien Springs High School, Berrien Spring, MI.
APPLICATION: Interviews required. Write for info. Deadline 4/1
CONTACT: Bruce Taiclet, Committee Chairman, Berrien Springs High School, Berrien Springs, MI 49102 TEL: (616)471-1748

FOUNDATION: The Vomberg Foundation
REQUISITE: Must be a student who resides in Eaton County,
APPLICATION: Interviews required. Write for info. Deadline December 1 of senior year.
CONTACT: 1023 Reynolds Rd., Charlotte, 48813 (517)543-0430

FOUNDATION: George W. & Sadie Marie Juhl Scholarship Fund
REQUISITE: Must be a student residing in Branch County, MI, who is planning to attend a school of higher education in MI.
APPLICATION: Write for info. No deadline listed.
CONTACT: c/o Southern MI National Bank, 51 W. Pearl St., Coldwater, MI 49036 TEL: (517)279-7511

FOUNDATION: Corwill & Margie Jackson Foundation
REQUISITE: Must be a 1st year university student from Ludington, MI.
APPLICATION: Write for info. No deadline listed.
CONTACT: c/o Detroit Bank & Trust Co., Comerica Bank-Detroit, Detroit,

MI 48275 TEL: (313)212-4000

FOUNDATION: Ida & Benjamin Alpert Foundation
REQUISITE: Must be a MI resident who has been accepted to or is enrolled in an accredited law school.
APPLICATION: Write for info. Submit applications to Judge Frank S. Szymanski, 1215 City Cnty Bldg, Detroit, MI 48226
CONTACT: Myron Alpert, Secty., 31275 Northwestern Highway 233, Farmington Hills, MI 48018
(We were not able to verify this listing; it may not be extant.)

FOUNDATION: The Fremont Area Foundation
REQUISITE: Must be a resident of Newaygo County, MI.
APPLICATION: Write for info. No deadline listed.
CONTACT: Elizabeth Cherin, 108 S. Stewart, Fremont, MI 49412
TEL: (616)924-5350

FOUNDATION: Grand Rapids Foundation
REQUISITE: Reside in Kent County (Greater Grand Rapids)
APPLICATION: Write or call for info. Student loan applications accepted between January 1 & April 1.
CONTACT: Diana R. Sieger, Exec. Dir., 209 C. Walters Building, 161 Ottawa, N.W., Grand Rapids, MI 49503 TEL: (616)454-1751

FOUNDATION: Kent Medical Foundation
REQUISITE: Must be a resident of Kent, MI, or a bordering county who is pursuing education in medicine, nursing, or related health fields.
APPLICATION: Interviews & at least 3 letters of recommendation required. Applications made through financial aid office at your high school. No deadline listed.
CONTACT: William G. McClimas, Exec. Dir., 1155 Front Ave., NW, Grand Rapids, MI 49504 TEL: (616)458-4157

FOUNDATION: Allen H. Meyers Foundation
REQUISITE: Scholarships granted to undergraduates seniors studying in Lenawee County Michigan only in the fields of Aviation, Engineering or Physical Sciences.
APPLICATION: Write for info. Application deadline is March 15th.
CONTACT: Box 100, Tecumseh, MI 49286 (517)467-4478

FOUNDATION: H. T. Ewald Foundation

REQUISITE: Undergraduate scholarships to any high school senior who is a resident of the metropolitan Detroit area.
APPLICATION: Interviews required. Write for info. Deadline 5/1
CONTACT: Henry T. Ewald, Pres., 15175 E. Jefferson Ave., Grosse Pointe Park, MI 48230 TEL: (313)821-2000

FOUNDATION: The John & Elizabeth Whiteley Foundation
REQUISITE: Must be a needy & deserving student whose parents live in Ingham County, MI, & is studying business education or Episcopal theology.
APPLICATION: Write for info. No deadline listed.
CONTACT: Joseph A. Caruso, c/o First of America Bank-Central, Trust Division, POB 21007, Lansing, MI 48909 TEL: (517)334-1600

FOUNDATION: Midland Foundation
REQUISITE: Must reside in the Midland County, MI, area.
APPLICATION: Call for info. No deadline listed.
CONTACT: Denise Spencer, 812 W. Main St., POB 289, Midland, MI 48640 (517)839-9661

FOUNDATION: Muskegon County Community Foundation, Inc.
REQUISITE: Must be a student in Muskegon County, MI.
APPLICATION: Interviews required for high school seniors. There is a $5.00 application fee. Call for info. Deadline April 16.
CONTACT: Bruce Walker, Frauenthal Building, Ste. 304, 425 W. Western Ave., Muskegon, 49440 TEL: (616)722-4538

FOUNDATION: Charles I. & Emma J. Clapp Scholarship Fund
REQUISITE: Non-interest-bearing student loans to any non-drinker. Any female applicant must also be a non-smoker.
APPLICATION: Write for info. No deadline listed.
CONTACT: John Withee, c/o First of America Bank-MI, N.A.-Otsego Office, 110 E. Allegan St., Otsego, MI 49078 TEL: (616)692-6281

FOUNDATION: The Pipp Foundation
REQUISITE: Must be a senior of Plainwell High School, MI, who ranks in the top 20 percent of their class.
APPLICATION: High school record required. Applications available from Plainwell High School, Plainwell, MI. Deadline 6/30
CONTACT: Dr. Robert J. Tisch, 235 N. Sunset, Plainwell, MI 49080 (616)685-8940

FOUNDATION: Deseranno Educational Foundation, Inc.
REQUISITE: Must be a student attending Madonna College, MI.
APPLICATION: Write for info. No deadline listed.
CONTACT: 21777 Hoober Rd., Warren, MI 48089 (810)776-8500

FOUNDATION: C.K. Eddy Family Memorial Fund
REQUISITE: Must be resident of Saginaw County, MI, for at least 1 year prior to application deadline.
APPLICATION: Write for info. Deadline May 1.
CONTACT: Tracy Swanson, c/o Second National Bank of Saginaw, Trust Dept., 101 N. Washington Ave., Saginaw, MI 48607 (517)776-7353

FOUNDATION: Michael Jeffers Memorial Foundation
REQUISITE: Must reside in Saginaw County, MI.
APPLICATION: Write for info. Deadline June 1 for new applications & renewals.
CONTACT: Tracy Swanson, c/o Second National Bank of Saginaw, Trust Dept., 101 N. Washington Ave., Saginaw, MI 48607 (517)776-7353

FOUNDATION: John W. & Rose E. Watson Foundation
REQUISITE: Must be a resident of Saginaw, MI, who is graduating from a Catholic High School.
APPLICATION: Interviews granted upon request. Write for info. Deadline 1 month prior to academic year.
CONTACT: Rose Watson, 1551 Avalon, Saginaw, MI 48603 (517)792-2301

FOUNDATION: Allen H. Meyers Foundation
REQUISITE: Must be a snr in Lenawee Cnty, MI, who is planning to study in the sciences or allied fields.
APPLICATION: Submit letter requesting application & intended field of study. Interviews required. Deadline March 15.
CONTACT: POB 100, Tecumseh, MI 49286 TEL: (517)467-4478

FOUNDATION: Swiss Benevolent Society of Chicago
REQUISITE: Undergraduate scholarships to any full-time student of Swiss descent who resides in IL, IN, IA, MI, or WI.
APPLICATION: Write for info. Deadline March 1.
CONTACT: Professor Jean Devaud, Chairman of S.B.S. Schlrshp Committee, 629 S. Humphrey Ave., Oak Park, IL 60304 (We were not able to verify this listing; it may not be extant.)

FOUNDATION: Wisconsin Public Service Foundation, Inc.
REQUISITE: Child of employee or customer of WI Pblc Service Corp
APPLICATION: Write for info. No deadline listed.
CONTACT: Wisconsin Public Service Foundation, Inc., Scholarship Program, College Scholarship Service, Sponsored Scholarships Program, CN 6730, Princeton, NJ 08541 TEL: (609)683-5655

FOUNDATION: Gerber Companies Foundation
REQUISITE: Schlrshps for children of employees of Gerber Products Co.
APPLICATION: Application deadline is April 1st.
CONTACT: Cynthia Ebert, c/o Gerber Products Company, 445 State Street, Fremont, MI 49413. TEL: (616)928-2759

FOUNDATION: Monroe Auto Equipment Company Foundation
REQUISITE: Scholarships for children of employees of Monroe Auto Equipment Company.
APPLICATION: Applications are accepted throughout the year.
CONTACT: c/o Comerica Bank, Detroit, MI 45275-1022. Kay Osgood, Trustee, Monroe Auto Equipment Company, One International Drive, Monroe, MI 48161 TEL: (313)243-8000

FOUNDATION: Whirlpool Foundation
REQUISITE: Scholarships for child of employees of Whirlpool Corp
APPLICATION: Write for application.
CONTACT: Colleen Keast, Exec. Dir., 400 Riverview Dr., Suite 410, Benton Harbor, MI 49022. TEL: (616)923-3461

FOUNDATION: Cooper Industries Foundation
REQUISITE: Scholarships for children of employees of Cooper Industries, Inc. in AL, CA, CT, GA, IL, IN, ME, MI, MO, MS, NJ, NY, NC, OH, OK, PA, SC, TN, TX, and VA.
APPLICATION: Applications are accepted throughout the year.
CONTACT: First City Tower, Suite 4000, POB 4446, Houston, TX 77210. Patricia B. Meinecke, Secretary. TEL: (713)739-5632

FOUNDATION: Clapp (Charles I. & Emma J.) Scholarship Fund
REQUISITE: Non-interest loans for students who are non-drinkers and non-smokers.
APPLICATION: Applications are accepted throughout the year.
CONTACT: First of America Bank-Michigan, N.A., Kalamazoo, MI 49007. Or John Withee, c/o First of America Bank-Michigan, N.A.-Otsego Office,

110 East Allegan St., Otsego, MI 49078. TEL: (616)692-6281

FOUNDATION: Eddy (C.K.) Family Memorial Fund
REQUISITE: Student loans for residents of Saginaw County, MI. They must have been residents for at least 1 year.
APPLICATION: Application deadline is May 1st.
CONTACT: Tracy Swanson, c/o Second National Bank of Saginaw, Trust Dept., 101 North Washington Ave., Saginaw, MI 48607. (517)776-7353

FOUNDATION: Jeffers (Michael) Memorial Foundation
REQUISITE: Edctnl loans for those who live in Saginaw Cnty
APPLICATION: Application deadline is June 1st.
CONTACT: Tracy Swanson, c/o Second National Bank of Saginaw, Trust Dept., 101 North Washington Ave., Saginaw, MI 48607. (517)776-7353

MINNESOTA

FOUNDATION: American Legion Auxiliary
REQUISITE: Scholarships granted to Minnesota resident high school seniors with a good scholastic record. Student must be studying fields in Vocational-Technical areas. Must demonstrate financial need and be of good character with ambition to continue studies.
APPLICATION: Write for info. Application deadline is March 15th.
CONTACT: State Veterans Service Building, St. Paul, MN 55155.
Tel: 612-224-7634

FOUNDATION: State Bank and Trust Company
REQUISITE: Scholarships granted to student that resided or graduated within a 30 mile radius of Fairfax Minnesota. This is for full-time undergraduate study only.
APPLICATION: Write for info. Application deadline is April 1st.
CONTACT: 100 N. Minnesota Street, New Ulm, MN 56073. 507-354-8215

FOUNDATION: American Legion Auxiliary
REQUISITE: Scholarships granted to members of an American Legion Auxiliary unit in the Dept. of Minnesota. Must be resident of Minnesota and maintain a "C" average or better in school.
APPLICATION: Write for info. Application deadline is March 15th.
CONTACT: State Veterans Service Building, St. Paul, MN 55155.
Tel: 612-224-7634

FOUNDATION: Marshall H. and Nellie Alworth Memorial Fund
REQUISITE: Scholarships granted to high school seniors at Northern Minnesota High Schools. Must be US citizen.
APPLICATION: Write for info. Application deadline is March 1st.
CONTACT: 506 Alworth Bldg., Duluth, MN 55802.
(We were not able to verify this listing; it may not be extant.)

FOUNDATION: Clem Jaunich Education Trust
REQUISITE: Scholarships granted to students who have attended public or parochial school in the Delano Minn School District or currently reside within 7 miles of the City of Delano Minn. to support undergraduate and graduate study in Theology or Medicine.
APPLICATION: Write for info. Application deadline is July 15th.
CONTACT: 5353 Gamble Dr., Suite 110, Minneapolis, MN 55416.
(We were not able to verify this listing; it may not be extant.)

FOUNDATION: Minnesota State Arts Board
REQUISITE: Scholarships granted to individual artists who are residents of Minnesota. These grants are not in support of degree requirements.
APPLICATION: Write for info. Application deadline is not specified.
CONTACT: 432 Summit Ave., St. Paul, MN 55102. (612)297-2603

FOUNDATION: Marshall H. and Nellie Alworth Memorial Fund
REQUISITE: Scholarships granted to Northern Minnesota residents that are high school seniors at Northern Minnesota High School. Must be US citizen.
APPLICATION: Write for info. Application deadline is March 1st.
CONTACT: 506 Alworth Bldg., Duluth, MN 55802. (218)722-9366

FOUNDATION: Alworth (Marshall H. & Nellie) Memorial fund
REQUISITE: Scholarships in basic sciences are awarded to high school graduates of northern Minnesota.
APPLICATION: Deadline is March 1st. You can submit your proposal between December and February. Write for info.
CONTACT: 604 Alworth Building, Duluth, MN 55802. Raymond W. Darland, President. (218)722-9366

FOUNDATION: Eddy (Edwin H.) Family Foundation
REQUISITE: Scholarships are awarded to college seniors or graduate students in communication disorders who are attending University of Minnesota-Duluth, MN.

APPLICATION: Application deadline is 3/31. Write for info.
CONTACT: c/o Norwest Bank Duluth, Capital Management and Trust Dept, Duluth , MN 55802, Murray George, Trustee. (218)723-2773

FOUNDATION: Jaunich (Clem) Education Trust
REQUISITE: Schlrshps for students who live in 7 mile radius of Delano, MN, or have gone to public or parochial schls there, and are going to accredited medical, pre-medical, seminary, or pre-seminary schools.
APPLICATION: Application deadline is 8/1. Write for info.
CONTACT: 5353 Gamble Drive, Suite 110, Minneapolis, MN 55416. Joseph L. Abrahamson, Trustee. (Apply at these specific schools.) TEL: (612)546-1555

FOUNDATION: Meyer (Roy E. & Merle) Foundation
REQUISITE: Schlrshps awarded to seniors of Red Wing Central High, who intend to pursue a career in engineering or science.
APPLICATION: Contact the school for application deadline.
CONTACT: 408 Main Street, Suite M-101, Red Wing, MN 55066. Tel.: (612)388-4788. Guidance Office, Red Wind Central High School, Red Wing, MN 55066. (Apply at these specific schools.)

FOUNDATION: Minnesota Foundation
REQUISITE: Scholarships for residents of Minnesota.
APPLICATION: Application deadline varies.
CONTACT: 1120 Norwest Center, St. Paul, MN 55101. Judith K. Healey, President. TEL: (612) 224-5463

FOUNDATION: Bush Foundation
REQUISITE: Scholarships granted to writers, visual artists, composers and choreographers who are residents of Minn., N. Dakota, or S. Dakota and is at least 25 years old. Must work full-time in their chosen art form.
APPLICATION: Write for info. Application deadline is October 30th, November 6th, and November 13th.
CONTACT: E900 First National Bank Bldg., St. Paul, MN 55101 (612)227-0891

FOUNDATION: St. Paul Foundation
REQUISITE: Scholarships for residents of St. Paul and Minneapolis, MN, and for children of employees of 3M Company.
APPLICATION: Write for more information.
CONTACT: 1120 Norwest Center, St. Paul, MN 55101. Paul A. Verret,

President. TEL: (612)224-5463

FOUNDATION: Tozer Foundation, Inc.
REQUISITE: Scholarships for high school seniors in 3 counties in MN
APPLICATION: Accepted throughout the year. Write for information.
CONTACT: Betsy Keyet, c/o First Trust N.A., SPFS0200 First Ntnl Bnk
Bldg, POB 64704, St. Paul, MN 55164. TEL: (612)224-0958

FOUNDATION: Wedum Foundation
REQUISITE: Student aid given to residents of Alexandria, MN area. Write
for information.
APPLICATION: Applications are accepted throughout the year.
CONTACT: 4721 Spring Circle, Minnetonka, MN 55345 or POB 644,
Alexandria, MN 56308. TEL: (612)762-7812

FOUNDATION: Whiteside (Robert B. & Sophia) Schlrshp Fndtn
REQUISITE: Schlrshps for graduates of Duluth, MN high schools
APPLICATION: Applications are accepted throughout the year and are
available from high school counselors.
CONTACT: Mary Anne Korfch, 1600 North Eighth Ave. East, Duluth, MN
55805. TEL: (218)728-6428

FOUNDATION: Winkleman (Emma) Trust B
REQUISITE: Scholarships for nursing students who live in or graduated
from high school in a 30-mile radius of Fairfax, MN.
APPLICATION: Deadline is April 1st.
CONTACT: State Bank & Trust Company, 100 North Minnesota St, POB
189, New Ulm, MN 56073. Trust Department. TEL: (507)354-8215

FOUNDATION: Wood (A.R.) Educational Trust
REQUISITE: Schlrshps for graduates of Luverne Hgh School, Luverne, MN
APPLICATION: Application deadline is August 3rd.
CONTACT: POB 1953, Sioux Falls, SD 57117-1953. Mary Jo Curtin
(605)339-7400

FOUNDATION: Graco Foundation
REQUISITE: Schlrshps to children of Graco employees.
APPLICATION: Deadlines 2/15, 5/15, 8/15 & 10/31
CONTACT: POB 1441, Minneapolis, MN 55440-1444. David L. Schoeneck,
Executive Director. TEL: (612)623-6679

FOUNDATION: Potlatch Foundation for Higher Education
REQUISITE: Scholarships awarded to undergraduates who live in areas of Potlatch Corporation operation.
APPLICATION: Application deadlines are February 1st for new application and July 1st for renewals.
CONTACT: POB 3591, San Francisco, CA 94119. George C. Check, President. TEL: (415)981-5980

FOUNDATION: Conwed Foundation
REQUISITE: Schlrshps for children of emplys of Conwed Corp.
APPLICATION: Application deadline is July 1st.
CONTACT: 620 Taft Street, N.E., Minneapolis, MN 55413. (612)623-1700

FOUNDATION: Dyco Foundation
REQUISITE: Scholarships for children of employees of Dyco Petroleum Corporation.
APPLICATION: Application deadline is March 30th.
CONTACT: 11000 Interchange Tower, Minneapolis, MN 55426. Alicia Ringstad, Director. (612)545-4021

FOUNDATION: Groves Foundation
REQUISITE: Scholarships for children of employees of S.J. Groves and Sons Company, and its subsidiaries.
APPLICATION: Applications are accepted throughout the year.
CONTACT: 10,000 Hghwy 55 West, POB 1267, Mnnpls, MN 55440 Elfriede M. Lobeck, Executive Director. TEL: (612)546-6943

FOUNDATION: Hotchkiss (W.R.) Foundation
REQUISITE: Scholarships for children of employees and ex-employees of Deluxe Check Printers, Inc.
APPLICATION: Application deadline is January 31st.
CONTACT: 1080 West County Road F, St. Paul, MN 55126. Michael J. Welch, W.R. Hotchkiss Scholarship Plan, POB 64399, St. Paul, MN 55146-0399 TEL: (612)483-7232

FOUNDATION: Valspar Foundation
REQUISITE: Schlrshps for children of employees Valspar Corp
APPLICATION: Application deadline is June 1st.
CONTACT: 1101 Third Street South, Minneapolis, MN 55415. Joanne Smith, Valspar Scholarship Committee, Personnel Department, POB 1461, Minneapolis, MN 55440. (612)332-7371

MISSOURI

FOUNDATION: Missouri League for Nursing
REQUISITE: Scholarships granted to any LPN/RN or MSN nursing student who is a resident of Missouri and going to school in Missouri. Must be US citizen.
APPLICATION: Write for info. Application deadline is September 30th. Application must be obtained through your Director of Nursing at respective school.
CONTACT: 1804 Southwest Blvd., Suite E, Jefferson City, MO 65101 314-635-5355

FOUNDATION: Missouri Coordinating Board for Higher Education
REQUISITE: Scholarships granted to Missouri residents. Undergraduate juniors and seniors with need. Loans will be forgiven if you teach in critical areas of need in Missouri.
APPLICATION: Write for info. Application deadline is June 1st.
CONTACT: POBOX 1438, 101 Adams St., Jefferson City, MO 65102 (314)751-2361

FOUNDATION: National FFA Center
REQUISITE: Scholarships granted to FFA member planning to enroll as a freshman in a 4-year undergraduate program at an accredited university or college in USA. Must be a USA citizen or legal resident. Must be a resident of Illinois and Missouri.
APPLICATION: Write for info. Application deadline is April 1st.
CONTACT: Scholarship Office, POBOX 15160, Alexandria, VA 22309. (703)360-3600

FOUNDATION: Ayres (Mildred L.) Trust
REQUISITE: Student loans and scholarships available for residents of MO attending Midwestern Baptist Seminary, William Jewell College, or the University of MO at Columbia. Money used to help student with theological and medical training and living expenses.
APPLICATION: Applications are accepted throughout the year and are available in high school financial aid offices.
CONTACT: c/o First National Bank of Kansas City, 14 West Tenth St, Kansas City, MO 64105. David P. Ross TEL: (816)234-7481

FOUNDATION: Barber (George & Hazel) Scholarship Trust
REQUISITE: Schlrshps for high school seniors in Marion County, MO, &

Pike County, IL.
APPLICATION: Deadline is April 1st. Application must be notarized and returned to local school official for forwarding.
CONTACT: POB 938, Hannibal, MO 63401. Guidance counselor of eligible high schools.
(We were not able to verify this listing; it may not be extant.)

FOUNDATION: Bour Memorial Scholarship Fund
REQUISITE: Scholarships awarded to needy high school graduates who live in Lafayette County, MO, who will be attending an accredited Missouri college.
APPLICATION: Application deadline is April 15th.
CONTACT: POB 38, Kansas City, MO 64141. Delores A. Fischer, Boatmen's Bank of Lexington, POB 428, Lexington, MO 64067. TEL: (816)259-4661

FOUNDATION: Ilgenfritz (May H.) Testamentary Trust
REQUISITE: Scholarships for resident of Sedalia, MO, area.
APPLICATION: Applications accepted throughout the year.
CONTACT: 108 West Pacific, Sedalia, MO 65301. John Pelham, Trustee. (816)826-3310

FOUNDATION: Lyons (Charles) Memorial Foundation, Inc.
REQUISITE: Scholarships for graduates of Lafayette County, MO, high schools who are residents of this county at application time.
APPLICATION: Application deadline is April 1st.
CONTACT: 2420 Pershing Rd, Suite 400, Kansas City, MO 64108. Hnrble H. Townsend Hader, Prsdnt, POB 236, Lexington, MO 64067 (We were not able to verify this listing; it may not be extant.)

FOUNDATION: Marymount (Mother Joseph Rogan) Foundation
REQUISITE: Scholarships and loan for students who are residents of the St. Louis, MO area.
APPLICATION: Applications are accepted throughout the year.
CONTACT: 2217 Clayville Court, Chesterfield, MO 63017. Joseph E. Lynch, Treasurer.
(We were not able to verify this listing; it may not be extant.)

FOUNDATION: Orscheln Industries Foundation, Inc.
REQUISITE: Scholarships for graduates of Cairo, Higbee, Moberly, and Westran high schools located in Randolph County, MO.

APPLICATION: Application deadline is April 1st.
CONTACT: Boatman's Frst Ntnl Bnk of Kansas Cty, POB 38, Kansas City, MO 64183. William E. Clark, Orscheln Industries Foundation Schlrshp Committee, POB 266, Moberly, MO 65270 (816)263-4900

FOUNDATION: Speas (Victor E.) Foundation
REQUISITE: Schlrshps and loans are awarded to medical students who attend the University of Missouri at Kansas City.
APPLICATION: Applications are accepted throughout the year. Call for more information.
CONTACT: c/o Boatmen's First National Bank of Kansas City, 14 West Tenth St., Kansas City, MO 64183. David P. Ross, Senior Vice-President (816)234-7481

FOUNDATION: Tilles (Rosalie) Nonsectarian Charity Fund
REQUISITE: Scholarships awarded to high school graduates who live in the city or cnty of St. Louis, MO.
APPLICATION: Application deadline is March 1st.
CONTACT: 705 Olive St, Suite 906, St. Louis, MO 63101. Susan Shrago, Secretary-Investigator. TEL: (314)231-1721

FOUNDATION: Westlake (James L. & Nellie M.) Schlrshp Fund
REQUISITE: Schlrshps for high school seniors who are residents of MO.
APPLICATION: Application deadline is March 1st.
CONTACT: c/o Mercantile Trust Co, POB 387, St. Louis, MO 63166. (314) 725-6410. Or 111 S. Bemiston, Suite 412, Clayton, MO 63105.

FOUNDATION: Gladish (Sarah Cora) Endowment Fund
REQUISITE: Scholarships awarded to accomplished artists, musicians, and composers and teachers of art who have lived in Lafayette, Johnson, or Jackson counties, MO for at least 3 yrs.
APPLICATION: Application deadline is July 1st.
CONTACT: c/o Margaret Lomax, Trustee, Forest Hills Estate, Apt. C-11, Lexington, MO 64067. TEL: (816)259-3643

FOUNDATION: MFA Foundation
REQUISITE: Scholarships awarded to MO students in areas where MFA Oil Company, MFA Inc., and Shelter Insurance operate.
APPLICATION: Application deadline is April 15th.
CONTACT: 615 Locust, Columbia, MO 65201. Ormal C. Creach, President. TEL: (314)442-0171

FOUNDATION: Block (The H&R) Foundation
REQUISITE: Scholarships for children of employees of H&R Block, Inc. who live within a 50-mile radius of Kansas City, MO including KS.
APPLICATION: Write for more details.
CONTACT: 4410 Main Street, Kansas City, MO 64111. Terrence R. Ward, Vice-President. TEL: (816)753-6900

FOUNDATION: Butler Manufacturing Company Foundation
REQUISITE: Scholarships for children of employees of Butler Manufacturing Company.
APPLICATION: Application deadline is March 15th, but you should approach before January 15th.
CONTACT: POB 419917, Kansas City, MO 64141-0197. Barbara Lee Fay, Foundation Administrator. TEL: (816)968-3208

FOUNDATION: Cooper Industries Foundation
REQUISITE: Scholarships for children of employees of Cooper Industries, Inc. in AL, CA, CT, GA, IL, IN, ME, MI, MO, MS, NJ, NY, NC, OH, OK, PA, SC, TN, TX, and VA.
APPLICATION: Applications are accepted throughout the year.
CONTACT: First City Tower, Suite 4000, POB 4446, Houston, TX 77210. Patricia B. Meinecke, Secretary. TEL: (713)739-5632

FOUNDATION: Emerson Charitable Trust
REQUISITE: Schlrshps for children of employees Emerson Electric Co.
APPLICATION: Employees notified of how and when to apply.
CONTACT: Emerson Electric Co, 8000 West Florissant Ave, POB 4100, St. Louis, MO 63136. R.W. Staley, Executive VP. TEL: (314)553-2000

FOUNDATION: Hall Family Foundation
REQUISITE: Schlrshps for children of employees of Hallmark.
APPLICATION: Applications available for employees only.
CONTACT: Charitable Crown Investment-323, POB 41950, Kansas Cty, MO 64141. Margaret Pence or Wendy Hockaday, Prgrm Drctrs (We were not able to verify this listing; it may not be extant.)

FOUNDATION: Ralston Purina Trust Fund
REQUISITE: Schlrshps for children emplys Ralston Purina Co.
APPLICATION: Applications are accepted throughout the year.
CONTACT: Checkerboard Square, St. Louis, MO 63164. Fred H. Perabo, Member, Board of Control. TEL: (314)982-3230

FOUNDATION: McDavid (G.N. & Edna) Dental Education Trust
REQUISITE: Student loans for residents of Missouri who attend accredited dental schools in Missouri. Preference is given to residents of Madison County, MO.
APPLICATION: Contact the Financial Aid Office of the dental school for application information.
CONTACT: Sharon Ebner, c/o Mercantile Bank, N.A., POB 387, Main Post Office, St. Louis, MO 63166. TEL: (314)425-2672

FOUNDATION: Young (Judson) Memorial Educational Foundation, Inc.
REQUISITE: Student loans for graduates Salem High School, MO.
APPLICATION: Application deadlines are August 15th for the fall term, 12/15 for winter term, and 5/15 for the summer term.
CONTACT: 101 West Fourth St., Salem, MO 65560. Max Coffman, Foundation Manager. (314)729-3137

MISSISSIPPI

FOUNDATION: Mississippi Board of Trustees of State Institutions of Higher Learning
REQUISITE: Scholarships granted to residents of Mississippi for at least one year who is currently licensed as a registered nurse in the state of Mississippi. Must be admitted into an accredited bachelor of science degree nursing program or a graduate degree program.
APPLICATION: Write for info. Application deadline is not specified.
CONTACT: 3825 Ridgewood Road, POBOX 2336, Jackson, MS 39225
601-982-6168

FOUNDATION: Mississippi Board of Trustees of State Institutions of Higher Learning
REQUISITE: Scholarships granted to full-time students who are enrolled as a Junior or Senior in an accredited institution who is majoring in education leading to a Class A certification in Math and/or Science. Must agree to work in critical shortage area in MS
APPLICATION: Write for info. Deadline is not specified.
CONTACT: 3825 Ridgewood Rd., POBOX 2336, Jackson, MS 39225
(601)982-6611

FOUNDATION: Biglane (D.A.) Foundation
REQUISITE: Scholarships for residents of Natchez, MS, area.
APPLICATION: No date given.

CONTACT: POB 966, Natchez, MS 39120. (We were not able to verify this listing; it may not be extant.)

FOUNDATION: First Mississippi Corporation Foundation
REQUISITE: Schlrshps given to valedictorians of local hgh schls
APPLICATION: Write for more information.
CONTACT: 700 North Street, POB 1249, Jackson, MS 39215-1249. Jay Dee Fountain, Executive Secretary. TEL: (601)948-7550

FOUNDATION: Cooper Industries Foundation
REQUISITE: Scholarships for children of employees of Cooper Industries, Inc. in AL, CA, CT, GA, IL, IN, ME, MI, MO, MS, NJ, NY, NC, OH, OK, PA, SC, TN, TX, and VA.
APPLICATION: Applications are accepted throughout the year.
CONTACT: First City Tower, Suite 4000, POB 4446, Houston, TX 77210. Patricia B. Meinecke, Secretary. TEL: (713)739-5632

FOUNDATION: Evinrude (The Ole) Foundation
REQUISITE: Scholarships for children of employees of Outboard Marine Corp in WI, IL, TN, MS, NC, GA, and NB.
APPLICATION: Application deadline is October 31st.
CONTACT: 100 Sea Horse Drive, Waukegan, IL 60085. F. James Short, Vice-President. (708)689-6200

FOUNDATION: Texas Industries Foundation
REQUISITE: Schlrshps for kids of employees of TX Industries, Inc.
APPLICATION: Application deadline is January 15th.
CONTACT: 8100 Carpenter Freeway, Dallas, TX 75247. James R. McCraw, Controller. (214)637-3100

FOUNDATION: Feild Co-Operative Association, Inc.
REQUISITE: Educational loans for Mississippi residents.
APPLICATION: Application deadline is six to eight weeks before the start of the semester.
CONTACT: POB 5054, Jackson, MS 39296-5054. Ann Stephenson (601)939-9295

FOUNDATION: Pickett & Hatcher Educational Fund, Inc.
REQUISITE: Undergraduate student loans for those who live in AL, FL, GA, KY, MS, NC, SC, TN, and VA. There is no support for those planning to study medicine, law, or ministry.

116

APPLICATION: Application deadline is May 15th. First-time applicants may request their application after October 1st.
CONTACT: 1800 Buena Vista Rd, P.O. Box 8169, Columbus, GA 31908. Robert Bennett, Executive Vice-President. TEL: (706)327-6586

MONTANA

FOUNDATION: Bair (Charles M.) Memorial Trust
REQUISITE: Scholarships awarded 2 graduates each of high schools listed: Harlowton H.S., MT, White Sulphur Springs H.S., MT, & 4 graduates of high school located in Meagher & Wheatland counties, MT.
APPLICATION: Application deadline is April 20th.
CONTACT: First Trust Company of Montana, POB 30678, Billings, MT 59115. Alberta M. Bair, Trustee. TEL: (406)657-8122

FOUNDATION: Treacy Company
REQUISITE: Scholarship is now $400 for students who live in or will be attending an institution of higher education in MT, IN, ND, & SD.
APPLICATION: Application deadline is June 15th.
CONTACT: Box 1700, Helena, MT 59624. James O'Connell (406)442-3632

FOUNDATION: Bryan (Dodd & Dorothy L.) Foundation
REQUISITE: Educational loans for students from Sheridan, Campbell, and Johnson counties, WY, and from Powder River, Rosebud, and big Horn counties, MT.
APPLICATION: Application deadline is July 15th.
CONTACT: P.O. Box 6287, Sheridan, WY 82801. J. E. Goar, Manager. TEL: (307)672-3535

NORTH CAROLINA

FOUNDATION: North Carolina Division of Vocational Rehabilitation Services
REQUISITE: Scholarships granted to North Carolina resident who has a mental or physical disability which is a handicap to employment. There must also be a reasonable expectation that as a result of vocational rehabilitation services the person may become employed.
APPLICATION: Write for info. Application deadline is not specified.
CONTACT: POBOX 26053, 620 North West St., Raleigh, NC 27611 919-733-3364

FOUNDATION: North Carolina Society for Medical Technology
REQUISITE: Scholarships granted to residents of North Carolina for one year studying Medical Technology or Medical Laboratory Technician. Must be US citizen.
APPLICATION: Write for info. Application deadline is June 30th.
CONTACT: 6722 Tattershale Ct., Raleigh, NC 27612 919-848-3609

FOUNDATION: Ferree Educational & Welfare Fund
REQUISITE: Student loans & scholarships for higher education limited to any resident of Randolph County, NC.
APPLICATION: Write for info by 5/1. Include financial statements with application & attend an interview. Deadln 6/15
CONTACT: Claire C. Sprouse, Administrative Dir., 101 Sunset Ave., POB 2207, Asheboro, NC 27204-2207 TEL: (910)629-2960

FOUNDATION: Foundation for the Carolinas
REQUISITE: Must be a student residing in NC or SC.
APPLICATION: Write for info. Contact fndtn for current deadline
CONTACT: Renee Peeler, POB 34769, Charlotte, NC 28234-4769 (704)376-9541

FOUNDATION: Wellons Foundation, Inc.
REQUISITE: Student loans for higher education.
APPLICATION: Write for info. No deadline listed.
CONTACT: Julia Gregory, POB 1254, Dunn, NC 28335 (910)892-3123

FOUNDATION: Elizabeth City Foundation
REQUISITE: Must be a student in Camden county, NC.
APPLICATION: Applications available at Wachovia Bank & Trust Co. & Camden High Schl. Deadline 4/1.
CONTACT: Ray S. Jones, Jr., Exec. Dir., POB 574, Elizabeth City, NC 27909 (We were not able to verify this listing; it may not be extant.)

FOUNDATION: James G.K. McClure Edctnl & Development Fund, Inc.
REQUISITE: Must be a resident of western NC, including these counties: Allegheny, Ashe, Avery, Buncombe, Burke, Caldwell, Cherokee, Clay, Graham, Haywood, Henderson, Jackson, Macon, Madison, McDowell, Mitchell, Polk, Rutherford, Swain, Transylvania, Watauga, & Yancey.
APPLICATION: Write for info. No deadline listed.
CONTACT: John C Ager, Exec. Dir., Hickory Nut Gap Farm, Rte. 6, Box 100, Fairview, NC 28730

118

North Carolina

(We were not able to verify this listing; it may not be extant.)

FOUNDATION: Emanuel Sternberger Educational Fund
REQUISITE: Must be a legal resident of NC. Educational loans only for use by any junior, senior, or graduate school student.
APPLICATION: In February request application. Transcript of college grades, 4 references, photo & interviews required. Deadline 4/30
CONTACT: Ms. Brenda Henley, Exec. Dir., POB 1735, Greensboro, NC 27402 TEL: (910)275-6316

FOUNDATION: Sigmund Sternberger Foundation, Inc.
REQUISITE: Must be a resident of Guilford County, NC, who is pursuing undergraduate studies at a college or university in NC or a child of a member of the Revolution Masonic Lodge.
APPLICATION: Please contact the following financial aid office at each of the following schools: The University of North Carolina at Greensboro, Greensboro College, Guilford College, North Carolina A & T State University, Bennett College, Elon College, High Point College, Guilford Technical Community College, Wake Forest University, Duke University, University of North Carolina at Chapel Hill, N.C. State University, N.C. School of the Arts.
CONTACT: Robert O. Klepfer, Jr., Exec. Dir., POB 3111, Greensboro, NC 27402 TEL: (919)373-1500

FOUNDATION: Close Foundation, Inc.
REQUISITE: Must be a resident of NC or Lancaster County, Chester Township of Chester County or Fort Mill Township, SC.
APPLICATION: Write for info. No deadline listed.
CONTACT: Charles A. Bundy, Pres., PO Drawer 460, Lancaster, SC 29720
(We were not able to verify this listing; it may not be extant.)

FOUNDATION: Blackwelder Foundation, Inc.
REQUISITE: Must reside in NC. Preference is given to any resident of Caldwell County, NC, & especially one whose parents work in an hospital.
APPLICATION: Write for info. Deadline July.
CONTACT: Lloyd M. Rash, Pres., POB 1431, Lenoir, NC 28645
(We were not able to verify this listing; it may not be extant.)

FOUNDATION: Huffman Cornwell Foundation
REQUISITE: Must be a high schl student of Burke County, NC.
APPLICATION: Write for info. No deadline listed.

CONTACT: Graham S. DeVane, Secty., POB 98, Morgantown, NC 28655 (We were not able to verify this listing; it may not be extant.)

FOUNDATION: James E. & Mary Z. Bryan Foundation, Inc.
REQUISITE: Must be a needy & worthy student who is a legal resident of NC & attends a specified educational institution, including trade schools, colleges, or universities.
APPLICATION: Write for info. Deadline January 31.
CONTACT: Bryon E. Bryan, Pres., First Citizens Bank & Trust Co., POB 151, Raleigh, NC 27602 TEL: (919)755-7101

FOUNDATION: Stonecutter Foundation, Inc.
REQUISITE: Be resident of the Rutherford or Polk Cnty, NC
APPLICATION: Write for info. No deadline listed.
CONTACT: J.T. Strickland, Treasurer, 300 Dallas St., Spindale, NC 28160 TEL: (704)286-2341

FOUNDATION: Percy B. Ferebee Endowment
REQUISITE: Scholarships to any resident of the NC counties of Cherokee, Clay, Graham, Jackson, Macon, or Swain, or the Cherokee Indian Reservation, for study only at any NC college or university. APPLICATION: Applications available from high school guidance counselors, the Cherokee Indian Reservation, & school superintendents. Submit completed applctns to schlrshp committee of your hgh schl. Interviews required. Deadln 2/15
CONTACT: E. Ray Cope, VP, Wachovia Bank & Trust Co., POB 3099, Winston-Salem, NC 27150 TEL: (919)748-5269

FOUNDATION: Senah C. & C.A. Kent Foundation
REQUISITE: Must be a student attending Wake Forest University, NC School of the Arts, or Salem College.
APPLICATION: Contact individual schools. Deadline July 1.
CONTACT: G. William Joyner, Jr., VP for Development, Wake Forest University, 7227 Reynolds Station, Winston-Salem, NC 27109 (919) 761-5265; or Patsy Braxton, Dir. of Financial Aid, NC School of the Arts, Box 12189, Winston-Salem, NC 27107 (919) 784-7170; or Mrs. Len Brinkley, Dir. of Financial Aid, Salem College, Winston-Salem, NC 27108

FOUNDATION: The Winston-Salem Foundation
REQUISITE: Student loans to any resident of NC. Scholarships primarily to any resident of Forsyth County, NC.

North Carolina

APPLICATION: Application must be submitted with a $20 application fee. Interviews sometimes required. Call for info. Deadlines January 1, April 1, May 1, July 1, & October 1.
CONTACT: 310 West Forest St., Suite 229, Winston-Salem, NC 27101.
TEL: (919)725-2382

FOUNDATION: Pickett & Hatcher Educational Fund, Inc.
REQUISITE: Must reside in the southeastern U.S., including AL, FL, GA, KY, MS, NC, SC, TN, & VA. No support for any student planning to enter fields of medicine, law, or the ministry.
APPLICATION: First-time applicants may request application after October 1. Write or call for info. Deadline May 15.
CONTACT: Robert E. Bennett, Exec. VP, 1800 Buena Vista Rd., POB 8169, Columbus, GA 31908 TEL: (706)327-6586

FOUNDATION: Camp Foundation
REQUISITE: Graduate of a high school in Southampton or Isle of Wight cnties, or Franklin, or Tidewater, VA, or northeastern NC
APPLICATION: Applicants must file with their high school principal who then files with foundation. Write for info. Deadlines Feb. 26 for filing with high school principals & March 15 for principals to file with fndtn.
CONTACT: Harold S. Atkinson, Exec. Dir., POB 813, Franklin, VA 23851
TEL: (804)562-3439

FOUNDATION: Nucor Foundation, Inc.
REQUISITE: Schlrshps for chldrn emplys of Nucor Fndtn, Inc.
APPLICATION: Application deadline is March 1st.
CONTACT: 4425 Randolph Rd., Charlotte, NC 28211. James Coblin (704)366-7000

FOUNDATION: Bailey Foundation
REQUISITE: Loans and scholarships for children of employees of Clinton Mills, Inc., its subsidiaries, or M.S. Bailey & Son, Bankers. Employees can be active or retired and must have two years of service.
APPLICATION: Application deadline is April 15th of the applicant's senior year in high school.
CONTACT: POB 1276, Clinton, SC 29325. H. William Carter, Jr., Administrator. TEL: (910)833-6830

FOUNDATION: Chatham Foundation, Inc.
REQUISITE: Scholarships for children of employees of Chatham

Manufacturing Company.
APPLICATION: Applications are accepted throughout the year.
CONTACT: Chatham Mnfctrng Co., 3100 Glen Ave., Elkin, NC 28621.
David Cline, Secretary-Treasurer. TEL: (910)835-2211

FOUNDATION: Cooper Industries Foundation
REQUISITE: Scholarships for children of employees of Cooper Industries,
Inc. in AL, CA, CT, GA, IL, IN, ME, MI, MO, MS, NJ, NY, NC, OH, OK, PA,
SC, TN, TX, and VA.
APPLICATION: Applications are accepted throughout the year.
CONTACT: First City Tower, Suite 4000, POB 4446, Houston, TX 77210.
Patricia B. Meinecke, Secretary. TEL: (713)739-5632

FOUNDATION: Evinrude (The Ole) Foundation
REQUISITE: Scholarships for children of employees of Outboard Marine
Corp in WI, IL, TN, MS, NC, GA, and NB.
APPLICATION: Application deadline is October 31st.
CONTACT: 100 Sea Horse Drive, Waukegan, IL 60085. F. James Short,
Vice-President. (708)689-6200

FOUNDATION: Fieldcrest Foundation
REQUISITE: Schlrshps for kids employees of Fieldcrest Mills, Inc.
APPLICATION: Application deadline is May 1st.
CONTACT: 326 East Stadium Drive, Eden, NC 27288; Tel.:(919)627-3126.
Or Calvin Barnhardt, c/o Fieldcrest Cannon, Inc., General Office, Eden,
NC 27288 TEL: (910)627-3000

FOUNDATION: Giles (The Edward C.) Foundation
REQUISITE: Scholarships for children of employees of Carauster
Industries, Inc. and its subsidiaries.
APPLICATION: Application deadline is April 15th.
CONTACT: 736 Hempstead Place, Charlotte, NC 28207. Or The Edward
C. Giles Foundation, POB 33056, Charlotte, NC 28233. (We were not able
to verify this listing; it may not be extant.)

FOUNDATION: North Carolina Association of Educators
REQUISITE: Scholarships granted for senior year of study at an
accredited undergraduate institution in North Carolina. Must be US
citizen or legal resident.
APPLICATION: Write for info. Application deadline is February 1st.
CONTACT: POBOX 27347, 700 S. Salisbury St., Raleigh, NC 27611

(919)832-3000

FOUNDATION: North Carolina Department of Public Instruction
REQUISITE: Scholarships granted to any N.C. resident interested in preparing to teach in N.C. public schools. Scholarships are awarded based on academic performance, scores on standardized tests, class rank, congressional district and recommendations. Must be US citizen.
APPLICATION: Write for info. Application deadline is March 1st.
CONTACT: 116 W. Edenton St., Office of Teachers Recruitment, Raleigh, NC 27603. Tel: (919)715-1000

FOUNDATION: Myers-Ti-Caro Foundation, Inc.
REQUISITE: Scholarships for children and dependents of employees of Ti-Caro, Inc..
APPLICATION: Application deadline is September.
CONTACT: POB 2208, Gastonia, NC 28053. Albert Meyers, Jr., President
TEL: (704)867-7271

FOUNDATION: Thomasville Furniture Industries Foundation
REQUISITE: Scholarships for children of employees of Thomasville Furniture Industries.
APPLICATION: Applications are accepted throughout the year.
CONTACT: c/o Wachovia Bank & Trust Company, POB 3099, Winston-Salem, NC 27150. David Taylor, Account Manager. TEL: (910)724-0581

FOUNDATION: Close Foundation, Inc.
REQUISITE: Student loans for residents of NC and Lancaster County, Chester Township of Chester County & Fort Mill Township, SC
APPLICATION: Write for application information.
CONTACT: P.O. Drawer 460, Lancaster, SC 29720. Charles Bundy, President. (We were not able to verify this listing; it may not be extant.)

FOUNDATION: Pickett & Hatcher Educational Fund, Inc.
REQUISITE: Undergraduate student loans for those who live in AL, FL, GA, KY, MS, NC, SC, TN, and VA. There is no support for those planning to study medicine, law, or ministry.
APPLICATION: Application deadline is May 15th. First-time applicants may request application after 10/1.
CONTACT: 1800 Buena Vista Rd, P.O. Box 8169, Columbus, GA 31908. Robert Bennett, Executive Vice-President. TEL: (706)327-6586

FOUNDATION: Sternberger (Emanuel) Educational Fund
REQUISITE: Educational loans for residents of North Carolina. They must be juniors, seniors, or graduate school students.
APPLICATION: Application deadline is April 30th.
CONTACT: P.O. Box 1735. Greensboro, NC 27402. Ms. Brenda Henley, Executive Director TEL: (919)275-6316

FOUNDATION: Wellons Foundation, Inc.
REQUISITE: Student loans for educational purposes.
APPLICATION: Applications are accepted throughout the year.
CONTACT: POB 1254, Dunn, NC 28335. Julia Gregory (910)892-3123

NORTH DAKOTA

FOUNDATION: Norther Dakota State Highway Department
REQUISITE: Scholarships granted to undergraduate students at accredited institutions in North Dakota. Must have completed at least 1 year of studies in Civil Engineering or Civil Engineering Technology.
APPLICATION: Write for info. Application deadline is February 15th.
CONTACT: 608 East Blvd. Ave., Human Resources Div., Bismarch, ND 58505. (701)328-2500

FOUNDATION: Bush Foundation
REQUISITE: Scholarships granted to writers, visual artists, composers and choreographers who are residents of MN, ND, or SD and are at least 25 years old. Must work full-time in their chosen art form.
APPLICATION: Write for info. Application deadline is October 30th, November 6th, and November 13th.
CONTACT: E900 First National Bank Bldg., St. Paul, MN 55101 Tel: (612)227-0891

FOUNDATION: Fargo-Moorhead Area Foundation
REQUISITE: Schlrshps for students in Fargo-Moorhead area.
APPLICATION: Deadline 4/15 Contact for more information.
CONTACT: 315 North Eighth Street, POB 1609, Fargo, ND 58107. Susan M. Hunke, Executive Director. TEL: (701)234-0756

FOUNDATION: Hatterscheidt Foundation, Inc.
REQUISITE: Scholarships for students for their first year in college and are graduating high school in the top 25 percent of the class in SD and a 100-mile radius of Jamestown, ND.

APPLICATION: Write for more information.
CONTACT: First Bnk-Aberdeen, POB 100, Aberdeen, SD 57402-1000.
Kaye DeYoung, First Bank-Aberdeen. TEL: (605)225-9400

FOUNDATION: Treacy Company
REQUISITE: Scholarships for undergraduate study for students who attend institutions in the northwest or reside there.
APPLICATION: Application deadline is June 15th.
CONTACT: Box 1700, Helena, MT 59624 James O'Connell (406)442-3632

FOUNDATION: Brown (Gabriel J.) Trust
REQUISITE: Student loans for those who live in North Dakota.
APPLICATION: Application deadline is June 15th.
CONTACT: 112 Ave E West, Bismarck, ND 58501. TEL: (701)223-5916

NEBRASKA

FOUNDATION: Hamilton Community Foundation, Inc.
REQUISITE: Schlrshps for students who live in Hamilton County
APPLICATION: Write for application.
CONTACT: POB 283, Aurora, NE 68818. TEL: (402)694-3200

FOUNDATION: Kiewit(Peter) Foundation
REQUISITE: Schlrshps for undergraduates in the Omaha area
APPLICATION: Application deadline is March 1st.
CONTACT: Woodmen Tower, Suite 900, Farnam at 17th, Omaha 68102.
Lyn Wallen Ziegenbein, Executive Drctr. TEL: (402)344-7890

FOUNDATION: Lane (Winthrop & Frances) Foundation
REQUISITE: Scholarships for students at Creighton University School of Law and the University of Nebraska College of Law.
APPLICATION: Applications accepted throughout the year.
CONTACT: Michael O'Mally, c/o FirsTier Bank, 17th and Farnam, Omaha, NE 68102. TEL: (402)348-6350

FOUNDATION: Leu Foundation, Inc.
REQUISITE: Schlrshps for students living in North Platte area
APPLICATION: Applications are accepted throughout the year.
CONTACT: 2409 Abbott Martin Rd, Nashville, TN 37315. Frank Leu
(We were not able to verify this listing; it may not be extant.)

FOUNDATION: Webermeier (William) Scholarship Trust
REQUISITE: Schlrshps for graduates of Milford H.S., Milford, NE
APPLICATION: Contact superintendent of Milford School District for application requirements.
CONTACT: c/o National Bank of Commerce, 13th and "O" St., Lincoln, NE 68508. Superintendent of Schools, Milford, NE. TEL: (402)434-4321

FOUNDATION: Weller Foundation, Inc.
REQUISITE: Scholarships for residents of Nebraska who attend a technical community college or other vocational institutions in fields such as nursing.
APPLICATION: Application deadline is June 1st for the fall semester and Nov. 1st for spring semester.
CONTACT: E Highway 20, POB 636, Atkinson, NE 68713 (402)925-2803

FOUNDATION: Evinrude (The Ole) Foundation
REQUISITE: Scholarships for children of employees of Outboard Marine Crprtn in WI, IL, TN, MS, NC, GA, and NB.
APPLICATION: Application deadline is October 31st.
CONTACT: 100 Sea Horse Drive, Waukegan, IL 60085. F. James Short, Vice-President. TEL: (708)689-6200

NEW HAMPSHIRE

FOUNDATION: New Hampshire Post-Secondary Education Commission
REQUISITE: Scholarships granted to New Hampshire residents who are accepted to or enrolled in an approved nursing program in the state of New Hampshire. Must be US citizen or legal resident.
APPLICATION: Write for info. Application deadline is 6/1, 1/January 5th and May 1st.
CONTACT: Two Industrial Park Drive, Concord, NH 03301 603-271-2555

FOUNDATION: Abbie Sargent Memorial Scholarship Inc.
REQUISITE: Scholarships granted to high school graduate of New Hampshire with good grades and character and ready to attend school as an undergraduate or graduate student.
APPLICATION: Write for info. Application deadline is March 15th.
CONTACT: RFD #10, Box 344D, Concord, NH 03301.
(We were not able to verify this listing; it may not be extant.)

FOUNDATION: Foundation for Biblical Research & Preservation of

Primitive Christianity
REQUISITE: Must be a graduating student of Fall Mountain Regional High School, Alstead, NH, who is at the freshman or sophomore level & attending an accredited institution for religious education.
APPLICATION: Write for info. Deadline April 1.
CONTACT: Jan L. Kater, Pres., 144 Main St., Box 373, Charlestown, NH 03603 TEL: (603)826-7751

FOUNDATION: The New Hampshire Charitable Fund
REQUISITE: Must be a NH resident pursuing undergraduate or graduate study at an accredited college, university, or vocational school.
APPLICATION: Applications available in April & May for assistance during the following academic year. Call for info. Deadline early May for upcoming academic year. Contact foundation for application deadline.
CONTACT: Judith Burrows, Dir., Student Aid, 37 Pleasant, POB 1335, Concord, NH 03301-4005 TEL: (603)225-6641

FOUNDATION: Kingsbury Fund
REQUISITE: Must be a high school senior who is a child of an employee of the Kingsbury Machine Tool Corporation, or an undergraduate student in a technical institute, college, or other accredited school.
APPLICATION: Must submit an essay & transcript of grades. Write for further info. Deadline March 30.
CONTACT: James E. O'Neil, Jr., Exec. Trustee, Kingsbury Mchn Tool Corp, 80 Laurel St., Keene, NH 03431 TEL: (603)352-5212

FOUNDATION: Andrew J. Scarlett Scholarship Fund
REQUISITE: Must be an undergraduate member of the Sigma Alpha Epsilon Fraternity at Dartmouth College, NH.
APPLICATION: Write for info. No deadline listed.
CONTACT: Clark A. Griffiths, Trustee, 74 Prospect St., Lebanon, NH 03766 (We were not able to verify this listing; it may not be extant.)

FOUNDATION: Henry C. Lord Scholarship Fund Trust
REQUISITE: Needy resident of Petersborough, NH, or nearby town
APPLICATION: Write for info. Deadlines April 30 for 1st-time applicants & June 15 each year thereafter.
CONTACT: Pamela D. Mallett, Trust Officer, c/o Amoskeag Bank, POB 150, Manchester, NH 03105 (We were not able to verify this listing; it may not be extant.)

FOUNDATION: Edward Wagner, Greg Hosser Schlrshp Fndtn Trust
REQUISITE: Must be a male resident of Manchester, NH.
APPLICATION: Write for info. Deadline April 30.
CONTACT: Pamela D. Mallett, Trust Officer, Amoskeag Bank, POB 150, Manchester, NH 03105 (We were not able to verify this listing; it may not be extant.)

FOUNDATION: Milford Educational Foundation
REQUISITE: Must reside in Milford, NH.
APPLICATION: Write for info. Deadlines May 25 for fall term & November 15 for spring term.
CONTACT: Allen G. White, Treasurer, POB 483, Milford 03055
(We were not able to verify this listing; it may not be extant.)

FOUNDATION: The Barker Foundation, Inc.
REQUISITE: Must reside in NH.
APPLICATION: Submissions must allow sufficient lead time for review by the trustees. Interviews sometimes required. Write for info. No deadline listed.
CONTACT: Allan M. Barker, Pres., POB 328, Nashua, NH 03061 (603)889-1763

FOUNDATION: Abbie M. Griffin Educational Fund
REQUISITE: Must reside in Merrimack, NH.
APPLICATION: Written applications accepted. Interviews required. No deadline listed.
CONTACT: S. Robert Winer, Trustee, Merrimack high school guidance office, 111 Concord St., Nashua, NH 03060 TEL: (603)882-5157

FOUNDATION: George T. Cogan Trust
REQUISITE: Must be a student who has resided in Portsmouth, NH, for at least 4 years prior to graduation from either Portsmouth High School or St. Thomas Aquinas High School.
APPLICATION: 2 letters of recommendation, copy of transcript, & Student Aid Report required. Write for info. Deadln 5/5
CONTACT: Wyman P. Boynton, Trustee, 82 Court St., Portsmouth, NH 03801 (We were not able to verify this listing; it may not be extant.)

FOUNDATION: Charles H. Berry Trust Fund
REQUISITE: Must be a male student from New Durham, Farmington, or Rochester, NH, who will be attending college in Strafford County, NH.

APPLICATION: Submit high school transcript with application. Write for info. No deadline listed.
CONTACT: George Findell, Jr., POB 2036, Rochester, NH (603)332-1670

FOUNDATION: Sarah E. Young Trust
REQUISITE: Scholarships to any needy resident of Strafford County, NH, who has completed at least 1 year of college.
APPLICATION: Include high school & college grades & show financial status. Write for further info. Deadline June 30.
CONTACT: Judi Tuttle, BankEast Trust Co., 22 S. Main St., Rochester, NH 03867 (We were not able to verify this listing; it may not be extant.)

FOUNDATION: Marjorie Sells Carter Boy Scout Schlrshp Fnd
REQUISITE: Former Boy Scout who resides in the New England
APPLICATION: Submit letter requesting application. No deadline listed.
CONTACT: Joan Shaffer, POB 527, West Chatham, MA 02669
(We were not able to verify this listing; it may not be extant.)

FOUNDATION: Milford Educational Foundation
REQUISITE: Student loans for residents of Milford, NH.
APPLICATION: Application deadlines are 5/25 for the fall term, and 11/15 for the spring term. CONTACT: P.O. Box 483, Milford, NH 03055. Allen White, Trsrr (We were not able to verify this listing; it may not be extant.)

FOUNDATION: Scarlett (Andrew J.) Scholarship Fund
REQUISITE: Student loans for undergraduate member of the Sigma Alpha Epsilon Fraternity at Darthmouth College, NH.
APPLICATION: Write for more information.
CONTACT: 74 Prospect St., Lebanon, NH 03766. Clark Griffiths, Trustee.
(We were not able to verify this listing; it may not be extant.)

FOUNDATION: Charles H. Hood Fund
REQUISITE: Must be a CT, MA, ME, NH, RI, or VT resident.
APPLICATION: Write for info. No deadline listed.
CONTACT: 500 Rutherford Ave., Boston, MA 02129 (We were not able to verify this listing; it may not be extant.)

FOUNDATION: New England Regional Student Program
REQUISITE: Must reside in 1 of the New England States: CT, ME, MA, NH, RI, or VT. You may attend a public college or unvrsty within the region at a reduced tuition rate for certain degree prgrms not offered by

their own state's pblc schls.
APPLICATION: Write for info. No deadline listed.
CONTACT: Office of the Regional Student Program, New Englnd Brd of Hghr Edctn, 45 Temple Place, Boston, MA 02111 TEL: (617)357-9620

FOUNDATION: Fred Forsyth Educational Trust Fund
REQUISITE: Must be a CT, MA, ME, NH, RI, or VT student.
APPLICATION: Write for info. No deadline listed.
CONTACT: Rosie Marie Bates, Fleet Bank, POB 923, Bangor, ME 04402-0923. (207)941-6000

NEW JERSEY

FOUNDATION: William M. Grupe Foundation Inc.
REQUISITE: Scholarships granted to residents of Bergen; Essex or Hudson Count NJ. Students must be plan on or is majoring in Medicine; Nursing; or Paramedical field. Must be US citizen.
APPLICATION: Write for info. Application deadline is March 1st.
CONTACT: 22 Old Short Hills Road, Livingston, NJ 07039.
(We were not able to verify this listing; it may not be extant.)

FOUNDATION: New Jersey Society of Architects
REQUISITE: Scholarships granted to New Jersey residents enrolled in an accredited School of Architecture. Must be US citizen.
APPLICATION: Write for info. Application deadline is April 1st.
CONTACT: Nine Hundred Route 9, Woodbridge, NJ 07095.
(We were not able to verify this listing; it may not b extant.)

FOUNDATION: Consulting Engineers Council of New Jersey
REQUISITE: Scholarships granted to undergraduate student who are of junior status at an ABET accredited institution in New Jersey. Must be in top half of their class and considering a career in Consulting Engineering and a USA citizen.
APPLICATION: Write for info. Application deadline is January 27th.
CONTACT: 66 Morrise Ave., Springfield, NJ 07081. (201)564-5848

FOUNDATION: Young Printing Executives Club
REQUISITE: Scholarships granted to residents of New York, New Jersey, and Connecticut who are enrolled at the Rochester Institute of Technology. Students should have at least a 3.0 GPA and be committed to a career in the Tri-State area.

APPLICATION: Write for info. Application deadline is 5/15 - 6/1.
CONTACT: 5 Penn Plaza, New York, NY 10001. (212)318-9608

FOUNDATION: Allied Educational Fund B
REQUISITE: Scholarships for graduating high school seniors who are the
family of Union members.
APPLICATION: Application deadline is March 15th.
CONTACT: 467 Sylvan Ave, Englewood Cliffs, NJ 07632. (212)695-7791

FOUNDATION: Bergen (Frank & Lydia) Foundation
REQUISITE: Educational support for worthy music students in NJ for
securing a musical education.
APPLICATION: Contact for more information.
CONTACT: c/o First Fidelity Bank, 55 Madison Ave., Morristown, NJ
07960. Jane Donnelly, Executive Director. TEL: (201)606-4321

FOUNDATION: Borden (The Mary Owen) Memorial Foundation
REQUISITE: Scholarships for graduates of Rumson-Fair Haven New
Jersey Regional High School, NJ.
APPLICATION: Contact for more information.
CONTACT: 11 Wisteria Drive, Fords, NJ 08863. Mary Miles, Secretary.
(We were not able to verify this listing; it may not be extant.)

FOUNDATION: Caldwell (Charles W.) Scholarship Fund
REQUISITE: Scholarships to males seniors who attend Princeton
University for postgraduate study.
APPLICATION: Write for information.
CONTACT: c/o State Street Bank & Trust Company, POB 351, Boston,
MA 02101. (617)786-3000

FOUNDATION: Grupe (William F.) Foundation, Inc.
REQUISITE: Scholarships for residents of Bergen, Essex, and Hudson
counties, NJ for study in medical, nursing, or paramedical, who plan to
practice in the state.
APPLICATION: Application deadline is March 1st.
CONTACT: 22 Old Short Hills Rd., Livingston, NJ 07039. Abdol H. Islami,
M.D., President. (We were not able to verify this listing; it may not be
extant.)

FOUNDATION: Horbach Foundation, The
REQUISITE: Scholarships for needy, gifted, people under the age of 20,

who live in NJ.
APPLICATION: Application deadline is August 1st.
CONTACT: c/o National Community Bank of New Jersey, 113 West Essex Street, Maywood, NJ 07607.
(We were not able to verify this listing; it may not be extant.)

FOUNDATION: Jewish Foundation for Education of Women
REQUISITE: Scholarships and loans to women who are legal residents of the greater NYC area which includes Long Island & NJ
APPLICATION: Application deadline is January 31st.
CONTACT: 330 West 58th St, Suite 5J, New York, NY 10019. Florence Wallach, Executive Director. TEL: (212)265-2565

FOUNDATION: Madison Scholarship Committee
REQUISITE: Schlrshps for graduates of Madison, NJ, hgh schls
APPLICATION: Application deadline is February 15th.
CONTACT: 3 Wilson Ln.,Madison, NJ 07940. Mrs. Willard Thatcher, Applications Chairman.
(We were not able to verify this listing; it may not be extant.)

FOUNDATION: Middlesex County Medical Society Fndtn, Inc.
REQUISITE: Scholarships for those who have lived in Middlesex County, NJ for 5 yrs, & plan to study medicine, nursing or pharmacy.
APPLICATION: Application deadline is February 1st.
CONTACT: POB 674, Franklin Park, NJ 08823. Mary Alice Bruno. (908)257-6800

FOUNDATION: Shreve (William A. & Mary A.) Foundation, Inc.
REQUISITE: Scholarships for students in New Jersey, PA & VT.
APPLICATION: Applications are accepted throughout the year.
CONTACT: c/o Robert M. Wood, Esquire, 200 Atlantic Ave., Mansquan, NJ 08736. Dr. Clifford G. Pollock, Route 1, Box 408, Wallingford, VT 05773 (We were not able to verify this listing; it may not be extant.)

FOUNDATION: Sussman (Otto) Trust
REQUISITE: Education expenses for residents of NY or NJ in need because of a death or illness in their immediate family or some other unfortunate or unusual circumstance.
APPLICATION: Applications are accepted throughout the year. Write for more information.
CONTACT: c/o Sullivan and Cromwell, 125 Broad Street, 28th floor, New

NewYork, NY 10004. TEL: (212)558-4000

FOUNDATION: Byas (The Hugh Fulton) Memorial Foundation
REQUISITE: Scholarships for English nationals or permanent residents of England only for study at colleges or universities in the Eastern U.S.
APPLICATION: Applications are accepted throughout the year.
CONTACT: 91 Shenandoah Drive, Spring Lake Heights, NJ 07782. William B. Nagle. (We were not able to verify this listing; it may not be extant.)

FOUNDATION: Reeves Brothers Foundation, Inc.
REQUISITE: Scholarship loans for employees or children of employees of Reeves Brothers, Inc., or subsidiaries, or students who in areas where Reeves or its subsidiaries are located.
APPLICATION: Application deadlines are May 15th for summer school and June 15th for full year.
CONTACT: 115 Summit Avenue, Summit, NJ 07901. Paschal Wilborn, Reeves Brothers, Inc., POB 1898, Spartanburg, SC 29304 (803)576-9210

FOUNDATION: Chubb Foundation
REQUISITE: Scholarships for qualified relatives of employees of Chubb Group Insurance Company, including Chubb and Son, Inc.,the Colonial Life Insurance Company of America and the Chubb Corporation.
APPLICATION: Application deadline is December 15th.
CONTACT: 15 Mountain View Road, POB 1615, Warren, NJ 07060. Alice Billick, Secretary. TEL: (908)903-2000

FOUNDATION: Cooper Industries Foundation
REQUISITE: Scholarships for children of employees of Cooper Industries, Inc. in AL, CA, CT, GA, IL, IN, ME, MI, MO, MS, NJ, NY, NC, OH, OK, PA, SC, TN, TX, and VA.
APPLICATION: Applications are accepted throughout the year.
CONTACT: First City Tower, Suite 4000, POB 4446, Houston, TX 77210. Patricia B. Meinecke, Secretary. TEL: (713)739-5632

FOUNDATION: CPC Educational Foundation
REQUISITE: Schlrshps for children of employees of CPC International Inc.
APPLICATION: Applications can be submitted between 8/30 and 11/30.
CONTACT: International Plaza, POB 8000, Englewood Cliffs, NJ 07632. Linda Salcito. (201)894-4000

FOUNDATION: Mueller (C.F.) Company Scholarship Fund

REQUISITE: Scholarships, grants, and student loans for children of employees of C.F. Mueller.
APPLICATION: Submit applications between 1/1 and 4/30
CONTACT: 180 Baldwin Ave, Jersey City 07360. Edwin Geils, Treasurer.
(We were not able to verify this listing; it may not be extant.)

FOUNDATION: Union Camp Charitable Trust
REQUISITE: Schlrshps for kids of employees of Union Camp Corp
APPLICATION: Write for more information.
CONTACT: c/o Union Camp Corporation, 1600 Valley Rd, Wayne, NJ 07470. Harold Hoss, VP & Trsrr. TEL: (201)628-2000

FOUNDATION: Yegen (Christian C.) Foundation
REQUISITE: Scholarships for children of employees of Yegen Holdings Corporation and affiliated companies. The family earnings with two or more dependents must not exceed $40,000.
APPLICATION: Deadline is before the end of the semester.
CONTACT: Jason W. Semel, Mack Center Drive, 5th Floor, Paramus, NJ 07652 TEL: (201)307-8800

FOUNDATION: The Horbach Fund
REQUISITE: Needy, gifted person under age 20 in CT, MA, NJ, NY, RI.
APPLICATION: Write for info. Deadline August 1.
CONTACT: c/o National Community Bank of NJ, 113 W. Essex St., Maywood, NJ 07607
(We were not able to verify this listing; it may not be extant.)

NEW MEXICO

FOUNDATION: Carlsbad Foundation, Inc.
REQUISITE: Student loans for medical and paramedical students in the South Eddy County and Carlsbad, NM, area. Scholarships for students who plan to have careers teaching.
APPLICATION: Write for more information.
CONTACT: 11 South Canyon Street, Carlsbad, NM 88220. John Mills, Executive Director. (505)887-1131

FOUNDATION: Viles Foundation, Inc.
REQUISITE: Scholarships for needy residents of San Miguel and Mora counties, NM. Funds are very limited.
APPLICATION: Application deadline is April 1st. Write for info.

CONTACT: c/o Sunwest Bank of Albuquerque, POB 26900, Alburquerque, NM 87125. (505)765-2211

FOUNDATION: Levi Strauss Foundation, Inc
REQUISITE: Scholarships for disadvantaged high school seniors in communities where Levi Strauss & Company has production or distribution facilities.
APPLICATION: Accepted throughout the year. Write for info.
CONTACT: 1155 Battery Street, POB 7215, SF, CA 94106. Martha M Brown, Drctr of U.S. Contributions. TEL: (415)544-6577

FOUNDATION: Maddox (J.F.) Foundation
REQUISITE: Student loans for residents of Lea County, NM.
APPLICATION: Applications are accepted throughout the year.
CONTACT: POB 2588, Hobbs, NM 88241. Robert Socolofsky, Executive Director. TEL: (505)393-6338

NEVADA

FOUNDATION: Levi Strauss Foundation
REQUISITE: Business Opportunity Scholarships for needy students who live in communities where Levi Strauss & Company has a production or distribution facility including AR, CA, GA, NV, NM, TX, and VA.
APPLICATION: Applications are accepted throughout the year.
CONTACT: 1155 Battery Street, POB 7215, San Francisco, CA 94106. Martha Montag Brown, Director of U.S. Contribution. (415)544-6577

NEW YORK

FOUNDATION: New York State Higher Education Services Corporation
REQUISITE: Scholarships granted to Vietnam Veterans who are New York residents and are enrolled at an approved vocational-technical institution within New York state.
APPLICATION: Write for info. Application deadline is September 1st.
CONTACT: 99 Washington Ave., Student Information, Albany, NY 12255. 518-473-1574

FOUNDATION: New York State Higher Education Services Corporation
REQUISITE: Scholarships granted to New York high school students who are planning to enroll full-time in nursing at an accredited 2-year or 4-year

post secondary institution in New York State. This scholarship includes hospital and registered nurse certification programs.
APPLICATION: Write for info. Application deadline is March 31st.
CONTACT: 99 Washington Ave., Student information, Albany, NY 12255 518-473-1574

FOUNDATION: Columbia University
REQUISITE: Competition open to young composers between the ages of 18-25. Students must compete in either of two categories for music composition. No one can enter more than one. Must be US citizen.
APPLICATION: Write for info. Application deadline is February 1st.
CONTACT: Department of Music, 703 Dodge Hall, New York, NY 10027 (212)854-3825

FOUNDATION: Young Printing Executives Club
REQUISITE: Scholarships granted to residents of New York, New Jersey, and Connecticut who are enrolled at the Rochester Institute of Technology. Students should have at least a 3.0 GPA and be committed to a career in the Tri-State area.
APPLICATION: Write for info. Application deadline is 4/15 - 6/1.
CONTACT: 5 Penn Plaza, New York, NY 10001. (212)318-9608

The capitalized center headings are counties.

ALBANY

FOUNDATION: Grace Appleton Student Loan Fund
REQUISITE: Must be Jr/Sr attending SUNY at Plattsburgh. Small grants made on a national basis.
APPLICATION: Write letter asking for application. No deadline.
CONTACT: Director of Financial Aid, State University College, Plattsburgh, NY 12901 (518)564-2040

FOUNDATION: Arthur Atwood Scholarship Fund
REQUISITE: Strictly for residents of Champlain or county of Clinton, NY. Preference given to male students accepted to Yale.
APPLICATION: Their application form is required. Deadline 4/15.
CONTACT: Prncpl, Champlain Central School, Champlain, NY 12919

FOUNDATION: Lois M. Brown Scholarship Fund
REQUISITE: For seniors at Lansingburgh High School, N Troy, NY.

APPLICATION: No deadline stated.
CONTACT: Prncpl, Lansingburgh High School, North Troy, NY 18182 (518)235-1910

FOUNDATION: Rachel Fiero Clarke Scholarship Fund
REQUISITE:Must be a graduate of Catskill High School.
APPLICATION:Write for information & application. 4/15 deadln
CONTACT:Catskill Board of Education, Catskill, NY 12414 (518)943-2300

FOUNDATION: Mary Smith Courtney Memorial Schlarshp Fnd
REQUISITE:For graduates of Albany High School
APPLICATION:Write for information & application. 6/1 deadline
CONTACT:Principal, Albany High School, 700 Washington Ave., Albany, NY 12203 TEL: (518)454-3987

FOUNDATION: General Steel Fabricators Cllg Schlrshp Fndtn
REQUISITE:For children of employees.
APPLICATION:Need high school transcript & proof of college acceptance. Write address below
CONTACT:R.J.Monroe, Trustee, (Foundation name), P.O. Box 636 Latham, NY 12110 (518)785-3221

FOUNDATION: J.H. Guido f/b/o K. Guido Scholarship
REQUISITE:Only for students of Maria College, Albany, NY.
APPLICATION:Write or phone.
CONTACT:FAO or Registrar, Maria College, Albany, 12203 (518)489-7436

FOUNDATION: C.M. & J.C. Harrington Scholarship Fund
REQUISITE:Limited to graduates of Plattsburgh NY high school.
APPLICATION:Deadline 4/1. Write requesting application & info.
CONTACT:%Key Trust Co., 60 State St, Albany 12207-2524 (518)486-8701

FOUNDATION: ¦Rose Brilleman Hessberg Trust for Samuel Hessberg Memorial Scholarship Fund
REQUISITE: Jewish & a resident of Albany.
APPLICATION: Deadline 4/15. Write for application & info.
CONTACT: Exec. Dir., Albany Jewish Family Services, 930 Madison Ave., Albany NY 12208 TEL: (518)482-8856

FOUNDATION: Andrew M. Johnston Award Fund
REQUISITE: Residents of Chateauguay, NY and attend one of several

local churches.
APPLICATION: No deadline. Write requesting application & info.
CONTACT: Superintendent of Schools, Chateauguay Central School, Chateauguay, NY 12901
(We were not able to verify this listing; it may not be extant.)

FOUNDATION: Linda B. Lange Trust
REQUISITE: Must be resident of Tannersville, NY and graduate of Hunter-Tannersville High School.
APPLICATION: Must write letter. Deadline 5/15.
CONTACT: Principal, Hunter-Tannersville High School, Tannersville, NY 12485 TEL: (518)589-5880

FOUNDATION: Douglas W. Lincoln Scholarship Fund
REQUISITE: For students of Albany High School only.
APPLICATION: Must write for application. Deadline 5/3.
CONTACT: Guidance Office, Albany High School, Albany, NY TEL: (518)454-3987

FOUNDATION: John M. Maslowski Scholarship Fund
REQUISITE: Must be a graduate of Chazy Central School.
APPLICATION: Write for application. Deadline 6/30.
CONTACT: Superintendent of Schools, Chazy Central Rural School, Chazy, NY 12921 (Apply at these specific schools.)

FOUNDATION: !Dr. Robert S. & Mary B. McDonald Mmrl Trst
REQUISITE:Must be a medical student residing in Plattsburgh or Clinton County, NY.
APPLICATION:Must write for application. Deadline 4/1.
CONTACT:McDonald Scholarship Fund, Key Trust Co., P.O. Box 1915, Albany, NY 12201 (518)486-8701

FOUNDATION: Edith Grace Reynolds Estate Residuary Trust
REQUISITE: Be from School District 1, in Rensselaer County
APPLICATION:Must include H.S. transcript with letter.
CONTACT:Micheline Cardillo, Trust Officer, Key Trust Co., 60 State St., P.O. Box 1965, Albany, NY 12207 TEL: (518)486-8701

FOUNDATION: Charles M. Stern Award Fund
REQUISITE:Must be graduate of Albany High School.
APPLICATION:Write for application. No deadline.

CONTACT:Principal, Albany High School, 700 Washington Ave., Albany, NY 12207 TEL: (518)454-3987

FOUNDATION: Joan D. Van Slyke Trust for SUNY at Albany Benevolent Association
REQUISITE:Must be a student at SUNY Albany.
APPLICATION:Write for application. No deadline.
CONTACT:Office of Financial Aid, SUNY at Albany, 1400 Washington Ave., Albany, NY 12222 (Apply at these specific schools.)

FOUNDATION: Sarah S. Vert Student Fund Trust
REQUISITE: Must be a current year graduate of the Plattsburgh City School District.
APPLICATION:Write for application. No deadline.
CONTACT:Norstar Bank of Upstate NY, Albany, NY 12201 TEL: (518)447-4000

ALLEGANY

FOUNDATION: John C. Robertson and Flora S. Whitman Memorial Educational Aid Fund
REQUISITE:Must be students of Central School, Cuba, NY.
APPLICATION:Write for application. No deadline.
CONTACT:Wesley J. Serra, 25 Schuyler, Belmont, NY 14813 (Apply at these specific schools.)

FOUNDATION: Wellsville Rotary Education Fund
REQUISITE:Must be graduating senior of Wellsville Cntrl Hgh Schl
APPLICATION:Write for application.
CONTACT:Frnk E. Jenson, POB 292, Wellsville, NY 14895-1016 TEL: (518)593-2291

BRONX

FOUNDATION: American Double Ditch League Inc.
REQUISITE:Submit educational profile.
APPLICATION:Send profile when requesting application.
CONTACT:David Walker Pres., 790 Concourse Village West Apt.7-D, Bronx, NY 10451
(We were not able to verify this listing; it may not be extant.)

BROOME

FOUNDATION: Pauline R.Parker Trust
REQUISITE:Must be under 25 years of age, attending either Broome Community College or Harpur College.
APPLICATION:Call or write Exec. Sec. for application.
CONTACT:Eugene Monroe, POB 323, Binghamton, NY 13902
(We were not able to verify this listing; it may not be extant.)

CATTARAUGUS

FOUNDATION: Walter and Beatrice J. Beigel Scholarship Trust
REQUISITE: Must be a student from Salamanca Cntrl Hgh Schl
APPLICATION: Write for application. No deadline stated.
CONTACT: Thomas DeBolski, Principal, Salamanca Central High School, 50 Iroquois Dr., Salamanca, NY 14779 TEL: (716)915-2400

CHAUTAUQUA

FOUNDATION: Chautauqua Region Cmmnty Fndtn, Inc.
REQUISITE: Must be from the Chautauqua area.
APPLICATION: Call or write for application. Deadline 2/28.
CONTACT: Donald J. Luscher, RM 104-106 Hotel Jamestown Bldg., Jamestown, NY 14701 TEL: (716)661-3390

FOUNDATION: Amelia G. Jachym Scholarship Fund
REQUISITE: Must be a graduate of Pine Valley Central Hgh Schl
APPLICATION: Write for application. No deadline stated.
CONTACT: Richard L. Earle, 412 Second St., South Dayton, NY 14138 TEL: (716)988-3632

CHEMUNG

FOUNDATION: James J. Bloomer Charitable Trust.
REQUISITE: Must be a Catholic student from Elmira, NY attending a Catholic college or University.
APPLICATION: Call or write for application. No deadline stated.
CONTACT: Trustees, Saint Patrick's Roman Catholic Church Society, Elmira, NY 14901 (607)733-6661

FOUNDATION: The Cmmnty Fndtn of the Chemung Cnty Area

REQUISITE: Must be from the Chemung County, NY area.
APPLICATION: Call or write for application on 12/15.
CONTACT: Suzanne Lee, Exec. Dir., 168 N. Main St., BOX 714, Elmira, NY 14902 TEL: (607)734-6412

FOUNDATION: Leo E. Considine Scholarship f/b/o Notre Dame
REQUISITE: Must be a student from Notre Dame High School.
APPLICATION: Call or write for application. No deadline stated.
CONTACT: School Chaplin and School Principal, Notre Dame High School, Elmira, NY 14904 TEL: (607)735-3200

FOUNDATION: Harrison Earl and Francis Smith Schlrshp Fnd
REQUISITE: Must be a graduate of Thomas A. Edison High School in Elmira Heights, NY.
APPLICATION: Call or write for application. No deadline.
CONTACT: Board of Education, Elmira Heights Central School District, Elmira Heights, NY 14903 TEL: (607)734-7114

CHENANGO

FOUNDATION: Chenango County Medical Society and Ostego County Medical Society, Trustees for the Van Wagner Scholarship
REQUISITE: Must be from Chenango or Ostego Co., NY
APPLICATION: Write for application. Deadline 6/15.
CONTACT: Mark S. Thompson, 210 Clinton Rd., Rte 12-B, New Hartford, NY 13413 TEL: (315)735-2204

FOUNDATION: Greater Norwich Foundation
REQUISITE: Must be from Norwich, NY area.
APPLICATION: Write for application. Deadlines 5/10 and 11/10.
CONTACT: Sandra Colton, c/o Natl. Bank and Trust Co. of Norwich, 52 South Broad St., Norwich, NY 13815 TEL: (607)337-6000

FOUNDATION: Christopher David Lyons Scholarship Fund
REQUISITE: Must be a senior from South New Berlin school district according to the map in 1982.
APPLICATION: Write for application. Deadline 5/1.
CONTACT: William Lyons R.D. 2, BOX 135A, South New Berlin, NY 13843 TEL: (607)334-5073

FOUNDATION: Jane Schneck Estate

REQUISITE: Must be a student from Afton or Greene Central School Districts.
APPLICATION: Write for loan application. No deadline stated.
CONTACT: c/o President, Board of Education or Superintendent, Greene Central School, Greene, NY 13778; Afton Central School, Afton, NY 13738
TEL: (607)639-8229

FOUNDATION: Otis A. Thompson Foundation, Inc.
REQUISITE: Must be from high schools in Chenango, DE, Ostego county, NY.
APPLICATION: Write for application. Deadline between 2/1 4/1
CONTACT: Sandra Colton, c/o The National Bank and Trust Co. of Norwich, 52 S. Broad St., Norwich, NY 13815-1646   (607)335-6193

CORTLAND

FOUNDATION: Sigma Delta Phi, Inc.
REQUISITE: Must be a student at SUNY Cortland pursuing a degree in medical education. Must have 3 letters of recommendation from persons associated with SUNY Cortland.
APPLICATION: Call or write for application. No deadline stated.
CONTACT: FAO, SUNY Cortland, Cortland, NY 13045 (607)753-2011

DELAWARE

FOUNDATION: Jennie Bradley Hanford Education Fund
REQUISITE: Must be member of the United Methodist Church.
APPLICATION: Write for application. No deadline.
CONTACT: Trustees, Untd Methodist Church, Walton, NY 13856   TEL: (607)865-5765

FOUNDATION: Charles O. and Elsie Haynes Trust
REQUISITE: Must be from Charlotte Valley Central Schl Dstrct
APPLICATION: Write for application. Deadline 6/1.
CONTACT: Thomas J. Trelease, HC 83-Box 262A, Davenport, NY 13750-9729 (Apply at these specific schools.)

FOUNDATION: Abel E. Peck Memorial Fund
REQUISITE: Must be a student from Walton Central Hgh Schl
APPLICATION: Call or write for application. Deadline 4/1.
CONTACT: Guidance Dept. Walton Central High School, Walton, NY

13856 TEL: (607)829-4116

FOUNDATION: Clarke Sanford Memorial Trust Fund
REQUISITE: Must be from Delaware Co., NY training to be a professional nurse.
APPLICATION: Call or write for application. Deadline 8/31.
CONTACT: Per A. Omland, Franklin Central School, Franklin, NY 13775
TEL: (607)829-3551

DUTCHESS

FOUNDATION: Elizabeth Wolf Scholarship Fund
REQUISITE: Must be a graduate of Beacon High School.
APPLICATION: Write for application. Must include biographic and scholastic info. with application. Deadline 6/1.
CONTACT: Anthony Pagones, c/o Pagones and Cross, 355 Main St., Beacon, NY 12508-3020 TEL: (914)838-3400

ERIE

FOUNDATION: Jesse H. Baker Education Fund
REQUISITE: None listed.
APPLICATION: Write for application. Deadline not listed.
CONTACT: c/o Marine Midland Bank, POB 803, Buffalo, NY 14240 TEL: (716)841-2424

FOUNDATION: Mabel Bookstaver Trust Scholarship
REQUISITE: Must be a graduate from Dunkirk High School.
APPLICATION: Guidance Department, Dunkirk High School
CONTACT: Sharon Austin,c/o Marine Midland Bank, 360 South Warren S., 1st Floor, Syracuse, NY 13202 TEL: (716)841-2424

FOUNDATION: The Buffalo Foundation
REQUISITE: Must be a local resident.
APPLICATION: Call or write for application between 3/1 and 5/10. Deadline 5/25.
CONTACT: Bffl Fndtn, 237 Main St., Bffl, 14203 TEL: (716)852-2857

FOUNDATION: Judge John D. Hillery Mmrl Schlrshp Fnd
REQUISITE: Must show financial need.
APPLICATION: Write for before school year begins.

CONTACT: David Hillary, 601 McKinley Pkwy., Buffalo, NY 14220 TEL: (716)826-3610

FOUNDATION: Arlee Moore Scholarship Fund
REQUISITE: Must be a graduate from Frewsburg Central Schools.
APPLICATION: Guidance Department, Frewsburg Central Schools
CONTACT: c/o Marine Midland Bank, Trust Administration Center, P.O. Box 4888, Syracuse, NY 13221 TEL: (716)841-2424

FOUNDATION: Rochester Telephone Corporation Edctnl Fnd
REQUISITE: None Listed.
APPLICATION: Write for application. Deadline not listed.
CONTACT: c/o Marine Midland Bank, N.A., P.O. Box 4203, Buffalo, NY 14240 (716)841-2424

FOUNDATION: Scalp and Blade Scholarship Trust
REQUISITE: Must be male graduate from an Erie Co. high school planning to attend a college outside Erie or Niagra Counties.
APPLICATION: Write for application. Deadline 5/1.
CONTACT: c/o Manufacturers and Traders' Trust Co., One M and T Plaza, Buffalo, NY 14240 TEL: (716)842-4200

FOUNDATION: Dr Clarence A. Tyler Scholarship Fund
REQUISITE: Must be a graduating senior from Alden Hgh Schl.
APPLICATION: Call or write for application prior to graduation.
CONTACT: Principal, Alden High School, Alden, NY 14004 TEL: (716)937-9116

ESSEX

FOUNDATION: Bruce L. Crary Foundation, Inc
REQUISITE: Be from Clinton, Essex, Franklin, Hamilton and Warren cnts.
APPLICATION: Call or write for application. Deadline 3/31.
CONTACT: Richard Lawrence, Hand House, River St., P.O. Box 396, Elizibethtown, NY 12932   TEL: (518)873-6496

FOUNDATION: Jon Eric Hofmann Memorial Scholarship Fund
REQUISITE: Must be graduating senior from Moriah Cntrl Schl
APPLICATION: Write for application. Deadline 5/10.
CONTACT: Harry Shaw, 38 Broad St., Port Henry 12974-1196 (518)546-3301

FULTON

FOUNDATION: Conrad H. and Anna Belle Gillen Trust
REQUISITE: Must be from Fulton Co.
APPLICATION: Write for application. Deadline not listed.
CONTACT: Brd of Edctn, Cty of Gloversville, Gloversville 12078 TEL: (518)725-2612

FOUNDATION: William G. and Rhonda B. Partridge Memorl Schlrshp Fnd
REQUISITE: None listed.
APPLICATION: Write for application. No deadline.
CONTACT: Sandra Colton, c/o Fulton County National Bank and Trust Co, 52 South Broad St., Norwich, NY 13815 TEL: (607)335-6193

FOUNDATION: Evelyn E. Stempfle Fund Trust
REQUISITE: Must be from Gloversville, NY.
APPLICATION: Write for application. Deadline not listed.
CONTACT: Sandra Colton, c/o Fulton County National Bank and Trust Co., 52 South Broad Street, Norwich, NY 13815 TEL: (607)335-6193

GENESEE

FOUNDATION: Children's Home Association of Genesee County
REQUISITE: Must be from Genesee Co.
APPLICATION: Call or Write for application. No deadline.
CONTACT: P.O. Box 130 Batavia, NY 14020
(We were not able to verify this listing; it may not be extant.)

GREENE

FOUNDATION: Sheldon N. Peck Memorial Scholarship Fund
REQUISITE: Must be graduating senior from Windham-Ashland-Jewett Central School in Windham.
APPLICATION: Write for application.
CONTACT: P.O. Box 423, Windham, NY 12496 (Apply at these specific schools.)

HERKIMER

FOUNDATION: Marion Brill Scholarship Foundation, Inc.
REQUISITE: Must be graduate of Ilion High School.

APPLICATION: Write for application. Deadline 4/15.
CONTACT: Jack Manley, Gdnce Office, Ilion Cntrl Schl, Ilion, NY 13357 (315)895-7471

JEFFERSON

FOUNDATION: Winifred Sperry Memorial Fund
REQUISITE: Must be from Malone, NY.
APPLICATION: Write for application, include academic record and college acceptance letter. Deadline 6/15.
CONTACT: Scholarship Committee of the Academic Board, Malone Central Schl Dstrct, Malone, NY 12953 (Apply at these specific schools.)

FOUNDATION: Watertown Foundation, Inc
REQUISITE: Must be from Jefferson County.
APPLICATION: Write for application. Deadlines 2/1 and 8/1.
CONTACT: James McVean, P.O. Box 6106, 120 Washington St, Watertown, NY 13601 (315)782-7110

KINGS

FOUNDATION: Elaine Elizabeth Barbiere Foundation
REQUISITE: Studying nursing.
APPLICATION: Write for application. Deadline not listed.
CONTACT: 1892 Gerritsen Ave., Brooklyn, NY 11229-2644
(We were not able to verify this listing; it may not be extant.)

FOUNDATION: Joel Braverman Foundation, Inc
REQUISITE: None listed.
APPLICATION: Write for application. Deadline not listed.
CONTACT: Dr. Joel Wolowelsky, 1609 Ave. J, Brooklyn 11230 TEL: (718)377-1100

FOUNDATION: New England Society in the City of Brooklyn
REQUISITE: Must be permanent resident of Brooklyn or Long Island, attending a New England college.
APPLICATION: Write for application. No deadline.
CONTACT: Harrison M. Davis, III, 215 Adams St., Apt. 2-J, Brooklyn, NY 11201 TEL: (718)625-1291

LEWIS

New York

FOUNDATION: The Pratt-Northam Foundation
REQUISITE: Must be from the Black River Valley, NY region.
APPLICATION: Write for application. No deadline.
CONTACT: Donald Exford, P.O. Box 104, Lowville, NY 13367
(We were not able to verify this listing; it may not be extant.)

LIVINGSTON

FOUNDATION: Livonia C.H.S. Trust
REQUISITE: Must be a graduate of Livonia Central High School.
APPLICATION: Write for application. Deadline not listed.
CONTACT: Livonia Cntrl Schl, Spring St., Livonia, NY 14487   TEL: (716)346-4040

MONROE

FOUNDATION: Adelphic Cornell Educational Fund, Inc.
REQUISITE: Must be a student at Cornell University.
APPLICATION: Write for application. No deadline.
CONTACT: Steven V. Ritchey, 122 Homer Ave., Cortland 13095

FOUNDATION: John Walker Bowron Scholarship Fund
REQUISITE: Resident of Village of Rouses Point or Town of Champlain for minimum of 10 yrs.
APPLICATION: Write for application. Deadline not listed.
CONTACT: Norstar Trust Co., One East Ave., Rochester NY 14638   TEL: (716)546-9085

FOUNDATION: The Branch - Wilbur Fund, Inc.
REQUISITE: Must be a student from or studying in Rochester.
APPLICATION: Write for application. Include financial status, school, and course of study.
CONTACT: John Branch, 65 Broad St., Rochester, NY 14614
(We were not able to verify this listing; it may not be extant.)

FOUNDATION: Joseph L. Briggs Trust
REQUISITE: Be graduate of East High School in Rochester.
APPLICATION: Write for application. Deadline not listed.
CONTACT: Patricia Carnahan, East High School, 1801 Main St. East, Rochester, NY 14609   TEL: (716)288-3130

147

FOUNDATION: Educational Fund of the Rochester New York Branch of the American Association of University Women
REQUISITE: Completed at least 2 years of study; obtaining a bachelor's or graduate degree. Resident or student in Monroe County (includes Rochester, NY & Brockport)
APPLICATION: Write for application. Deadline not listed.
CONTACT: Board of Trustees, 494 East Ave., Rochester, NY 14607-1911 (716)244-8890

FOUNDATION: William H. Coe Medical & Surgical Fnd for Edctn
REQUISITE: Auburn, NY school district. Medical education.
APPLICATION: Write for application. Deadline not listed.
CONTACT: Norstar Trst Co., One East Ave., Rochester, NY 14604-2205 (716)546-9085

FOUNDATION: Delta Sigma Delta Educational Foundation
REQUISITE: Dentistry.
APPLICATION: Contact Delta Sigma Delta at participating dental schl
CONTACT: 1005 Temple Bldg., Rochester, NY 14604 (We were not able to verify this listing; it may not be extant.)

FOUNDATION: Katherine Fitter Scholarship Fund
REQUISITE: Must be from Penfield, NY.
APPLICATION: Write for application. No deadline.
CONTACT: Norstar Trst Co., One East Ave., Rochester 14638   TEL: (716)546-9085

FOUNDATION: Harry S. Fredenburgh Scholarship Trust
REQUISITE: Be graduate of Myderse Academy in Seneca Falls
APPLICATION: Write for application. Deadline not listed.
CONTACT: c/o Superintendent, Seneca Falls Central School District, 76 State St., Seneca Falls, NY 13148 TEL: (315)568-5874

FOUNDATION: Gould Scholarship Fund
REQUISITE: Must be an employee of Gould Pumps, Inc.
APPLICATION: Write for application. Deadline not listed.
CONTACT: Mrs. M.J. Catoe, c/o Gould Pumps, Inc., 240 Falls St., Seneca Falls, NY 13148   (315)568-2811

FOUNDATION: Madeline Hurbert Scholarship Award Trust
REQUISITE: Graduate of Victor High School, Victor, NY

New York

APPLICATION: Write for application. Deadline not listed.
CONTACT: William Guiffre, Principal, Victor Central School, High St., Victor, NY 14564 TEL: (716)924-3252

FOUNDATION: Godfrey J. Jacobsen Memorial Schlrshp Fnd
REQUISITE: Must be graduates of James E. Sperry High School, Henrietta, NY.
APPLICATION: Write for application. No deadline listed.
CONTACT: c/o George Wolf, 150 Perinton Hills Office Park, Fairport, NY 14450-9107 TEL: (716)223-2034

FOUNDATION: Jewish Children's Home of Rochester, NY, Inc., Fnd
REQUISITE: Must be an undergraduate college student.
APPLICATION: Write for application. No deadline.
CONTACT: Nathan J. Robfogle, 200 Midtown Tower, Rochester, NY 14604
(We were not able to verify this listing; it may not be extant.)

FOUNDATION: King Scholarship Fund
REQUISITE: Must be a resident from Auburn or Cayuga County.
APPLICATION: Write for application. Deadline not listed.
CONTACT: Norstar Trst Co., 1 East Ave., Rochester 14604-2220
(716)546-9085

FOUNDATION: Harry E. Knight Scholarship Fund
REQUISITE: Must be from Plattsburgh, NY.
APPLICATION: Write for application. No deadline.
CONTACT: Dr. George H. Amedore, Plattsburgh City School District, 1 Clifford, Suite 101, Plattsburgh, NY 12901 TEL: (518)561-6670

FOUNDATION: Cornelius and Elizabeth Lynch Schlrshp Trust
REQUISITE: Must be high school graduate of Geneva, NY.
APPLICATION: Write for application. Deadline not listed.
CONTACT: 44 Exchange St. Rochester, NY 14614 (716)546-4500
(We were not able to verify this listing; it may not be extant.)

FOUNDATION: Bernard W. McCormick Scholarship Fund
REQUISITE: Must be from Troy, NY.
APPLICATION: Write for application, include school transcript. No deadline.
CONTACT: Principal, Catholic Central High School, Troy, NY (518)235-7100

FOUNDATION: Olmsted-Leroy High School Scholarship Fund
REQUISITE: Must be from Leroy Central School District.
APPLICATION:Write for application. Deadline not listed.
CONTACT:Norstar Trst Co., 1 East Ave., Rochester NY 14638   TEL: (716)546-9085

FOUNDATION: Madge Preston Scholarship Fund
REQUISITE: Be graduate from Red Jacket Cntrl Schl Dstrct.
APPLICATION: Write for application. Deadline not listed.
CONTACT:Norstar Trst Co., 1 East Ave., Rochester, NY 14604-2220 TEL: (716)546-9085

FOUNDATION: Ward H. Preston Scholarship Fund Trust
REQUISITE: Must be a graduate of Red Jacket Central School District.
APPLICATION: Write for application. Deadline not listed.
CONTACT: Principal, Red Jacket Central Schl, Shortville, NY 14548 TEL: (716)289-3964

FOUNDATION: Tibbets Scholarship Trust
REQUISITE: Graduate of North Salem Central Schl Dstrct, NY.
APPLICATION: Write for application. Deadline not listed.
CONTACT: William A. Zeralsky, Principal, North Salem Central School District, Route 124, North Salem, NY 10560 TEL: (914)669-5414

FOUNDATION: David H. Utter Memorial Scholarship Fund
REQUISITE: Be graduate of Marcus Whitman Cntrl Schl Dstrct
APPLICATION: Write for application. Deadline not listed.
CONTACT: Gary F. Shultz, Asst. V.P., c/o Chase Lincoln First Bank, N.A., Five Seneca St., Geneva, NY 14456 TEL: (315)789-7700

FOUNDATION: The Anne Walker Scholarship Fund
REQUISITE: Be a male graduating snr from Dunkirk Hgh Schl
APPLICATION: Write for application. Deadline not listed.
CONTACT: Norstar Trst Co., 1 East Ave., Rochester, NY 14638 TEL: (716)546-9085

FOUNDATION: E.R. Woelfel Memorial Scholarship Fund
REQUISITE: Must be a student in the Newark New York school area.
APPLICATION: Write for application. Deadline not listed.
CONTACT: c/o Chase Lincoln First Bank, N.A., P.O. Box 1412, Rochester, NY 14603-1412 (716)258-6000

New York

MONTGOMERY

FOUNDATION: Children's Aid Association of Amsterdam
REQUISITE: Must be from Montgomery County.
APPLICATION: Write for application. Deadline 3/30.
CONTACT: Skyline Dr., Palatine Bridge, NY 13428 TEL: (518)673-2335

FOUNDATION: David & Michele Cudmore Scholarship Fund
REQUISITE: Be a graduating senior of Amsterdam Hgh Schl
APPLICATION: Write for application. No deadline.
CONTACT: 13 Evelyn St., Amsterdam, NY 12010-1203.

FOUNDATION: David Wasserman Scholarship Fund, Inc.
REQUISITE: Must be an undergraduate student who is a bona fide resident of Montgomery County.
APPLICATION: Write for application. No deadline.
CONTACT: 107 Division St., Amsterdam, NY 12010-3107

NASSAU

FOUNDATION: Rose L. Abrams Gemileth Chesed Assctn, Inc.
REQUISITE: None listed.
APPLICATION: Write for application. No deadline.
CONTACT: Eliezer Horowitz, Pres., 42 Stevens Place, Lawrence, NY 11559

FOUNDATION: Hugh Jms Ashford D.C. Memorial Scholarship Fund, Inc.
REQUISITE: Must be 9th semester student enrolled in accredited Chiropractic College.
APPLICATION: Write for application. No deadline.
CONTACT: 54 West Millpage Dr., Bethpage, NY 11714-4818

FOUNDATION: The Frank J. Becker Educational Foundation
REQUISITE: Limited to Lynbrook, Malverne, East Rockaway, Valley Stream and Rockville Center residents. Graduate of an accredited high school.
APPLICATION: Write for application. Deadline April I.
CONTACT: Robert Becker, V.P., 173 Earle Ave., Lynbrook, NY 11563

FOUNDATION: Dion Foundation, Inc.
REQUISITE: Must be students of Greek ancestry.

151

APPLICATION: Write for application. Deadline 1/3l.
CONTACT: Nicholas MaGoulias, Pres., 110 Cathedral Ave., Hempstead 11550

FOUNDATION: Jodi Ann Wollman Glioblastoma Foundation, Inc.
REQUISITE: None listed.
APPLICATION: Write for application. Deadline not listed.
CONTACT: 13 Cloverfield Rd. South, Valley Stream, NY 11581-2421

FOUNDATION: Kane Paper Scholarship Fund, Inc.
REQUISITE: Must be from New York City.
APPLICATION: Write for application. No deadline.
CONTACT: James T. Kane, 2365 Milburn Ave., Baldwin, NY 11510-3384

FOUNDATION: The William R. Larkin Memorial Foundation
REQUISITE: Must be a college student.
APPLICATION: Write for application. No deadline.
CONTACT: Edward Larkin, 191 Cathedral Ave., West Hempstead, NY 11550

FOUNDATION: Harvey R. Lewis Foundation
REQUISITE: Must be resident of Port Washington or Manhasset.
APPLICATION: Write for application. Deadline not listed.
CONTACT: Robert Brady, Director, 277 Main St., Port Washington, NY 11050-2703

FOUNDATION: The Li Foundation
REQUISITE: Must be Chinese and attend school in China.
APPLICATION: Write for application. No deadline.
CONTACT: E. Leon Way, Pres., 66 Herbhill Rd., Glen Cove, NY 11542

FOUNDATION: Edith Reisner Mmrl College Assistance Fnd
REQUISITE: Be a graduating snr from Wyandanch Hgh Schl
APPLICATION: Write for application. Deadline not listed.
CONTACT: c/o Alan Reisner, 137 South Babylon Tpke., Merrick, NY 11566-3518 (516)491-1022

FOUNDATION: Shoppers Village/ Maureen Nolan Mmrl Fnd
REQUISITE: Must be from West Hempstead School District.
APPLICATION: Write for application. Deadline 11/25
CONTACT: Robert W. O'Brien, Secy., P.O. Box 536, 138 Woodfield Rd.,

New York

West Hempstead, NY 11552-0536

NEW YORK

FOUNDATION: Consortium of Metropolitan Law Schools
REQUISITE: Scholarships granted to minority students primarily for the first year of Law School at Brooklyn; Fordham; New York; St. Johns; Seton Hall; Rutgers or Pace University Law Schools.
APPLICATION: Write for info. Application deadline is not specified.
CONTACT: 230 Park Avenue, New York, NY 10169. 212-661-4000

FOUNDATION: New York University
REQUISITE: Scholarships granted to undergraduate and graduate students enrolled in the Gallatin Division of New York University studying Publishing.
APPLICATION: Write for info. Application deadline is not specified.
CONTACT: 715 Broadway 6th Floor, NY, NY 10003   212-598-7077

FOUNDATION: New York State Education Department
REQUISITE: Scholarships granted to New York resident for undergraduate or graduate study leading to teaching certification in Science; Math; or other designated area.
APPLICATION: Write for info. Application deadline is not specified.
CONTACT: Attn. Bureau of Higher and Professional Testing, Albany, NY 12230. (518)474-3852

FOUNDATION: New York State Education Department
REQUISITE: Scholarships granted to New York residents of at least one year who is enrolled in a New York post-secondary institution in program requiring state license. Must be willing to accept guidelines for funding.
APPLICATION: Write for info. Application deadline is not specified.
CONTACT: Attn. Bureau of Higher and Professional Testing, Albany, NY 12230. (518)474-3852

FOUNDATION: Boy Scouts of America-Dr. Harry Britenstool Scholarship Committee
REQUISITE: Scholarships granted to undergraduate students who have been NYC Boy Scout or Explorer Scout for at least the last 2 year. Students must have need and excellent academic record. Students must also show service to NYC Council and strong scout participation. Must be a US citizen.

APPLICATION: Write for info. Application deadline is June 1st.
CONTACT: 345 Hudson Street, New York, NY 10014. (212)242-1100

FOUNDATION: New York City
REQUISITE: Summer management internship program provides undergraduate or graduate students with work experience on a full-time basis in city government from mid-June to mid-August. Must be a resident of New York City and US citizen.
APPLICATION: Write for info. Application deadline is February 1st.
CONTACT: 220 Church St Rm 338 NY, NY 10013 (212)233-0489 EX 0535

FOUNDATION: New York City
REQUISITE: Fellowships provides one academic year of full-time work experience in Urban government. Students must be senior, recent graduate or in a graduate program. Must be US citizen.
APPLICATION: Write for info. Application deadline is February 15th.
CONTACT: 220 Church St Rm 338 NY, NY 10013 (212)233-0489 EX 0535

FOUNDATION: Allaverdy Foundation
REQUISITE: Grants made on national basis. Awardees must be direct or indirect descendants of natives of the Caucasus.
APPLICATION:Write for application. No deadline indicated.
CONTACT: Allaverdy Foundation, Constanine Sidamon-Eristoff, Trustee, 630 Fifth Ave., Ste. 2350, New York 10111

FOUNDATION: Chauncey Stillman Benevolent Fund
REQUISITE: Requisite not clearly stated, but financially generous. Grants made on national basis.
APPLICATION: Write for application. No deadline indicated.
CONTACT: Chauncey Stillman Benevolent Fund, %Kelley, Drye & Warren, 101 Park Ave., New York 10178 (We were not able to verify this listing; it may not be extant.)

FOUNDATION: Stony Wold-Herbert Fund Inc.
REQUISITE:Only those living in greater NY area, 16 years or older, & having respiratory illness. Supplementary scholarships for college or vocational school students.
APPLICATION: Write or call for initial approach and deadline.
CONTACT: Mrs. C.S. Friedman, Exec. Dir., Stony Wold-Herbert Fnd Inc., 136 E 57th St., Rm. 1705, NY 10022 TEL: (212)753-6565

154

FOUNDATION: David Aronow Foundation, Inc.
REQUISITE: Made on national basis. No requisites stated.
APPLICATION: No deadline. Write for application.
CONTACT: Write foundation, %J.D. Leinwand, 10 West 47th St., NY 10036-3301 (We were not able to verify this listing; it may not be extant.)

FOUNDATION: The Theodore H. Barth Foundation, Inc.
REQUISITE: None stated. Grants made on national basis.
APPLICATION: No deadline. Write for application.
CONTACT: Irving P. Berelson, 1211 Ave. of the Americas, NY 10036 (We were not able to verify this listing; it may not be extant.)

FOUNDATION: The James Gordon Bennett Memorial Crprtn
REQUISITE: Employees or immediate family of New York City Daily Newspapers.
APPLICATION: Write for application. Deadline 3/1.
CONTACT: %Eleanor H. Keil, NY University, P.O. Box 908, Madison Square Station, NY 10154   TEL: (212)998-1212

FOUNDATION: Blakely Memorial Scholarship Fund Trust
REQUISITE: 6 scholarships for students who for the past 3 years have attended Evander Childs High School in the Bronx.
APPLICATION: Write for application. No deadline indicated.
CONTACT: Evander Childs Hgh Schl, Schlrshp Cmmttee, 99 Park, Suite 1600, Bronx, NY 10016 TEL: (212)490-0400

FOUNDATION: Brown Brothers, Harriman & Co. Undergraduate Fnd
REQUISITE: Given primarily in NY, NJ, MA & PA. Limited to children of employees of The Brown Brothers, Harriman & Co.
APPLICATION: Write for application. No deadline indicated.
CONTACT: % Personnel Dept., 59 Wall St., NY 10005-2818   TEL: (212)483-1818

FOUNDATION: Chinese Christian Fellowship, Inc.
REQUISITE: None stated. Grants made on national basis.
APPLICATION: Write for application, include references and recommendations. No deadline indicated.
CONTACT: %CCF Scholarship Committee, 549 West 123rd St., NY 10027-5026 TEL: (212)666-3230

FOUNDATION: The Clark Foundation

REQUISITE: Mainly for students living in the Cooperstown area. Also those living in NYC & upstate NY
APPLICATION: Write for application. No deadline indicated.
CONTACT: Edward W. Stack, Secy., 30 Wall St., NY 10005 TEL: (212)269-1833

FOUNDATION: Joseph Collin Foundation
REQUISITE: Undergraduate medical student, with the recommendation of med. school authorities. Maximum award is $2,500 for tuition and/or subsistence. Grants made on national basis. Not for pre-med or post-doctoral.
APPLICATION: Obtain application form from medical school. Write full proposal initially. Submission time is 1/1 to 3/1.
CONTACT: %Augusta L. Packer, Secy.-Treas., One Citicorp Center, 153 East 53rd St., NY 10022.
(We were not able to verify this listing; it may not be extant.)

FOUNDATION: The Cornell Delta Phi Educational Fund
REQUISITE: Must be student of Cornell University. Must submit academic record, evidence of need and good character.
APPLICATION: Submit in fall or spring semester. Request their application form.
CONTACT: Rogers & Wells, 200 Park Ave., NY 10166 (212)878-8000

FOUNDATION: Daughters of the Cincinnati
REQUISITE: High school senior and daughter of regular Army, Air Force, Navy, Coast Guard, or Marine Commissioned Officer. Grants made on national basis.
APPLICATION: Application form a must. Deadline 4/15.
CONTACT: % Mrs. J. Walthausen, Scholarship Administrator., 122 East 58th St., NY 10022 TEL: (212)319-6915

FOUNDATION: Jerome Lowell Dejur Trust
REQUISITE: Student of CCNY majoring in creative writing.
APPLICATION: Instead of applctn submit manuscript by 4/1.
CONTACT: %Chairman, English Department, %City College Fund, Convent Ave., 138th St., NY 10031

FOUNDATION: Deke Foundation
REQUISITE: None stated. Grants made on national basis.
APPLICATION: Write for application. No deadline indicated.

CONTACT: 16 East 64th St., NY 10021-7291
(We were not able to verify this listing; it may not be extant.)

FOUNDATION: Diamond Jubilee Fund of King Solomon-Beethoven Lodge No.232
REQUISITE: Medical education is primary interest. Grants made on national basis.
APPLICATION: Write for application. No deadline indicated.
CONTACT: %Robert L. Lippman, 201 East 79th St., NY 10021 (212) 425-0625 (We were not able to verify this listing; it may not be extant.)

FOUNDATION: The Ned Doyle, Maxwell Dane and William Bernbach Scholarship Fund
REQUISITE: Must Be the Sibling of a Doyle, Dane, Bernbach International, Inc., employee.
APPLICATION: Write for application. Deadline 2/14.
CONTACT: DDB Scholarship Consultant, Two Bryan Ave., Malvern, PA 19355 TEL: (215)896-1350

FOUNDATION: Endowment Fund of the 5th Masonic District
REQUISITE: Be child of a member of the Fifth Masonic District.
APPLICATION: Write for application. Deadline not listed.
CONTACT: Frank Messemer, 2905 39th St., Lng Island Cty 11101
(We were not able to verify this listing; it may not be extant.)

FOUNDATION: The Eta Chapter Sigma Alpha Mu Fndtin, Inc.
REQUISITE: Must be a member of the Eta chapter of Sigma Alpha Mu Fraternity.
APPLICATION: Write for application. Deadline 11/30.
CONTACT: Leonard Rubin, 14 Morton Center, Lawrenceville, NJ 08648

FOUNDATION: Molly M. Forster Trust
REQUISITE: None listed.
APPLICATION: Write for application. Deadline not listed.
CONTACT: Lawrence Morgan, 420 Lexington Ave., Rm. 2400, NY 10017
(We were not able to verify this listing; it may not be extant.)

FOUNDATION: James P. and Ruth C. Gillory Foundation, Inc.
REQUISITE: Must be from New York, NY.
APPLICATION: Write for application. Deadline 2 months prior to need.
CONTACT: Edmund Grainger, 501 Fifth St., Rm. 907, NY 10017

New York

(We were not able to verify this listing; it may not be extant.)

FOUNDATION: Gilman paper Company Foundation, Inc.
REQUISITE: Children of Gilman Paper employees.
APPLICATION: Write for application. Deadline not listed.
CONTACT: 111 West 50th St., New York, NY 10020 (212)246-3300

FOUNDATION: Harpsichord Music Society, Inc.
REQUISITE: Must be a Music student.
APPLICATION: Write for applctn & include resume. Deadline not listed.
CONTACT: Louise Crane, 820 5th Ave, NY 10021 TEL: (212)838-3147

FOUNDATION: William Randolph Hearst Foundation
REQUISITE: Not available to individuals
APPLICATION: Write for listing of schools where it is available.
CONTACT: Robert M. Frehse, Exec. Dir., 888 Seventh Ave., 27th Floor, New York, NY 10106 TEL: (212)586-5404

FOUNDATION: Howard Memorial Fund
REQUISITE: Must be from the Greater NYC area.
APPLICATION: Write for application. Deadline 5/30.
CONTACT: 500 East 62nd St., New York, NY 10021 (We were not able to verify this listing; it may not be extant.)

FOUNDATION: Jewish Foundation for Education of Women
REQUISITE: Must be from the Greater NYC area.
APPLICATION: Write for application. Deadline 10/30.
CONTACT: Florence Wallach, Exec. Dir., 330 West 58th St., 5J, New York, NY 10019 (212)265-2565

FOUNDATION: Dr. Martin Luther King, Jr. Scholarship Fund
REQUISITE: Must be a child of a member of the IUE Local 431.
APPLICATION: Write for application, include a copy of college acceptance letter. Deadline 4/1-6/1
CONTACT: Nancy Bunch, Cornell Unvrsty, Empire State College, 225 Verrick St., New York, NY 10014 TEL: (212)647-7800

FOUNDATION: Kosciuszko Foundation, Inc.
REQUISITE: Must be an American student wanting to study in Poland or a Polish student studying in the U.S.
APPLICATION: Write for application. Deadline not listed.

New York

CONTACT: 15 East 65th St., New York, NY 10021 TEL: (212)734-2130

FOUNDATION: Laboratories for Therapeutic Research, Inc.
REQUISITE: Must be studying Medical Research.
APPLICATION: Write for application. Deadline not listed.
CONTACT: c/o L. Effman, 425 West 59th St., NY, NY 10019 (We were not able to verify this listing; it may not be extant.)

FOUNDATION: Lyric Foundation for Traditional Poetry, Inc.
REQUISITE: None listed.
APPLICATION: Write for application. Deadline not listed.
CONTACT: The Lyric, 307 Dunton Dr., S.W., Blacksburg, VA 24060
(We were not able to verify this listing; it may not be extant.)

FOUNDATION: Anne O'Hare McCormick Memorial Fund, Inc.
REQUISITE: Must be accepted by the Columbia University School of Journalism and female.
APPLICATION: Write for application. Deadline not listed.
CONTACT: c/o Newswomens' Club of New York, 15 Gramercy Park, New York, NY 10003 TEL: (212)777-1612

FOUNDATION: National Sculpture Society, Inc.
REQUISITE: Must be a Sculpture student.
APPLICATION: Write for application, include background and photos of sculptures. Deadline mid-January.
CONTACT: 15 E 26th St., NY, NY 10010-1505 (We were not able to verify this listing; it may not be extant.)

FOUNDATION: The NY Council Navy League Schlrshp Fnd
REQUISITE: Must be dependents of officers or enlisted men of the regular Navy or Marine Corps.
APPLICATION: Write for application or call. Deadline 4/15.
CONTACT: One E 60th St., NY, NY 10022 (We were not able to verify this listing; it may not be extant.)

FOUNDATION: North American Phillips Foundation
REQUISITE: Children of Phillips Electronic North American Corp. employees.
APPLICATION: Write for application. Deadline 3/1.
CONTACT: 100 East 42nd St., New York, NY 10017 (212)850-5000

FOUNDATION: Open Society Fund, Inc.
REQUISITE: Available upon request.
APPLICATION: Write for application. Deadline not listed.
CONTACT: Gary Gladstein, 888 Seventh Ave., New York, NY 10106 TEL: (212)757-2323

FOUNDATION: Osceola Foundation, Inc.
REQUISITE: None listed.
APPLICATION: Write for application. Deadline not listed.
CONTACT: Walter Beinecke, Jr., Pres., 51 E 42nd St, Ste 1601, NY, NY 10017 (We were not able to verify this listing; it may not be extant.)

FOUNDATION: Painting Industry Promotion Fund
REQUISITE: Children of house painters in good standing with painters' union; must be high school senior maintaining at least "B" average, cannot attend community college or trade school.
APPLICATION: Write for application.
CONTACT: Arnold Merritt, Administrator, Association of Master Painters and Decorators of the City of New York, 50 East 42nd St., New York, NY 10017 TEL: (212)867-4384

FOUNDATION: Realty Foundation of New York
REQUISITE: Must be a child of employee at Realty Foundation in Manhattan.
APPLICATION: Write for application. Deadline not listed.
CONTACT: Scholarship Aid Committee, %31 Fifth Ave., Suite 921, New York, NY 10017 (212)697-2510

FOUNDATION: Elnr Roosevelt Newspaper Women's Mmrl Fund, Inc.
REQUISITE: None listed.
APPLICATION: Write for application. Deadline not listed.
CONTACT: 15 Gramercy Park, NY, NY 10003-1796 (212)777-1610

FOUNDATION: The Rothbert Fund, Inc.
REQUISITE: Edge given to those considering teaching as a vocation.
APPLICATION: Write for application in January. Deadline 3/1.
CONTACT: Jacob van Rossum, Admin. Secy., 475 Riverside Dr., Rm.252, New York, NY 10115 TEL: (212)870-3116

FOUNDATION: Leopold Schepp Foundation
REQUISITE: Must show need.

New York

APPLICATION: Write for application, include SASE.
CONTACT: 551 Fifth Ave, Ste 3000 NY NY 10176   (212)986-3078

FOUNDATION: The Scholarships Foundation, Inc.
REQUISITE: None listed.
APPLICATION: Write for application. Deadline not listed.
CONTACT: P.O. Box 170, Canal St. Station, NY, NY 10013
(We were not able to verify this listing; it may not be extant.)

FOUNDATION: Annie Sonnenblick Scholarship Fund, Inc.
REQUISITE: Children of Republic National Bank employees.
APPLICATION: Write for application. Deadline not listed.
CONTACT: Evelyn Hansen, c/o Republic National Bank of NY, 452 Fifth Ave., NY, NY 10018-2706 TEL: (212)525-5000

FOUNDATION: Virginia E. Stauffer Scholarship Fund
REQUISITE: Must be a student from a high schl within 10 mile radius from Exchange Bank of Olean, NY
APPLICATION: Write for application. Deadline not listed.
CONTACT: c/o The Bank of New York, Tax Dept., 48 Wall St., New York, NY 10015 TEL: (212)635-6747

FOUNDATION: Chauncey Stillman Benevolent Fund
REQUISITE: None listed.
APPLICATION: Write for application. Deadline not listed.
CONTACT: Kelley, Drye and Warren, 101 Park Ave., NY, 10178
(We were not able to verify this listing; it may not be extant.)

FOUNDATION: Stony Wold - Herbert Fund, Inc.
REQUISITE: Must be a student from the NYC area with respiratory illness.
APPLICATION: Write for application. Deadline not listed.
CONTACT: Mrs. Cheryl S. Friedman, Exec. Dir., 136 East 57th St., Rm. 1705, New York, NY 10022 TEL: (212)753-6565

FOUNDATION: Otto Sussman Trust
REQUISITE: Must show need.
APPLICATION: Write for application. Deadline not listed.
CONTACT: POB 1374, Trainsmeadow Station, Flushing, NY 11370

FOUNDATION: J.T. Tai and Company Foundation, Inc.
REQUISITE: Medical Education.

161

APPLICATION: Write for application. Deadline not listed.
CONTACT: J.T. Tai, Pres., 18 East 67th St., NY, NY 10021   TEL: (212)288-5253

FOUNDATION: Taraknath Das Foundation
REQUISITE: Must be from India and studying in the U.S.
APPLICATION: Write for application. Deadline 7/31.
CONTACT: Dr. Leonard A. Gordon, V.P., c/o 11th Floor International Affairs Bldg., Columbia Unvrsty, 420 W 118th St., NY, NY 10027-7296 TEL: (212)854-1754

FOUNDATION: Teamsters BBYO Scholarship Fund
REQUISITE: None listed.
APPLICATION: Write for application. Deadline not listed.
CONTACT: 225 Park Ave. South, New York, NY 10003
(We were not able to verify this listing; it may not be extant.)

FOUNDATION: Marcus Wallenberg Foundation
REQUISITE: Must be studying Business or International Studies.
APPLICATION: Write for application. Deadline not listed.
CONTACT: c/o Sulivan and Cromwell, 250 Park Ave., NY, 10017   TEL: (212)558-4000

FOUNDATION: Women's Aid Society of 1844, Inc.
REQUISITE: Must show need.
APPLICATION: Write for application. Deadline not listed.
CONTACT: Dorothy C. Moore, Secy.-Tres., 150 East 45th. St., NY, NY 10-017 (We were not able to verify this listing; it may not be extant.)

FOUNDATION: Women's Medical Association of New York
Financial Assistance Fund
REQUISITE: Must be a third or fourth year medical student in the Greater NYC area.
APPLICATION: Write for application. Deadline 4/1.
CONTACT: Anne Carter, M.D., Tres., 33 East 70th St., New York, NY 10021-4946 TEL: (212)545-0022

FOUNDATION: Youth Foundation, Inc.
REQUISITE: Must show need and ability.
APPLICATION: Write for application, include a self-addressed stamped envelope. Deadline 4/15.

CONTACT: Edward Bruen VP 36 W 44th St, NY 10036 (212)840-6291

NIAGARA

FOUNDATION: Oppenheim Students' Fund, Inc.
REQUISITE: Must be from Niagara County and male.
APPLICATION: Write for application, include transcript and three letters of recommendation before start of semester.
CONTACT: Anne Lascelle, Brd of Edctn, 607 Walnut Ave., Niagara Falls, NY 14301-1729 (Were not able to verify this listing; it may not be extant.)

ONEIDA

FOUNDATION: Alpha Delta Phi Memorial Scholarship Fund
REQUISITE: Must be an undergraduate of Hamilton college and a member of the society.
APPLICATION: Write for application. Deadline not listed.
CONTACT: 37 Williams St., Clinton, NY 13323-1705 TEL: (315)853-6673

FOUNDATION: Cogar Foundation
REQUISITE: Be a student or grad of Herkimer Cmmnty Cllg.
APPLICATION: Write during first quarter of the year.
CONTACT: c/o Director of Financial Aid, Herkimer Community College, Reservoir Rd., Herkimer, NY 13350 TEL: (315)886-0300

FOUNDATION: Harden Foundation, Inc.
REQUISITE: Must be from the central New York area.
APPLICATION: Write for application. No deadline.
CONTACT: David Harden, c/o Harden Furniture Co., McConnellsville, NY 13401 TEL: (315)245-1000

ONONDAGA

FOUNDATION: Amos Foundation, Inc.
REQUISITE: Must be within the community.
APPLICATION: Write for application. Deadline not listed.
CONTACT: John Amos, Pres., 1204 James St., Syracuse, NY 13203 TEL: (315)471-1187

FOUNDATION: Dikaia Foundation, Inc.
REQUISITE: Must be a student from Syracuse University.

APPLICATION: Write before 12/1 & show proof of financial need
CONTACT: P.O. Box 10, Syracuse, NY 13205 (We were not able to verify this listing; it may not be extant.)

FOUNDATION: Harry and Estella D. Eno Memorial Fund Trst
REQUISITE: Must be graduating senior from Charles W. Baker High School in Baldwinsville, NY.
APPLICATION: Write for application. Deadline 5/1.
CONTACT: Charles F. Coleman, Principal, Charles W. Baker High School, Baldwinsville, NY 13027 TEL: (315)638-6000

FOUNDATION: Peggy Hunter Memorial Scholarship Fndtn
REQUISITE: Must be a graduate of Marcellus High School.
APPLICATION: Write for application. Deadline not listed.
CONTACT: Guidance Office, Marcellus Central High School, Marcellus, NY 13108 TEL: (315)673-0298

FOUNDATION: Gretchen Landers Business Edctn Schlrshp Trst
REQUISITE: Must be a graduate of Liverpool High School in Liverpool, NY majoring in Business Education.
APPLICATION: Write for application. Deadline not listed.
CONTACT: Principal, Liverpool High School, Liverpool, NY 13088 TEL: (315)453-1500

FOUNDATION: Rinker Robinson Memorial Scholarship Fund
REQUISITE: Medical technology student at SUNY HSC at Syracuse.
APPLICATION: Write for application. Deadline varies.
CONTACT: c/o Upstate Medical Center, Clinical Pathology Dept., 750 East Adams St., Syracuse, NY 13210 TEL: (315)464-5540

FOUNDATION: Skaneateles Central School Endowment Fndtn
REQUISITE: Be graduating snr from Skaneateles Cntrl Schl
APPLICATION: Write for application. Deadline 4/30.
CONTACT: 49 East Elizabeth St., Skaneateles, NY 13152 (315)685-8361

FOUNDATION: Peter N. Whitcher Trust
REQUISITE: Son or daughter of a member in good standing of the Iron Workers District Counsel and from western NY Area.
APPLICATION: Write for application. Deadline 2/1.
CONTACT: PO Box 259, Skaneateles, NY 13152
(We were not able to verify this listing; it may not be extant.)

New York

ONTARIO

FOUNDATION: Ontario Childrens Home
REQUISITE: Must be from Ontario County, NY.
APPLICATION: Write for application. Deadline not listed.
CONTACT: PO Box 82, Canandaigua, NY 14424-0383   (716)396-4546

ORANGE

FOUNDATION: Carol A. Gregory & Angelo Calabrese Mmrl Trst
REQUISITE: Must be from Orange or Ulster Counties, NY. and furthering occupational training.
APPLICATION: Write for application. Deadline not listed.
CONTACT: William Calabrese, Orange/Ulster County BOCES, Gibson Rd., Goshen, NY 10924-9802   TEL: (914)294-5431

OSTEGO

FOUNDATION: Cooperstown Community Foundation
REQUISITE: Must be from Cooperstown, NY.
APPLICATION: Write for application. Deadline not listed.
CONTACT: Five Pine Blvd., Cooperstown, NY 13326-1020
(We were not able to verify this listing; it may not be extant.)

FOUNDATION: Carolyn Jenkins Trust f/b/o Scott Jenkins Fund
REQUISITE: Must be from State University College Oneonta.
APPLICATION: Write for application. Deadline not listed.
CONTACT: Donald Moore, 4015, State University College Oneonta, Oneonta, NY 13820 (607)436-3500

FOUNDATION: Phillip E. Potter Foundation
REQUISITE: Must be from Delaware or Ostego Counties, NY.
APPLICATION: Write for application. Deadline not listed.
CONTACT: c/o Henry L. Hulbert, Six Ford Ave., Oneonta, NY 13820
TEL: (607)432-6720

PUTNAM

FOUNDATION: Cris Foster Schlrshp Fund Charitable Trust
REQUISITE: Must be a Carmel High School graduating senior.
APPLICATION: Write for application. Deadline 4/1.

CONTACT: Carmel Hgh Schl, Carmel, NY 10512 TEL: (914)225-8441

QUEENS

FOUNDATION: Eddie Barnes Mmrl Music Schlrshp Fndtn
REQUISITE: Study of Music.
APPLICATION: Write for application. Deadline not listed.
CONTACT: Norli Bollag, Pres., 212-75 Whitehall Trc, Queens Village, NY 11427-1892 (We were not able to verify this listing; it may not be extant.)

FOUNDATION: Davis And Warshow Schlrshp Fndtn, Inc.
REQUISITE: Must be a full-time student.
APPLICATION: Write for application. Deadline 12/31.
CONTACT: Stanley Factor, 57-22 48th St., Maspeth, NY 11377 TEL: (718)937-9500

FOUNDATION: Nancy Kalinsky Scholarship Fund, Inc.
REQUISITE: Must be from NYC .
APPLICATION: Write for application. Deadline 6/1.
CONTACT: 45-40 218th St., Bayside, NY 11361-3538
(We were not able to verify this listing; it may not be extant.)

FOUNDATION: William F. Treacy Scholarship Fund
REQUISITE: None listed.
APPLICATION: Write for application. Deadline 6/1.
CONTACT: 115-06 Myrtle Ave., Richmond Hill, NY 11418
(We were not able to verify this listing; it may not be extant.)

RENSSELAER

FOUNDATION: Clarence Isham Pi Kappa Alpha Loan Fund
REQUISITE: Contact your college financial aid office.
APPLICATION: Write for application. Deadline 3/15.
CONTACT: 2144 Burdett Ave., Troy, NY 12180-3704

FOUNDATION: Clifford W. & Beryl H. Moul and West Sand Lake Grange # 949 Scholarship Fund
REQUISITE: Must be resident of Rensselaer County and be a student in certain fields related to agriculture.
APPLICATION: Write for application.
CONTACT: Charles L. Ballard, Chairman, Scholarship Committee, West

Sand Lake Grange #949, Box 3, Poestenkill, NY 12140

RICHMOND

FOUNDATION: Chesed Avrhom Hacohn Foundation
REQUISITE: Must be in rabbinical studies.
APPLICATION: Write for application. Deadline 4/1.
CONTACT: A. Romi Cohn, 5422 14th Ave., Brooklyn, NY 11219
(We were not able to verify this listing; it may not be extant.)

ROCKLAND

FOUNDATION: Ada Janow Jacobs Scholarship Fund, Inc.
REQUISITE: None listed.
APPLICATION: Write for application. Deadline 5/1.
CONTACT: Hugh Janow, Pres., 16 Deer Meadow Dr., West Nyack, NY
10994-1836 (We were not able to verify this listing; it may not be extant.)

FOUNDATION: Mayne Educational Fund
REQUISITE: None listed.
APPLICATION: Write for application. Deadline not listed.
CONTACT: Katherine Bartlett, 127 W Main St., Stony Point, NY 10980-1817 (We were not able to verify this listing; it may not be extant.)

SARATOGA

FOUNDATION: Hawley Foundation for Children
REQUISITE: Must be from Saratoga County, NY.
APPLICATION: Write or call for application. Deadline not listed.
CONTACT: Chamber of Commerce Bldg., 494 Broadway, Saratoga
Springs, NY 12866 TEL: (518)584-3255

FOUNDATION: Jehova Jireh,Inc.
REQUISITE: Protestant biblical, missionary, or theological student.
APPLICATION: Write for application. Deadline not listed.
CONTACT: Larry Deason, P.O. Box 795, Clinton Park, NY 12065 (We were not able to verify this listing; it may not be extant.)

SCHENECTADY

FOUNDATION: John Alexander Memorial Scholarship Fund

New York

REQUISITE: Be Schenectady resident attending law schl in NY.
APPLICATION: Write for application. Deadline 8/15.
CONTACT: Konray & Konray, 525 State St., Schenectady, NY 12305
TEL: (518)374-1200

FOUNDATION: The Golub Foundation
REQUISITE: Must be from area served by Price Chopper Sprmrkt.
APPLICATION: Write for application. Deadline 4/1.
CONTACT: Scholarship Committee, c/o Golub Corp., P.O. Box 1074,
Schenectady, NY 12301   TEL: (518)355-5000

FOUNDATION: The Schenectady Foundation
REQUISITE: Must be from Schenectady County, NY.
APPLICATION: Write for application. Deadline not listed.
CONTACT: P.O. Box 380, Schenectady, NY 12301 TEL: (518)372-4761

SCHUYLER

FOUNDATION: Northrup Educational Foundation, Inc.
REQUISITE: Must be from Schuyler County, NY.
APPLICATION: Write for application. Deadline 4/1.
CONTACT: Jane Isley, 116 11th St., Watkins Glenn, NY 14891-9809
(607)535-7438

STEUBEN

FOUNDATION: Lynn E. and Mattie McConnell Schlrshp Fnd
REQUISITE: 3 worthy protestant student in Prattsburg school dstrct.
APPLICATION: Write for application. Deadline 6/1.
CONTACT: Bath National Bank, 44 Liberty St., Bath, NY 14810   TEL:
(607)776-9661

SUFFOLK

FOUNDATION: Yvonne Bellew Daher Memorial Scholarship
REQUISITE: Be a graduating senior from West Islip Hgh Schl
APPLICATION: Write for application. Deadline not listed.
CONTACT: Director of Guidance, West Islip High School, West Islip, NY
11795 TEL: (516)422-1500

FOUNDATION: Eagalton War Memorial Scholarship Fund

REQUISITE: Be graduating snr from Bridgehampton Hgh Schl
APPLICATION: Write for application. Deadline not listed.
CONTACT: L. Alan Birtwhistle, Box 980, Bridgehampton 11932 TEL: (516)537-0271

FOUNDATION: EESCO Foundation, Inc.
REQUISITE: Must be from Greenport, NY.
APPLICATION: Get applications through schools.
CONTACT: Mike Burden, POB 530, Greenport, NY 11944-1719 TEL: (516)477-0265

FOUNDATION: The Joseph Monitto Memorial Fndtn, Inc.
REQUISITE: Must be the child of a full-time employee of Monitor Aerospace Corporation.
APPLICATION: Write for application. Deadline 11/1.
CONTACT: Dr. Claude Casey, 9897 NW 83rd Place, Ocala,. FL 32675 (We were not able to verify this listing; it may not be extant.)

FOUNDATION: Peter Donald Schild Memorial Scholarship Fund
REQUISITE: Must be from Huntington High School and have athletic achievement.
APPLICATION: Write for application. Deadline end of schl yr
CONTACT: 11 Maurice Ln., Huntington, NY 11743-1842 (516)673-2001

SULLIVAN

FOUNDATION: Lazare and Charlotte Kaplan Foundation, Inc.
REQUISITE: Must be a graduate from one of these four local schools: Jeffersonville, Rosco, Liberty, and Livinston Manner.
APPLICATION: Write for application. Deadline 5/1.
CONTACT: Irving Avery, P.O. Box 216, Livingston Manor, NY 12758 TEL: (914)439-4544

FOUNDATION: Charles P. and Pauline M. Kautz Foundation
REQUISITE: Must be from Delaware Senior High School.
APPLICATION: Write for application. Deadline not listed.
CONTACT: c/o Sylvia F. Mitterwager, United National Bank, Callicoon, NY 12723 TEL: (914)887-5305

FOUNDATION: Sawyer Scholarship Foundation
REQUISITE: None listed.

APPLICATION: Write for application. Deadline not listed.
CONTACT: United National Bank, Callicoon, NY 12723
(We were not able to verify this listing; it may not be extant.)

FOUNDATION: Judge Louis B. Scheinman Mmrl Schlrshp Fnd
REQUISITE: Must be from a Sullivan County high school.
APPLICATION: Write for application. Deadline not listed.
CONTACT: Stangel Dr., Woodbourne, NY 12788 TEL: (914)434-4110

TIOGA

FOUNDATION: Dale Allan Lampila Trust Fund
REQUISITE: Must be from Springville-Griffith Institute or Spencer-Van Etten Central School.
APPLICATION: Write for application. Deadline not listed.
CONTACT: Martin L. Fisher II, One Main St., Spencer, NY 14883-9767
(We were not able to verify this listing; it may not be extant.)

TOMPKINS

FOUNDATION: Alpha Psi of Chi Psi Educational Trust
REQUISITE: Must be a member of Chi Psi fraternity.
APPLICATION: Write for application. Deadline 4/30.
CONTACT: David Dunlop, 480 Brooktondale Rd., Brooktondale, NY 14817
(We were not able to verify this listing; it may not be extant.)

FOUNDATION: Coleman Student Fund, Inc.
REQUISITE: Must be graduate of Trumansburg Central School.
APPLICATION: Write for application. Deadline not listed.
CONTACT: 16 Elm St., Trumansburg, NY 14886
(We were not able to verify this listing; it may not be extant.)

WARREN

FOUNDATION: The Glens Falls Foundation
REQUISITE: Be graduating snr from a Glens Falls area hgh schl.
APPLICATION: Write or call for application. Deadline end of March, June, September, or December.
CONTACT: G. Nelson Lowe, P.O. Box 311, Glens Falls, NY 12801 TEL: (518)792-1151

FOUNDATION: Stephen J. Potter Memorial Foundation, Inc.
REQUISITE: Must be a graduate from Ticonderoga high school.
APPLICATION: Write for application. Deadline not listed.
CONTACT: John Austin, 47 Sunnyside East, Queensburg, NY 12804 TEL: (518)793-3712

FOUNDATION: The E. Leo and Louise F. Spain Schlrshp Fndtn
REQUISITE Must be from Saint Mary's Academy or other Glens Falls area high schools.
APPLICATION: Write for application. Deadline not listed.
CONTACT: Robert J. O'Brien, 83 Bay St., Box 785, Glens Falls, NY 12801
TEL: (518)793-5173

WASHINGTON

FOUNDATION: Belle C. Burnett Foundation
REQUISITE: Be a graduating senior from Salem Cntrl Hgh Schl
APPLICATION: Write for application. Deadline 6/1.
CONTACT: Salem Central School, Guidance Office, E Broadway, Salem, NY 12865 (We were not able to verify this listing; it may not be extant.)

WESTCHESTER

FOUNDATION: Joseph B. Corpina, Jr. Mmrl Foundation, Inc.
REQUISITE: Have been stdnt at Iona Grammar Schl, Scarsdale
APPLICATION: Write for application. Deadline not listed.
CONTACT: Joseph B. Corpina, 46 Candlewood Rd., Scarsdale, NY 10583-6041 TEL: (914)633-7744

FOUNDATION: Arthur J. Gavrin Foundation, Inc.
REQUISITE: Be a graduating senior of New Rochelle Hgh Schl
APPLICATION: Write for application. Deadline 4/1.
CONTACT: Marvin Bookbinder, Guidance Dept., New Rochelle High School, New Rochelle, NY TEL: (914)576-4500

FOUNDATION: Andrea Nadel Griffin Memorial Fndtn, Inc.
REQUISITE: None listed.
APPLICATION: Write for application. Deadline not listed.
CONTACT: Murray Nadel, 433 Beechmont Dr., New Rochelle 10804-4617
TEL: (914)937-5141

FOUNDATION: Humanas, Inc.
REQUISITE: None listed.
APPLICATION: Write for application 6 months prior to schl yr
CONTACT: Herbert Gstalder, 15 Croosridge Rd., Chappaqua, NY 10514-2103 (We were not able to verify this listing; it may not be extant.)

FOUNDATION: Rye Rotary Foundation, Inc.
REQUISITE: Must be from Rye High School, NY.
APPLICATION: Write for application. Deadline 3/1.
CONTACT: c/o Alfano and Alfono, P.C., 350 Theo. Fremd Ave., Rye, NY 10580
(We were not able to verify this listing; it may not be extant.)

FOUNDATION: Tyler Foundation, Inc.
REQUISITE: None listed.
APPLICATION: Write for application. Deadline not listed.
CONTACT: Parker Tyler, Jr., POB 536, Nine Hunts Ln., Chappaqua, NY 10514-0536 (We were not able to verify this listing; it may not be extant.)

FOUNDATION: Adolph Vanpelt Foundation, Inc.
REQUISITE: Must be a Native American student.
APPLICATION: Write for application. Deadline 4/15.
CONTACT: Olga Karch, Fargo Ln., Irvington, NY 10533
(We were not able to verify this listing; it may not be extant.)

FOUNDATION: Visiting Nurse Association of Rye, Inc.
REQUISITE: Must be from Rye, NY studying Medical Edctn
APPLICATION: Write for application. Deadline 4/15.
CONTACT: Michael Grean, 15 Elm Place, Rye, NY 10580 (914)666-7616

FOUNDATION: The Horbach Fund
REQUISITE: Must be a needy, gifted, young person under the age of 20 who resides in CT, MA, NJ, NY, or RI.
APPLICATION: Write for info. Deadline August 1.
CONTACT: c/o National Community Bank of NJ, 113 W. Essex St., Maywood, NJ 07607
(We were not able to verify this listing; it may not be extant.)

FOUNDATION: Dan River Foundation
REQUISITE: Scholarships for employees, or children of current, deceased, or retired employees of Dan River, Inc. in NY, Virginia, or South Carolina.

APPLICATION: Deadline is the last day of February.
CONTACT: POB 261, Danville, VA 24541. Or Chairman, Scholarship Committee, Dan River Foundation, POB 2178, Danville, VA 24541. TEL: (804)799-7000

OHIO

FOUNDATION: Cleveland Area Citizens League for Nursing
REQUISITE: Scholarships granted to Cleveland area residents in Cuyahoga; Geauga; Lake; Lorain counties who will agree to work in a health-care facility in this area for at least one year after graduation. Must be US citizen.
APPLICATION: Write for info. Application deadline is 2/1 - 5/1.
CONTACT: 2800 Euclid Ave Ste 235, Cleveland, OH 44115 216-781-7222

FOUNDATION: Cuyahoga County Medical Foundation
REQUISITE: Scholarships granted to residents of Cuyahoga county who are enrolled in an accredited professional school for Medicine; Dentistry; Pharmacy; Nursing; or Osteopathy. Must be US citizen.
APPLICATION: Write for info. Application deadline is June 1st.
CONTACT: 11001 Cedar Ave., Cleveland, OH 44106 Tel: 216-229-2200

FOUNDATION: Academy of Medicine of Clevelan Auxiliary
REQUISITE: Scholarships granted to residents of Cuyahoga cnty accepted to an accredited Cuyahogo County Professional school and is able to demonstrate financial need. Must have at least a 2.0 GPA.
APPLICATION: Write for info. Application deadline is April 1st.
CONTACT: 11001 Cedar Ave., Cleveland, OH 44106 216-229-2200

FOUNDATION: Cuyahoga County Medical Foundation
REQUISITE: Scholarships granted to residents of Cuyahoga County who are accepted into or enrolled in an accredited institution majoring in Medicine; Dentistry; Pharmacy; Nursing or Osteopathy.
Must be US citizen.
APPLICATION: Write for info. Application deadline is June 1st.
CONTACT: 11001 Cedar Ave., Cleveland, OH 44106. (216)443-7000

FOUNDATION: Ohio Arts Council
REQUISITE: Scholarships granted to high school seniors that are residents of Ohio who wish to continue their arts training and education at an accredited institution in the state of Ohio.

APPLICATION: Write for info. Application deadline varies.
CONTACT: 727 E. Main St., Columbus, OH 43205. (614)466-2613

FOUNDATION: Dr. R.S. Hosler Memorial Educational Fund
REQUISITE: Must be a high school graduate of Teays Valley or Amanda Clearcreek, OH, school systems.
APPLICATION: Write for info. No deadline listed.
CONTACT: Vaundell White, Trustee, 154 E. Main St., Ashville, OH 43103 (Apply at these specific schools.)

FOUNDATION: Charles F. High Foundation
REQUISITE: Must be a male resident of OH who plans to attend OH State University.
APPLICATION: Write for info. Deadline June 1.
CONTACT: John R. Clime, Secty.-Treasurer, 1520 Melody Dr., Bucyrus, OH 44820 TEL: (419)562-2074

FOUNDATION: August Michael Rocco Scholarship Foundation
REQUISITE: Must be a graduate of Central Catholic High School or St. Thomas Aquinas in Stark County, OH, who plans to attend Notre Dame University IN.
APPLICATION: Write for info. No deadline listed.
CONTACT: Christine E. Sutton-Kruman, AmeriTrust Co., 237 Tuscarawas St. W., Canton, OH 44702 TEL: (216)833-0310

FOUNDATION: Chester A. & Ethel J. Seran Scholarship Fund
REQUISITE: Must be an undergraduate student who is a member of Westbrook Park United Methodist Church, enrolled at Otterbein or Malone cllgs, or from the Stark County area.
APPLICATION: Submit letter requesting application. No deadln
CONTACT: Christine Sutton-Kruman, AmeriTrust Co. National Association, 237 Tuscarawas St. W., Canton, OH 44702 TEL: (216)833-0310

FOUNDATION: The Stark County Foundation
REQUISITE: Must be a student who resides in Stark Cnty
APPLICATION: Interviews, references, & grade records required. Applications not reviewed by foundation. Separate board reviews & interviews applicants. Deadline March 1.
CONTACT: Cynthia Lazor, VP Progammer, Untd Bnk Bldg., 331 Market Ave S, Canton, OH 44702-2107 TEL: (216)454-3426

FOUNDATION: Eleanor M. Webster Testamentary Trust
REQUISITE: Must be a student who has completed at least 1 year of study at an OH college or university. Preference given to any resident of Stark County, OH.
APPLICATION: Submit letter requesting application. No deadln
CONTACT: Steven N. More, AmeriTrust Co., 237 Tuscarawas St. W., Canton, OH 44702 (216)833-0310

FOUNDATION: William P. Anderson Foundation
REQUISITE: Must reside in Cincinnati, OH, or Boston, MA.
APPLICATION: Submit letter for application. No deadln
CONTACT: Paul D. Myers, Secty., 3552 Bayard Rd., Cincinnati, OH 45208
(We were not able to verify this listing; it may not be extant.)

FOUNDATION: Scripps Howard Foundation
REQUISITE: Must be a professional print & broadcast journalist or a student who is pursuing this career.
APPLICATION: Deadline 12/20 for initial submission consisting of a self-addressed typewritten mailing label with the words "Scholarship Application," only. Application packets will be mailed by the fndtn in late December, & must be returned by 2/25
CONTACT: Albert J. Schottelkotte, Pres., POB 5380, Cincinnati, OH 45201
TEL: (513)977-3035

FOUNDATION: New Orphan Asylum Scholarship Foundation
REQUISITE: Must be a resident of, or a graduate of a high school in the greater Cincinnati, OH, area.
APPLICATION: Write for info. Deadline July 31.
CONTACT: Norma Lane, 2340 Victory Parkway, Ste. 1, Cincinnati, OH 45206 TEL: (513)961-6626

FOUNDATION: The Ratner, Miller, Shafran Foundation
REQUISITE: Must reside in Cuyahoga County, OH.
APPLICATION: Write for info. Deadline May 1.
CONTACT: Nathan Shafran, 10800 Brookpark Rd., Cleveland, OH 44130
TEL: (216)267-1200

FOUNDATION: Meftah Scholarship Foundation
REQUISITE: Must be a recent immigrant or a refugee youth who is planning to study in a college in OH.
APPLICATION: Interviews required. Write for info. No deadln

CONTACT: Michael Meftah, M.D. or Patricia Meftah, 2777 McCoy Rd., Columbus, OH 43220
(We were not able to verify this listing; it may not be extant.)

FOUNDATION: George J. Record School Foundation
REQUISITE: Must be a legal resident of Ashtabula County, OH.
APPLICATION: Interviews required. Write for info. Deadline May 20 for freshmen & June 20 for upperclassmen.
CONTACT: Charles N. Lafferty, Pres. & Exec. Dir., POB 581, Conneaut, OH 44030 TEL: (216)599-8283

FOUNDATION: Coshocton Foundation
REQUISITE: Must reside in Coshocton County, OH.
APPLICATION: Apply through high schools.
CONTACT: Orville Fuller, Treasurer, or Sam C. Clow, Chairman, Distribution Committee, POB 15, Coshocton, OH 43812 (614)622-0010

FOUNDATION: Harry W. & Margaret Moore Foundation, Inc.
REQUISITE: Undergraduate student from Dayton area who plans to attend a local public, non-sectarian university.
APPLICATION: Write or call for info. No deadline listed.
CONTACT: Mary Ann Price, Secty.-Treasurer, 5051 Kitridge Rd., Dayton, OH 45424 TEL: (513)233-0233

FOUNDATION: Charles Kilburger Scholarship Fund
REQUISITE: Must be a resident of Fairfield County, OH, & be recommended by a guidance counselor at a high school or college.
APPLICATION: Interviews required. Individual application without recommendation of a guidance counselor will not be accepted. Write for further info. No deadline listed.
CONTACT: Scott Shephard, Equitable Bldg., Lancaster, OH 43130 TEL: (614)654-6711

FOUNDATION: The Flickinger Memorial Trust, Inc.
REQUISITE: Must reside in OH.
APPLICATION: Interviews required. Write for info. No deadline
CONTACT: F. Miles Flickinger, M.D., Chairman, 115 W. North St., POB 1255, Lima, OH 45802 (We were not able to verify this listing; it may not be extant.)

FOUNDATION: The Wagnalls Memorial

Ohio

REQUISITE: Graduate of a high school in Bloom Township, OH.
APPLICATION: Submit letter for application. Deadline June 15.
CONTACT: Jerry W. Neff, Exec. Dir., 150 E. Columbus St., POB 217, Lithopolis, OH 43136 TEL: (614)837-4765

FOUNDATION: The Community Fndtn of Greater Lorain Cnty
REQUISITE: Must reside in Lorain County, OH.
APPLICATION: Applications for Nord Scholarships may be obtained from any Lorain County high school counselor; applications for Chronicle-Telegram Scholarships available from the newspaper's offices in Elyria; applications for other scholarship programs available from foundation. Write for more info. Deadline 4/15 for Lake Erie Electric Scholarships & April 21 for Elyria Chronicle-Telegram Scholarships & Nord Scholarships.
CONTACT: Carol G. Simonetti, Exec. Dir., 1865 N. Ridge Rd. East, Ste. A, Lorain, OH 44055 TEL: (216)277-0142

FOUNDATION: James R. Nicholl Memorial Foundation
REQUISITE: Medical school scholarships only. Must be a needy student who has been a resident of Lorain County, OH, for at least 2 years & intends to return to Lorain County to practice.
APPLICATION: Write for info. No deadline listed.
CONTACT: David E. Nocjar, Trust Officer, c/o The Central Trust Co. of Northern OH, Trust Dept., 1949 Broadway, Lorain, OH 44052 TEL: (216)244-1965

FOUNDATION: Martha Holden Jennings Foundation
REQUISITE: Scholarships granted to Ohio classroom teachers that carry out projects which they believe may improve the quality of education in their schools.
APPLICATION: Write for info. Application deadline is not specified.
CONTACT: C/O Business Manager; 4225 Mayfield #102A, South Euclid, OH 44121. (216)589-5700

FOUNDATION: The S.N. Ford & Ada Ford Fund
REQUISITE: Must reside in Richland County, OH.
APPLICATION: Write for info. No deadline listed.
CONTACT: Ralph H. LeMunyon, Distribution Committee, 35 N. Park St., Mansfield, OH 440901 TEL: (419)526-3493

FOUNDATION: The Richland County Fndtn of Mansfield, Ohio
REQUISITE: Must be a full-time undergraduate student who is a resident

of Richland County, OH.
APPLICATION: Submit your grade transcript along with your application. You must also file a Financial Aid Form (FAF) with College Scholarship Service using foundation's code number (which appears on the application form). Applications available from foundation after January 1 for following academic year. No deadline listed.
CONTACT: Amy Marinelli, 24 West Third St., Suite 100, Mansfield, OH 44902 TEL: (419)525-3020

FOUNDATION: The Paul & Adelyn C. Shumaker Foundation
REQUISITE: Must be a resident of Richland County, OH, who is a graduate student studying for the medical profession.
APPLICATION: Write for info. No deadline listed.
CONTACT: R. J. Sutter, Senior VP, c/o Bank One, Trust, 28 Park Ave. W., Mansfield, OH 44902   (419)525-5700

FOUNDATION: John Q. Shunk Association
REQUISITE: Must be a graduate of Bucyrus High School, Colonel Crawford High School, Wynford High School, or Buckeye Central High School in Crawford County, OH.
APPLICATION: Applications available at guidance offices of the specified high schools. Write for complete info. Deadline February 15. Scholarships must be renewed each year.
CONTACT: Jane C. Peppard, 1201 Timber Ln., Marion, OH 43302 TEL: (614)389-3132

FOUNDATION: The Gardner Foundation
REQUISITE: Must be a graduating senior of Middletown or Hamilton County, OH. Must also be a student planning to attend a non tax-supported college.
APPLICATION: Write for info. Deadline April 1.
CONTACT: Calvin F. Lloyd, Secty., POB 126, Middletown 45042
(We were not able to verify this listing; it may not be extant.)

FOUNDATION: Edwin L. & Louis B. McCallay Edctnl Trst Fnd
REQUISITE: Must be a graduate of a high school in the Middletown, OH, city school district, including Fenwick Hgh Schl.
APPLICATION: Applications can be obtained at high schools in the Middletown, OH, city school district. No deadline listed.
CONTACT: Trust Officer, First National Bank of Southwestern Ohio, 2 North Main, Middletown, OH 45042 TEL: (513)425-7674

FOUNDATION: Beta Theta Pi Fraternity Founders Fund
REQUISITE: Must be a member of any Beta Theta Pi fraternity.
APPLICATION: Write for info. Deadline April 15.
CONTACT: Thomas A. Beyer, Administrative Secty., 208 E. High St., POB
111, Oxford, OH 45056 TEL: (513)523-7591

FOUNDATION: Kibble Foundation
REQUISITE: Must be a graduate of a high school in Meigs County, OH,
pursuing a 4-year degree or a lesser technical degree on a full-time basis.
APPLICATION: Write for info. No deadline listed.
CONTACT: POB 723, Pomeroy, OH 45769
(We were not able to verify this listing; it may not be extant.)

FOUNDATION: The Simmons Charitable Trust
REQUISITE: Music scholarship to any student of Steubenville High
School, OH.
APPLICATION: Write for info. No deadline listed.
CONTACT: c/o Miners & Mechanics Savings & Trust Co., 124 N. Fourth
St., Steubenville, OH 43952   TEL: (614)284-5600

FOUNDATION: Scholarship Fund, Inc.
REQUISITE: Must be a needy student with a good academic record who
resides in the northwest OH area, with emphasis on anyone pursuing a
baccalaureate degree. Preference given to any student who is upper
class, highly ranked, & is commuting.
APPLICATION: Interviews required. Write for info. No deadline
CONTACT: c/o Dean Ernest Weaver, Jr., Secty., University of Toledo,
2801 W. Bancroft St., Toledo, OH 43606 TEL: (419)537-4632

FOUNDATION: The Van Wert County Foundation
REQUISITE: Must reside in Van Wert County, OH.
APPLICATION: Interviews required. Write for info. Deadlines 5/25 & 11/25.
CONTACT: Robert W. Games. Exec. Secty., 101-1/2 E. Main St., Van
Wert, OH 45891   (419)238-1743

FOUNDATION: The Hauss-Helms Foundation, Inc.
REQUISITE: Must be needy graduating high school student who resides
in Auglaize or Allen counties, OH
APPLICATION: Submit letter for application. Deadline 1/5.
CONTACT: James E. Weger, Pres., People's National Bank Bldg., POB
25, Wapakoneta, OH 45895 TEL: (419)738-4911

FOUNDATION: Frank F. Bentley Trust
REQUISITE: Must be a graduate of a hgh schl in Trumbull Cnty
APPLICATION: Submit letter for application by mid-summer.
CONTACT: Lawrence Turner, Turner & May, 185 High St. Northeast, Warren, OH 44481 (216) 399-8801

FOUNDATION: Alice A. Andrus Foundation
REQUISITE: Graduate of Wellington High School, Wellington, OH.
APPLICATION: Must submit letter, including amount & purpose. No deadline listed.
CONTACT: Robert F. Shaffer, Jr., Principal, Wellington Hgh Schl, 629 N. Main St., Wellington, OH 44090

FOUNDATION: John W. Landis Scholarship Trust
REQUISITE: Must be a resident of Wayne County, OH, who is a high school graduate & desires further education, not necessarily leading to a degree, in agriculture, horticulture, home economics, farm economics, animal husbandry, soil & water conservation, or forestry.
APPLICATION: Available from, & returned to, Wayne Cnty Sprntndnt of Schls, 2534 Burbank Rd., Wooster, OH 44691 by 3/15
CONTACT: c/o D. Williams Evans, Jr., 1670 Christmas Run, Wooster, OH 44691 (We were not able to verify this listing; it may not be extant.)

FOUNDATION: Veronica Willo Scholarship Fund
REQUISITE: Must be a graduating senior of a Mahoning County, OH, high school who has been nominated for this award.
APPLICATION: Nominations are to be made by Mahoning Cnty hgh schl principals. Individual applications will not be accepted.
CONTACT: c/o Bank One of Eastern OH, N.A., POB 359, Youngstown, OH 44501 TEL: (216)744-5041

FOUNDATION: Esther Hamilton Alias Santa Claus Club Schlrshp Fnd
REQUISITE: Must be a graduating senior in the top 25 percent of your class of all city, county, or parochial high schools in Mahoning County, OH. You must also be planning to attend Youngstown State University.
APPLICATION: Interviews required. Applications available from high school principals. Deadline June of graduation year.
CONTACT: Herbert H. Pridham, Sr., VP, Dollar Savings & Trust Co., POB 450, Youngstown, OH 44501 (We were not able to verify this listing; it may not be extant.)

FOUNDATION: John McIntire Educational Fund
REQUISITE: Must be a resident of Zanesville, OH, who is single & under 21 years of age.
APPLICATION: Write for info. Deadline May 1.
CONTACT: R. L. Hecker, Snr Trust Officer, First National Bank, Trust Dept., POB 2668, 422 Main St., Zanesville, OH 43701 (614)452-8444

FOUNDATION: Blanche & Thomas Hope Memorial Fund
REQUISITE: Must be a student who is graduating from a high school in Boyd or Greenup counties, KY, or Lawrence County,
APPLICATION: Interviews required. Write for info by 3/1.
CONTACT: National City Bank, POB 1270, Ashland, KY 41105 TEL: (606)329-2900

FOUNDATION: Avon Products Foundation, Inc.
REQUISITE: Must be a child of a current Avon Products, Inc. employee or a high school senior who resides in proximity to an Avon location.
APPLICATION: Write for info. Deadline November 2.
CONTACT: Glenn S. Clarke, Pres., Nine W. 57th St., New York, NY 10019 TEL: (212)546-6015

FOUNDATION: Amcast Industrial Foundation
REQUISITE: Scholarship for children of employees of Amcast Industrial Corporations.
APPLICATION: Applications are accepted throughout the year.
CONTACT: 3931 South Dixie Avenue, Kettering, OH 45439. Thomas Amato, Secretary-Treasurer. TEL: (513)291-7000

FOUNDATION: Austin Powder Foundation
REQUISITE: Scholarships for children and wards of full-time employees of the Austin Powder Corporation.
APPLICATION: Applications are accepted throughout the year.
CONTACT: c/o Austin Powder Company, 3690 Orange Place, Cleveland, OH 44122. Dr. Walter Nosal, Scholarship Committee. (216)464-2400

FOUNDATION: Caldwell (James R.) Scholarship Fund
REQUISITE: Scholarships for children of full-time employees of Rubbermaid, Inc. with at least two years of service.
APPLICATION: Application deadline is March 15th.
CONTACT: Send a postcard requesting an application to this address: c/o Rubbermaid, Inc., 1147 Akron Rd.,Wooster, OH 44691;

Tel.:(216)264-7119. Or c/o Wayne County National Bank, Public Square, Box 550, Wooster, OH 44691. Tel.:(216)264-1222.

FOUNDATION: Cooper Industries Foundation
REQUISITE: Scholarships for children of employees of Cooper Industries, Inc. in AL, CA, CT, GA, IL, IN, ME, MI, MO, MS, NJ, NY, NC, OH, OK, PA, SC, TN, TX, and VA.
APPLICATION: Applications are accepted throughout the year.
CONTACT: First City Tower, Suite 4000, POB 4446, Houston, TX 77210. Patricia B. Meinecke, Secretary. TEL: (713)739-5632

FOUNDATION: Crosset Family Fund
REQUISITE: Scholarships and loans for children of employees of The Crosset Company, Inc..
APPLICATION: Write for info on application requirements.
CONTACT: 205 Central Ave., Cincinnati, OH 45202. Richard Crosset, Trustee. TEL: (513)421-5511

FOUNDATION: Kuntz Foundation
REQUISITE: Scholarships for children of employees of The Peter Kuntz Company.
APPLICATION: Contact for current application requirements.
CONTACT: 120 W 2nd Street, Dayton, OH 45402. TEL: (513)294-4787

FOUNDATION: Marathon Oil Foundation, Inc.
REQUISITE: Scholarships and awards for children of employees of Marathon Oil Company studying for a B.A.
APPLICATION: Applications are accepted from October 1st to January 1st of their senior year.
CONTACT: 539 South Main St., Room 4125, Findlay, OH 45840. J.S. Dimling, Vice-President. TEL: (419)422-2121

FOUNDATION: National Machinery Foundation, Inc.
REQUISITE: Scholarships for high school seniors or first-year graduates who are children of employees of National Machinery.
APPLICATION: Write for application information.
CONTACT: Greenfield Street, PO Box 747, Tiffin, OH 44883. D.B. Bero, Administrator. (419)447-5211

FOUNDATION: Premier Industrial Foundation
REQUISITE: Scholarships for employees, and their close relatives, of

Premier Industrial Corporation.
APPLICATION: Applications are accepted throughout the year.
CONTACT: 4500 Euclid Ave., Cleveland, OH 44103. Morton Mandel, Trustee. TEL: (216)391-8300

FOUNDATION: Taft(Hulbert) Jr. Memorial Schlrshp Fndtn
REQUISITE: Scholarships for children of employees of the Taft Broadcasting Company.
APPLICATION: Application deadline is February 27th.
CONTACT: c/o Taft Broadcasting Company, 1718 Young Street, Cincinnati, OH 45210. Dudley Taft, President.

FOUNDATION: Timken Company Educational Fund, Inc.
REQUISITE: Scholarships for children of employees of the Timken Company.
APPLICATION: Contact for application deadlines.
CONTACT: 1835 Dueber Ave., S.W., Canton, OH 44706. Thomas Grove, Supervisor-Education Programs. TEL: (216)438-3000

FOUNDATION: TRW Foundation
REQUISITE: Schlrshps for children of employees of TRW Inc
APPLICATION: Contact for more information.
CONTACT: 1900 Richmond Road, Cleveland, OH 44124. Donna Cummings, Manager. TEL: (216)291-7164

FOUNDATION: Ohio Baptist Education Society
REQUISITE: Scholarships granted to Ohio residents that are members of an Ohio Baptist Convention Church. Undergraduate sophomores at an accredited institution are eligible. Must be USA citizen or legal resident. Must demonstrate need.
APPLICATION: Write for info. Application deadline is April 1st.
CONTACT: POBOX 288, Granville, OH 43023. Tel: (614)349-9136

FOUNDATION: Flickinger Memorial Trust, Inc.
REQUISITE: Student loans for residents of Ohio.
APPLICATION: Applications are accepted throughout the year.
CONTACT: 115 West North Street, P.O. Box 1255, Lima, OH 45802. F. Miles Flickinger, M.D., Chairman.
(We were not able to verify this listing; it may not be extant.)

FOUNDATION: Moore (Harry W. & Margaret) Foundation, Inc.

REQUISITE: Low-interest loans for undergraduates who plan to attend local public, non-sectarian schools.
APPLICATION: Applications are accepted throughout the year.
CONTACT: 5051 Kietridge Rd., Dayton, OH 45424. A.C. Reiger, Jr., Secretary-Treasurer. (513)233-0233

OKLAHOMA

FOUNDATION: Lippoldt (Arthur H.)Trust
REQUISITE: Scholarships for students who attend the University of Oklahoma and meet the academic requirements.
APPLICATION: Contact for application and more information.
CONTACT: 4123 North Spenser Road, Spencer, OK 73084. Ed J. Poole, Trustee. (We were not able to verify this listing; it may not be extant.)

FOUNDATION: Sussman (Otto) Trust
REQUISITE: Education expenses for residents of Oklahoma who are in need due to illness or death in their immediate family or some other unusual or unfortunate circumstance.
APPLICATION: Applications accepted all year. Write for more information.
CONTACT: POB 1374, Trainsmeadow Station, Flushing, NY 11370

FOUNDATION: Ullery Charitable Trust
REQUISITE: Scholarships for students studying at Presbyterian theological seminaries.
APPLICATION: Applications accepted all year. Write for more information.
CONTACT: c/o Liberty Bank and Trust Company, N.A., POB 1, Tulsa, OK 74193. Marilyn Pierce, Trust Officer. TEL: (918)586-5845

FOUNDATION: Cooper Industries Foundation
REQUISITE: Scholarships for children of employees of Cooper Industries, Inc. in AL, CA, CT, GA, IL, IN, ME, MI, MO, MS, NJ, NY, NC, OH, OK, PA, SC, TN, TX, and VA.
APPLICATION: Applications are accepted throughout the year.
CONTACT: First City Tower, Suite 4000, POB 4446, Houston, TX 77210. Patricia B. Meinecke, Secretary. TEL: (713)739-5632

FOUNDATION: Dyco Foundation
REQUISITE: Scholarships for children of employees of Dyco Petroleum Corporation.
APPLICATION: Application deadline is March 30th.

CONTACT: 1100 Interchange Tower, Minneapolis, MN 55426. Alicia Ringstad, Director. (612)545-4021

FOUNDATION: Educational Fund for Children of Phillips Petroleum Company Employees
REQUISITE: Scholarships for children of present or deceased full-time employees of Phillip Petroleum Company. They must have been employed at least three year.
APPLICATION: Application deadline is March 7th.
CONTACT: 180 Plaza Office Building, Batlesville, OK 74004. Bill Dausses, Administrator. (918)661-6600

FOUNDATION: Noble (The Samuel Roberts) Foundation, Inc.
REQUISITE: Scholarships for children of employees of Noble-affiliated companies.
APPLICATION: Write for more information.
CONTACT: POB 2180, Ardmore, OK 73402. John F. Snodgrass, President. TEL: (405)223-5810

FOUNDATION: Phillips (Frank) Educational Loan Fund
REQUISITE: Loans for children of present, deceased, or retired employees of the Phillips Petroleum Company.
APPLICATION: Application deadline is August 1st.
CONTACT: c/o Phillips Petroleum Company, 750A Plaza Office Building, Bartlesville, OK 74004. Or Bill F. Dausses, Director, Educational Funds, 180 Plaza Office Building, Bartlesville, OK 74004 (918)661-6600

FOUNDATION: Fields (Laura) Trust
REQUISITE: Student loans for residents of Comanche County,
APPLICATION: Applications are accepted throughout the year.
CONTACT: 2106 Atlanta, Lawton, OK 73505. Jay Dee Fountain, Executive Secretary. TEL: (405)355-3733

FOUNDATION: Johnson (Dexter G.) Edctnl & Benevolent Trst
REQUISITE: Educational loans for residents of Oklahoma.
APPLICATION: Applications are accepted throughout the year.
CONTACT: 900 First City Place, Oklahoma City, OK 73102. Phil Daugherty, Trustee.
(We were not able to verify this listing; it may not be extant.)

OREGON

FOUNDATION: Oregon State Scholarship Commission
REQUISITE: Scholarships granted to Oregon residents who have been accepted to or are enrolled in a School of Barbering; Hair Design; Cosmetology or Manicure which is located in the state of Oregon. Must be US citizen or legal resident.
APPLICATION: Write for info. Application deadline is December 1st.
CONTACT: 1445 Willamette Street, Eugene, OR 97401. 503-686-4166

FOUNDATION: Verne Catt McDowell Corporation
REQUISITE: Member of the Christian Church, Disciples of Christ, & use the scholarship for graduate theological studies.
APPLICATION: Interviews required. Write for info. No deadline
CONTACT: Katherine Buike, BX 128, Albany 97321
(We were not able to verify this listing; it may not be extant.)

FOUNDATION: Tektronix Foundation
REQUISITE: Must be a child of a Tektronix, Inc., employee or a student who attends high school in Clackamas, Washington, or Multnomah county, OR, or in Clark County, WA.
APPLICATION: Interviews required for finalists. Write for further info. Deadline March 15.
CONTACT: Thomas O. Williams, Administrator, Y 3-439, POB 500, Beaverton, OR 97077   (503)627-7111

FOUNDATION: Bend Foundation
REQUISITE: Scholarships to any resident of Bend or Deschutes Cnty, OR, who is a graduate of Bend or Mountain View High Schools.
APPLICATION: Guidelines available from Administrative School District No. 1, Bend, OR. Write for further info. Deadline April.
CONTACT: Michael P. Hollern, Trustee, 416 NE Greenwood, Bend, OR 97701 TEL: (503)382-1662

FOUNDATION: Bowerman Foundation
REQUISITE: Scholarships & research grants primarily to any resident of Eugene, OR.
APPLICATION: Write for info. & include your name, address, transcripts, grades & tuition fees. No deadline listed.
CONTACT: Donald A. Gallagher, Jr., Secty., 825 E. Park St., Eugene, OR 97401 (We were not able to verify this listing; it may not be extant.)

Oregon

FOUNDATION: Collins-McDonald Trust Fund
REQUISITE: Scholarships for higher education limited to any graduate of a Lake County, OR, high school.
APPLICATION: Interviews required. Write for info. Deadln 5/14
CONTACT: James C. Lynch, Trustee, 620 N. First St., POB 351, Lakeview, OR 97630   (503)947-2196

FOUNDATION: Bernard Daly Educational Fund
REQUISITE: Schlrshps to student in Lake Cnty for study at any OR state-supported university, college, or technical school.
APPLICATION: Write Trst for info & application deadline.
CONTACT: James C. Lynch, Secty., POB 351, Lakeview, OR 97630 TEL: (503)947-2196

FOUNDATION: Burt Snyder Educational Foundation
REQUISITE: Graduate from a Lake County, OR, area hgh schl
APPLICATION: Contact foundation for current application info. No deadline listed.
CONTACT: Jim Lynch, 620 N. First St., POB 351, Lakeview, OR 97630 TEL: (503)947-2196

FOUNDATION: Virginia A. Archer Scholarship Trust Fund
REQUISITE: Scholarships to any graduating senior of a Multnomah County, OR, high school planning to attend an OR college or university.
APPLICATION: Submit letter for application Deadline 4/1
CONTACT: Ralph J. Shepherd, 319 S.W. Washington, Ste. 920, Portland, OR 97204 TEL: (503)224-3015

FOUNDATION: The Saidie Orr Dunbar Nursing Education Fund
REQUISITE: Scholarships to any individual accepted in a master's or doctoral nursing degree program in OR which emphasizes the education of community health nurses. You must practice in OR upon graduation.
APPLICATION: Interviews required of finalists. Write or call for info. Deadline between 12/1 & 3/30.
CONTACT: Evelyn Schindler, Chrmn, American Lung Association of OR, 9320 S.W. Barbur Blvd., Portland, OR 97219 TEL: (503)246-1997

FOUNDATION: Ben Selling Scholarship
REQUISITE: OR resident who is attending an OR school.
APPLICATION: School transcript & proof of enrollment required. Write for further info. Deadline 8/15. Applications accepted between 6/1 & 8/15.

CONTACT: Charles D. Woodcock, Trst Officer, 1st Interstate Bank of OR, POB 2971, Portland, OR 97208

FOUNDATION: Harley & Mertie Stevens Memorial Fund
REQUISITE: Graduate of a Clackamas County, OR, high school who is attending a college or university supported by OR state or owned & operated by any Protestant church organization.
APPLICATION: Interviews for scholarship finalists required. Additional info. may be obtained from foundation. Deadlines May 15 for scholarships & between June 1 & June 15 for loans.
CONTACT: Jami Fabianek, c/o U.S. National Bank of OR, POB 7369, Clamath Falls, OR 97603 TEL: (503)225-3174

FOUNDATION: Merle S. & Emma J. West Scholarship Fund
REQUISITE: High school graduate residing in Klamath Cnty
APPLICATION: Interviews required. For application info. contact Francis S. Landrum, Chairman, West Scholarship Committee, 740 Main St., Klamath Falls, OR 97601
CONTACT: Jami Fabianek, c/o U.S. National Bnk of OR, POB 7369, Clamath Falls, OR 97603 TEL: (503)883-3857

FOUNDATION: Ochoco Scholarship Fund
REQUISITE: Resident of the Prineville (Crook Cnty), OR, area who has been in college at least one year.
APPLICATION: Write for info. Deadline is in August.
CONTACT: David Doty, Trustee, Crook County High School, E. First St., Prineville, OR 97754 TEL: (503)447-5661

FOUNDATION: Millar Scholarship Fund
REQUISITE: Must be a high school graduate of Reynolds High School or Columbia High School, OR, who is planning to attend a post-secondary institution in OR.
APPLICATION: Write for info. Deadline March 30.
CONTACT: Reynolds High School, 1200 NE 201st, Troutdale, OR 97060 TEL: (503)667-3186

FOUNDATION: Blue Mountain Area Foundation
REQUISITE: Scholarships to any graduate of hgh schl in the Blue Mountain area, including Walla Walla, Columbia, Garfield, Benton, or Franklin cnties in southeastern WA or Umatilla Cnty in northeastern OR
APPLICATION: Write for info. Deadln vary between 4/15 & 6/1

CONTACT: Eleanor S. Kane, Administrator, 12 E. Main St., POB 603, Walla Walla, WA 99362 TEL: (509)529-4371

FOUNDATION: Bohemia Foundation
REQUISITE: Scholarships for entry-level college students who are children of employees of Bohemia, Inc.
APPLICATION: Application deadline is April 15th.
CONTACT: 2280 Oakmont Way, Eugene, OR 97401. Ms. Ardis Hughes, Bohemia Inc., POB 1819, Eugene, OR 97440. (We were not able to verify this listing; it may not be extant.)

FOUNDATION: Halton Foundation
REQUISITE: Schlrshps for children of employees who have worked for Halton Tractor Co and related companies for at least one year, or are disabled, retired, or deceased. The student must be under the age of 28, and are planning to be full-time students.
APPLICATION: Application deadline is January 31st. Applications can be obtained from the personnel office in Portland or the Foundation.
CONTACT: 3114 N.W. Verde Vista Terrace, Portland, OR 97210. Susan Findlay, Manager. TEL: (503)288-6411

FOUNDATION: Rosenkrans (Fred A.) Trust
REQUISITE: Loans for those attending OR State Unvrsty
APPLICATION: Applications are accepted throughout the year.
CONTACT: c/o First Interstate Bank of Oregon, N.A., P.O. Box 2971, Portland, OR 97208. Charles Woodcock, Trust Officer. (503)225-3174

FOUNDATION: Selling (Ben) Scholarship
REQUISITE: Low-interest loans for those attending OR Schls.
APPLICATION: Applications are accepted from 6/1 to 8/15
CONTACT: c/o First Interstate Bank of Oregon, P.O. Box 2971, Portland, OR 97208. Charles Woodcock, Trust Officer. TEL: (503)225-3174

FOUNDATION: Tektronix Foundation
REQUISITE: Must be a child of a Tektronix, Inc., employee or a student attending a high school in Clackamas, Washington, or Multnomah counties, OR, or in Clark County, WA.
APPLICATION: Interviews for finalists. Write for info. Deadln 3/15
CONTACT: Thomas O. Williams, Admnstrtr, Y 3-439, POB 500, Beaverton, OR 97077 (503)627-7111

FOUNDATION: Oregon PTA
REQUISITE: Scholarships granted to outstanding Oregon residents pursuing a career in education on an elementary or secondary level. Scholarship may be used to attend any Oregon Public School.
APPLICATION: Write for info. Application deadline is March 1st.
CONTACT: 531 S.E. 14TH, Portland, OR 97214. Tel: (503)234-3928

PENNSYLVANIA

FOUNDATION: Pennsylvania League for Nursing
REQUISITE: Scholarships granted to Pennsylvania League members for nursing. Applicants may also be a dependent of member or sponsored by a member of the league. This is for final year of study at any level.
APPLICATION: Write for info. Application deadline is November 1st.
CONTACT: 2001 North Front Street, Suite 110, Harrisburg, PA 17102.

FOUNDATION: Pennsylvania Medical Society
REQUISITE: Loans granted to residents of Pennsylvania who demonstrate financial need while seeking a medical degree in a four or two year health program of study in the USA.
APPLICATION: Write for info. Application deadline is 4/1 to 6/1.
CONTACT: 20 Erford Road, Lemoyne, PA 17043. (717)558-7750

FOUNDATION: Penn State University
REQUISITE: Scholarships granted to outstanding undergraduate students accepted to or enrolled in Penn State's College of Earth and Mineral Sciences with at least a 3.15 GPA
APPLICATION: Write for info. Application deadline is not specified.
CONTACT: 104 Deike Bldg, University Park, PA 16802. (814)865-7482

FOUNDATION: Mercyhurst College
REQUISITE: Scholarships granted to talented young musicians who are ready to start their college education at the D'Angelo School of Music of Mercyhurst College. Must be full-time student in undergraduate study.
APPLICATION: Write for info. Application deadline is April.
CONTACT: Glenwood Hills, Erie, PA 16546. (814)824-2000

FOUNDATION: Chatman College
REQUISITE: Scholarships to women only for full-time undergraduate study at Chatham College. Scholarships are open to talented young vocalists who are accepted for admission and pass their audition.

APPLICATION: Write for info. Application deadline is March 1st.
CONTACT: Woodland Rd., Office of Admissions, Pittsburgh, PA 15232
(412)365-1290

FOUNDATION: Waverly Community House Inc.
REQUISITE: Scholarships granted to residents of Abingtons or Pocono
Northeastern region of Pennsylvania. Students must submit proof of
exceptional ability in chosen field. Students studying in the following
fields may apply: Painting, Sculpture, Music, Drama, Dance, Literature,
Architecture, Photography, Printmaking or Film.
APPLICATION: Write for info. Application deadline is December 15th.
CONTACT: Scholarships Selection Committee, Waverly, PA 18471
(717)586-8191

FOUNDATION: Pennsylvania Higher Education Assistance Agency
REQUISITE: Scholarships granted to Penn. residents with high academic
grades/scores and have an eager desire to pursue a career in teaching
at a Pennsylvania secondary school.
APPLICATION: Write for info. Application deadline is May 1st.
CONTACT: Towne House, Harrisburg, PA 17102. Tel: (717)257-2850

FOUNDATION: Pennsylvania Higher Education Assistance Agency
REQUISITE: Scholarships granted to high school seniors that are Penn.
residents for at least 1 year. Must be pursuing education major at
accredited institution in Penn. Must be US citizen & legal resident.
APPLICATION: Write for info. Application deadline is May 1st.
CONTACT: Towne House, Harrisburg, PA 17102. Tel: (717)257-2850

FOUNDATION: Bloch-Selinger Educational Trust Fund
REQUISITE: Scholarships for honor students who are graduating from
Danville High School, Danville, PA.
APPLICATION: Applications are accepted throughout the year.
CONTACT: Commonwealth Bank & Trst Co, N.S., POB 308, Williamsport,
PA 17703. Or Superintendent of Schools, Danville Area School District,
POB 139, Danville, 17821 TEL: (717)275-4111

FOUNDATION: Clark (Morris J.) Medical Education Foundation
REQUISITE: Scholarship and fellowships for students who attend the
University of Pittsburgh School of Medicine.
APPLICATION: Contact Fndtn for current application info
CONTACT: Helen Collins, c/o Mellon Bank, N.A., One Mellon Bank

Center, Rm. 3845, Pittsburgh, PA 115258. TEL: (412)234-4695

FOUNDATION: Clarke-Aff League Memorial Fund
REQUISITE: Scholarships for students who attend medical school in Philadelphia, PA, including podiatry students.
APPLICATION: Contact local school financial aid offices for current information.
CONTACT: Fran Smith, c/o Mellon Bank (East) N.A., POB 7236, Philadelphia, PA 19101. (215)553-2596

FOUNDATION: Clements (H. Loren) Scholarship
REQUISITE: Scholarships for graduates of North Pocono High School in Moscow, PA.
APPLICATION: Application deadline is April 15th.
CONTACT: c/o Third National Bank, 130 Wyoming Ave., Scranton, PA 18501. TEL: (717)348-8230

FOUNDATION: Daly (Nathan & Harry) Scholarship
REQUISITE: Scholarships for deserving students who are from Butler County, PA, and attend Duquesne University.
APPLICATION: Contact the foundation for current info
CONTACT: Mellon Bank N.A., One Mellon Bank Center - 3845, Pittsburgh PA 15258. Helen Collins, Assistant Trust Officer. TEL: (412)234-4695

FOUNDATION: Dozzi (Eugene) Charitable Foundation
REQUISITE: Scholarships for Pennsylvania residents, preference given to those in the Pittsburgh area.
APPLICATION: Contact for more information.
CONTACT: 2000 Lincoln Rd., Pittsburg, PA 15235.
(We were not able to verify this listing; it may not be extant.)

FOUNDATION: Eldred (Ruby March) Scholarship Trust
REQUISITE: Scholarships for students from Meadville, PA, area and western Crawford County, PA.
APPLICATION: Application deadline is March 1st.
CONTACT: c/o marine Bank Trust Division, POB 8480, Erie, PA 16553. Or Honorable Robert Walker, Crawford County Courthouse, Meadville, PA 16335.
(We were not able to verify this listing; it may not be extant.)

FOUNDATION: Erie Community Foundation

REQUISITE: Scholarships for college for students attending the four public hgh schls of Erie County, PA.
APPLICATION: Write for more information.
CONTACT: 419 G. Daniel Baldwin Building, POB 1818, Erie, PA 16507. Edward C. Doll, Chairman. (Apply at these specific schools.)

FOUNDATION: Goldman (William) Foundation
REQUISITE: Scholarships for residents of Philadelphia, PA, for graduate or medical study at specific Philadelphia institutions.
APPLICATION: Application deadline is March 15th. Write for information on institutions.
CONTACT: 1700 Walnut Street, Suite 800, Philadelphia, PA 19103. Marilyn Klein, Executive Director.
(We were not able to verify this listing; it may not be extant.)

FOUNDATION: Goodwin (Howard D. & Rose E.) Schlrshp Fnd
REQUISITE: Scholarships for students who live in the Antietam School District, Berks County, PA, and who have graduated form Mt. Penn High School. The student must show a need for financial assistance.
APPLICATION: Applications are accepted throughout the year.
CONTACT: Meridian Trst Company, POB 1102, Reading, PA 19603-1102. R. Kemp. (We were not able to verify this listing; it may not be extant.)

FOUNDATION: Hassel Foundation
REQUISITE: Schlrshps for snrs at Reading Snr Hgh Schl, Reading & Exeter Township Snr Hgh Schl, Exeter Township.
APPLICATION: Applications are accepted throughout the year.
CONTACT: 1845 Walnut Street, Suite 1409, Philadelphia, PA 19103. Herman H. Krekstein, Secretary. (Apply at these specific schools.)

FOUNDATION: Hershey (Andrew J.) Foundation
REQUISITE: Scholarships for graduates of Spring Grove, PA, and York County, PA, area high schools.
APPLICATION: Application deadline is April 1st.
CONTACT: Steve Seldmann, c/o York Bank & Trust Company, POB 869, York, PA 17401. (717)843-8651

FOUNDATION: Hoyt Foundation
REQUISITE: Scholarships for students in Lawrence County, PA. Awards are based on need.
APPLICATION: Application deadlines are 7/15 and 12/15

CONTACT: Jaimie Kopp, c/o First National Bank Building, POB 1488, New Castle, PA 16103 TEL: (412)652-5511

FOUNDATION: Lancaster County Foundation
REQUISITE: Limited number of scholarships for people who live in Lancaster County, PA.
APPLICATION: Application deadline is 10/15. Write for info.
CONTACT: 29 East King Street, Lancaster, PA 17602. Nancy L. Neff, Executive Secretary. TEL: (717)397-1629

FOUNDATION: Leidy-Rhoads Foundation Trust
REQUISITE: Scholarships for residents of Boyertown, PA.
APPLICATION: Application deadline is February. Write for info.
CONTACT: Mellon Bnk (East) N.A., POB 7899, Philadelphia, PA 19101-7899 TEL: (215)553-3000

FOUNDATION: Lesher (Margaret & Irvin)
REQUISITE: Scholarships for graduates of Union High School, Clarion County, PA.
APPLICATION: Write for more information.
CONTACT: POB 374, Oil City, PA 16301. Stephen P. Kosak, Consultant. TEL: (814)677-5085

FOUNDATION: McKaig (Lalita Nash) Foundation
REQUISITE: Schlrshps for residents Bedford & Somerset cntys
APPLICATION: Application deadline is May 31st.
CONTACT: c/o Pittsburgh National Bank, Trust Charitable Division, One Oliver Plaza, Pittsburgh, PA 15265. Henry C. Flood, VP, Pittsburgh Ntnl Bnk. TEL: (412)762-2000

FOUNDATION: Nestor (Mary Margaret) Foundation
REQUISITE: Scholarships for residents of Lykens area.
APPLICATION: Applications are accepted throughout the year. Write for more information.
CONTACT: Reiff & West Streets, Lykens, PA 17048. Robert E. Nestor. TEL: (717)453-7113

FOUNDATION: Packer (Horace B.) Foundation, Inc.
REQUISITE: Scholarships for students in medical school who intend to work in Tioga County, PA.
APPLICATION: Applications accepted throughout the year.

Pennsylvania

CONTACT: POB 35, Wellsboro 16901 Charles G. Webb, Prsdnt
(We were not able to verify this listing; it may not be extant.)

FOUNDATION: Peckitt (Leonard Carlton) Scholarship Fund
REQUISITE: Scholarships for graduates Catasauqua Hgh Schl
APPLICATION: Application deadline is May 15th.
CONTACT: c/o Catasauqua High School, 850 Pine Street, Catasauqua, PA 18032. TEL: (610)264-0506

FOUNDATION: Roth Foundation
REQUISITE: Scholarships for nursing students attending a Pennsylvania institution.
APPLICATION: Applications accepted throughout the year.
CONTACT: 410 Vernon Rd, Jenkintown, PA 19046. Linda Schwartz, Trustee. TEL: (215)576-1191

FOUNDATION: Schramm Foundation
REQUISITE: Scholarships only to graduates of high schools in the West Chester, PA area, for studying business or engineering. Recipients are recommended by their high schools.
APPLICATION: Talk to counselor.
CONTACT: 800 East Virginia Ave., West Chester, PA 19380. Norman Greet, Personnel Officer. TEL: (610)696-2500

FOUNDATION: Shreve (William A. & Mary A.) Foundation, Inc.
REQUISITE: Scholarships for students in Pennsylvania.
APPLICATION: Applications are accepted throughout the year. Write for more information.
CONTACT: Robert M. Wood, Esquire, 200 Atlantic Ave., Manasquan, NJ 08736. Or Dr. Clifford G. Pollock, Rte 1, Box 408, Wallingford, VT 05773. (We were not able to verify this listing; it may not be extant.)

FOUNDATION: Snayberger, Harry E & Florence W Mmrl Fndtn
REQUISITE: Scholarships for residents of Schuylkill County
APPLICATION: Application deadline is February 28th.
CONTACT: c/o Pennsylvania National Bank & Trust Company, One South Center Street, Pottsville, PA 17901-3003. Tel.:(717)622-4200. Paul J. Hanna, II, Senior Vice-President and Trust Officer, Pennsylvania National Bank & Trust Company.

FOUNDATION: Sussman (Otto) Trust

REQUISITE: Education expenses to residents of Pennsylvania who are in need due to an illness or death in the immediate family or some other unusual circumstance.
APPLICATION: Applications are accepted throughout the year.
CONTACT: POB 1374, Trainsmeadow Station, Flushing, NY 11370

FOUNDATION: Thomson (The John Edgar) Foundation
REQUISITE: Schlrshps for daughters deceased railroad emplys
APPLICATION: Applications are accepted throughout the year.
CONTACT: The Rittenhouse Claridge, Suite 318, Philadelphia, PA 19103. Glida Verstein, Director. TEL: (215)545-6083

FOUNDATION: Vincent (Anna M.) Trust
REQUISITE: Scholarships for long-term residents of Delaware Valley, PA, for undergraduate or graduate study.
APPLICATION: Application deadline is March 1st.
CONTACT: c/o Mellon Bank (East), POB 7236, Three Mellon Bank Center, Philadelphia, PA 19101-7236, Pat Kling, Trust Officer, Mellon Bank (East). TEL: (215)553-3000

FOUNDATION: Warren Foundation
REQUISITE: Scholarships for residents of Warren County, PA.
APPLICATION: Write for more information.
CONTACT: c/o Warren National Bank, PO Drawer 69, Warren, PA 16365. Holger N. Elmquist, Director.
(We were not able to verify this listing; it may not be extant.)

FOUNDATION: Weber (Jacques) Foundation Inc.
REQUISITE: Scholarships for residents who live within a 70-mile radius of Bloomsburg, Pa, to be used for textile study only.
APPLICATION: Application deadline is November 30th.
CONTACT: 1460 Broadway, New York, NY 10036. Or Sandra Grasley, Jacques Weber Foundation, Inc.,POB 420, Bloomsburg, PA 17815. TEL: (717)784-7701

FOUNDATION: Wolf (Benjamin & Fredora K.) Foundation
REQUISITE: Scholarships awarded upon recommendations by high school principals and counselors, for graduates of Philadelphia, PA, area high schools.
APPLICATION: Applications accepted throughout the year.
CONTACT: Park Towne Place - North Building 1205, Prkway at 22nd

Street, Philadelphia, PA 19130. David Horowitz, Administrator. (We were not able to verify this listing; it may not be extant.)

FOUNDATION: Brice (Helen) Scholarship Fund
REQUISITE: Scholarships for undergraduates that are by nomination only. These scholarships are for students who have attended Uniontown, PA, area high schools.
APPLICATION: Talk to counselors.
CONTACT: Helen Collins, c/o Mellon Bank N.A., Mellon Bank Center, Rm. 3845, Pittsburg, PA 15258-0001. TEL: (412)234-5000

FOUNDATION: Demarest (Eben) Trust
REQUISITE: Grants by nomination only for students studying archaeology or the arts and are exceptionally gifted.
APPLICATION: Talk to counselor.
CONTACT: Mellon Bank, N.A., POB 185, Pittsburgh, PA 15230. Eileen Wilhem, Assistant Vice-President. TEL: (412)234-4695

FOUNDATION: Hirtzel (Orris C.) Memorial Foundation
REQUISITE: Scholarships by nomination only to students attending institutions in northeast PA.
APPLICATION: Talk to counselor.
CONTACT: Helen Collins, c/o Mellon Bank N.A., Mellon Bank Center, Rm. 3845, Pittsburgh, PA 15258-0001. TEL: (412)234-5000

FOUNDATION: Berwind (Charles G.) Foundation
REQUISITE: Scholarships for children of Berwind Corporation employees & occasional schlrshps for residents in company areas.
APPLICATION: Application deadline is November 30th.
CONTACT: 3000 Center Sq West, 1500 Market St, Philadelphia, PA 19102. Betty Olund, Administrator. TEL: (215)563-2800

FOUNDATION: Golub Foundation
REQUISITE: Scholarships for graduating high school students in areas served by Price Chopper Supermarkets.
APPLICATION: Application deadline is April 1st.
CONTACT: 501 Duanesburg Rd., Schenectady, NY 12306. Scholarship Committee, c/o Golub Corporation, POB 1074, Schenectady, NY 12301 TEL: (518)356-9390

FOUNDATION: Hall Foundation

REQUISITE: Scholarships for children of employees or customer of Hall's Motor Transit Company.
APPLICATION: Deadline 3 months prior to fall semester.
CONTACT: 444 S 2nd St, Harrisburg, PA 17104. John N. Hall, President. (We were not able to verify this listing; it may not be extant.)

FOUNDATION: Steinman (James Hale) Foundation
REQUISITE: Scholarships for newspaper carriers and children of employees of Steinman Enterprises, in Lancaster, PA.
APPLICATION: Application deadline is February 28th.
CONTACT: POB 128, Lancaster, PA 17603. M. Steven Weaver, Eight West King St, Lancaster, PA 17603
(We were not able to verify this listing; it may not be extant.)

FOUNDATION: Westinghouse Educational Fund
REQUISITE: Schlrshps for kids of employees of Westinghouse and its U.S.A. subsidiaries, any freshman woman entering the field of engineering, students who are 4-H members working under the supervision of the Extension Service and wishing to compete in the 4-H Electrics Awards Program. Scholarships are also awarded in the Science Talent Search. Students who are in their last year of high school and expect to complete college entrance qualifications before October 1st, and have not participated in the talent search before, are encouraged to.
APPLICATION: Write for details and application deadlines.
CONTACT: Westinghouse Electric Company, Westinghouse Building, Gateway Center, Pittsburgh, PA 15222. Walter A. Schratz, Executive Director. TEL: (412)244-2000

FOUNDATION: Alcoa Foundation
REQUISITE: Scholarships for children of employees of Aluminum Company of America.
APPLICATION: Applications are accepted throughout the year.
CONTACT: 1501 Alcoa Building, Pittsburg, PA 15219. Earl Gadbery, President. TEL: (412)553-4545

FOUNDATION: Blank (Samuel A.) Scholarship Fund
REQUISITE: Scholarships for children of employees of Continental Bank, Philadelphia, PA.
APPLICATION: Write for more information.
CONTACT: c/o Jeffrey Blank, 300 Jenkintown Commons, Jenkintown, PA 19046. Ruth or Robert Blank, Trustees. TEL: (215)887-5555

Pennsylvania

FOUNDATION: Bruder (Michael A.) Foundation
REQUISITE: Scholarships for children of employees of M.A. Bruder and Sons, Inc.
APPLICATION: Write for more information.
CONTACT: 600 Reed Road, P.O. Box 600, Broomall,PA 19008.
(We were not able to verify this listing; it may not be extant.)

FOUNDATION: Cooper Industries Foundation
REQUISITE: Scholarships for children of employees of Cooper Industries, Inc. in AL, CA, CT, GA, IL, IN, ME, MI, MO, MS, NJ, NY, NC, OH, OK, PA, SC, TN, TX, and VA.
APPLICATION: Applications are accepted throughout the year.
CONTACT: First City Tower, Suite 4000, POB 4446, Houston, TX 77210. Patricia B. Meinecke, Secretary. TEL: (713)739-5632

FOUNDATION: Downs Foundation
REQUISITE: Scholarships for children of employees of Downs Carpet Company, Inc.
APPLICATION: Write for information.
CONTACT: POB 475, Davisville Rd & Turnpike Dr, Willow Grove, PA 19090. T. George Downs, Trustee. TEL: (215)672-1100

FOUNDATION: Evans (D.A. & J.A.) Memorial Foundation
REQUISITE: Schlrshps for kids emplys of Ellwood Cty Corp
APPLICATION: Write for more information.
CONTACT: Robert Barensfeld, Ellwood City Forge Corp, Ellwood City, PA 16117. (We were not able to verify this listing; it may not be extant.)

FOUNDATION: Founder's Mmrl Fund of the American Streilizer Co.
REQUISITE: Scholarships for children of employees of the American Sterilizer Co..
APPLICATION: Write for more information.
CONTACT: 2222 W Grandview Blvd, Erie, PA 16509 (814)452-3100

FOUNDATION: Hoffman (Bob) Foundation
REQUISITE: Scholarships for children of employees of the York Bar Bell Co., Inc., and its affiliates.
APPLICATION: Applications are accepted throughout the year.
CONTACT: c/o York Bar Bell Co., The, P.O. Box 1707, York, PA 17405. Michael Dietz, Trustee. TEL: (717)767-6481

FOUNDATION: Hunt Manufacturing Company Foundation
REQUISITE: Scholarships for children of employees of the Hunt Manufacturing Company. The employees must have at least one year of service as of April 15th of the year the application is made.
APPLICATION: Application deadline is April 15th.
CONTACT: 230 South Broad Street, Philadelphia, PA 19102. Vice-President of Human Resources. TEL: (215)732-7700

FOUNDATION: McCain Foundation, Inc.
REQUISITE: Scholarships for full-time students of non-stockholding employees of the Erie Concrete & Steel Supply Company, Perry Mill Supply Company, and Dobi Plumbing and Heating Supply Company.
APPLICATION: Applications are accepted throughout the year.
CONTACT: c/o Erie Concrete and Steel, P.O. Box 10336, Erie, PA 16514-0336. Fund Manager. TEL: (814)453-4969

FOUNDATION: Merit Gasoline Foundation
REQUISITE: Scholarships for children of full-time employees of Merit Oil Company and its affiliates. The employees must have at least two years of service and can be active, retired, deceased, or disabled.
APPLICATION: Application deadline is April 1st.
CONTACT: 551 West Lancaster Ave., Haverford, PA 19041. Robert Harting, Executive Director. TEL: (610)527-7900

FOUNDATION: Pennsylvania Steel Foundry Foundation
REQUISITE: Scholarships for employees and the children of employees of PA Steel Foundry and Machine Co, Hamburg, PA.
APPLICATION: Applications are accepted throughout the year.
CONTACT: c/o Meridian Trust Company, P.O. Box 1102, Reading, PA 19603. Elizabeth Clapper, Secretary (610)655-2000

FOUNDATION: Pennwalt Foundation
REQUISITE: Scholarships for high school seniors of employees of Pennwalt Corporation.
APPLICATION: Applications are accepted throughout the year.
CONTACT: Pennwalt Building, Three Benjamin Franklin Parkway, Philadelphia, PA 19102. George Hagar, Executive Secretary. TEL: (215)419-7000

FOUNDATION: Potlatch Foundation for Higher Education
REQUISITE: Scholarships for undergraduates that live in areas of Potlatch

Corporation operations.
APPLICATION: Application deadline is February 1st for new applications, and July 1st for renewals.
CONTACT: P.O. Box 3591, San Francisco, CA 94119. George Check, President. TEL: (415)576-8800

FOUNDATION: Quaker Chemical Foundation
REQUISITE: Schlrshps for employees of Quaker Chemical Corp
APPLICATION: Application deadline is April 30th.
CONTACT: Elm and Lee Streets, Conshohocken, PA 19428. Karl Spaeth, Chairman. TEL: (610)832-4000

FOUNDATION: Smith Kline Beckman Foundation
REQUISITE: Scholarships for children of deceased or disabled employees of Smith Kline Beckman Corp and its subsidiaries.
APPLICATION: Write for application information.
CONTACT: One Franklyn Plaza, P.O. Box 7929, Philadelphia, PA 19101. William Grala, President. TEL: (215)751-4000

FOUNDATION: Superior-Pacific Fund
REQUISITE: Scholarships for kids of employees of the Superior Tube Co. Employees must have at least three years of service.
APPLICATION: Application deadline is January 1st. Applications can be obtained from personnel office of the Superior Tube Co.
CONTACT: Seven Wynnewood Rd, Wynnewood, PA 19096. Or Superior Tube Company Scholarship Committee, P.O. Box 616, Devault, PA 19432; TEL: (610)489-5200

FOUNDATION: Thomson (Frank) Scholarship Trust
REQUISITE: Scholarships for high school seniors who are the sons of employees of Conrail, or Penn Central, and Amtrak who where employed by the Penn Central Transportation Company or Pennsylvania Railroad Company before April 1st, 1976.
APPLICATION: Application deadline is March 31st.
CONTACT: c/o Fidelity Bank, N.A., Trustee, 135 South Broad Street, Philadelphia, PA 19109. Frank Thomson, Chairman Selection Committee TEL: (215)985-6000

FOUNDATION: West (Herman O.) Foundation
REQUISITE: Schlrshps for kids of employees of The West Co.
APPLICATION: Application deadline is February 28th.

CONTACT: P.O. Box 808, Phoenixville, PA 19460.
(We were not able to verify this listing; it may not be extant.)

FOUNDATION: Women's Aid of the Penn Central Transportation Co.
REQUISITE: Scholarships for children of employees of Conrail, or Penn Central, and Amtrak who where employed by the Penn Central Transportation Co. or Pennsylvania Railroad Co.
APPLICATION: Application deadline is April 1st.
CONTACT: c/o Consolidated Rail Corporation, Six Penn Center, Room 1010, Philadelphia, PA 19103. J.P. Fox, Human Resources Department; TEL: (215)209-2000

FOUNDATION: Abrams (Samuel L.) Foundation
REQUISITE: Non-interest loans for students in greater Harrisburg, PA area
APPLICATION: Deadline is May 15th. Write for info
CONTACT: Abrams & Sons Inc., c/o Richard E. Abrams, 1616 N. Cameron St., Harrisburg, PA 17103 TEL: (717)234-4344.

FOUNDATION: Gibson (Addison H.) Foundation
REQUISITE: Loans for male students who live in western Pennsylvania after having participated at least one year in an undergraduate or graduate degree program.
APPLICATION: Contact foundation for deadlines and info.
CONTACT: Two PPG Place, Suite 310, Pittsburgh, PA 15222. Charlotte Kisseleff, Secretary TEL: (412)261-1611

FOUNDATION: Klemstine (G. William) Foundation
REQUISITE: Edctnl loans for residents of Cambria and Somerset cnts.
APPLICATION: Applications are accepted throughout the year.
CONTACT: Pittsburgh National Bank C. & I. Trust Dept., One Oliver Plz, Pittsburgh, PA 15265. TEL: (412)762-2000

FOUNDATION: Lalitta Nash McKaig Foundation
REQUISITE: Scholarships to any resident of Bedford or Somerset counties, PA, Mineral or Hamshir counties, WV, or Allegany or Garrett counties, MD, for undergraduate, graduate, or professional edctn at any accredited cllg or unversty in U.S.
APPLICATION: Application forms available from Cumberland, MD, area high school guidance offices, Frostburg State College & Allegany Community College financial aid offices, the Pittsburgh National Bank, or the foundation's Cumberland office, POB 1360, Cumberland, MD 21502

(301) 777-1533. Must submit Financial Aid Form (FAF) & Supplement directly to College Scholarship Service. Interviews required. Deadline 5/31 CONTACT: Henry C. Flood, VP, Pittsburgh Ntnl Bnk, Trust Charitable Division, One Oliver Plaza, Pittsburgh, PA 15265 (412)762-4000

PUERTO RICO

FOUNDATION: Harvey Foundation, Inc.
REQUISITE: Scholarships only for residents of Puerto Rico.
APPLICATION: Contact Foundation for more information.
CONTACT: 1st Federal Bldg 1519 Ponce de Leon Ave Ste 507 Santurce, PR 00909 (We were not able to verify this listing; it may not be extant.)

RHODE ISLAND

FOUNDATION: Rhode Island Higher Education Assistance Authority
REQUISITE: Scholarships granted to Rhode Island residents who are enrolled or planning to enroll at least 1/2 time at an eligible vocational-technical institution. Must be US citizen or legal resident.
APPLICATION: Write for info. Application deadline is March 1st.
CONTACT: 560 Jefferson Blvd., Warwick, RI 02886. 401-277-2050

FOUNDATION: Rhode Island State Council on the Arts
REQUISITE: Scholarships granted to individual professional artists who are residents of the State of Rhode Island.
APPLICATION: Write for info. Application deadline is March 15th.
CONTACT: 95 Cedar St., #103, Providence, RI 02903. (401)277-3880

FOUNDATION: Mary E. Hodges Fund
REQUISITE: Must be an individual who has a masonic affiliation or who has been a resident of RI for 5 years or more.
APPLICATION: Write for info. Deadline June 1.
CONTACT: Arthur Medley, Secty., 2115 Broad St., Cranston, RI 02905 (We were not able to verify this listing; it may not be extant.)

FOUNDATION: The Suttell Foundation
REQUISITE: Undergraduate educational grants or loans only to any resident of RI. Preference will be given to grants for medical studies or work with youth.
APPLICATION: Submit letter requesting application. Must include brief resume of academic qualifications, course of study & expense involved

along with application. Individuals should submit name of college & address. Deadline September 1.
CONTACT: T. Earl Haworth, Pres., c/o St. Paul's Church, 50 Park Place, Pawtucket, RI 02860 TEL: (401)728-4300

FOUNDATION: George Abrahamian Foundation
REQUISITE: Must be a local student of Armenian ancestry who plans to attend a college or university primarily in RI.
APPLICATION: Initial approach by in-person visit through the Armenian churches in the area. Interviews required before final selections are made. Write for further info. Deadline September.
CONTACT: A. G. Abraham, Trsrr, 945 Admiral St, Providence RI 02904 (401)831-0008 (Were not able to verify this listing; it may not be extant.)

FOUNDATION: Marjorie Sells Carter Boy Scout Schlrshp Fnd
REQUISITE: Former Boy Scout who resides in New England.
APPLICATION: Submit letter requesting application by April 1.
CONTACT: Joan Shaffer, POB 527, West Chatham, MA 02669
(We were not able to verify this listing; it may not be extant.)

FOUNDATION: The Horbach Fund
REQUISITE: Must be a needy, gifted, young person under the age of 20 who resides in CT, MA, NJ, NY, or RI.
APPLICATION: Write for info. Deadline August 1.
CONTACT: Ntnl Community Bnk NJ 113 W Essex St, Maywood, NJ 07607
(We were not able to verify this listing; it may not be extant.)

FOUNDATION: Rhode Island Higher Education Assistance Authority
REQUISITE: Scholarships granted to undergraduates at a Rhode Island institution. Students must be pursuing a teaching career. Must be US citizen or legal resident.
APPLICATION: Write for info. Application deadline is June 15th.
CONTACT: 560 Jefferson Blvd., Warwick, RI 02886 (401)736-1100

FOUNDATION: Cranston Foundation
REQUISITE: Scholarships for children of employees (not including those of directors or officers) of the Cranston Print Works Company, its divisions or subsidiaries. The scholarships are for two years only.
APPLICATION: Application deadline is April 15th.
CONTACT: c/o Administrator, 1381 Cranston St., Cranston, RI 02920. TEL: (401)943-4800

Rhode Island

FOUNDATION: Charles H. Hood Fund
REQUISITE: Must be a CT, MA, ME, NH, RI, or VT resident.
APPLICATION: Write for info. No deadline listed.
CONTACT: 500 Rutherford Ave., Boston, MA 02129

FOUNDATION: New England Regional Student Program
REQUISITE: Must reside in 1 of the New England States: CT, ME, MA, NH, RI, or VT. You may attend a public college or university within the region at a reduced tuition rate for certain degree programs that are not offered by their own state's public institutions.
APPLICATION: Write for info. No deadline listed.
CONTACT: Office of the Regional Student Program, New England Board of Hghr Edctn, 45 Temple Plc, Boston, MA 02111

FOUNDATION: Massachusetts/Rhode Island League for Nursing
REQUISITE: Must be a member of the MA/RI League for Nursing for at least 1 year prior to applying; a resident of MA or RI; & a registered nurse who has been in full-time practice for at least 1 year immediately prior to acceptance into a graduate program. You must also be accepted into a National League for Nursing accredited graduate program for nursing or be already enrolled in such a program & be continuing for a 2nd year.
APPLICATION: References, written presentation of goals, & at the discretion of the scholarship committee a personal interview.
Submit letter requesting application & include a self-addressed stamped business envelope. Deadline May 1.
CONTACT: Mary B. Conceison Scholarship Committee, One Thompson Square, Charlestown, MA 02129 TEL: (617)242-3009

FOUNDATION: Massachusetts/Rhode Island League for Nursing
REQUISITE: Resided in the MA/RI League for Nursing geographical area for the 4 years immediately prior to the receipt of the scholarship. You may also be either a registered nurse that is accepted into a program leading to a baccalaureate degree in nursing; a generic student who is entering the snr year in any undergraduate nursing program; or a student who has successfully completed 4 months of a practical nursing prgrm.
APPLICATION: Submit letter requesting application along with a self-addressed stamped business size envelope. Deadline June 1. Recipients notified by August 15.
CONTACT: Scholarship Committee, Nursing Scholarship, One Thompson Square, Charlestown, MA 02129 TEL: (617)242-3009

FOUNDATION: Fred Forsyth Educational Trust Fund
REQUISITE: Must be a CT, MA, ME, NH, RI, or VT student.
APPLICATION: Write for info. No deadline listed.
CONTACT: Rose Marie Bates, Fleet Bank, Investment Services, POB 923, Bangor, ME 04402-0923   TEL: (201)941-6000

FOUNDATION: The Horbach Fund
REQUISITE: Must be a needy, gifted, young person under the age of 20 who resides in CT, MA, NJ, NY, or RI.
APPLICATION: Write for info. Deadline August 1.
CONTACT: c/o National Community Bank of NJ, 113 W. Essex St., Maywood, NJ 07607

SOUTH CAROLINA

FOUNDATION: Coastal Advertising Federation
REQUISITE: Scholarships   granted   to   undergraduates   in Hobby/Georgetown County residents who has completed at least their sophomore year of study at an accredited college or university. Must have 3.0 GPA or better. USA citizens only.
APPLICATION: Write for info. Application deadline is March 31st.
CONTACT: Mary Miller, POBOX 1414, Myrtle Beach, SC   29578 (803)497-6925

FOUNDATION: National FFA Center
REQUISITE: Scholarships granted to FFA member planning to enroll as a freshman in a 4-year undergraduate program at an accredited university or college in USA. Must be a USA citizen or legal resident. Must be a resident of CA;FL;SC;TN; or TX.
APPLICATION: Write for info. Application deadline is April 1st.
CONTACT: Scholarship Office, POBOX 15160, Alexandria, VA   22309. (703)360-3600

FOUNDATION: Alsobrooks (Miriam E.) Educational Fund
REQUISITE: Schlrshps for graduates McColl Hgh Schl, McColl
APPLICATION: Write for more information.
CONTACT: Wachovia Bank, 1401 Main Street, Columbia, SC 29226. Trust Department. (803)771-3475

FOUNDATION: Byrnes (James F.) Foundation
REQUISITE: Scholarships for South Carolina residents who have lost one

or both parents by death.
APPLICATION: Application deadline is 3/1. Write for info.
CONTACT: POB 9596, Columbia, SC 29290. Margaret Courtney, Executive Secretary. (803)776-1211

FOUNDATION: Cameron (The Dave) Educational Foundation
REQUISITE: Scholarships for undergraduate students who live within the York, SC area, and who maintain at least a 2.0 GPA.
APPLICATION: Applications are accepted throughout the year.
CONTACT: Margaret Adkins, POB 181, York, SC 29745   (803)684-4968

FOUNDATION: Doyle (Dr. Edgar Clay) & Mary Cherry Doyle Mmrl Fnd
REQUISITE: Scholarships for residents and graduates of high school in Oconee County, SC, for use at a South Carolina college.
APPLICATION: Application deadline is March 1st.
CONTACT: Cheryl Vaeth, c/o South Carolina National Bank, Trust Department, 1401 Main St., Ste. 501, Columbia, SC 29226. Or South Carolina Foundation of Independent Colleges, Scholarship Committee, POB 6998, Greenville, SC 29606. TEL: (803)765-3657

FOUNDATION: Fairey (Kittie M.) Educational Fund
REQUISITE: Scholarships for residents of South Carolina to attend an institution in South Carolina.
APPLICATION: Application deadline is March 31st.
CONTACT: Cheryl Vaeth, c/o The South Carolina National Bank, 1401 Main St., Ste. 501, Columbia, SC 29226. TEL: (803)765-3657

FOUNDATION: Foundation for the Carolinas
REQUISITE: Scholarship and loans to residents of NC & SC.
APPLICATION: Write for more information.
CONTACT: 1043 East Morehead, POB 34769, Charlote, NC 28234-4769. Barbara T. Hautau, Vice-President. TEL: (704)376-9541

FOUNDATION: Fuller (C.G.) Foundation
REQUISITE: Scholarships for South Carolina residents to attend colleges or universities within the state.
APPLICATION: Application deadline is March 31st.
CONTACT: c/o Nations Bank, POB 448, Columbia, SC 29202. Thomas W. Duke, Jr. TEL: (803)765-8011

FOUNDATION: Graham Memorial Fund

REQUISITE: Scholarships for post-secondary education for residents of Bennettsville, SC.
APPLICATION: Application deadline is June 1st.
CONTACT: POB 533, Bennettsvillle, SC 29512. (We were not able to verify this listing; it may not be extant.)

FOUNDATION: Horne (Dick) Foundation
REQUISITE: Scholarships for residents of the trading area by Horne Motors of Orangeburg, SC.
APPLICATION: Applications are accepted throughout the year.
CONTACT: POB 30, Orangeburg, SC 29116. Tel.:(803)534-2096. Or Andrew Berry, Manager, 360 Russell Street, S.E., Orangeburg, SC; Lenora R. Player, 595 Calhoun Drive, Orangeburg, SC; or John F. Shuler, 250 Keitt Street, N.E., Orangeburg, SC.

FOUNDATION: Kennedy (Francis Nathaniel & Katheryn Padgett) Fndtn
REQUISITE: Scholarships for students in South Carolina who study at a college for the ministry in the Southern Baptist Church and for foreign mission work or Christian education in their local church.
APPLICATION: Application deadline is May 15th.
CONTACT: POB 1178, Greenwood, SC 29648. Sam Smith. (803)942-1400

FOUNDATION: Moore (Alfred) Foundation
REQUISITE: Scholarships and loans for residents of Spartanburg and Anderson counties, SC.
APPLICATION: Application deadline is March 29th.
CONTACT: c/o C.L. Page Enterprises, Inc., POB 18426, Spartanburg, SC 29318. Cary L.Page, Jr., Chairman. TEL: (803)573-5298

FOUNDATION: Slocum-Lunz Foundation, Inc.
REQUISITE: Scholarships for students studying marine biology or closely related natural sciences.
APPLICATION: Application deadline is April 1st.
CONTACT: Grice Marine Biological Laboratory, 205 Fort Johnson, Charleston, SC 29412. Dr. Charles K. Biernbaum, Chairman, Scholarship Committee. TEL: (803)762-5550

FOUNDATION: Weber (Jacques) Foundation, Inc.
REQUISITE: Scholarships for residents of Abbeville area
APPLICATION: Application deadline is November 30th.
CONTACT: 1460 Broadway, New York, NY 10036. Or Sandra Grasley,

Scholarship Committee, Jacques Weber Fndtn, Inc., POB 420, Bloomsburg, PA 17815 TEL: (717)784-7701

FOUNDATION: Bailey Foundation
REQUISITE: Loans and scholarships for children of employees of Clinton Mills, Inc., it subsidiaries, or M.S. Bailey & Son, Bankers. Employees must have been employed at least two years, continuously and can be retired.
APPLICATION: Deadline is April 15th of the senior year.
CONTACT: POB 1276, Clinton, SC 29325. H. William Carter,Jr., Administrator. TEL: (803)833-1910

FOUNDATION: Cooper Industries Foundation
REQUISITE: Scholarships for children of employees of Cooper Industries, Inc. in AL, CA, CT, GA, IL, IN, ME, MI, MO, MS, NJ, NY, NC, OH, OK, PA, SC, TN, TX, and VA.
APPLICATION: Applications are accepted throughout the year.
CONTACT: First City Tower, Suite 4000, POB 4446, Houston, TX 77210. Patricia B. Meinecke, Secretary. TEL: (713)739-5632

FOUNDATION: Daniel Foundation of South Carolina
REQUISITE: Scholarships for children of employees of Daniel International Corporation.
APPLICATION: Application deadline is March 15th.
CONTACT: POB 9278, Greenville, SC 29604-9278. Barbara C. Lewis, Secretary-Treasurer (803)281-4400

FOUNDATION: Gregg-Graniteville Foundation, Inc.
REQUISITE: Scholarships for children of employees of Graniteville Company.
APPLICATION: Contact foundation for current deadlines.
CONTACT: POB 418, Graniteville, SC 29829. Joan F. Phibbs, Secretary-Treasurer. TEL: (803)663-7231

FOUNDATION: Inman-Riverdale Foundation
REQUISITE: Scholarships for kids of employees of Inman Mills.
APPLICATION: Write for more information.
CONTACT: Inman Mills, Inman, SC 29349. W. Marshall Chapman, Chairman. TEL: (803)472-2121

FOUNDATION: Coastal Advertising Federation

REQUISITE: Scholarships granted to undergraduate Horry/Georgetown County residents who have completed at least their sophomore year of study at any accredited 4-year college or university. Must have at least 3.0 GPA or better. Must be USA citizen.
APPLICATION: Write for info. Application deadline is March 31st.
CONTACT: POBOX 1414, Myrtle Beach, SC 29578. (803)497-6190

FOUNDATION: Post & Courier Foundation
REQUISITE: Scholarships for news-carriers of Post & Courier who have at least two years of service.
APPLICATION: Write for more information.
CONTACT: 134 Columbus Street, Charleston, SC 29402. J.F. Smoak, Secretary-Treasurer. TEL: 9803)577-7111

FOUNDATION: Close Foundation, Inc.
REQUISITE: Student loans for residents of North Carolina and Lancaster County, Chester Township of Chester County and Fort Mill Township, South Carolina.
APPLICATION: Write for application information.
CONTACT: P.O. Drawer 460, Lancaster, SC 29720. Charles Bundy, President. TEL: (803)286-2181

FOUNDATION: Pickett & Hatcher Educational Fund, Inc.
REQUISITE: Undergraduate student loans for those who live in AL, FL, GA, KY, MS, NC, SC, TN, and VA. There is no support for those planning to study medicine, law, or ministry.
APPLICATION: Application deadline is May 15th. First-time applicants may request their application after October 1st.
CONTACT: 1800 Buena Vista Rd, P.O. Box 8169, Columbus, GA 31908. Robert Bennett, Executive Vice-President. TEL: (404)327-6586

FOUNDATION: Dan River Foundation
REQUISITE: Scholarships for employees, or children of current, deceased, or retired employees of Dan River, Inc. in New York, Virginia, or SC.
APPLICATION: Deadline is the last day of February.
CONTACT: POB 261, Danville, VA 24541. Or Chairman, Scholarship Committee, Dan River Foundation, POB 2178, Danville, VA 24541. TEL: (804)799-7000

SOUTH DAKOTA

FOUNDATION: Bush Foundation
REQUISITE: Scholarships granted to writers, visual artists, composers and choreographers who are residents of Minn., N. Dakota, or S. Dakota and is at least 25 years old. Must work full-time in their chosen art form.
APPLICATION: Write for info. Application deadline is October 30th, November 6th, and November 13th.
CONTACT: E900 First National Bank Bldg., St. Paul, MN 55101 Tel: (612)227-0891

FOUNDATION: Hatterscheidt Foundation, Inc.
REQUISITE: Scholarships for the first year of college for high school seniors graduating in the top 25% of their class in SD.
APPLICATION: Apply to college financial aid office.
CONTACT: c/o First Bank-Aberdeen, 320 South First Street, Aberdeen, SD 57401. Markyn S. Hearnen, Trust Officer, First Bank-Aberdeen TEL: 9605)225-9400

FOUNDATION: Treacy Company
REQUISITE: Scholarships for undergraduate study only for residents or students attending schools in SD.
APPLICATION: Application deadline is June 15th.
CONTACT: Box 1700, Helena, MT 59624. James O'Connell TEL: (406)442-3632

TENNESSEE

FOUNDATION: Tennessee Arts Commission
REQUISITE: Scholarships granted to artists who are residents of the State of TN for only one year.
APPLICATION: Write for info. Application deadline is January 12th.
CONTACT: 320 Sixth Ave. North #100, Nashville, TN 37219 Tel: (615)298-4072

FOUNDATION: National FFA Center
REQUISITE: Scholarships granted to FFA member planning to enroll as a freshman in a 4-year undergraduate program at an accredited university or college in USA. Must be a USA citizen or legal resident. Must be a resident of CA;FL;SC;TN; or TX.
APPLICATION: Write for info. Application deadline is April 1st.

CONTACT: Scholarship Office, POBOX 15160, Alexandria, VA 22309. (703)360-3600

FOUNDATION: Chattanooga, The Community Foundatn of Greater, Inc.
REQUISITE: Scholarships to residents of Chattanooga, TN, who will work in advanced social work or nursing.
APPLICATION: Write for more information.
CONTACT: 736 Market St., Ste. 1700, Chattanooga, TN 37402 William A. Walter, Executive Secretary TEL: (615)265-0586

FOUNDATION: Hurley (Ed E. & Gladys) Foundation
REQUISITE: Scholarships for students attending Scarritt College for Christian Workers, TN.
APPLICATION: Application deadline is May 31st.
CONTACT: c/o Premier Bank, POB 2116, Shreveport, LA 71154. TEL: (318)226-2382

FOUNDATION: Westend Foundation, Inc.
REQUISITE: Scholarships and grants for those who live in the Chattanooga, TN area.
APPLICATION: Applications are accepted throughout the year.
CONTACT: c/o American National Bank and Trust Company, 736 Market Street, Chattanooga, TN 37402. Raymond B. Witt, Jr., Secretary TEL: (615)265-8881

FOUNDATION: Jewell (The Daniel Ashley & Irene Houston) Mmrl Fndtn
REQUISITE: Undergraduate scholarships for children of employees that work for Crystal Springs Printwork, Inc., Chickamauga, GA, and for high school seniors that live in the area of Dade, Catoosa, or Walker counties, GA to attend college in GA, AL, or TN.
APPLICATION: Applications are accepted throughout the year.
CONTACT: c/o American National Bank & Trust Company, POB 1638, Chattanooga, TN 37401. Peter T. Cooper, Treasurer. (615)757-3661

FOUNDATION: Austin Scholarship Foundation
REQUISITE: Scholarships for children of full-time employees and seasonal employees. They must have been employed for at least 10 weeks for five seasons.
APPLICATION: Applications are accepted throughout the year.
CONTACT: POB 1360, Greeneville, TN 37743-1360. John Waddle, Jr.
(We were not able to verify this listing; it may not be extant.)

FOUNDATION: Binswanger (S.E.) Memorial Fund, Inc.
REQUISITE: Scholarships for children of employees of Binswanger Glass Company.
APPLICATION: Application deadline is April 15th.
CONTACT: POB 171173, Memphis, TN 38117-1173. Or Regina Sisson, c/o Binswanger Glass Company, 965 Ridge Lake Boulevard, Memphis Tn. 38117. TEL: (901)767-7111

FOUNDATION: Cooper Industries Foundation
REQUISITE: Scholarships for children of employees of Cooper Industries, Inc. in AL, CA, CT, GA, IL, IN, ME, MI, MO, MS, NJ, NY, NC, OH, OK, PA, SC, TN, TX, and VA.
APPLICATION: Applications are accepted throughout the year.
CONTACT: First City Tower, Suite 4000, POB 4446, Houston, TX 77210. Patricia B. Meinecke, Secretary. TEL: (713)739-5631

FOUNDATION: Evinrude (The Ole) Foundation
REQUISITE: Scholarships for children of employees of Outboard Marine Crprtn in WI, IL, TN, MS, NC, GA, and NB.
APPLICATION: Application deadline is October 31st.
CONTACT: Denise Charts, 100 Sea Horse Drive, Waukegan, IL 60085. TEL: (708)689-6200

FOUNDATION: Hyde (J.R.) Foundation, Inc.
REQUISITE: Schlrshps for kids of employees of Malone & Hyde
APPLICATION: Applications are accepted throughout the year. Available funds are distributed in August.
CONTACT: 3030 Poplar Ave., Memphis, TN 38111. Margaret Hyde, President. TEL: (901)325-4245

FOUNDATION: Lee (Arthur K. & Sylvia S.) Scholarship Fndtn
REQUISITE: Scholarships for children of employees (company not listed).
APPLICATION: Write for more information.
CONTACT: 5300 Maryland Way, Brentwood, TN 37027. James B. Ford, Secretary-Treasurer.
(We were not able to verify this listing; it may not be extant.)

FOUNDATION: North American Royalties Inc. Welfare Fund
REQUISITE: Scholarships for children of employees of North American Royalties, Inc.
APPLICATION: Application deadline is March 1st.

CONTACT: 200 East Eighth Street, Chattanooga, TN 37402. Gordon L. Smith, Jr., Vice-President, Planning TEL: (615)265-3181

FOUNDATION: Pickett & Hatcher Educational Fund, Inc.
REQUISITE: Undergraduate student loans for those who live in AL, FL, GA, KY, MS, NC, SC, TN, and VA. There is no support for those planning to study medicine, law, or ministry.
APPLICATION: Application deadline is May 15th. First-time applicants may request their application after October 1st.
CONTACT: 1800 Buena Vista Rd, P.O. Box 8169, Columbus, GA 31908. Robert Bennett, Executive Vice-President TEL: (404)327-6586

TEXAS

FOUNDATION: Texas Electric Cooperatives Inc.
REQUISITE: Scholarships granted to Texas residents graduating from high school who are active members of a local Texas chapter of the Future Homemakers of America. Must be attending an accredited institution. Must be US citizen.
APPLICATION: Write for info. Application deadline is March 1st.
CONTACT: POBOX 9589, Austin, TX 78766   512-454-0311

FOUNDATION: Good Samaritan Foundation
REQUISITE: Scholarships granted to all nursing students at "Texas" schools who have attended the clinical level of their nursing education. Must be full-time student at an accredited institution with an accredited nursing program. Must be US citizen.
APPLICATION: Write for info. Application deadline is not specified.
CONTACT: 5615 Kirby Dr., Suite 308, Houston, TX 77005. 713-529-4647

FOUNDATION: National FFA Center
REQUISITE: Scholarships granted to FFA member planning to enroll as a freshman in a 4-year undergraduate program at an accredited university or college in US. Must be a US citizen or legal resident. Must be a resident of CA, FL, SC, TN or TX.
APPLICATION: Write for info. Application deadline is April 1st.
CONTACT: Scholarship Office, POBOX 15160, Alexandria, VA 22309. (703)360-3600

FOUNDATION: May & Wallace Cady Memorial Trust
REQUISITE: Scholarships only to graduates of United Presbyterian Homes

of Synod, TX, for use at Washington University in St. Louis, MO.
APPLICATION: Applications accepted throughout the year. Initial approach by letter.
CONTACT: G. L. Wedemeier, Assistant VP, Commerce Bank of St. Louis, N.A., 8000 Forsyth Blvd., Clayton, MO 63105　(314)726-2255

FOUNDATION: Amarillo Area Foundation, Inc.
REQUISITE: Scholarships for residents of the 26 most northern counties of the Texas Panhandle.
APPLICATION: Write or call for info. Deadline　October 1.
CONTACT: Jack Cromartie, Exec. Dir., 801 S. Fillmore, Suite 700, Amarillo, TX 79101 TEL:　(806)376-4521

FOUNDATION: Mary E. Bivins Foundation
REQUISITE: Scholarships are awarded to residents of TX whose major & institution are religious.
APPLICATION: Deadline to apply is October 31. Include in your letter of request religious preference, background, your reasons for applying, future plans, needs, etc.
CONTACT: Lindsay Ward, 6214 Elmhurst, Amarillo, TX 79106

FOUNDATION: Lindsay Student Aid Fund
REQUISITE: Undergraduate & graduate loans to students attending TX colleges or universities.
APPLICATION: Awards made in July.
CONTACT: Texas Commerce Bank-Austin, POB 550, Austin, TX 78739 TEL:　(512)476-6611

FOUNDATION: Fay T. Barnes Scholarship Trust
REQUISITE: Scholarships for deserving students of Williamson & Travis counties, TX.
APPLICATION: High school principal or counselor for complete application info.　Deadline for applying is January 15.
CONTACT: TX Cmmrce Bnk, Trst Dept., POB 550, Austin 78789

FOUNDATION: Texas Electric Cooperatives Inc. (Ann Lane Homemaker Scholarship)
REQUISITE: Must be an active member of a Texas chapter of The Future Homemakers of America and a graduating seniors.
APPLICATION: Based on grades, need, and community leadership and involvement.　Deadline March 1. Write for application and guidelines.

CONTACT: Dennis Engelke, POB 9589, Austin, TX 78766 (512)454-0311

FOUNDATION: Opal G. Cox Charitable Trust
REQUISITE: Awardee must be enrolled at Baylor University or S.W. Baptist Theological Seminary. Preference is given to students in the top 25% of their class & studying as missionaries or foreign students.
APPLICATION: Write for guidelines to S.W. Baptist Theological Seminary (deadline 4/1) or Baylor University (deadline 5/18)
CONTACT: Judy Bollom, NCNB N.A., Trust Division, 6th & Congress, Austin, TX 78781 (512)397-2586

FOUNDATION: American College of Musicians and National Guild Of Piano Teachers
REQUISITE: Must be a student of the American college of Musicians or National Guild of Piano Teachers.
APPLICATION: Write for application and other guidelines.
CONTACT: P.O. Box 1807, Austin, TX 78767 TEL: (512)478-5775

FOUNDATION: B.M. Woltman Foundation
REQUISITE: Scholarships to students from TX or who are studying in TX, & preparing for the Lutheran ministry or for teaching in Lutheran schools.
APPLICATION: Must be submitted before the school year begins. Completion of formal application required.
CONTACT: Frederick Boden, Exec. Dir., Lutheran Church Synod, 7900 U.S. 290 E., Austin, TX 78724

FOUNDATION: State Scholarship Program for Ethnic Rcrtmnt
REQUISITE: Must have SAT score of 800 or ACT score of 18. Transfer students must have a GPA of at least 2.75. Scholarship good for 1 academic year; non-renewable.
APPLICATION: Contact the financial aid at the public senior college in which they plan to enroll for deadline dates.
CONTACT: TX College & Univrsty System Coordinating Board, POB 12788, Capitol Station, Austin, TX 78711 TEL: (512)462-6400

FOUNDATION: Aupree Foundation
REQUISITE: For residents of Fannin County, TX.
APPLICATION: Write for application anytime.
CONTACT: M. Sorrells, 518 N. Ctr., Bonham, TX 75418 (214)583-5614

FOUNDATION: Astin Charitable Trust

REQUISITE: Must be a senior at either Bryan High School or A&M Consolidated High School in College Station, TX.
APPLICATION: Contact the counselor at either high school for application. Deadline May 1.
CONTACT: Dean Dier, First City National Bank, Trust Dept., PO Drawer 913, Bryan, TX 77805 TEL: (409)776-5402

FOUNDATION: First Cavalry Division Association
REQUISITE: Must be the child of a soldier who died while serving in the First Cavalry Division during the Vietnam War.
APPLICATION: Write for guidelines and application.
CONTACT: 302 N. Main, Copperas Cove, TX 76522

FOUNDATION: Coastal Bend Community Foundation
REQUISITE: Must live in Aransas, Bee, Jim Wells, Kleberg, Nueces, Refugio or San Patricio county.
APPLICATION: Write letter requesting application & guidelines.
CONTACT: Dr. Dana Williams, 1201 N Shoreline, Corpus Christi, TX 78403 TEL: (512)882-9745

FOUNDATION: Paul & Mary Haas Foundation
REQUISITE: Undergraduate scholarships to needy college & vocational school students exclusively in the Corpus Christi area
APPLICATION: Deadline preferably 3 months prior to each semester. Applications accepted throughout the year. Initial approach should be made 4 months prior to each semester. Completion of written application required. Interviews required.
CONTACT: Nancy Wise Somers, Dir., POB 2928, Corpus Christi, TX 78403 TEL: (512)888-9301

FOUNDATION: M.C. & Mattie Caston Foundation, Inc.
REQUISITE: Graduate & undergraduate scholarships for residents of Navarro, TX, & surrounding counties (including Ellis, Limestone, & Freestone) who are applying for or presently attending Navarro College.
APPLICATION: Info. available in high schools & colleges in January. Deadline for applying is March 1.
CONTACT: Ken Walker, Navarro College, Corsicana, TX 75110 TEL: (214)874-6501

FOUNDATION: Harry Bass Foundation
REQUISITE: Must live in Dallas, TX & be a member of a numismatic

organization.
APPLICATION: Deadline November 1 of each year.
CONTACT: Harry W. Bass, Jr., 333 Douglas Ave., Ste. 1400, Dallas, TX 75225 TEL: (214)696-0525

FOUNDATION: Clements Foundation
REQUISITE: Be recommended by faculty of history dept. SMU
APPLICATION: Forms available upon request. No deadline
CONTACT: Dept. of History, SMU, Dallas, TX 75275, Att. Daniel Orlovsky, Chairman TEL: (214)692-2967

FOUNDATION: Haggar Foundation
REQUISITE: For the son, daughter, brother, sister, or spouse of any active employee of the Haggar Corporation.
APPLICATION: Write for applications. Completed forms must arrive at The Schlrshp Office, the University of N. TX, by 4/30
CONTACT: Rosemary Vaugan, 6310 Lemon Ave., Dallas, TX 75209 TEL: (214)352-8481

FOUNDATION: Hayes Foundation #8998-00
REQUISITE: Only Dallas County residents. Must attend Baylor University or Southwestern Theological Seminary in Ft. Worth. Full tuition scholarship awarded to a student.
APPLICATION: Contact foundation.
CONTACT: NCNB, N.A., POB 241, Dallas, TX 75221·

FOUNDATION: Hayes Fndtn #8998-01   Another schlrshp identical to above.

FOUNDATION: Holley Trust
REQUISITE: For worthy girls of Dallas County, TX who desire to attend Wellesley College, Boston, MA, for liberal education.
APPLICATION: Please request application forms. Deadline for entering freshmen is April 30, continuing students June 30.
CONTACT: NCNB Trust Administrator, Alice Gayle, POB 241, Dallas, TX 75221 TEL: (214)977-4410

FOUNDATION: Hurley Foundation
REQUISITE: Theological majors who reside in AR, LA or TX.
APPLICATION: April 15 deadline. Apply to address below.
CONTACT: NCNB, N.A., Alice Gayle, POB 83791, Dallas, TX 75283 TEL:

(214)922-5035

FOUNDATION: M K B Foundation
REQUISITE: For residents of Coleman county for college or vocational school.
APPLICATION: Send letter, no deadline.
CONTACT: Julie Bushman, POB 83791, Dallas, TX 75283 (214)977-4655

FOUNDATION: Maffett Scholarship Trust
REQUISITE: Scholarships for TX residents attending accredited college or university & a declared pre (med or nursing) major. Also good for TX medical schools or AMA approved nursing schools. Limestone county residents given preference.
APPLICATION: Application accompanied by official transcript. April 1 deadline.
CONTACT: Margaret Gregory, Dir. Financial Aid, Southern Methodist Univ., Dallas, TX 75275 TEL: (214)692-3417

FOUNDATION: National Home Fashions League Inc. (Design Fellowship Competition)
REQUISITE: For Interior Design majors open to 2nd - 4th year students as well as graduate students at accredited universities.
APPLICATION: Deadline February 1. Write for more guidelines.
CONTACT: 107 World Trade Center, P.O. Box 58045, Dallas, TX 75258 TEL: (214)747-2406

FOUNDATION: Ryrie Foundation
REQUISITE: & APPLICATION: Request & complete scholarship application provided by foundation; state educational background, objectives, current educational status, financial needs, & autobiography. No deadline.
CONTACT: Charles Ryrie, 3310 Fairmount #5D, Dallas, TX 75201 TEL: (214)522-6220

FOUNDATION: Summers Foundation
REQUISITE: Must be involved in study & teaching of science of self-government in TX.
APPLICATION: Apply by letter with resume & other supporting material.
CONTACT: Gordon Carpenter, Exec. Dir., 325 N. Saint Paul #3210, Dallas, TX 75201 TEL: (214)220-2128

FOUNDATION: Texas Industries Scholarship Foundation
REQUISITE: For employees and dependents only. Must use scholarships at an accredited institution.
APPLICATION: Annual deadline 1/15 Write for application.
CONTACT: TX Industries Foundation, Scholarship Coordinator, 7610 Stemmons Freeway, Dallas, TX 75247 TEL: (214)647-6700

FOUNDATION: Ann Bradshaw Stokes Foundation
REQUISITE: Scholarships to students majoring in theater & drama at colleges & universities in TX.
APPLICATION: Completion of formal application required. Institutional recommendation of applicant's potential required.
CONTACT: Foundation at 3204 Beverly Dr., Dallas, TX 75205 TEL: (214)528-1924

FOUNDATION: Sunnyside, Inc.
REQUISITE: Educational aid to underprivileged children residing in TX to provide for their intellectual needs.
APPLICATION: Applications accepted throughout the year. Completion of formal application required.
CONTACT: Mary Rothenflue, Exec. Dir., 8609 N.W. Plaza Dr., Ste. 201, Dallas, TX 75225 (214)692-5686

FOUNDATION: Watson Foundation
REQUISITE: Limited to high schl graduates of Tarrant or Dallas county, TX & who attend college in TX.
APPLICATION: Write for application, March 31 deadline.
CONTACT: NCNB N.A., Janne Wolfe, POB 241, Dallas, TX 75221 TEL: (214)977-4444

FOUNDATION: Puett Foundation
REQUISITE: Check with high school counselors.
APPLICATION: Ask for school procedures.
CONTACT: Dell City ISD, Mrs. Leslie Harlan, Sprntndt., POB 37, Dell City, TX 79837 (915)964-2663

FOUNDATION: Munson Foundation Trust
REQUISITE: For educational, medical & cultural purposes in the county of Grayson, TX.
APPLICATION: Letter stating purpose & purposed application of funds.
CONTACT: TX American Bank, Brent Reed, POB 341, Denison, TX 75020

Texas

(We were not able to verify this listing; it may not be extant.)

FOUNDATION: Temple-Inland Foundation
REQUISITE: Scholarships only to children of employees who have completed 3 years of continuous full-time service as of April 1 of the year of application at Temple-Inland, Inc. or its subsidiaries (except Inland Container Corporation).
APPLICATION: Deadline March 15. Completion of formal application & interviews required. Application forms & info. can be obtained in the offices of Temple-Inland, Inc. & its subsidiaries as well as from the foundation.
CONTACT: James R. Wash, Secty.-Treasurer, 303 S. Temple Dr., PO Drawer 338, Diboll, TX 75941 TEL: (409)829-5511

FOUNDATION: Robert Schreck Memorial Fund
REQUISITE: Must be El Paso County resident for at least 2 years and U.S. citizen or legal resident. Fields of study include Architecture, Chemistry, Engineering, Episcopal clergy, Medicine, Vet Medicine, and Physics.
APPLICATION: Deadlines 7/15 and 11/15. Write for guidelines.
CONTACT: Terry Crenshaw, Charitable Services Officer, c/o Texas Commerce Bank Trust Dept., P.O. Drawer 140, El Paso, TX 79980 TEL: (915)546-6515

FOUNDATION: El Paso Community Foundation
REQUISITE: El Paso area residents & must be enrolled in higher learning institute.
APPLICATION: Write for guidelines.
CONTACT: Janice Windle, Exec. Dir., 201 East Main, Ste. 1616, El Paso, TX 79901 TEL: (915)533-4020

FOUNDATION: The Mary L. Peyton Foundation
REQUISITE: Assistance only to legal residents or children of living residents of El Paso County, TX. Preference is given to children of needy present or former employees of Peyton Packing Company.
APPLICATION: Applications accepted throughout the year. Initial approach by letter explaining economic situation causing the need for assistance for basic services & itemization of those for which assistance is requested. Completion of formal application required. Interviews granted upon request.
CONTACT: James M. Day, Exec. Administrator, Texas Commerce Bank Building, Ste. 1706, El Paso, TX 79901 TEL: (915)858-6632

FOUNDATION: J.F. Maddox Foundation
REQUISITE: Student loans primarily for residents of NM & Western TX.
APPLICATION: No deadline. Initial approach by letter requesting application. Completion of formal application required.
CONTACT: Robert Socolofsky, Exec. Dir., POB 5410, Hobbs, NM 88241
TEL: (505)393-6338

FOUNDATION: Farah Foundation
REQUISITE: The scholarships are for students from El Paso attending UT at El Paso.
APPLICATION: Write for applications.
CONTACT: Grant Administrator, The Farah Foundation, P.O. Box 140, El Paso, TX 79980
(We were not able to verify this listing; it may not be extant.)

FOUNDATION: USPA & IRA Educational Foundation
REQUISITE: Limited to members of active duty, retired or deceased military family who are needy. Scholarship limited to $1,000 for undergraduate education only.
APPLICATION: Write for applications, no deadline.
CONTACT: G. Norman Coder, POB 2387, Ft. Worth, TX 76113 TEL: (817)731-8621

FOUNDATION: C.L. Rowan Charitable & Educational Fund, Inc.
REQUISITE: Grants to TX residents attending TX universities.
APPLICATION: Applications accepted throughout the year. Initial approach by letter.
CONTACT: Elton Hyder, Jr., 1918 Commerce Bldg., Fort Worth, TX 76102
TEL: (817)332-2327

FOUNDATION: Carter Star Telegram Employees
REQUISITE: Scholarships go only to children of employees of Fort Worth Star Telegram.
APPLICATION: Initially write a letter.
CONTACT: Mrs. Nenetta Tatum, 400 West 7th Street, Fort Worth, TX 76102 TEL: (817)390-7400

FOUNDATION: GLWJ Foundation
REQUISITE: Must be a high school graduate from Tarrant County, TX or a present college enrollee below Junior standing with at least a 3.0 GPA beginning with the 9th grade.

APPLICATION: Write for application. Deadline Dec 31 for following fall.
CONTACT: Frank P. Turrel, 2000 Tam O'Shanter, Ft. Worth, TX 76111
(We were not able to verify this listing; it may not be extant.)

FOUNDATION: Dallas-Fort Worth Association of Black Communicators
Scholarships
REQUISITE: Financial assistance to minority students in TX who are
interested in careers in print, broadcasting, or photojournalism. Must be
a minority high school senior or college freshmen & be a resident of TX.
APPLICATION: Deadline January of each year.
CONTACT: Dallas-Fort Worth/Association of Black Communicators,
Anthony Davis Bldg., 3103 Martin Luther King Blvd., Fort Worth, TX 75215
(We were not able to verify this listing; it may not be extant.)

FOUNDATION: Richardson Memorial Fund
REQUISITE: Must be a spouse, child, or grandchild presently employed
full time or a retired employee at Sid W. Richardson.
APPLICATION: Request application, include name, place & date of service
of qualifying employee. Apply by March 31.
CONTACT: Jo Helen Rosacker, 309 Main St., Ft. Worth, TX 76102 TEL:
(817)336-0494

FOUNDATION: Taylor Family Trust
REQUISITE: Limited to TX residents majoring in Home Economics.
APPLICATION: Obtain applications through the Home Economics Dept.
at TX cllg or university. May 1 deadline.
CONTACT: Texas American Bank, Suzanne Jennings, POB 2050, Ft.
Worth, TX 76113
(We were not able to verify this listing; it may not be extant.)

FOUNDATION: Wrightsman Educational Fund, Inc.
REQUISITE: Show financial need, be worthy or needy, good moral
character and have good grades. Also available for summer school.
Limited to payments on tuition and direct school expenses.
APPLICATION: Write for application, no deadline, include the following
information: the school you are attending, your classification, copy of your
grades or transcript, the yearly cost of school, your financial status, and
info on other form of financial assistance. Must reapply each semester.
CONTACT: Mr. Whitfield Collins, 801 Cherish St., Ste. 2100, Ft. Worth, TX
76102 TEL: (817)332-9396

FOUNDATION: Texas Osteopathic Medical Association
REQUISITE: Must be a Texas resident enrolled in college of osteopathic medicine.
APPLICATION: Deadline May 1. Write for guidelines.
CONTACT: 226 Bailey Ave., Fort Worth, 76107 TEL: (817)294-2788

FOUNDATION: August W. Klingelhoefer Needy Student Assistance Fund
REQUISITE: Scholarships to residents of Fredericksburg, TX.
APPLICATION: Deadline for applying is May 1. Completion of formal application required along with a student financial assistance form including info. regarding need, ambition, merit, scholastic ability, & financial data.
CONTACT: John Clawson, Principal, Fredericksburg High School, Fredericksburg, TX 78624 TEL: (210)997-7551

FOUNDATION: Hill Country Student Help--
REQUISITE: Must have lived for 2 years & graduated from a Gilespie County, TX high school. $1000 loan per year for 4 years for expenses while attending post secondary school.
APPLICATION: Request application form. No deadlines.
CONTACT: John Benson, POB 151, Fredericksburg, TX 78624 TEL: (210)997-9865

FOUNDATION: Pearce Educational Foundation
REQUISITE: For young residents of Galveston City who want college or professional education.
APPLICATION: Applications accepted from January-April. Write for application & guidelines.
CONTACT: United States National Bank, Judith T. Whelton, POB 8210, Galveston, TX 77553 TEL: (409)763-1151

FOUNDATION: Harris & Eliza Kempner Fund
REQUISITE: Interest-free student loans only to residents of TX; no grants. Limit per student of $10,000 over the 3-or 4-year program.
APPLICATION: Deadlines 7/1 & 10/1. Applications accepted all year. Initial approach by letter. Co-signers required.
CONTACT: POB 119, Galveston, TX 77553 TEL: (409)762-1603

FOUNDATION: The Moody Foundation
REQUISITE: Schlarships for graduates of hgh schls of Galveston Cnty TX
APPLICATION: Applications through school in September of senior year.

CONTACT: Peter M. Moore, Grants Officer, 2302 Post Office St., Ste. 704, Galveston, TX 77550 TEL: (409)763-5333

FOUNDATION: Seibel Foundation
REQUISITE: TX residents enrolled in an accredited TX College & the student is in good standing.
APPLICATION: Write for application. February 28 is deadline.
CONTACT: United States National Bank, Judith Whelton, POB 8210, Galveston, TX 77553 409-763-1151

FOUNDATION: Live Oak Foundation
REQUISITE: For the poorer high school students in the southern counties of TX who wish to continue their education in a vocational field.
APPLICATION: Write a resume of academic record. No deadln
CONTACT: Alfred West Ward, POB 1202, George West, TX 78022
(We were not able to verify this listing; it may not be extant.)

FOUNDATION: Elam Scholarship Trust Fund
REQUISITE: Resident of Hamilton County, TX & attending public school in the county.
APPLICATION: Deadline is May 10.   Include in application name & address, name & income of parent(s), school activities & awards, personal references, goals, vocational interests & the reasons you applied.
CONTACT: Guarantee Bank, Bill Barkley, POB 873, Hamilton, TX 76531 TEL: (817)386-8937

FOUNDATION: Ollege & Minnie Morrison Foundation
REQUISITE: Scholarships only to graduating seniors of the Livingston Intermediate School District, Livingston, TX, area.
APPLICATION: Write for info. No deadline listed.
CONTACT: Fndtn, TX Commerce Bank, POB 2558, Houston, TX 77252

FOUNDATION: Shell Companies Foundation, Inc
REQUISITE: Must be the child of an employee of participating Shell Co. in the US.   Also must compete successfully in the corporations qualifications test. Apply your junior year in high school.
APPLICATION: Write for guidelines and application.
CONTACT: Two Shell Plaza, P.O. Box 2099, Houston, TX 77001   TEL: (713)241-3078

FOUNDATION: American Junior Brahman Association (Ladies of the A.B.B.A. Scholarship)
REQUISITE: Member of the Junior Brahman Association, a full time undergraduate student studying agriculture.
APPLICATION: Apply your junior year in high school.
CONTACT: 1313 La Concha Ln., Houston 77054 TEL: (713)795-4444

FOUNDATION: Cooper Industries Foundation
REQUISITE: Scholarships only to children of employees of Cooper Industries, Inc. in AL, CA, CT, GA, IL, IN, ME, MI, MO, MS, NJ, NY, NC, OH, OK, PA, SC, TN, TX and VA.
APPLICATION: Applications accepted throughout the year. Initial approach by letter.
CONTACT: Patricia B. Meinecke, Secty., 1001 Fannin, Ste. 4000, POB 4446, Houston, TX 77002 TEL: (713)739-5632

FOUNDATION: Gregory Foundation
REQUISITE: Awards are for primarily East TX residents majoring in religion, education, or cultural studies.
APPLICATION: No deadline or standard application form.
CONTACT: Temple Webber, Jr., 1001 Fannin, Ste. 4360, Houston, TX 77002 TEL: (713)951-9544

FOUNDATION: The Robert A. Welch Foundation
REQUISITE: Grants to full-time faculty members of TX educational institutions to do research in basic chemistry.
APPLICATION: Deadline to apply is Feb 1. Initial approach by phone. Completion of formal application required. Interviews required.
CONTACT: Norbert Dittrich, Exec. Manager, 4605 Post Oak Place, Ste. 200, Houston, TX 77027 TEL: (713)961-9884

FOUNDATION: George & Mary Josephine Hamman Foundation
REQUISITE: Undergraduate scholarships only to graduating high school seniors in the Houston, TX, area.
APPLICATION: Deadline for applying is March 15. Initial approach before Nov. by letter including name, address, & name of high school you are attending. Completion of formal application & interviews required.
CONTACT: Thomas P. Stone, Operating Manager, 910 Travis, Ste. 1990, Houston, TX 77002 TEL: (713)658-8345

FOUNDATION: Leola W. & Charles H. Hugg Trust

REQUISITE: Scholarships for students from Williamson County to attend colleges & universities in TX.
APPLICATION: Deadline for applying is May 1. Application forms & guidelines are available upon request from participating high schools, or from the dir. of the Texas Baptist Children's Home in Round Rock, TX, or the Office of Student Financial Aid at Southwestern University in Georgetown, TX.
CONTACT: Foundation c/o Carroll Sunseri, Texas Commerce Bank, POB 809, Houston, TX 77001 TEL: (713)216-4865

FOUNDATION: Knox Charitable Foundation
REQUISITE: Must attend Austin College
APPLICATION: Apply by letter; no deadline.
CONTACT: The Nations Bank-Houston, Carl Schumacher, POB 2518, Houston, TX 7252 TEL: (713)787-5441

FOUNDATION: Conrad and Marcel Schlumberger Schlrshp Fnd
REQUISITE: Must be the son or daughter of a Schlumberger employee. Must be a high school senior or an entering freshman.
APPLICATION: Deadln 3/31. Write for guidelines & application.
CONTACT: Scholarship Committee, POB 2175, Houston 77001

FOUNDATION: Parry Foundation
REQUISITE: Priority given to nursing majors attending universities in TX or OK & intending to practice in TX or the SW.
APPLICATION: Submit application through the institution you are or will attend. These institutions have established criteria.
CONTACT: W.W. Vann, POB 2538, Houston 77252, TEL: (713)651-0641

FOUNDATION: Student Aid Foundation Enterprise, Inc.
REQUISITE: Primarily for underprivileged youths from Houston area, but all requests are considered. Matching funds for U of H and Rice, also available for foreign students.
APPLICATION: Write for application or submit request in letter
CONTACT: Frank T. Abraham, 800 Commerce St., Houston, TX 77002 TEL: (713)222-7211

FOUNDATION: Worthing Scholarship Fund
REQUISITE: Applicant must have graduated from a high school in HISD, attend an accredited college in TX, maintain a "C" average & take a full course load.

APPLICATION: State background & goals on application. May 1 deadline for fall semester.
CONTACT: NCNB N.A., F.D.Woesley, 119 E St.,Houston 77018

FOUNDATION: American Women in Radio & Television
REQUISITE: Paid internships granted to students with Junior, Senior or Graduate status at a Houston area college or university for a period of 8 weeks at a company chosen to suit student's interest.
APPLICATION: Write for info. Application deadline is April 15th.
CONTACT: Cathy Coers, KLTR-FM, 10333 Richmond, Suite 693, Houston, TX 77042.
(We were not able to verify, this listing; it may not be extant.)

FOUNDATION: The David & Eula Wintermann Foundation
REQUISITE: Scholarships to area high school seniors whose intended field of study is in the medical field.
APPLICATION: Deadline to apply is April.   Initial approach by letter, including high School transcript, statement of financial need, field of intended study, & a character reference, required.
CONTACT: Daniel Thorton (409) 234-5551 or (713) 346-1735

FOUNDATION: Boy Scouts of America / J. Edgar Hoover Foundation Scholarship
REQUISITE: Must be a registered active Explorer in a post specializing in Law Enforcement. Must be a high school senior and have an interest in Law Enforcement.
APPLICATION: Deadline March 31.   Also ask about the Boy Scout Directory of scholarships and loans for all areas of study. Write for guidelines and application.
CONTACT: 1325 Walnut Hill Ln., Irving, TX 75038 (214)580-2000

FOUNDATION: D.D. Hachar Charitable Trust Fund
REQUISITE: Scholarships & loans primarily to resident of Laredo & Webb County, TX, for higher education or to students with a degree from a TX college or a non-resident with a B.A. from a TX school.
APPLICATION: Initial approach by phone or letter. Complete a formal application. Interview required. Deadlines last Friday in April & October.
CONTACT: Margie H. Weatherford, Administrator, c/o Laredo National Bank, POB 59, Laredo, TX 78042 TEL: (210)723-1151

FOUNDATION: Lubbock Area Foundation

REQUISITE: Must be from the Lubbock area.
APPLICATION: Deadline Feb 1. Write for information and application.
CONTACT: Kathleen Stocco, Exec.Dir., 1655 Main St. #209, Lubbock, TX
79401 TEL: (806)762-8061

FOUNDATION: S.D. Scholarship Fund
REQUISITE: Employees of the Newsprint Operation in Lufkin & Sheldon
Mills are eligible for scholarships.
APPLICATION: Info. & application are available upon request.
CONTACT: T.J. McComber, Highway 103 E., POB 149, Lufkin, TX 75901
(We were not able to verify this listing; it may not be extant.)

FOUNDATION: The Luling Foundation
REQUISITE: Scholarships to residents of Caldwell, Gonzales, &
Guadalupe cnties, working toward an agricultural degree.
APPLICATION: Deadline for applying is May 15. Completion of formal ap-
plication required.
CONTACT: Archie Abrameit, Manager, 523 S. Mulberry Ave., PO Drawer
31, Luling, TX 78648
(We were not able to verify this listing; it may not be extant.)

FOUNDATION: Lewer Foundation
REQUISITE: Awards are for students studying in Lutheran Church schools
Missouri Synod.
APPLICATION: By letter; no deadline.
CONTACT: Mr. & Mrs. Buck Busse, Rte. 2, Box 130, Lyford, TX 78569
TEL: (210)347-3470

FOUNDATION: Mead Educational Trust
REQUISITE: For residents of Marion, Harrison, Cass, Morris, Gregg or
Upshur counties, TX to receive academic scholarships to institutions of
higher learning.
APPLICATION: Write for applications.
CONTACT: Rev. Malcolm Proudy, 309 S. Frio, Jefferson, TX 75675, Mrs.
Enid King, POB 297A, Hughes Springs, TX 75656 or H. V. Hackney, 1300
E. Austin, Marshall, TX 75670
(We were not able to verify this listing; it may not be extant.)

FOUNDATION: Tartt Scholarship Fund
REQUISITE: Student must attend non-state supported college or
university & must be a resident of Harrison, Panola, Gregg, Upshur or

Marion Counties, TX.
APPLICATION: Guidelines & application sent upon request.
CONTACT: Rev. James Heflin, POB 1964, Marshall, TX 75671
(We were not able to verify this listing; it may not be extant.)

FOUNDATION: Loring Cook Foundation
REQUISITE: Must be a local high school graduate.
APPLICATION: Write before March 1 to McAllen Memorial High School counselor for procedures on how to apply.
CONTACT: Vannie E. Cook, Jr., POB 1060, McAllen, TX 78502
TEL: (512)686-5491

FOUNDATION: Heard Foundation of Collin County, TX
REQUISITE: Student must be resident of Collin County, TX.
APPLICATION: Applications available upon request.   Submit before semester, but scholarships are limited by availability of funds.
CONTACT: W.B. Hope, POB 661, McKinney, TX 75069 (214)542-1773

FOUNDATION: Fasken Foundation
REQUISITE: Apply through the high school. Must be a resident of TX.
Must be a graduate from a Midland County high school.
APPLICATION: Write for specific forms which spell out data requirements.
CONTACT: B.L. Jones, 500 W. Texas, Ste. 1160,Midland, TX 79701, TEL: (915)683-5401

FOUNDATION: Manna Foundation
REQUISITE: Three letters of recommendation, educational institute, course of study, cost & need. Submit most recent grades & GPA. MUST MAINTAIN "C" average.
APPLICATION: Write for application.
CONTACT: Elizabeth A. Blackmore, 200 W. Illinois, Ste. 200, Midland, TX 79701 (We were not able to verify this listing; it may not be extant.)

FOUNDATION: Scarborough Foundation
REQUISITE: No specifications.
APPLICATION: Write letter describing need for grant.
CONTACT: Evelyn Lineberry, POB 1536, Midland, TX 79702
(We were not able to verify this listing; it may not be extant.)

FOUNDATION: McKinney Foundation
REQUISITE: Church related.

APPLICATION: Apply by letter.
CONTACT: H. Wade Miller, POB 8, Nacogdoches, TX 75963
(We were not able to verify this listing; it may not be extant.)

FOUNDATION: Nelda C. & H.J. Lutcher Stark Foundation (Administered by Texas Interscholastic League Foundation)
REQUISITE: Must be high school senior, rank top 25% of graduating class, place 1st, 2nd or 3rd in Interscholastic league contest in science, number sense, calculator application or ready writing. Scholarships limited to residents of TX & southwest LA.
APPLICATION: Applications accepted throughout the year.   Initial approach by letter.
CONTACT: Clyde V. McKee, Jr., Secty.-Treasurer, 602 W. Main St., POB 909, Orange, TX 77631-0909 TEL: (409)883-3513

FOUNDATION: McMillan, Jr. Foundation, Inc.
REQUISITE: Generally for graduates of high schools in a 15 mile radius of Overton, TX.
APPLICATION: Write for application & guidelines. Deadln 6/15
CONTACT: Ralph Ward, POB 9, Overton 75684 TEL: (903)834-3148

FOUNDATION: Fellowship of United Methodist in Worship, Music and Other Arts
REQUISITE: Must be a member of the United Methodist Church at least one year prior to application. Must be an undergraduate planning a career in music, worship, or related arts in the Methodist Church.
APPLICATION: Deadline June 1. Write for guidelines and application.
CONTACT: P.O. Box 603, Paducah, TX 79240 TEL: (806)492-3321

FOUNDATION: Haverlah Foundation
REQUISITE: Students wishing to attend 4 yr college or university in TX.
APPLICATION: Deadline May 8. Write for application.
CONTACT: H.L. Brown, 901 N. Mallard, Palestine, TX 75801
(We were not able to verify this listing; it may not be extant.)

FOUNDATION: Burch-Settoon Student Loan Fund
REQUISITE: Restricted to high school graduates of Brisco, Castro, Floyd, Hale, Lamb or Swisher counties of TX.
APPLICATION: Apply before April 30. Applications & guidelines are available upon request.
CONTACT: First United Methodist Church Board of Stewards, Plainview,

TX 79072 TEL: (806)293-3658

FOUNDATION: Snyder Trust
REQUISITE: Write for restrictions. Must be graduate from Plainview High, Boys Ranch, Girls Town.
APPLICATION: Write for application. Deadline precedes fall registration.
CONTACT: First National Bank, Trust Dept., POB 580, Plainview TX 79073 TEL: (806)296-0396

FOUNDATION: Ryan Foundation
REQUISITE: Must be a resident of TX & have a yearly income less than $30,000. For N. TX State U. in Denton & UT in Dallas & Richardson.
APPLICATION: Write for more info.
CONTACT: Ann E. O'Neal, 4975 Preston Park Blvd., Ste. 375, Plano, TX 75075 (We were not able to verify this listing; it may not be extant.)

FOUNDATION: Harding Foundation
REQUISITE: Seminary students only.
APPLICATION: Letter explaining need. No deadline.
CONTACT: Harding Foundation P.O. Box 130,Raymondville, TX 78580 TEL: (210)689-2706

FOUNDATION: San Antonio Area Foundation
REQUISITE: Scholarships primarily to high school snrs in Bexar County, TX. One fund limited to San Antonio residents in religious education.
APPLICATION: Get applications through counselor of schools.
CONTACT: Katherine Netting Folbre, Exec. Dir., Bear County Scholarship Clearing House, 800 Northwest, Loop 410, Ste. 200, San Antonio, TX 78216 TEL: (210)525-8494

FOUNDATION: Professional Engineers Scholarship Fund, Inc.
REQUISITE: Scholarships to residents within the geographic boundaries of the Bexar Chapter TX Society of Professional Engineers to attend accredited engineering colleges.
APPLICATION: Deadline for applying is 11/1. Completion of formal application required using current NSPE Educational Foundation Scholarship application form. Interviews required.
CONTACT: Mr. Michael Couch, Secty., 6735 Carters Bluff, SA, TX 78239 (We were not able to verify this listing; it may not be extant.)

FOUNDATION: Minnie Stevens Piper Foundation

REQUISITE: Student loans for undergraduate juniors or seniors, or graduate students who are residents of TX attending TX colleges, universities, or graduate schools.
APPLICATION: Loan applications must be made through recipient's college or university. Completion of formal application required. Application should be accompanied by transcript of grades & letter of recommendation regarding character & ability from head of dept. of student's major or dean of students.
CONTACT: Michael J. Balint, Exec. Dir., GPM S. Tower, Ste. 530, 800 NW Loop 410, San Antonio 78216-5699 TEL: (210)525-8494

FOUNDATION: Classen Memorial Scholarship Fnd
REQUISITE: Preferably students attending TX Lutheran College or some other Lutheran college.
APPLICATION: Send background info., academic record, & need requirements to either TX Lutheran College or the address below asking for application form.
CONTACT: Frost National Bank, Susan Palmer, POB 1600, San Antonio, TX 78296 TEL: (210)220-4363

FOUNDATION: Non Commissioned Officers Association
REQUISITE: Must be the child of a member and be under 25 years old for initial grant.
APPLICATION: Submit SAT or ACT scores and an essay on Patriotism-What America and the American Way of Life Means to Me. Based on academic ability. Deadline 3/31. Write for guidelines & application.
CONTACT: P.O. Box 33610, San Antonio, TX 78233
(We were not able to verify this listing; it may not be extant.)

FOUNDATION: Phi Sigma Iota-Office of the Executive Secretary (Scholarship Fund)
REQUISITE: Must be an active member of Phi Sigma Iota (Foreign Languages Honor Society) and maintain a "B" average.
APPLICATION: Deadline March 1. Write for guidelines.
CONTACT: c/o Modern Language Dept./Southwest Texas State University, San Marcos, TX 78666 TEL: (512)245-2138

FOUNDATION: Welder Wildlife Foundation
REQUISITE: The scholarships are limited to the study of conservation, range management or wildlife.
APPLICATION: Write for application & guidelines.

CONTACT: John Welder, POB 1400, Sinton, TX 78387 (512)364-2643

FOUNDATION: Nettie Millhollon Educational Trust
REQUISITE: Educational loans ($1,500.00 per semester) to needy residents of TX. Must take at least 12 semester hours, maintain 2.5 average. After initial screening will arrange a personal interview.
APPLICATION: Write for info. July 1 deadline for fall semester; January 2 deadline for spring semester. No funds available for summer semester or graduate school.
CONTACT: Millhollon Educational Trust Estate, 309 W St. Anna, P.O. Box 643, Stanton, TX 79782 TEL: (915)756-2261

FOUNDATION: Wilson Plastics Employee Scholarships
REQUISITE: For Ralph Wilson Plastic Co. in Temple, TX employees' children.
APPLICATION: Write for application.
CONTACT: Gail Benavidez, 600 General Bruce Dr., Temple, TX 76501 TEL: (817)778-2711

FOUNDATION: Scottish Rite Edctnal & Fellowshp Prgrm of TX
REQUISITE: Fellowships to TX residents for doctoral degree studies at universities in TX having accredited curricula in public school administration. Special consideration will be given to individuals with family Masonic connections.
APPLICATION: Applications accepted throughout the year. Completion of formal application required.
CONTACT: N. Lee Dunham, Chairman, Awards Committee, 2632 Lake Oaks Rd., Waco, TX 76710 TEL: (817)754-3942

FOUNDATION: Meat Cutters Educational Trust
REQUISITE: Must be a member of a Local UFCW or a child of a member & a high school senior, under 20, who will graduate in the spring.
APPLICATION: Write for application. Deadline December 31.
CONTACT: UFCW Scholarship Program, Office of Education, 1775 K Street N.W., Washington, DC 20006
(We were not able to verify this listing; it may not be extant.)

FOUNDATION: M.E. Singleton Scholarship Trust
REQUISITE: Scholarships only to students who graduate from high schools in Ellis County, TX, & are unable to enter college without financial assistance.

APPLICATION: Applications accepted throughout the year. Initial approach by letter requesting application. Completion of formal application required.
CONTACT: George H. Singleton, Pres., POB 717, Waxahachie, TX 75165
(We were not able to verify this listing; it may not be extant.)

FOUNDATION: Gentry Scholarship Fund Trust
REQUISITE: Scholarship limited to $150.00 each.
APPLICATION: Must apply within 3 months of graduation from high school. Written application & personal interview necessary. Tell about scholastic standing & economic need.
CONTACT: Sue Plowman, c/o Texas Bank, POB 760, Weatherford, TX 76086 TEL: (817)594-8721

FOUNDATION: Hawes Foundation, Inc.
REQUISITE: Must be a student in TX, Wharton County.
APPLICATION: No deadline, make request by letter.
CONTACT: Albert W. Clay, 309 N. Resident St., Wharton, TX 77488
(We were not able to verify this listing; it may not be extant.)

FOUNDATION: Godwin Foundation, Inc.
REQUISITE: Must be a resident of Grayson County, TX.
APPLICATION: In letter requesting schlrshp or loan state cost of tuition & room & board. Indicate college major & future plans. No deadline.
CONTACT: Carl Bryan, POB 10, Whitesboro, TX 76273
(We were not able to verify this listing; it may not be extant.)

FOUNDATION: Edith Hardin Foundation for Wichita County
REQUISITE: Must be Midwestern State University attendee.
APPLICATION: Deadlines are 4/1 for summer, 7/1 for fall, 11/1 for spring semester. Apply at financial aid office at the college.
CONTACT: Joseph N Sherrill, Jr, PO Drawer S&P, Wichita Falls, TX 76307
(We were not able to verify this listing; it may not be extant.)

FOUNDATION: Frank & Bea Wood Foundation
REQUISITE: Undergraduate educational grants.
APPLICATION: Applications accepted throughout the year. Completion of formal application required.
CONTACT: Martha Kay Hendrickson, 2304 Midwestern Parkway, Ste. 204, Wichita Falls, TX 76308
(We were not able to verify this listing; it may not be extant.)

FOUNDATION: The M.L. Shanor Foundation
REQUISITE: Student loans primarily to residents of Cherokee, Midland, Wichita, & Wilbarger counties, TX.
APPLICATION: Deadline for applying is August 1. Completion of formal application required.
CONTACT: J.B. Jarratt, Pres., POB 7522, Wichita Falls, TX 76307
(We were not able to verify this listing; it may not be extant.)

FOUNDATION: West Foundation
REQUISITE: Residents of Wichita Falls, TX area.
APPLICATION: Write for application.
CONTACT: Lane West, 1632 Hursh, Wichita Falls, TX 76302
(We were not able to verify this listing; it may not be extant.)

FOUNDATION: Rooke Foundation Inc.
REQUISITE: Must be a Refugio County high school graduate.
APPLICATION: Applications at Refugio Cnty Hgh Schls.
CONTACT: Frank J. Scanio, Jr., POB 7, Woodsboro, TX 78393
TEL: (512)543-4533

FOUNDATION: Transportation Clubs International
REQUISITE: Scholarships granted to students who have graduated from a Texas high school and is now attending an accredited college or university in a degree or vocational program in Transportation or Traffic Management.
APPLICATION: Write for info. Application deadline is April 15th.
CONTACT: 203 E. Third Street, Suite 201, Sanford, FL 32771.
(We were not able to verify this listing; it may not be extant.)

FOUNDATION: Levi Strauss Foundation
REQUISITE: Business Opportunity Scholarships to disadvantaged high school seniors in U.S. communities where Levi Strauss & Co. has production or distribution facilities including AR, CA, GA, NV, NM, TX, & VA. Foundation also awards international scholarships.
APPLICATION: Applications accepted throughout the year. Initial approach by letter requesting application. Completion of formal application required.
CONTACT: Martha Montag Brown, Dir. of U.S. Contributions, 1155 Battery St., POB 7215, SF, CA 94106 TEL: (415)544-6577

FOUNDATION: Transportation Clubs International (Texas Traffic and

Transportation Scholarship)
REQUISITE: Must be a Texas high school graduate attending an accredited university and majoring in Transportation or Traffic Management.

APPLICATION: Deadline is April 15. Write information.
CONTACT: 1040 Woodcock Rd, Orlando, FL 32803
(We were not able to verify this listing; it may not be extant.)

HOUSTON LIVESTOCK SHOW & RODEO SCHOLARSHIPS
(See CONTACT: for application)

FOUNDATION: Four-year Scholarships
REQUISITE: Must be a graduating high school senior who ranks academically in the upper one-fourth of the graduating class at the end of the 1st semester or equivalent of your senior year. You must also satisfy all other criteria, rules & procedures presented in the scholarship application. 100, four year, $8,000 awards given annually. Must be 4-H or FFA member.
CONTACT: Scholarship Director, Houston Livestock Show & Rodeo, POB 20070, Houston, TX 77225, for further information.

FOUNDATION: Metropolitan Scholarship Program
REQUISITE: You must be a graduating high school senior who ranks academically in the upper one-fourth of the graduating class at the end of the 1st semester of your senior year or a midterm graduate of the semester immediately preceding the award of the scholarship. 26, four year, $8,000 awards given annually to students in Harris and surrounding counties.
CONTACT: Scholarship Director, Houston Livestock Show & Rodeo, POB 20070, Houston, TX 77225, for further info.

FOUNDATION: School Art Program Scholarships
REQUISITE: Recipients are selected from the school districts participating in the Houston Livestock Show & Rodeo School Art Program. Each year school district representatives present the program in their respective districts in the fall. Beginning in early January-mid-February, committee members & judges schedule, attend & judge art shows in each participating school district. 4, one year $2,000 and 1, 4 year, $8,000 awards given annually.
CONTACT: Scholarship Director, Houston Livestock Show & Rodeo, POB 20070, Houston, TX 77225, for further information.

FOUNDATION: Cowboy Artist of America/Schreiner College Scholarships
REQUISITE: Recipients are selected through an application process. Application forms are given to all 11th & 12th grade students in each participating school district who are "Best of Show" or "Gold Medal" winners. Interviews are required.
CONTACT: For further information, contact Scholarship Director, Houston Livestock Show & Rodeo, POB 20070, Houston, TX 77225.

FOUNDATION: Go Texan Scholarships
REQUISITE: Must be a graduating high school senior who ranks academically in the upper one-fourth of your graduating class at the end of the 2nd 6 weeks grading period or equivalent of your senior year. 57, one year, $2,000 awards and one, 4 year, $8,000 award given annually.
CONTACT: Scholarship Director, Houston Livestock Show & Rodeo, POB 20070, Houston, TX 77225, for further information.

FOUNDATION: Endowed Scholarships
REQUISITE: Must be an existing college/university student who has demonstrated financial need & who is a permanent citizen of the U.S. You must also be an undergraduate student selected by the college/school/dept. of agriculture scholarship selection committee. You must have & maintain an authorized major in an agricultural field of study in the college/school/dept. of agriculture at the institution throughout the duration of the scholarship.
CONTACT: Scholarship Director, Houston Livestock Show & Rodeo, POB 20070, Houston, TX 77225, for further information

FOUNDATION: Doctor of Veterinary Medicine
REQUISITE: Acceptance to Texas A&M DVM School. One, one year scholarship for $4,000.
CONTACT: Scholarship Director, Houston Livestock Show & Rodeo, POB 20070, Houston, TX 77225, for further information.

UTAH

FOUNDATION: Utah State Office of Education
REQUISITE: Scholarships granted to outstanding Utah high school graduates or college freshman. Open to undergrads on a sophomore/junior or senior level.
APPLICATION: Write for info. Application deadline is March 1st.
CONTACT: 250 E. 500 SO., Salt Lake City, UT 84111. (801)538-7500

FOUNDATION: Bank One Scholarship Trust
REQUISITE: Scholarships for high school seniors who will attend the University of Utah or another institution and major in banking and finance.
APPLICATION: Get applications through office of development at University of Utah.
CONTACT: Bank One, 80 West Broadway, Suite 210, Salt Lake City, UT 84101. University of Utah, College of Business, 202 Park Bldg, Salt Lake Cty, UT 84112. TEL: (801)481-5350

FOUNDATION: Ruth Eleanor Bamberger & John Ernest Bamberger Memorial Foundation
REQUISITE: Must be a UT resident, with preference given to student nurses. Occasional loans awarded for medical education.
APPLICATION: Attend an interview. Write for info. Deadline not listed.
CONTACT: William H. Olwell, Secty.-Treasurer, 1201 Walker Ctr., Salt Lake City, UT 84111 TEL: (801)364-2045

VIRGINIA

FOUNDATION: Virginia Baptist General Board
REQUISITE: Scholarships granted to residents of Virginia who are enrolled as an undergraduate student at a southern baptist convention school studying to become a southern baptist minister and a member of a church association of Virginia.
APPLICATION: Write for info. Application deadline is August.
CONTACT: POBOX 8568, Richmond, VA 23226 (804)672-2100

FOUNDATION: Virginia Museum of Fine Arts
REQUISITE: Fellowships granted to undergraduate and graduate students that are residents of Virginia for at least 5 years of the last 10 years. Students must have need for financial assistance.
APPLICATION: Write for info. Application deadline is March 9th.
CONTACT: Virginia Museum Blvd and Grove Ave., Richmond, VA 23221. Tel: (804)367-0844

FOUNDATION: Northern Virginia Board of Realtors Inc.
REQUISITE: Scholarships granted to residents of Northern Virginia ONLY. Undergraduate or graduate students at an accredited college or university.
APPLICATION: Write for info. Application deadline is April 30th.

Virginia

CONTACT: 8411 Arlington Blvd., Fairfax, VA 22116. (703)207-3200

FOUNDATION: Mark and Catherine Winkler Foundation
REQUISITE: Must be a single mother and reside in VA.
APPLICATION: Submit letter requesting application. Deadline not listed.
CONTACT: Harold Winkler, VP, 4900 Seminar Rd., Ste. 900, Alexandria, VA 22311 TEL: (703)998-0400

FOUNDATION: The English Foundation-Trust
REQUISITE: Must reside in the Campbell County, VA, area.
APPLICATION: Submit letter requesting application. No deadline listed.
CONTACT: Betty Roger, 1522 Main St, Altavista VA 24517 (804)791-2294

FOUNDATION: Womack Foundation
REQUISITE: Student loans by recommendation of local referral agencies for any resident of the city of Danville or Pittsylvania County, VA.
APPLICATION: Interviews required. Applications without local referral recommendations not accepted. Write for info. No deadline listed.
CONTACT: POB 521, Danville, VA 24543 TEL: (804)793-5134

FOUNDATION: Sigma Nu Educational Foundation, Inc.
REQUISITE: Must be a member of Sigma Nu Fraternity.
APPLICATION: Write for info. No deadline listed.
CONTACT: Maurice E. Littlefield, Exec. VP, POB 1869, Lexington, VA 24450 TEL: (703)463-2164

FOUNDATION: Rangeley Educational Trust
REQUISITE: Must reside in the city of Martinsville or Henry Cnty, VA.
APPLICATION: Interviews required. Write for info. Deadline 5/1
CONTACT: Paul J. Turner, VP, Personal Financial Services, c/o Crestar Bank, POB 4911, Martinsville, VA 24115
(We were not able to verify this listing; it may not be extant.)

FOUNDATION: The Lincoln-Lane Foundation
REQUISITE: Must be a college student who is a permanent resident of the Norfolk-Virginia Beach, VA, area.
APPLICATION: Interviews required. Write or call for info. Applications available after October 1. No deadline listed. Recipients notified in April.
CONTACT: 112 Grammy, Ste. 300, Norfolk, VA 23510 (804)622-2557

FOUNDATION: The Norfolk Foundation

REQUISITE: Must reside in Norfolk, VA, or an area within 50 miles of its boundaries.
APPLICATION: Write or call for info. Deadline 12/1-3/1
CONTACT: 1410 Nations Bank, Norfolk, VA 23510 TEL: (804)622-7951

FOUNDATION: Petersburg Methodist Home for Girls
REQUISITE: Must reside in Southside, VA.
APPLICATION: Write for info. Deadlines July & February.
CONTACT: Hilde T. Atkinson, Secty., 910 Northampton Rd., Petersburg, VA 23805
(We were not able to verify this listing; it may not be extant.)

FOUNDATION: Clifford D. Grim & Virginia S. Grim Edctnl Fnd
REQUISITE: Must reside in the Winchester, VA, area.
APPLICATION: Interviews required. Write for info. Deadline May 1 for following fall & spring semesters.
CONTACT: Bill Daisley, c/o First Union, POB 1000, Winchester, VA 22601
TEL: (703)667-2000

FOUNDATION: Levi Strauss Foundation
REQUISITE: Business Opportunity Scholarships to any disadvantaged high school senior in a U.S. community where Levi Strauss & Co. has production or distribution facilities including AR, CA, GA, NV, NM, TX, & VA. Foundation also awards international scholarships.
APPLICATION: Write for info. No deadline listed.
CONTACT: Martha Montag Brown, Dir. of U.S. Contributions, 1155 Battery St., POB 7215, SF, CA 94106 TEL: (415)544-6577

FOUNDATION: Pickett & Hatcher Educational Fund, Inc.
REQUISITE: Be a resident of the southeastern U.S., including AL, FL, GA, KY, MS, NC, SC, TN, & VA. No support for any student planning to enter fields of medicine, law, or the ministry.
APPLICATION: Write or call for info. Any first-time applicant may request an application form after October 1. Deadline 5/15
CONTACT: Robert E. Bennett, Exec. VP, 1800 Buena Vista Rd., POB 8169, Columbus, GA 31908

FOUNDATION: Avon Products Foundation, Inc.
REQUISITE: Must be a child of a current Avon Products, Inc., employee or a high school senior who resides in proximity to an Avon location.
APPLICATION: Write for info. Deadline November 2.

CONTACT: Glenn S. Clarke, Pres., Nine West 57th St., New York, NY 10019 TEL: (212)546-6731

FOUNDATION: The Slemp Foundation
REQUISITE: Must reside in Lee or Wise County, VA.
APPLICATION: Write for info. Deadline October 1.
CONTACT: c/o The First National Bank of Cincinnati, POB 1118, mail location 7155, Cincinnati, OH 45201 TEL: (513)632-4585

FOUNDATION: Westmoreland Coal Co. & Penn VA Corp Fndtn
REQUISITE: Must be a child of an employee of Westmoreland Coal Co. or Penn Virginia Corp. or their subsidiaries who is employed at a VA or WV division of either co. or a coal mining subsidiary of Westmoreland, or resides within the following locations: Lee, Scott or Wise counties, VA; Boone, Fayette, Greenbrier, Logan, Nicholas, Raleigh, or Wyoming counties, WV, or Delta County, CO.
APPLICATION: Interviews required. Write for info. Applications accepted beginning of fall. Deadline December 1.
CONTACT: Philip D. Weinstock, Manager, 2500 Fidelity Bldg., Philadelphia, PA 19109 TEL: (215)545-2500

FOUNDATION: Circuit City Foundation
REQUISITE: Scholarships for children of employees of Wards Company, Inc., and Circuit City Stores, Inc.
APPLICATION: Write for information.
CONTACT: 2040 Thalbro Street, Richmond, VA 23230. (804)527-4000

FOUNDATION: Cooper Industries Foundation
REQUISITE: Scholarships for children of employees of Cooper Industries, Inc. in AL, CA, CT, GA, IL, IN, ME, MI, MO, MS, NJ, NY, NC, OH, OK, PA, SC, TN, TX, and VA.
APPLICATION: Applications are accepted throughout the year.
CONTACT: First City Tower, Suite 4000, POB 4446, Houston, TX 77210. Patricia B. Meinecke, Secretary. TEL: (713)739-5632

FOUNDATION: Dan River Foundation
REQUISITE: Scholarships for employees, or children of current, deceased, or retired employees of Dan River, Inc. in New York, Virginia, or South Carolina.
APPLICATION: Deadline is the last day of February.
CONTACT: POB 261, Danville, VA 24541. Or Chairman, Scholarship

Committee, Dan River Foundation, POB 2178, Danville, VA 24541. TEL: (804)799-7000

FOUNDATION: Fairchild Industries Foundation, Inc.
REQUISITE: Scholarships for children of employees of Fairchild Industries, Inc. and its subsidiaries.
APPLICATION: Applications are accepted throughout the year.
CONTACT: POB 10803, Chantilly, VA 22021-9998. John D. Jackson, President. TEL: (703)478-5800

FOUNDATION: Virginia State Council of Higher Education
REQUISITE: Scholarships granted to Virginia residents in top 10% of their high school class and is enrolling in a full-time teacher education program. Must be US citizen or legal resident.
APPLICATION: Write for info. Application deadline is not specified.
CONTACT: 101 N.14TH St., James Monroe Building, Richmond, VA 23219. Tel: (804)225-2141

FOUNDATION: Grim (Clifford D. & Virginia S.) Eductnl Fund
REQUISITE: Edctnl loans for students in Winchester, VA, area
APPLICATION: Application deadline is May 1st for the following fall and spring semester.
CONTACT: c/o First Union Trust Department, P.O. Box 1301, McLean, VA 22101-1340. Or Bill Daisley, c/o First Union, P.O. Box 1000, Winchester, VA 22601 TEL: (703)667-2000

FOUNDATION: Pickett & Hatcher Educational Fund, Inc.
REQUISITE: Undergraduate student loans for those who live in AL, FL, GA, KY, MS, NC, SC, TN, and VA. There is no support for those planning to study medicine, law, or ministry.
APPLICATION: Application deadline is May 15th. First-time applicants may request their application after October 1st.
CONTACT: 1800 Buena Vista Rd, P.O. Box 8169, Columbus, GA 31908. Robert Bennett, Executive VP

FOUNDATION: Rangeley Educational Trust
REQUISITE: Loans for students in Martinsville & Henry Cnty
APPLICATION: Application deadline is May 1st.
CONTACT: c/o Crestar Bank, P.O. Box 4911, Martinsville, VA 24115. Betty Settler, Personal Financial Services. TEL: (703)666-8200

FOUNDATION: Virginia Baptist General Board
REQUISITE: Scholarships granted to residents of Virginia who are pursuing a career as a nursing missionary and is a member of a church associated with the Baptist General Association of Virginia.
APPLICATION: Write for info. Application deadline is August.
CONTACT: POBOX 8568, Richmond, VA 23226.

FOUNDATION: Womack Foundation
REQUISITE: Student loans by recommendation only for those living in Danville and Pittsylvania County, VA.
APPLICATION: Write for more information.
CONTACT: 513 Wilson St., Danville, VA 24541; Tel.:(804)791-4179. Or Mrs. Lalor Earle,P.O. Box 521, Danville, VA 24543.

VERMONT

FOUNDATION: Stratton Arts Festival
REQUISITE: Awards are granted to Vermont residents that are undergraduate or graduate students for continuing study in the areas of Arts, Photography and Crafts. Must be USA citizen or legal resident.
APPLICATION: Write for info. Application deadline is September 5th.
CONTACT: POBOX 576 Stratton Mountain, VT 05155. (802)297-3265

FOUNDATION: Faught Memorial Scholarship Trust
REQUISITE: Must be a graduate of Bellows Falls Union High School, District 27, VT.
APPLICATION: Submit letter requesting application, stating educational goals & financial situation, & include a transcript of school record. Deadline June 1.
CONTACT: Joyce H. Miller, Trust Officer, Bellows Falls Trust Co., POB 399, Bellows Falls, VT 05101 TEL: (802)463-3944

FOUNDATION: Olin Scott Fund, Inc.
REQUISITE: Must be a young man in Bennington County, VT.
APPLICATION: Write or call for info. No deadline listed.
CONTACT: Melvin A. Dyson, Treasurer, 100 S. St., POB 1208, Bennington, VT 05201 TEL: (802)447-1096

FOUNDATION: Augustus & Kathleen Barrows Mmrl Trst Fnd
REQUISITE: Must be a woman under 25 who resides in VT
APPLICATION: Two reference letters &, if applicable, a college transcript.

Vermont

Write for info. Deadline July prior to next schl yr.
CONTACT: Maureen T. McNeil, 271 S. Union St., Burlington, VT 05401
TEL: (802)863-4531

FOUNDATION: General Educational Fund, Inc.
REQUISITE: Must reside in VT.
APPLICATION: Write for info. No deadline listed.
CONTACT: David W. Webster, Pres., c/o The Merchants Trust Co., POB
1009, 123 Church St., Burlington, VT 05402 TEL: (802)658-3400

FOUNDATION: The Windham Foundation, Inc.
REQUISITE: Undergraduate level (including "trade" school) or college.
Scholarship available to any resident of Windham Cnty
APPLICATION: Write foundation for current dates & other info.
CONTACT: Stephen A. Morse, Exec. Dir., POB 70, Grafton, VT 05146
TEL: (802)843-2211

FOUNDATION: Eleanor White Trust
REQUISITE: Must reside in Fair Haven, VT.
APPLICATION: Interviews granted upon request. Write for info.
Deadline July 31.
CONTACT: Richard S. Smith, Trustee, POB 147, Rutland VT 05701
(We were not able to verify this listing; it may not be extant.)

FOUNDATION: William A. & Mary A. Shreve Foundation, Inc.
REQUISITE: Must be a student in NJ, PA, or VT.
APPLICATION: Write for info. No deadline listed.
CONTACT: Dr. Clifford G. Pollock, Rte. 1, Box 408, Wallingford, VT 05773
(We were not able to verify this listing; it may not be extant.)

FOUNDATION: Marjorie Sells Carter Boy Scout Schlrshp Fnd
REQUISITE: Former Boy Scout who resides in New England
APPLICATION: Submit letter for application. Deadline April 1.
CONTACT: Joan Shaffer, POB 527, West Chatham, MA 02669
(We were not able to verify this listing; it may not be extant.)

FOUNDATION: The Golub Foundation
REQUISITE: Graduating high school student in an area served by Price
Chopper Supermarkets, including NY, MA, PA, & VT.
APPLICATION: Write for info. Deadline April 1.
CONTACT: Scholarship Committee, c/o Golub Corp., Duans Burg Rd.,

Schenectady, NY 12306 TEL: (518)356-9390

FOUNDATION: Scott (Olin) Fund, Inc.
REQUISITE: Student loans for young men living in Bennington Cnty, VT.
APPLICATION: Applications are accepted throughout the year.
CONTACT: 100 South St., P.O. Box 1208, Bennington, VT 05201. Melvin
Dyson, Treasurer. TEL: (802)447-1096

FOUNDATION: Charles H. Hood Fund
REQUISITE: Must be a CT, MA, ME, NH, RI, or VT resident.
APPLICATION: Write for info. No deadline listed.
CONTACT: 500 Rutherford Ave., Boston, MA 02129

FOUNDATION: New England Regional Student Program
REQUISITE: Must reside in 1 of the New England States: CT, ME, MA,
NH, RI, or VT. You may attend a public college or university within the
region at a reduced tuition rate for certain degree programs that are not
offered by their own state's public institutions.
APPLICATION: Write for info. No deadline listed.
CONTACT: Office of the Regional Student Program, New England Board
of Higher Education, 45 Temple Place, Boston, MA 02111 (617)357-9620

FOUNDATION: Fred Forsyth Educational Trust Fund
REQUISITE: Must be a CT, MA, ME, NH, RI, or VT student.
APPLICATION: Write for info. No deadline listed.
CONTACT: Rose Marie Bates, c/o Fleet Bank, Fleet Investment Services,
POB 923, Bangor, ME 04402-0923 TEL: (207)941-6000

VIRGIN ISLANDS

FOUNDATION: Virgin Island Board of Education
REQUISITE: Scholarships granted to bonafide residents of the Virgin
Islands who are enrolled in an accredited music program.
APPLICATION: Write for info. Application deadline is March 31st.
CONTACT: POBOX 11900, St. Thomas, VI 00801. (809)774-4546

FOUNDATION: Virgin Island Board of Education
REQUISITE: Scholarships granted to bonafide residents of the Virgin
Islands who are accepted by an accredited school of Nursing or an
accredited institution offering courses in health-related fields.
APPLICATION: Write for info. Application deadline is March 31st.

Washington

CONTACT: POBOX 11900, St. Thomas, VI 00801. Tel: 809-774-4546

WASHINGTON

FOUNDATION: Women in Communications
REQUISITE: Scholarships granted to women only who are Washington resident undergraduate juniors or seniors or graduate students attending an accredited institution in the state of WA studying Communications.
APPLICATION: Write for info. Application deadline is March 1st.
CONTACT: 604 Lloyd Bldg., Seattle, WA 98101. Tel: 206-682-9424

FOUNDATION: Auxiliary to the Washington Optometric Association
REQUISITE: Scholarships granted to Washington state residents who are attending or have been excepted into an accredited school of Optometry.
APPLICATION: Write for info. Application deadline is December 15th.
CONTACT: 555 116th Ave Ste 166, Bellevue, WA 98004   (206)455-0874

FOUNDATION: American Federation of Musicians Local 451
REQUISITE: High schools seniors in Whatcom county, WA who are interested in attending Western Washington State University in Bellingham Washington. Students must be able to perform on the guitar or other band instruments.
APPLICATION: Write for info. Application deadline is April 30th.
CONTACT: 61 East Sunset Drive, Bellingham, Washington 98225.
(We were not able to verify this listing; it may not be extant.)

FOUNDATION: Nellie Martin Scholarship Committee
REQUISITE: Scholarships granted to student residing in Washington for at least 5 years. Open to high school seniors in King; Pierce; and Snohomish-WA Counties. For undergraduate study at school in Washington in all areas except music; sculpture; drawing; interior design & home economics. Must be US citizen. Must maintain a 3.0 GPA and does not get married.
APPLICATION: Write for info. Application deadline is March 15th.
CONTACT: Your school counselor or 1121 244th St. SW, Bothell, WA 98021 (We were not able to verify this listing; it may not be extant.)

FOUNDATION: E.K. & Lillian F. Bishop Foundation
REQUISITE: Student who has resided in Grays Harbor County, WA, at least 1 year immediately prior to date of application.
APPLICATION: Write for info. Deadline June 1.

CONTACT: Bishop Scholarship Committee, c/o Security Pacific Bank, Grays Harbor Branch, POB 149, Aberdeen, WA 99520   (206)533-1000

FOUNDATION: W.F. & Blanche E. West Educational Fund
REQUISITE: Must be a graduate of W.F. West High School, Chehalis, WA, & who has lived in Lewis County, WA, at least 2 years.
APPLICATION: Interviews required. Applications available at school. Deadline April 15.
CONTACT: c/o First Interstate Bank of WA, Trust Dept., 473 N. Market Blvd., POB 180, Chehalis, WA 98532 TEL: (206)740-8565

FOUNDATION: Walter E Lundquist Schlrshp Testamentary Trst
REQUISITE: Must be a graduate of Kalama High School, WA, who has resided in WA for at least 1 year.
APPLICATION: Write for info. Deadline April 1.
CONTACT: Superintendent, Kalama School District, POB 1097, Kalama, WA 98625 TEL: (206)673-5225

FOUNDATION: The Rachel Royston Permanent Scholarship Foundation of Alpha Sigma State of the Delta Kappa Gamma Society International
REQUISITE: Scholarships only for graduate study to any female educator who is a bona fide resident of the state of WA.
APPLICATION: Submit letter requesting application. Interviews required including: list of names from who board will directly receive endorsement, official transcripts of all undergraduate & graduate work, full statement of proposed program of study, letter of acceptance by the institution if working in a field of special interest, or from grad schl if working towards graduate degree, & an official statement indicating the stage of doctoral progress, if applicable, usually from the advisor. Deadln January 1.
CONTACT: Gwen Page, 14607 S.E. 267th St., Kent, WA 98042

FOUNDATION: George A. Cady Educational Trust
REQUISITE: Be a graduating senior from Valley High School, Menlo, WA.
APPLICATION: Your GPA, name of college or university you plan to attend, & future plans are required along with application which are available from Valley High School guidance counselor; (206) 942-5855.
CONTACT: c/o First Interstate Bank of WA, POB 21927, Seattle, WA 98111 TEL: (206)292-3522

FOUNDATION: Nellie Martin Carman Scholarship Trust
REQUISITE: Must be a student graduating from a public high school in

King, Snohomish, or Pierce counties, WA, & planning to attend a college or university in WA State.
APPLICATION: Write for info. Deadlines March 15 for 1st-time applicants & April 2 for renewals.
CONTACT: Mrs. Warren E. Kraft, Jr., Secty., c/o Seattle Trust & Savings Bank, POB 12907, Seattle, WA 98111
(We were not able to verify this listing; it may not be extant.)

FOUNDATION: Leona M. Hickman Trust
REQUISITE: Must be a male resident of King County, WA, under age 26.
APPLICATION: Write for info. No deadline listed.
CONTACT: Jean V. Tennant, Trust Officer, U.S. Bank of WA, WWH 271, Trust Division, Seattle, WA 98111   TEL: (206)344-0720

FOUNDATION: Arthur & Doreen Parrett Scholarship Trst Fnd
REQUISITE: Must be a WA resident who is in a school of engineering, science, medicine, or dentistry.
APPLICATION: Submit letter for application. Deadline July 31.
CONTACT: George H. Carpenter, Trust Officer, c/o U.S. Bank of WA, N.A., POB 720, Trust Division, Seattle, WA 98111   TEL: (206)344-3685

FOUNDATION: Pemco Foundation
REQUISITE: Must be student resident of WA at the time of acceptance.
APPLICATION: Your principal must submit a letter stating your academic qualifications. Write for info. Deadline not listed.
CONTACT: Stanley O. McNaughton, Secty.-Treasurer, 325 Eastlake Ave., Seattle, WA 98109   TEL: 9206)628-4000

FOUNDATION: Poncin Scholarship Fund
REQUISITE: Must be an individual engaged in medical research in a recognized institution of learning within the state of WA.
APPLICATION: Write for info. No deadline listed.
CONTACT: Jennifer Sorenfen, c/o Sea-First National Bank, Charitable Trust, Administration, POB 3586, Seattle, WA 98124   (206)358-3384

FOUNDATION: Helen Martha Schiff Foundation
REQUISITE: Must reside in WA.
APPLICATION: Write for info. No deadline listed.
CONTACT: %Bank of CA, N.A., POB 3095, Seattle, 98114 (206)587-6100

FOUNDATION: University Students Club, Inc.

REQUISITE: Scholarships for any student of Japanese ancestry who attends the University of WA at Seattle on a full-time basis.
APPLICATION: Application forms available at the University of WA. Completed application should be sent to Scholarship Chairman, University Students Club, Inc., 400 Boylston Ave. E. No. 106, Seattle, WA 98102. Deadline March 15 for following or next school year.
CONTACT: Ken Sato, Pres., 1414 S. Weller St., Seattle, WA 98144
TEL: (206)543-2100 ext. 2536

FOUNDATION: John & Mary Wilson Foundation
REQUISITE: Scholarships only to any medical student (freshmen-seniors) who attends the University of WA.
APPLICATION: Request application & financial aid form from the University of WA Medical School, Seattle, WA 98195. No deadline listed.
CONTACT: Sharon Trail, c/o First Interstate Bank of WA, POB 21927, Seattle, WA 98111 TEL: (206)292-3522

FOUNDATION: Foundation Northwest Fund
REQUISITE: Must be a student living in western Spokane or Lincoln counties, WA, or Bonner County, ID.
APPLICATION: Write for info. Deadline April 1.
CONTACT: c/o Citizen Scholarship Foundation of America, POB 297, St. Peter, MN 56082 TEL: 1(800)537-4180

FOUNDATION: Berniece A.B. Keyes Trust
REQUISITE: Must be an individual in the Tacoma, WA, area.
APPLICATION: Applications available through college counselors at local high schools. Write for further info. No deadline listed.
CONTACT: John A. Cunningham, Trust Officer, Key Bank, POB 1150, Tacoma, WA 98411-5052 TEL: (206)305-7215

FOUNDATION: Belle Smith Scholarship Fund
REQUISITE: Must be a graduate of a high school in Peninsula Consolidated School District 401, located in Gig Harbor, WA.
APPLICATION: Write for info. No deadline listed.
CONTACT: Margy McGroarty, c/o Greater Tacoma Community Foundation, POB 1995, Tacoma, WA 98401-1121 TEL: (206)383-5622

FOUNDATION: Blue Mountain Area Foundation
REQUISITE: Must be a graduate of a high school in the Blue Mountain area, including Walla Walla, Columbia, Garfield, Benton, & Franklin

counties in southeastern WA & Umatilla County in northeastern OR.
APPLICATION: Write for info. Deadlines between 4/15 & 6/1
CONTACT: Eleanor S. Kane, Administrator, 12 E. Main St., POB 603,
Walla Walla, WA 99362 TEL: (509)529-4371

FOUNDATION: George T. Welch Testamentary Trust
REQUISITE: Scholarships for any 3 undergraduate years to any unmarried
needy student who is a resident of Walla Walla County, WA, & is enrolled
in a 4-year college.
APPLICATION: Meeting needed. Applications open by Jan 1 - May 1.
CONTACT: Bettie Loiacono, Trust Officer, c/o Baker-Boyer Ntnl Bank,
POB 1796, Walla Walla, WA 99362 TEL: (509)525-2000

FOUNDATION: George Washington Foundation
REQUISITE: Must be a local high school graduating senior, primarily to
attend a community college.
APPLICATION: Interviews required. Applications available from local public
high school principals or counselors. Deadline April 1.
CONTACT: Leslie Tripp, Secty.-Treasurer, 3012 Tieton Dr., Yakima, WA
98902 (We were not able to verify this listing; it may not be extant.)

FOUNDATION: The ITT Rayonier Foundation
REQUISITE: Student graduating from a high schl or residing in an area
of co. operations in Nassau County, FL, Wayne County, Georgia, or
Clallem, Mason, & Grays Harbor counties, WA.
APPLICATION: Applications available from principals of high school in
areas of co. operations. No deadline listed.
CONTACT: Jerome D. Gregoire, VP, 1177 Summer St., Stamford, CT
06904 TEL: (206)348-7000

FOUNDATION: Treacy Co.
REQUISITE: Scholarships for undergraduate study only to any
resident of, or students attending institutions of higher education in the
NW, including ID, MT, ND, SD, & WA.
APPLICATION: Write for info. Deadline June 15.
CONTACT: James O'Connell, Box 1700, Helena, MT 59624 (406)442-3632

FOUNDATION: Tektronix Foundation
REQUISITE: Must be a child of a Tektronix, Inc., employee or a student
attending a high school in Clackamas, Washington, or Multnomah
counties, OR, or in Clark County, WA.

APPLICATION: Finalists must interview. Write for info. Deadline 3/15.
CONTACT: Thomas O. Williams, Administrator, Y 3-439, POB 500, Beaverton, OR 97077 TEL: (503)627-7111

FOUNDATION: Pigott (Paul) Scholarship Foundation
REQUISITE: Scholarships for children of employees of PACCAR, Inc. and its subsidiaries for the freshman college year.
APPLICATION: Deadline is November 1st.
CONTACT: POB 1518 Bellevue, WA 98009 E.A.Carpenter. (206)455-7400

FOUNDATION: Hickman (Leona M.) Trust
REQUISITE: Student loans for male student living in King County, WA. They must also be under the age of 26.
APPLICATION: Applications are accepted throughout the year.
CONTACT: U.S. Bank of Washington, WWH 271, Trust Division, Seattle, WA 98111. Jean Tennant, Trust Officer. TEL: (206)344-3687

FOUNDATION: Arthur & Doreen Parrett Scholarship Trust Fund
REQUISITE: Scholarships granted to Washington residents attending an undergraduate accredited institution majoring in Engineering, Science, Medicine or Dentistry. Must be a US citizen.
APPLICATION: Write for info. Application deadline is July 31st.
CONTACT: C/O U.S. Bank of Washington, POBOX 720, Trust Dept., Seattle, Washington 98111.
(We were not able to verify this listing; it may not be extant.)

FOUNDATION: Washington Pulp & Paper Foundation
REQUISITE: Scholarships granted to students accepted into the University of Washington majoring in the Pulp & Paper Science curriculum. Must be US citizen or legal resident.
APPLICATION: Write for info. Application deadline in March 1st.
CONTACT: C/O University of Washington (AR-10), Seattle, WA 98195. Tel: (206)543-2763

FOUNDATION: Nellie Martin Scholarship Committee
REQUISITE: Scholarships granted to Washington resident for at least 5 years. Open to high school seniors in King; Pierce and Snohomish-WA Counties. Scholarships granted to all majors except Music, Sculpture, Drawing, Interior Design and Home Economics.
APPLICATION: Write for info. Application deadline is March 15th.
CONTACT: 1121 244TH ST. SW, Bothell, WA 98021.

(We were not able to verify this listing; it may not be extant.)

WISCONSIN

FOUNDATION: Wisconsin Higher Education Air Board
REQUISITE: Scholarships granted to Wisconsin residents who are enrolled at least half-time at the University of Wisconsin or Wisconsin State Vocation-Technical and/or adult education programs. Must have satisfactory academic standing and financial need.
APPLICATION: Write for info. Application deadline is not specified.
CONTACT: POB 7885, 25 W Main St, Madison, WI 53702 608-267-2206

FOUNDATION: Wisconsin League for Nursing, Inc.
REQUISITE: Scholarships granted to Wisconsin residents enrolled in a National League for nursing accredited program in Wisconsin. Must be at least half-way through academic program and have a 3.0 GPA. Must be recommended by your Dean or Director. Must be US citizen.
APPLICATION: Write for info. Application deadline is Aug. & March.
CONTACT: 2121 East Newport Ave., Milwaukee, WI 53211 414-332-6271

FOUNDATION: Wisconsin Dental Association Foundation
CONTACT: Loans granted to Wisconsin residents who are undergraduate juniors or seniors enrolled full-time in an accredited Pre-Dentistry Program. Must be US citizen.
APPLICATION: Write for info. Application deadline is April 30th.
CONTACT: 633 W. Wisconsin Ave., Suite 523, Milwaukee, WI 53203.
Tel: 414-276-4520

FOUNDATION: Ripon College
REQUISITE: Scholarships granted to students who maintains a 2.7 GPA one year and a 3.0 GPA the following years to recognize and encourage academic potential and accomplishment in Music, Debate-Forensics.
APPLICATION: Write for info. Application deadline is March 1st.
CONTACT: POBOX 248, 300 Seward St., Admissions Office, Ripon, WI 54971. (414)748-8102

FOUNDATION: Wisconsin Parents and Teachers Inc.
REQUISITE: Scholarships granted to Wisconsin residents that are seniors in public high school who intend to pursue a career in Education.
APPLICATION: Write for info. Application deadline is March 15th.
CONTACT: 223 North Baldwin, Madison, WI 53703.

(We were not able to verify this listing; it may not be extant.)

FOUNDATION: Caestecker (The Charles & Marie)Foundation
REQUISITE: Scholarships for students who have attended Green Lake Public High Schools, Green Lake, WI, for at least two years and plan to pursue a baccalaureate degree at a 4-year college or university.
APPLICATION: Application deadline is February 1st of graduation year.
CONTACT: c/o Frank Karaba, 111 West Monroe Street, Suite 2200E, Chicago, IL 60603. Guidance Counselor, c/o Green Lake Public High School, Green Lake, WI 54941. TEL: (414)294-6411

FOUNDATION: Fort Howard Paper Foundation, Inc.
REQUISITE: Schlrshps to graduating hgh schl snrs in Brown Cnty
APPLICATION: Application deadline is 11/1. Write for details.
CONTACT: 1919 South Broadway, POB 11325, Green Bay, WI 54307-1325. Scholarship Selection Committee. TEL: (414)435-8821

FOUNDATION: Frautschy (John Cowles) Scholarship Trst Fnd
REQUISITE: Scholarships for male Protestant seniors of Monroe High School, Monroe, WI.
APPLICATION: Applications can be obtained from guidance counselors of Monroe High School.
CONTACT: c/o First National Bank of Monroe, 1625 Tenth Street, Monroe, WI 53566. TEL: (608)328-5160

FOUNDATION: Fromm (Walter & Mabel) Scholarship Trust
REQUISITE: College and nursing school scholarships for students who graduated from Merrill Senior Public High School in Merrill, WI.
APPLICATION: Write for more details.
CONTACT: c/o First Star, POB 2054, Milwaukee, WI 53201. G. Lindermann. TEL: (414)765-4321

FOUNDATION: Janesville Foundation, Inc.
REQUISITE: Scholarships for Janesville, WI, high school graduates only. Application deadline is May 1st.
APPLICATION: Applications obtained from high schl principals.
CONTACT: 121 North Parker Drive, POB 1492, Janesville, WI 53547. Alan W. Dunwiddie, Jr., Executive Director. TEL: (608)752-1032

FOUNDATION: King's Daughters of Wisconsin Foundation, Inc.
REQUISITE: Scholarships and grants for students in current

graduating classes in these high schools: Appleton, Kaukauna, Lake Mills, Menasha, Nennah, Sheboygan, Sheboygan Falls. These are to be used at an accredited college or university in the state of Wisconsin.
APPLICATION: Application deadline is April 15th.
CONTACT: Bailey Gordon, Scholarship Committee, 4010 West Spencer St., Appleton, WI 54913. TEL: (414)739-6311

FOUNDATION: Kohler Foundation
REQUISITE: Scholarships for graduating high school seniors living in Sheboygan County, WI. They have to be recommended by their schools.
APPLICATION: Application deadline is April 15th.
CONTACT: 104 Orchard Road, Kohler, WI 53044. Eleanor Jung, Executive Director. TEL: (414)458-1972

FOUNDATION: Krause (Charles A.) Foundation
REQUISITE: Undergraduate schlrshps for those living in WI
APPLICATION: Application deadline is 1130. Write for details.
CONTACT: c/o Krause Consultants, Ltd., 330 East Kilbourne Avenue, Two Plaza East 570, Milwaukee, WI 53202. Charles A. Krause, Secretary-Treasurer. (We were not able to verify this listing; it may not be extant.)

FOUNDATION: La Crosse Foundation
REQUISITE: Scholarships are for residents of La Crosse, WI.
APPLICATION: Write for more details.
CONTACT: POB 489, La Crosse, WI 54602-0489. Carol B. Popelka, Program Director TEL: (608)782-3223

FOUNDATION: Marshall & Ilsley Bank Foundation, Inc.
REQUISITE: For child of full-time employee at Marshall & Ilsley Bank
APPLICATION: Write for more details.
CONTACT: 770 North Water St Milwaukee, WI 53202 (414)765-7700

FOUNDATION: Menn (Gregory) Foundation
REQUISITE: Scholarships for students and graduates of Appleton High School-East, Appleton, WI.
APPLICATION: Application deadline is May 1st.
CONTACT: c/o The Marine Trust Co., N.A., POB 1308, Milwaukee, WI 53201. Claude Radtke, Appleton High School-East Guidance Office, Appleton, WI 54911. TEL: (414)832-6203

FOUNDATION: Milwaukee Music Scholarship Foundation

REQUISITE: Financial assistance for residents of WI, who are worthy, needy, and talented, and plan to pursue an education or training in music.
APPLICATION: Application deadline is 2/1 for spring audition.
CONTACT: c/o First Star Trust, 777 East Wisconsin Ave., Milwaukee, WI 53202. M. Gregis. TEL: (414)765-5000

FOUNDATION: Oshkosh Foundation
REQUISITE: Scholarships for graduating seniors of Oshkosh, WI, high schl. These are to be used for a four-year term in cllg.
APPLICATION: Applications are accepted throughout the year.
CONTACT: 404 N. Main St., Oshkosh, WI 54902 TEL: (414)424-4200

FOUNDATION: Rutledge (Edward) Charity
REQUISITE: Scholarships for high school graduates who live in Chippewa County, WI.
APPLICATION: Application deadline is July 1st.
CONTACT: POB 758, 404 North Bridge Street, Chippewa Falls, WI 54729. John Frampton, President. TEL: (715)723-6618

FOUNDATION: Salem Lutheran Foundation
REQUISITE: Scholarships for men only, who are studying to become Lutheran ministers in the Wisconsin Evangelical Lutheran Synod.
APPLICATION: Application deadline is July 1st.
CONTACT: c/o Clark A. Harmon, Trustee, 760 Northlawn Drive, Columbus, OH 43214. Or Rev. Marc Schroder, Prince of Peace Lutheran Church, 6470 Centennial Drive, Reynoldsburg, OH 43088 (614)863-3124

FOUNDATION: Suder-Pick Foundation, Inc.
REQUISITE: Schlrships for graduating snrs of West Bend Hgh Schl, WI
APPLICATION: Applications are accepted throughout the year.
CONTACT: c/o Foley & Lardner, 777 East Wisconsin Avenue, Milwaukee, WI 53202. Harold J. McComas. TEL: (414)271-2400

FOUNDATION: Swiss Benevolent Society of Chicago
REQUISITE: Undergraduate scholarships for full-time students who are of Swiss descent and live in IL, IN, IA, MI, or WI.
APPLICATION: Application deadline is March 1st.
CONTACT: POB 2137, Chicago, IL 60609. Or Professor Jean Devaud, Chairman of S.B.S. Scholarship Committee, 629 South Humphrey Avenue Oak Park, IL 60304.

FOUNDATION: Wagner (R.H.) Foundation
REQUISITE: Scholarships for those interested in aviation schl
APPLICATION: Applications are accepted throughout the year. Write for more details.
CONTACT: 441 Milwaukee Avenue, Burlington, WI 53105. P B Edwards Trustee.(We were unable to verify this listing; it may not be extant.)

FOUNDATION: Racine Community Foundation
REQUISITE: Scholarships by nomination only are available for those living in Racine County, WI.
APPLICATION: Write for application.
CONTACT: 818 Sixth Street, Ste. 201, Racine, WI 53403. Helen M. Underwood, Executive Secretary. TEL: (414)632-8474

FOUNDATION: Oshkosh B'Gosh Foundation, Inc.
REQUISITE: Undergraduates scholarships for student who live in areas where Oshkosh B'Gosh, Inc. plants are located. These scholarships are also available for children of employees of Oshkosh B'Gosh, Inc.
APPLICATION: Write for application.
CONTACT: POB 300, Oshkosh, WI 54902. William P. Jacobsen, Treasurer. TEL: (414)231-8800

FOUNDATION: Wisconsin Public Service Foundation, Inc.
REQUISITE: Scholarships for children of employees or customers of Wisconsin Public Service Corporation in Wisconsin and Upper Michigan.
APPLICATION: Applications are accepted throughout the year.
CONTACT: 700 North Adams Street, POB 19001, Green Bay, WI 54307. Or Wisconsin Public Service Foundation, Inc., Scholarship Program, College Scholarship Service, Sponsored Scholarships Program, CN 6730, Princeton, NJ 08541.TEL: (414)448-7260

FOUNDATION: Marshall & Ilsley Bank Foundation, Inc
REQUISITE: Scholarships for residents of greater Milwaukee, WI, area.
APPLICATION: Contact for more information.
CONTACT: 770 N Water St, Milwaukee, WI 53202 (414)765-7700

FOUNDATION: Briggs & Stratton Corporation Foundation, Inc.
REQUISITE: Scholarships for children of employees of the Briggs & Stratton Corporation, Inc.
APPLICATION: Application deadline is January 31st.
CONTACT: 12301 West Wirth Street, Wauwatosa, WI 53222. K.K. Preston,

Secretary-Treasurer. TEL: (414)259-5333

FOUNDATION: DeLong (James E.) Foundation, Inc.
REQUISITE: Scholarships for children of employees of the Waukesha
Engine Division.
APPLICATION: Application deadline is the first Monday in April.
CONTACT: c/o Waukesha Engine Division, 1000 West St. Paul Ave.,
Waukesha, WI 53188. Tel.:(414)549-2773. Or Selection Committee on
Scholarships, c/o President, Carroll College, 100 North East Ave.,
Waukesha, WI 53186 TEL: (414)547-3311

FOUNDATION: Evinrude (The Ole) Foundation
REQUISITE: Scholarships for children of employees of Outboard Marine
Corp in WI, IL, TN, MS, NC, GA, and NB.
APPLICATION: Application deadline is October 31st.
CONTACT: 100 Sea Horse Drive, Waukegan, IL 60085. Denise Charts
TEL: (708)689-6200

FOUNDATION: Johnson Controls Foundation
REQUISITE: Scholarships for children of the employees of Johnson
Controls, Inc.
APPLICATION: Write for more information.
CONTACT: 5757 North Green Bay Ave., PO Box 591, Milwaukee, WI
53201. (414)274-4000

FOUNDATION: Oilgear Ferris Foundation, Inc.
REQUISITE: Scholarships for children of employees of The Oilgear Co.
APPLICATION: Application deadline is March 31st.
CONTACT: 2300 South 51st Street, Milwaukee, WI 53219. C.L. Gosewehr,
President. TEL: (414)327-1700

FOUNDATION: Oshkosh Truck Foundation, Inc.
REQUISITE: Scholarships for local high school student of employees of
Oshkosh truck Corporation.
APPLICATION: Write for more information.
CONTACT: 2307 Oregon Street, PO Box 2566, Oshkosh, WI 54903. Peter
Mosling. TEL: (414)235-9150

FOUNDATION: Pfister & Vogel Tanning Company, Inc. Fndtn
REQUISITE: Scholarships for children of employees of Pfister & Vogel
Tanning Company, Inc.

APPLICATION: Write for more information.
CONTACT: c/o First Wisconsin Trust Company, PO Box 2054, Milwaukee, WI 53201. TEL: (414)765-5000

FOUNDATION: Rahr Foundation
REQUISITE: Scholarships for children of employees of Rahr Malting Company and affiliates.
APPLICATION: Applications are accepted throughout the year.
CONTACT: PO Box 130, Manitowoc, WI 54220. Ms. JoAnn Weyenberg. TEL: (414)682-5631

FOUNDATION: Rexnord Foundation, Inc.
REQUISITE: Scholarships for children of employees of Rexnord, Inc. and its subsidiaries.
APPLICATION: Application deadline is May 11th.
CONTACT: Rexnord, Inc., 350 North Sunny Slope Rd., Brookfield, WI 53005. Robert MacQueen, Vice-President. TEL: (414)643-3000

WEST VIRGINIA

FOUNDATION: Ethel N. Bowen Foundation
REQUISITE: Student from coal mining areas of south or se WV
APPLICATION: Write for info. & include a resume & biographical outline. Interviews required. Applications accepted from 1/1-4/30
CONTACT: R.W. Wilkenson, Secty.-Treasurer, Frst Ntnl Bnk of Bluefield, 500 Fdrl St., Bluefield, WV 24701 TEL: (304)325-8181

FOUNDATION: Berkeley Minor & Susan Fontaine Minor Fndtn
REQUISITE: Must reside in WV.
APPLICATION: Any student who attends WV University or Marshall University should apply directly to the foundation. Any applicant must be admitted to & recommended for financial aid by the University of Charleston, The University of VA, or the Protestant Episcopal Theological Seminary of VA. Write for info. Deadline 8/1
CONTACT: c/o John L. Ray, 1210 One Valley Square, Charleston, WV 25301 (We were not able to verify this listing; it may not be extant.)

FOUNDATION: The Greater Kanawha Valley Foundation
REQUISITE: Scholarships primarily to any resident of WV for undergraduate, graduate, vocational, or technical education.
APPLICATION: Write for info. No deadline listed.

CONTACT: Betsy B. VonBlond, Exec. Dir., POB 3041, Charleston, WV 25331 TEL: (304)346-3620

FOUNDATION: James Harless Foundation, Inc.
REQUISITE: Must reside in the Gilbert, WV, area.
APPLICATION: Write for info. No deadline listed.
CONTACT: Ruth Phipps, Secty., PO Drawer D, Gilbert, WV 25621
TEL: (304)664-3227

FOUNDATION: Herschel C. Price Educational Foundation
REQUISITE: Scholarships primarily to any undergraduate who resides in WV &/or attends a WV college or university.
APPLICATION: Interviews required. Submit application from February-March, or from August-September. Deadlines April 1 for fall semester awards & October 1 for spring semester awards.
CONTACT: E. Joann Price, Trustee, POB 412, Huntington, WV 25708-0412 TEL: (304)529-3852

FOUNDATION: George E. Stifel Scholarship Fund
REQUISITE: Scholarships only to any needy resident, aged 17-25, of Ohio County, WV, who is a graduate of the Wheeling, WV, public high school.
APPLICATION: Interviews required. Write for info. Deadline spring for the following academic year.
CONTACT: Endowment Trustee, c/o Security National Bank & Trust Co., 1114 Market St., Wheeling, WV 26003
(We were not able to verify this listing; it may not be extant.)

FOUNDATION: Lalitta Nash McKaig Foundation
REQUISITE: Scholarships to any resident of Bedford or Somerset counties, PA, Mineral or Hamshir counties, WV, or Allegany or Garrett counties, MD, for undergraduate, graduate, or professional education at any accredited cllg or unvrsty in US
APPLICATION: Forms available from Cumberland, MD area high school guidance offices, Frostburg State College & Allegany Community College financial aid offices, the Pittsburgh National Bank, or the foundation's Cumberland office, POB 1360, Cumberland, MD 21502 (301) 777-1533. Submit Financial Aid Form directly to College Scholarship Service. Interviews required. Deadline May 31.
CONTACT: Henry C. Flood, VP, PNC Bank, Trust Charitable Division, One Oliver Plaza, Pittsburgh, PA 15265 TEL: (412)762-2000

FOUNDATION: Harless (James) Foundation, Inc.
REQUISITE: Schlrshp, loans for students in Gilbert, WV, area
APPLICATION: Applications are accepted throughout the year.
CONTACT: Drawer D, Gilbert, WV 25621. Ruth Phipps,
Secretary. TEL: (304)664-3227

FOUNDATION: Westmoreland Coal Co. & Penn VA Corp. Fndtn
REQUISITE: Must be a child of an employee of Westmoreland Coal Co.
or Penn Virginia Corp. or their subsidiaries who is employed at a VA or
WV division of either co. or a coal mining subsidiary of Westmoreland, or
resides within the following locations: Lee, Scott or Wise counties, VA;
Kentucky, Martin, Letcher, Calbell, Floyd, Jackson, Kanawha, Lincoln,
Pike, Putnam, Wyoming, Raleigh, Wayne, WV.
APPLICATION: Interviews required. Write for info. Applications accepted
beginning of fall. Deadline December 1.
CONTACT: Philip D. Weinstock, Manager, 700 The Bellezue, 200 South
Broad St., Philadelphia, PA 19102 TEL: (215)545-2500

WYOMING

FOUNDATION: Davis-Roberts Scholarship Fund, Inc.
REQUISITE: Scholarships for members or former member of the Order of
DeMolay or Jobs Daughters Bethel in Wyoming, for use of
full-time study at any college or university.
APPLICATION: Application deadline is June 15th.
CONTACT: 116 Lummis Court, Cheyenne, WY 82007. Charles H. Moore,
Secretary-Treasurer. TEL: (307)632-2948

FOUNDATION: Perkins (B.F. & Rose H.) Foundation
REQUISITE: Scholarships and loans to graduates of Sheridan County
High School, WY. First time applicants under age 20
APPLICATION: Application deadline is June 1st.
CONTACT: POB 1064, Sheridan, WY 82801. TEL: (307)674-8871

FOUNDATION: Stock (Paul) Foundation
REQUISITE: Grants and scholarships for residents of Wyoming,
preference given to the Cody area.
APPLICATION: Application deadline is 6/30 and 11/30
CONTACT: 1130 Rumsey Ave., POB 2020, Cody, WY 82414. Kenneth S.
Bailey, Secretary-Treasurer. TEL: (307)587-5275

FOUNDATION: Bryan (Dodd & Dorothy L.) Foundation
REQUISITE: Educational loans for students from Sheridan, Campbell, and Johnson counties, WY, and from Powder River, Rosebud, and big Horn counties, MT.
APPLICATION: Application deadline is July 15th.
CONTACT: P.O. Box 6287, Sheridan, WY 82801. J. E. Goar, Manager.
TEL: (307)672-3535

FOUNDATION: Whitney Benefits, Inc.
REQUISITE: Non-interest loans for student graduates of Sheridan County, WY, high schools, and are pursuing a baccalaureate degree.
APPLICATION: Applications submitted between March & June
CONTACT: P.O. Box 691, Sheridan, WY 82801. Jack Hufford, Secretary-Treasurer. TEL: (307)674-7303

AGRICULTURE

FOUNDATION: Soil Conservation Society of America
REQUISITE: Scholarships granted to any undergraduate who has completed two years at an accredited school and has interest in Conservation and related areas. Must have a minimum 2.5 GPA. Must be US citizen or legal resident.
APPLICATION: Write for info. Application deadline is April 1st.
CONTACT: 7515 NE Ankeny Road, Ankeny, IA 50021.
(We were not able to verify this listing; it may not be extant.)

FOUNDATION: United Agribusiness League
REQUISITE: Scholarships granted to UAL member employees and their dependent children to support undergraduate or graduate study in the agribusiness at a recognized school.
APPLICATION: Write for info. Application deadline is March 31st.
CONTACT: 54 Corporate Park, Irvine, CA 92714. (714)975-1424

FOUNDATION: United Dairy Industry Association
REQUISITE: Scholarships granted to undergraduates other than freshmen enrolled in an accredited agricultural program in the USA. Student must have at least a 2.5 GPA. Scholarship is to encourage qualified applicants to pursue a career in dairy marketing.
APPLICATION: Write for info. Application deadline is April 1st.
CONTACT: 6300 N. River Road, Rosemont, IL 60018. (708)803-2000

FOUNDATION: National Junior Horticultural Association
REQUISITE: Scholarships granted to students for one year of horticultural study and work experience program in Scotland at the Threave School of Practical Gardening. Must have previous horticulture experience and be between the ages of 18-21. Must be US citizen.
APPLICATION: Write for info. Application deadline is October 1st.
CONTACT: 1847 Hess Lake Drive, Newaygo, MI 49337.
(We were not able to verify this listing; it may not be extant.)

FOUNDATION: Moorman Company Fund
REQUISITE: Scholarships granted to undergraduate students at 28 Land grant colleges of agriculture in the USA. Must have good academic record, leadership qualities, & financial need. Must be US citizen.
APPLICATION: Write for info. Application deadline is not specified.
CONTACT: 1000 N. 30th St., Quincy, IL 62301. (217)222-7100

FOUNDATION: National Association of County Agriculture Agents
REQUISITE: Scholarships granted to undergraduate members of the National Association of County Agricultural Agents. Must be US citizen or legal resident.
APPLICATION: Write for info. Application deadline is not specified.
CONTACT: POBOX 367, Conway, NH 03818.
(We were not able to verify this listing; it may not be extant.)

FOUNDATION: Farm Foundation
REQUISITE: Scholarships granted to agriculture extension workers. Must be US citizens.
APPLICATION: Write for info. Application deadline is March 1st.
CONTACT: 1211 West 22nd St., Oak Brook, IL 60521. (708)571-9393

FOUNDATION: Dairy Remembrance Fund
REQUISITE: Loans granted to citizens of the USA and Canada who are in good academic standing in the fields of dairy science and food science to support undergraduate study.
APPLICATION: Write for info. Application deadline is not specified.
CONTACT: 6245 Executive Blvd., Rockville, MD 20852.
(We were not able to verify this listing; it may not be extant.)

FOUNDATION: Dairy Shrine-21st Century Genetics Cooperative
REQUISITE: Scholarships granted to college juniors and seniors majoring in Dairy Science and planning to work in field after graduation.

APPLICATION: Write for info. Application deadline is April 1st.
CONTACT: POB 469, 100 MBC Drive, Shawano, WI 54166 (715)526-2141

FOUNDATION: Dekalb Agrisearch Inc.
REQUISITE: Scholarships granted to students who are/have been 4-H members with at least one year 4-H work and in good academic standing.
APPLICATION: Write for info. Application deadline is not specified.
CONTACT: 3100 Sycamore Road, DeKalb, IL 60115.
(We were not able to verify this listing; it may not be extant.)

FOUNDATION: Continental Grain Company-Wayne Feed Division
REQUISITE: Scholarships granted to undergraduate students who are present or former 4-H members with at least one year of 4-H work. Must be US citizen or legal resident.
APPLICATION: Write for info. Application deadline is October 1st.
CONTACT: 10 South Riverside Plaza, Chicago, IL 60606. (312)930-1050

FOUNDATION: American Junior Brahman Association
REQUISITE: Scholarships granted to members of the Junior Brahman Association attending undergraduate school full-time.
APPLICATION: Write for info. Application deadline is not specified.
CONTACT: 1313 La Concha Lane, Houston, TX 77054.

FOUNDATION: Bedding Plants Inc.
REQUISITE: Scholarships granted to undergraduates and graduates in horticulture with a specific interest in bedding plants.
APPLICATION: Write for info. Application deadline is May 1st.
CONTACT: POBOX 27517, Lansing, MI 48909.
(We were not able to verify this listing; it may not be extant.)

FOUNDATION: American Institute of Cooperation
REQUISITE: Awards given from the American Institute of Cooperation to five undergraduates who write outstanding term papers on topic involved in agricultural cooperatives. Must be in junior or senior year.
APPLICATION: Write for info. Application deadline is June 15th.
CONTACT: 50 F St. NW #900, Washington, DC 20001. (202)458-3000

FOUNDATION: National FFA Center
REQUISITE: Scholarships granted to FFA member planning to enroll as a freshman in a 4-year undergraduate program that is an accredited institution in the USA. Must be USA citizen or legal resident.

APPLICATION: Write for info. Application deadline is April 1st.
CONTACT: Scholarship Office, POBOX 15160, Alexandria, VA 22309.
Tel: (703)360-3600

FOUNDATION: Farm Foundation
REQUISITE: Scholarships granted to agriculture extension workers.
Priority is given to those on the administrative level. Must be US citizen.
APPLICATION: Write for info. Application deadline is March 1st.
CONTACT: 1211 West 22ND ST., Oak Brook, IL 60521. (708)986-9393

FOUNDATION: Farm Foundation
REQUISITE: Scholarships granted to agricultural workers. Priority given
to those on the administrative level. Those being trained to assume
administrative responsibilities are also considered. Must be US citizen.
APPLICATION: Write for info. Application deadline is March 1st.
CONTACT: 1211 West 22ND ST, Oak Brook, IL 60521. (708)571-9393

FOUNDATION: Soil Conservation Society of America
REQUISITE: Scholarships granted to Society members currently
employed in natural resource related field and wish to return to school to
improve their technical or administrative skills.
APPLICATION: Write for info. Application deadline is April 1st.
CONTACT: 7515 Northeast Ankeny Rd, Ankeny, IA 50021 (515)964-4295

FOUNDATION: Soil Conservation Society of America
REQUISITE: Scholarships granted to any undergraduate who has
completed at least 2 years of study at an accredited institution majoring
in Conservation, Earth Science or related areas. Must have at least a 2.5
GPA. Must be US citizen.
APPLICATION: Write for info. Application deadline is April 1st.
CONTACT: 7515 NE Ankeny Rd., Ankeny, IA 50021. (515)964-1883

ARCHITECTURE

FOUNDATION: Society of Environmental Graphic Designers
REQUISITE: Scholarships granted to undergraduates and graduates in
various fields of architecture at an accredited institution. Award is to
encourage students to pursue a career in environmental graphic design.
APPLICATION: Write for info. Application deadline is March 18th.
CONTACT: 47 Third Street, Cambridge, MA 02141. (617)868-3381

FOUNDATION: Landscape Architecture Foundation
REQUISITE: Scholarships granted to women in their senior year of undergraduate study in an accredited USA or Canadian institution. Must have excellent design ability and sensitivity to the environment and quality of life.
APPLICATION: Write for info. Application deadline is 4/15 - 5/15.
CONTACT: C/O Wimmer Yamada & Assoc., 516 Fifth Ave., San Diego, CA 92101. (We were not able to verify this listing; it may not be extant.)

FOUNDATION: Landscape Architecture Foundation
REQUISITE: Scholarships granted for undergraduates and graduates in practical educational research of benefit to the profession and the general public while allowing students to expand their knowledge of their field of interest and develop innovative and creative projects.
APPLICATION: Write for info. Application deadline is 04/15 - 05/15.
CONTACT: 1733 Connecticut Ave SW, Wshngtn DC 20009 (202)686-2752

FOUNDATION: Landscape Architecture Scholarship Fund
REQUISITE: Scholarships granted to any undergraduate or graduate student who is in need of financial assistance. Students must submit a 2 page explanation of how the money is to be used. In addition, 3 letters of reference from professors/employers should accompany letter of need.
APPLICATION: Write for info. Application deadline is 04/15 - 05/15.
CONTACT: 1733 Connecticut Ave SW, Wshngtn DC 20009 (202)686-2752

FOUNDATION: National Association of Women in Construction
REQUISITE: Scholarships granted to undergraduate sophomore women in 4-year institution in CA. Awards given for jr year of study. US citizen.
APPLICATION: Write for info. Application deadline is May 1st.
CONTACT: 550 Sunol Street, San Jose, CA 95126. (408)379-3280

FOUNDATION: National Institute for Architectural Education
REQUISITE: Traveling fellowships tenable at the American Academy in Rome Italy. Must be USA citizen about to receive their first professional degree in Architecture.
APPLICATION: Write for info. Application deadline is April 20th.
CONTACT: 30 West 22ND ST., New York, NY 10010. (212)924-7000

FOUNDATION: National Institute for Architectural Education
REQUISITE: Competition in architectural design. Open to students who have or are to receive their first professional degree in Architecture.

APPLICATION: Write for info. Application deadline is June 2nd.
CONTACT: 30 West 22nd St., New York, NY 10010. (212)924-7000

FOUNDATION: Smithsonian Institution
REQUISITE: Internships granted at the Cooper-Hewitt Museum to undergraduate or graduate students enrolled in an accredited institution.
APPLICATION: Write for info. Application deadline is not specified.
CONTACT: Cooper-Hewitt Museum, 2 East 91st ST., New York, NY 10128. Tel: (212)860-6898

FOUNDATION: Society of Environmental Graphic Designers
REQUISITE: Scholarships granted to undergraduates and graduates studying different fields of architecture. Students must pursue this area of interest as a career.
APPLICATION: Write for info. Application deadline is March 18th.
CONTACT: 47 Third St., Cambridge, MA 02141. Tel: (617)868-3381

FOUNDATION: Webb Institute of Naval Architecture
REQUISITE: Scholarships granted to high school students aged 16-24 who are in the top 10% of their class and have at least a 3.2 GPA. Students must be pursuing a career in Naval Architecture or Marine Engineering and be willing to interview. Must be US citizen.
APPLICATION: Write for info. Application deadline is February 15th.
CONTACT: Crescent Beach Rd., Glen Cove, NY 11542. (516)671-2213

ARTS MILIEU

FOUNDATION: National School Orchestra Association
REQUISITE: Competition is open to original unpublished composition suitable for the average senior high school string orchestra in the US. Must submit 5 minute composition.
APPLICATION: Write for info. Application deadline is May 15th.
CONTACT: 811 Highland Terrace NE, Atlanta, GA 30306.
(We were not able to verify this listing; it may not be extant.)

FOUNDATION: National Federation of Music Clubs Scholarship and Awards Program
REQUISITE: Scholarships granted to young musicians age 16-25 who are either group or individual members of the National Fed. of Music Clubs.
APPLICATION: Write for info. Application deadline is not specified.
CONTACT: 1336 N. Delaware St., Indianapolis, IN 46202 (317)638-4003

FOUNDATION: National Foundation for Advancement in the Arts
REQUISITE: Open to all high school seniors with talent in the arts such as dance; music; theater; visual arts; film; video; writing, etc. Awards may be used anywhere and for anything. Must be US citizen.
APPLICATION: Write for info. Application deadline is 5/15 and 10/1.
CONTACT: 3915 Biscayne Blvd., Miami, FL 33137. (305)377-1140

FOUNDATION: National Guild of Community Schools of the Arts
REQUISITE: Scholarships granted to students aged 13-18 who are enrolled in a secondary school, musical school or engaged in private study of music with an established teacher in the US or Canada. Must be US citizen or legal resident.
APPLICATION: Write for info.
CONTACT: 40 N Van Brunt St Ste 32 Englewood NJ 07631 201-871-3337

FOUNDATION: Music Assistance Fund
REQUISITE: Scholarships granted to minority students of orchestras planning to or currently enrolled in recognized conservatory or university music program. An audition is required. Must be US citizen.
APPLICATION: Write for info. Application deadline is not specified.
CONTACT: C/O NY Philharmonic, Avery Fischer Hall, Broadway, NY 10023. (212)875-5000

FOUNDATION: National Association of Teachers of Singing
REQUISITE: Scholarships granted to young singers who are ready for professional careers and to encourage them to carry on the tradition of fine singing. Applicants should be ages 21-35 years old and must have studied with a N.A.T.S. teacher for at least one academic year.
APPLICATION: Write for info. Application deadline is not specified.
CONTACT: 2800 University Blvd. N Jacksonville, FL 32211 (904)744-9022

FOUNDATION: Loren L. Zachary Society for the Performing Arts
REQUISITE: Competition open to young opera singers to find them employment in European Opera Houses.
APPLICATION: Write for info. Application deadlines Feb, April & May.
CONTACT: 2250 Gloaming Way, Beverly Hills, CA 90210. (310)276-2731

FOUNDATION: Liederkranz Foundation
REQUISITE: Scholarships granted to voice/piano applicants. Awards can be used anywhere.
APPLICATION: Write for info. Application deadline varies.

Arts Milieu

CONTACT: John Balme Music Director, 6 East 87th, New York, NY 10128. (212)534-0880

FOUNDATION: Glenn Miller Birthplace Society
REQUISITE: Scholarship competition is open to high school seniors and undergraduate freshmen at accredited institutions and music schools for instrumental music. Audition is required.
APPLICATION: Write for info. Application deadline is April 2nd.
CONTACT: 711 N. 14th St., Clarinda, IA 51632. (712)542-2461

FOUNDATION: Fresno Philharmonic
REQUISITE: Competition is open to music students between the ages of 20-34 who are residents or are enrolled in an accredited program in various states. Categories vary.
APPLICATION: Write for info. Application deadline is January 2nd.
CONTACT: 1300 N Fresno St Ste 201B Fresno, CA 93703 (209)261-0600

FOUNDATION: Deluis Association of North Florida Inc.
REQUISITE: Competition is open in 3 categories: vocal, keyboard, and chamber music. Contest is open to all age groups.
APPLICATION: Write for info. Application deadline is October 15th.
CONTACT: C/O College of Fine Arts/Jacksonville University, Jacksonville, FL 32211. (904)744-3650 ext.3370

FOUNDATION: Crown Princess Sonja International Music Competition
REQUISITE: Competition open to any pianist between the ages of 18-25.
APPLICATION: Write for info. Application deadline is February 1st.
CONTACT:POB 1568 VIKA, N-0116 OSLO 1 Norway.Ph +47 2 41 60 65

FOUNDATION: Curtis Institute of Music
REQUISITE: Scholarships granted to students studying music, voice or opera full-time at the Curtis Institute of Music.
APPLICATION: Write for info. Application deadline is January 15th.
CONTACT: 1726 Locust St., Admissions Office, Philadelphia, PA 19103. (215)893-5252

FOUNDATION: American Scty of Composers, Authors & Pblshers Fndtn
REQUISITE: Competition is open to any young composer who is under 30 years of age as of March 15 of the year of application. Winning compositions selected by panel of judges.
APPLICATION: Write for info. Application deadline is March 15th.

CONTACT: ASCAP Building, 1 Lincoln Plaza, New York, NY 10023.
Tel: (212)621-6000

FOUNDATION: Aspen Music School
REQUISITE: Scholarships granted to aspiring young and professional musicians. Students must be enrolled in the nine-week summer session at the Aspen Music School for undergraduate or graduate credit.
APPLICATION: Write for info. Application deadline is May 1st.
CONTACT: Box AA, Aspen, CO 81611. (303)925-3254

FOUNDATION: Associated Male Choruses of America
REQUISITE: Scholarships granted to undergraduate deserving male vocal students to further their training while they are in college.
APPLICATION: Write for info. Application deadline is February 1st.
CONTACT: C/O Mr. Leo Berg, POBOX 482, New Ulm, MN 56073.
(We were not able to verify this listing; it may not be extant.)

FOUNDATION: American Federation of Musicians
REQUISITE: Scholarships granted to young string instrumentalists between 16-23 years of age. Winners go on to study and perform for six weeks during the summer.
APPLICATION: Write for info. Application deadline is February.
CONTACT: 1501 Broadway #600, New York, NY 10036. (212)869-1330

FOUNDATION: Fine Arts Work Center in Provincetown
REQUISITE: Scholarships for lodging and/or studio space at the center. Considerees are emerging writers or artists who have created work which can be presented in the form of slides/photographs or manuscripts.
APPLICATION: Write for info. Application deadline is February 1st.
CONTACT: POBOX 565, 24 Pearl Street, Provincetown, MA 02657.
Tel: (508)487-9960

FOUNDATION: University of Alabama at Birmingham
REQUISITE: Competition open to talented new American playwrights. Plays must be original, unproduced, unpublished and full-length. UAB reserves the rights for the premiere production of the winning play without royalties.
APPLICATION: Write for info. Application deadline is January 1st.
CONTACT: University Station, School of Arts and Humanities, Dept. of Theatre and Dance, Birmingham, AL 35294. Tel: (205)934-3236

FOUNDATION: Stanley Drama Award
REQUISITE: Competition is open to students for best play or musical. Students should be recommended by a theatre professional.
APPLICATION: Write for info. Application deadline is June 1st.
CONTACT: C/O Wagner College, Drama Department, 631 Howard Ave., Staten Island, NY 10301. (718)390-3100

FOUNDATION: National Federation of State Poetry Societies, Inc.
REQUISITE: Scholarships granted to undergraduate juniors and seniors attending an accredited institution in the USA.
APPLICATION: Write for info. Application deadline is February 1st.
CONTACT: % G.F.Walker, 915 Aberdeen Ave., Baton Rouge, LA 70808. Must send self-addressed stamped #10 envelope.
(We were not able to verify this listing; it may not be extant.)

FOUNDATION: Jacksonville University
REQUISITE: Bi-annual competition open to playwrites who submit an original unproduced play (full-length or one-act) or musical.
APPLICATION: Write for info, rules, and guidelines. Send self-addressed stamped #10 envelope. Application deadline is January 1 of even numbered years.
CONTACT: College of Fine Arts, Department of Theatre Arts, Jacksonville, FL 32211. (904)744-3950

FOUNDATION: Beverly Hills Theatre Guild
REQUISITE: Competition is open to any US citizen. Must submit a full-length (90 minutes) unproduced and unpublished play written for the theatre. Musicals, 1-Act plays, Adaptations, Translations and Plays entered in other competitions are not eligible.
APPLICATION: Write for info. Application deadline is Nov. 1st.
CONTACT: 2815 N. Beachwood Dr Los Angeles, CA 90068 (310)273-3033

FOUNDATION: American College Theatre Festival
REQUISITE: Scholarships to undergraduates or graduates whose plays are produced as part of the festival. Not restricted to these productions.
APPLICATION: Write for info. Application deadline is December 10th.
CONTACT: JFK Center for the Performing Arts, Washington, DC 20566.
(We were not able to verify this listing; it may not be extant.)

FOUNDATION: Alpha Delta Kappa
REQUISITE: Scholarships granted to assist in additional study and/or in

271

a project the applicant might have in mind to further his/her artistic skills. Specific Performing Art & Fine Art categories change each biennium.
APPLICATION: Write for info. Deadline is 6/1 of even-numbered year.
CONTACT: 1615 West 92nd ST., Kansas City, MO 64114. (816)363-5525

FOUNDATION: Artists Foundation
REQUISITE: Competition for high school students. For full-time study in the field of Arts.
APPLICATION: Write for info. Application deadline is January 2nd.
CONTACT: 10 Park Plaza, Boston, MA 02116. (617)859-3810

FOUNDATION: American Colleges for the Applied Arts
REQUISITE: Scholarships granted to high school students who are going to a 2-or 4-year program at one of the American colleges for the Applied Arts is Atlanta, Los Angeles or London.
APPLICATION: Write for info. Application deadline is May 1st.
CONTACT: 3330 Peachtree Rd. NE, Admissions Office, Atlanta, GA 30326. (404)231-9000

FOUNDATION: American Art Therapy Association
REQUISITE: Scholarships granted to professional art therapists performing significant research in the art therapy field. Research must be unrelated to requirements for a Master's thesis or Doctoral dissertation. Must have professional membership with AATA.
APPLICATION: Write for info. Application deadline is Spring.
CONTACT: 505 E. Hawley St., Mundelein, IL 60060. (708)919-6064

FOUNDATION: Academy of Motion Picture and Sciences
REQUISITE: Competition is to support and encourage film-makers without previous professional experience who are enrolled in an accredited institution.
APPLICATION: Write for info. Application deadline is April 1st.
CONTACT: 8949 Wilshire Blvd., Beverly Hills, CA 90211 (310)247-3200

FOUNDATION: Pastel Society of American
REQUISITE: Scholarships granted to talented pastel artists at all levels of study. Awards are for the study of pastel arts at the Art Students League, PSA studio or with a private PSA teacher.
APPLICATION: Write for info. Application deadline is August 1st.
CONTACT: 15 Gramercy Park South, New York NY 10003 (212)533-6931

FOUNDATION: Photographic Art and Science Foundation
REQUISITE: Scholarships granted to high school graduates who have 2 more semesters of formal portraiture photography study remaining and plan to become a professional and who has the recommendation of the Dean of their school. Must be US or Canadian Citizen.
APPLICATION: Write for info. Application deadline is February 1st.
CONTACT: F. Quellmalz Sec 111 Stratford Road, Des Plaines, IL 60016.
(We were not able to verify this listing; it may not be extant.)

FOUNDATION: Money for Women
REQUISITE: Scholarships granted to feminists active in the arts. Awards are to support and recognize artistic work that speaks for peace, social justice, condition of women and self-realization. Must be US citizen or legal resident.
APPLICATION: Write for info. Application deadline is not specified.
CONTACT: POBOX 40-1043, Brooklyn, NY 11240
(We were not able to verify this listing; it may not be extant.)

FOUNDATION: National Foundation for Advancement in the Arts
REQUISITE: Talent search is open to all high school seniors with talent in the arts such as dance, music, theater, visual arts, film, video, writing, etc. Awards can be used anywhere for any purpose. Must be US citizen or legal resident.
APPLICATION: Write for info. Application deadline is 5/15 and 10/1.
CONTACT: 3915 Biscayne Blvd., Miami, FL 33137. (305)377-1140

FOUNDATION: Nissan Focus Awards
REQUISITE: Scholarships granted to any student enrolled in a US college, university, institute or film school who has made a film on a non-commercial basis. Nine categories are available. Films must be on 16mm.
APPLICATION: Write for info. Application deadline is not specified.
CONTACT: 1140 Avenue of the Americas, 5th floor, NY, NY 10036.
(We were not able to verify this listing; it may not be extant.)

FOUNDATION: National Home Fashions
REQUISITE: Fellowships granted to undergraduates with at least one year of study completed and graduate students enrolled in an accredited institution or college with Schools of Design/Crafts or Arts.
APPLICATION: Write for info. Application deadline is February 1st.
CONTACT: 107 World Trade Center, POBOX 58045, Dallas, TX 75258.

(We were not able to verify this listing; it may not be extant.)

FOUNDATION: Memphis College of Arts
REQUISITE: Scholarships granted to excellent visual art portfolios submitted by either high school students or transfer students. Students must submit SAT or ACT scores, if you are an incoming freshman. Awards are tenable at the Memphis College of Arts only.
APPLICATION: Write for info. Application deadline is March 1st.
CONTACT: Memphis College of Arts/Overton Park, Memphis, TN 39112. Tel: (901)726-4085

FOUNDATION: Millay Colony for the Arts
REQUISITE: Scholarships granted to provide 60 residences per year for professional artists. There is no cash grant given, nor is there a residency fee charged.
APPLICATION: Write for info. Application deadline is not specified.
CONTACT: Steepletop, POBOX 3, Austerlitz, NY 12017. (518)392-9971

FOUNDATION: Ladies Auxiliary to the Veterans of Foreign Wars of the United States
REQUISITE: Scholarships granted to high school students to display their artistic talents and their ideas on America and at the same time are eligible for funds to further their art education. Must be US citizen.
APPLICATION: Write for info. Application deadline is April 15th.
CONTACT: 406 W. 34th St., Kansas City, MO 64111. (816)561-8655

FOUNDATION: Haystack Mountain School of Crafts
REQUISITE: Scholarships granted to students studying in Graphics, Ceramics, Weaving, Jewelry, Glass, Blacksmithing, Fabric and Wood. Must be planning to attend the School of Crafts for the five summer sessions.
APPLICATION: Write for info. Application deadline is April 1st.
CONTACT: Admissions Office, Deer Isle, ME 04627. (207)348-2306

FOUNDATION: Home Fashion Products Association
REQUISITE: Competition is open to any undergraduate student who is enrolled in an accredited institution for Art or Design.
APPLICATION: Write for info. Application deadline is not specified.
CONTACT: POBOX 5126, 35 Adams St., Old Ridge, NJ 08857.
(We were not able to verify this listing; it may not be extant.)

FOUNDATION: Fashion Institute of Technology
REQUISITE: Scholarships granted to eligible applicants who wish to attend the institute.
APPLICATION: Write for info. Application deadline is not specified.
CONTACT: Financial Aid Office, 227 West Twenty-Seventh Street, New York, NY 10001. Tel: (212)760-7673

FOUNDATION: Academy of Motion Picture and Sciences
REQUISITE: Fellowships granted to any US citizen who is preparing for a career as a screenwriter and who has not as yet been paid to write a screenplay or teleplay.
APPLICATION: Write for info. Application deadline is June 1st.
CONTACT: 8949 Wilshire Blvd., Beverly Hills, CA 90211. (213)247-3000

FOUNDATION: University Film and Video Foundation
REQUISITE: Scholarships granted to undergraduates and graduates enrolled in film and video programs at an accredited institution.
APPLICATION: Write for info. Application deadline is not specified.
CONTACT: Dr. R. W. Wagner, Department of Photography and Cinema, Ohio State University, Columbus, OH 43210. (614)292-4920

FOUNDATION: University Film and Video Association
REQUISITE: Scholarships granted to undergraduates and graduates sponsored by a faculty member active in the film and video association.
APPLICATION: Write for info. Application deadline is June 15th.
CONTACT: STEVE HANK, Dept of Drama & Communication, University of New Orleans/Lake Front, New Orleans, LA 70124. (504)286-6000

FOUNDATION: Society of Illustrators
REQUISITE: Scholarships granted to students who are enrolled in undergraduate illustration and graphic arts programs. This will lead to a scholarship show which is a judged art competition. Students must have their instructor contact organization for information.
APPLICATION: Write for info (Instructors only). Deadline not specified.
CONTACT: 128 East 63rd Street, New York, NY 10021. (212)838-2560

FOUNDATION: Solomon R. Guggenheim Museum
REQUISITE: Internships open to students studying Arts Administration or Art History who have completed at least 2 years of undergraduate study or is a recent graduate or first year graduate student.
APPLICATION: Write for info. Application deadline is March 15th.

275

CONTACT: 1071 Fifth Ave., New York, NY 10128. (212)423-3500

FOUNDATION: American College Theatre Festival
REQUISITE: Scholarships granted to undergraduates and graduates who are writers of best comedy entered into the student play-writing awards program.
APPLICATION: Write for info. Application deadline is December 20th.
CONTACT: JFK Center for Performing Arts, Washington, DC 20566.
(We were not able to verify this listing; it may not be extant.)

BUSINESS ADMINISTRATION

FOUNDATION: Business and Professional Women's Foundation
REQUISITE: Scholarships granted to women age 30 or older who are within 24 months of completing their undergraduate program of study in health related professions in the USA.
APPLICATION: Write for info. Deadline is October 1st through April 1st. Send self-addressed stamped #10 envelope with 55 cents postage.
CONTACT: 2012 Massachusetts Ave. NW, Washington, DC 20036.
Tel: 202-293-1200

FOUNDATION: Dairy Remembrance Fund
REQUISITE: Low-interest loans granted to citizens of the USA or Canada who are in good academic standing in the Dairy Science or Food Service fields. For undergraduate study. Preference to non-freshman students but not limited to.
APPLICATION: Write for info. Application deadline is not specified.
CONTACT: 6245 Executive Blvd., Rockville, MD 20852 301-984-1444

FOUNDATION: National Electronic Distributor Association Edctn Fndtn
REQUISITE: Scholarships granted to full-time undergraduate students majoring in a discipline related to electronic distribution. Student must be attending an accredited institution and be citizen or legal resident.
APPLICATION: Write for info. Application deadline is June 1st.
CONTACT: 35 E Wecker Dr, Ste 3202 Chicago, IL 60601 312)558-9114

FOUNDATION: State Farm Companies Foundation
REQUISITE: Scholarships granted to exceptional undergraduate juniors and seniors majoring in Business related fields, Computer Science, Prelaw or Mathematics. Students must have nomination from their Dean or Department Head. Must be USA citizen.

APPLICATION: Write for info. Application deadline is February 28th.
CONTACT: One State Farm Plaza, Bloomington, IL 61710. (309)766-2039

FOUNDATION: Institute of Business Designers
REQUISITE: Scholarships granted for students to solve a design problem. Presentation is on design boards. Must solve at least 4 total problems each year and is available only at participating schools. For undergraduate study only.
APPLICATION: Write for info. Application deadline is January.
CONTACT: 1155 Merchandise Mart, Chicago, IL 60654.
(We were not able to verify this listing; it may not be extant.)

FOUNDATION: Statler Foundation
REQUISITE: Scholarships granted to undergraduates or graduates accepted or enrolled full-time at US institution in an accredited program in Food Management; Culinary Arts; Hotel-Motel Management.
APPLICATION: Write for info. Application deadline is April 1st.
CONTACT: Statler Towers, Ste 508, Buffalo, NY 14202. (716)52-1104

FOUNDATION: Technical Marketing Society of America
REQUISITE: Scholarships granted to dependent of member or member of the TMSA who is enrolled in an undergraduate degree program in Marketing, Business or Engineering at an accredited four-year university or college and maintains a 3.0 GPA.
APPLICATION: Write for info. Application deadline is October 31st.
CONTACT: 3711 Long Beach Blvd., Suite 609, Long Beach, CA 90807.
(We were not able to verify this listing; it may be extant.)

FOUNDATION: Transportation Clubs International
REQUISITE: Scholarships granted to TCI members and dependents who are enrolled in an accredited institution in a degree or vocational program in Transportation; Traffic Management or related area and considering this field as a career.
APPLICATION: Write for info. Application deadline is April 15th.
CONTACT: 203 E. Third Street, Suite 201, Sanford, FL 32771.
(We were not able to verify this listing; it may not be extant.)_

FOUNDATION: American Accounting Association
REQUISITE: Scholarships granted to undergraduates and master degree candidates for study at accredited USA institutions offering accounting degrees. Selections based on merit not need; 40 awards per year.

APPLICATION: Write for info. Application deadline is April 1st.
CONTACT: 5717 Bessie Drive, Sarasota, FL 34233. (813)921-77472

FOUNDATION: National Society of Public Accountants Schlrshp Fndtn
REQUISITE: Scholarships granted to undergraduate study leading to a degree or diploma in accounting. Students in a US accredited night school, 2 or 4 year school. 4 year students must be in 3rd or 4th year.
APPLICATION: Write for info. Application deadline is February 28th.
CONTACT: 1010 North Fairfax St., Alexandria, VA 22314. (703)549-6400

FOUNDATION: American Institute For Economic Research
REQUISITE: Summer Fellowships given to undergraduates who have completed their junior year and graduate students.
APPLICATION: Write for info. Application deadline is March 31st.
CONTACT: Division St, Great Barrington, MA 01230. (413)528-1216

FOUNDATION: U.S. Department of Health and Human Services
REQUISITE: Scholarships granted to anyone accepted to or enrolled in full-time bachelor's degree program in accounting at an accredited institution in the US.
APPLICATION: Write for info. Application deadline May 15th.
CONTACT: 5600 Fishers Lane, Room 6-12, Rockville, MD 20857. (301)443-6197

FOUNDATION: American Institute of Certified Public Accountants
REQUISITE: Scholarships granted to undergraduate minority attending accredited colleges or universities. Must be citizen or legal resident. 400 scholarships awarded per year.
APPLICATION: Write for info. Deadlines between 7/1 & 12/1.
CONTACT: 1211 Avenue of the Americas, NY, NY 10036. (212)596-6200

FOUNDATION: American Institute of Real Estate Appraisers
REQUISITE: Scholarships granted to undergraduates attending an accredited college or university. Must be a US citizen. 10 to 15 awards given per year.
APPLICATION: Write for info. Application deadline is February 15th.
CONTACT: 430 North Michigan Ave., Chicago, IL 60611. (312)335-4100

FOUNDATION: American Management Association
REQUISITE: Scholarships granted to high school & college students to attend 6-10 day training seminars on leadership & management skills.

APPLICATION: Write for info. There is no application deadline.
CONTACT: PO BOX 88, Hamilton, NY 13346. (315)824-2000

FOUNDATION: American Production and Inventory Control Scty, Inc.
REQUISITE: Scholarships granted to undergraduate and graduate students for best paper dealing with operations, production, or industrial management or business administration. Open to US or Canadian colleges & universities.
APPLICATION: Write for info. Application deadline is June 1st.
CONTACT: 500 W. Annadale Rd, Falls Church, VA 22046 (703)237-8344

FOUNDATION: American Society of Travel Agents
REQUISITE: Scholarships granted to undergraduates & graduates with a 3.0 GPA, enrolled in an accredited 2 or 4 year proprietary school. Must be a US or Canadian citizen.
APPLICATION: Write for info. Application deadline is June 25th.
CONTACT: Asta Scholarship Foundation, POBOX 23992, Washington, DC 20026. (703)739-2782

FOUNDATION: Charles Price School of Advertising and Journalism
REQUISITE: Scholarships granted to undergraduate juniors & seniors and graduates at Charles Price School of Advertising and Journalism. Must be US citizen.
APPLICATION: Write for info. Application deadline is May 31st.
CONTACT: 110 South 16TH ST, Philadelphia, PA 19102. (215)634-1718

FOUNDATION: Club Managers Associations of America
REQUISITE: Scholarships granted to students with club management interest. Must have completed freshman year at an accredited college or university in US. Must have satisfactory academic performance and need.
APPLICATION: Write for info. Application deadline is May 1st.
CONTACT: 7615 Winterberry Pl., Bethesda, MD 20817.
(We were not able to verify this listing; it may not be extant.)

FOUNDATION: Griffith Foundation for Insurance Education
REQUISITE: Scholarships granted to undergraduate juniors/seniors and graduate students. Students attending a university with a Gamma Iota Sigma Insurance Fraternity branch will be given priority over those attending a university or college where this fraternity is not found.
APPLICATION: Write for info. There is no application deadline.
CONTACT: 1775 College Rd., Columbus, OH 43210. (614)442-8357

FOUNDATION: James S. Kemper Foundation
REQUISITE: Scholarships granted to students who are enrolled as an undergraduate freshman at participating colleges & universities in the US. Must be a US citizen.
APPLICATION: Write for info. There is no application deadline.
CONTACT: Kemper Insurance Center, Long Grove, IL 60049.
(We were not able to verify this listing; it may not be extant.)

FOUNDATION: National Assn of Real Estate Editors
REQUISITE: Scholarships granted to students attending an accredited college or university studying to become a real estate/business writer; editors or broadcasters.
APPLICATION: Write for info. Application deadline is May 15th.
CONTACT: POBOX 324, North Olmsted, OH 44070.
(We were not able to verify this listing; it may not be extant.)

FOUNDATION: National Association of Realtors
REQUISITE: Scholarships awarded to undergraduates and graduates who intend to pursue a career in real estate. Must be enrolled in an accredited institution. Open to all nationalities.
APPLICATION: Write for info. Dadlines are 12/15, 4/15 and 10/15.
CONTACT: 430 North Michigan Ave., Chicago, IL 60611 (312)329-8296

FOUNDATION: Phi Gamma Nu National Fraternity
REQUISITE: Scholarships granted to jnrs and snrs who are members of Phi Gamma Nu National Business Fraternity and in good standings.
APPLICATION: Write for info. Application deadline is October 31st.
CONTACT: 6745 Cheryl Ann Drive, Seven Hills, OH 44131.
(We were not able to verify this listing; it may not be extant.)

FOUNDATION: Radio Free Europe/Radio Liberty
REQUISITE: Internships in West Germany for undergraduates who have or will have completed 3 years of college by the time award is being given. Must be a US citizen or legal resident.
APPLICATION: Write for info. Application deadline is February 14th.
CONTACT: Mr. Alan Dodds, 1201 Connecticut Ave. SW, Washington, D.C. 20036. 202-457-6900

FOUNDATION: Real Estate Educators Assn
REQUISITE: Scholarships granted to undergraduates with 2 completed college semesters and graduates. Must be full-time student at accredited

US school, have a 3.2 GPA and intend to pursue a career in Real Estate.
APPLICATION: Write for info. Application deadline is December 1st.
CONTACT: 230 N Michigan Ave., Ste 1200 Chcg IL 60601 (312)201-0101

FOUNDATION: Society of Real Estate Appraisers
REQUISITE: Scholarships granted to undergraduates and graduates studying Real Estate Valuation, Real Estate or an allied field at an accredited college or university.
APPLICATION: Write for info. Application deadline is February.
CONTACT: 225 North Michigan Ave., Blvd. TWR-N, 7TH FL., Chicago, IL 60601 (312)819-2400

FOUNDATION: College of Insurance
REQUISITE: Scholarships granted to student attending the College of Insurance only. Must be US citizen, high school graduate, 3-years C.P.Math, SAT-1000 or ACT 24 Composite.
APPLICATION: Write for info. Application deadline is May.
CONTACT: 101 Murray Street, Admissions Office, New York, NY 10007. (212)962-4111

FOUNDATION: National Commercial Finance Association
REQUISITE: Scholarships granted in the form of an essay contest. Undergraduates and graduates attending an accredited college or university are eligible. Subject of essay is Asset-Based Lending.
APPLICATION: Write for info. Application deadline is June 30th.
CONTACT: 225 W. 34th St., New York, NY 10001.
(We were not able to verify this listing; it may not be extant.)

COMMUNICATION

FOUNDATION: Central Newspaper Inc.
REQUISITE: Internships granted to recent graduates and seniors who will receive their bachelor's degree by June. Internship is 10-weeks of work and study at one of CMI's Newspapers in Indianapolis or Phoenix.
APPLICATION: Write for info. Application deadline is March 1st.
CONTACT: C/O Editor, The Indianapolis News, Indianapolis, IN 46206. Tel: 317-633-9208

FOUNDATION: Charles Price School of Advertising and Journalism
REQUISITE: Scholarships granted to juniors and seniors and graduates studying Advertising, Journalism or Public Relations at Charles Price

School of Advertising and Journalism. Must be US citizen.
APPLICATION: Write for info. Application deadline is May 31st.
CONTACT: 110 South 16th St Philadelphia, PA 19102 215-665-1330

FOUNDATION: Chicago Association of Black Journalists
REQUISITE: Scholarships granted to juniors, seniors or graduates who are members of a minority and enrolled in an accredited print or broadcast journalism program at a Chicago area institution.
APPLICATION: Write for info. Application deadline April 30th.
CONTACT: POBOX 297, St. Peter, MN 56082 507-931-1682

FOUNDATION: Cox Newspapers
REQUISITE: Scholarship granted to Atlanta area high school seniors who are minority students with at least a "B" average and an interest in journalism as a career. Must be attending Georgia State University or one of the Colleges in the Atlanta University Center. Scholarships include paid internship.
APPLICATION: Write for info. Application deadline is April 29th.
CONTACT: POBOX 4689, Atlanta, GA 30302 404-526-5091

FOUNDATION: Delta Sigma Theta Sorority
REQUISITE: Scholarships granted to financial members of Delta Sigma Theta studying Communications. Must submit grade report.
APPLICATION: Write for info. Application deadline is March 1st.
CONTACT: 1707 New Hampshire Ave. NW, Washington, DC 20009. Tel: 202-483-5460

FOUNDATION: Dog Writer's Educational Trust
REQUISITE: Scholarships granted to students whose parents, grandparents or other close relatives are or have been involved in the world of dogs as exhibitors, breeders, handlers, judges, club officers or other capacities and who are studying Veterinary Medicine, Animal Behavior or Journalism on an undergraduate or graduate level.
APPLICATION: Write for info. Application deadline is December 31st.
CONTACT: C/O Mrs. R.H. Futh, Kinney Hill Road, Washington Depot, Ct 06794 Tel: 203-868-2863

FOUNDATION: Dow Jones Newspaper Fund Inc.
REQUISITE: Internships granted to undergraduate juniors who work on their school's newspaper.
APPLICATION: Write for info. Deadline is Thanksgiving Day.

Communication

CONTACT: POBOX 300, Princeton, NJ 08543   609-452-2820

FOUNDATION: Dow Jones Newspaper Fund Inc.
REQUISITE: Internships granted to minority students who are seniors studying Journalism.
APPLICATION: Write for info. Application deadline is November 15th.
CONTACT: POBOX 300, Princeton, NJ 08543   609-452-2820

FOUNDATION: Dow Jones Newspaper Fund Inc.
REQUISITE: Internships granted to minority students who are seniors studying Journalism and not returning to school once the internship ends. Must be US citizen.
APPLICATION: Write for info. Application deadline is November 15th.
CONTACT: POBOX 300, Princeton, NJ 08543   609-452-2820

FOUNDATION: Dow Jones Newspaper Fund Inc.
REQUISITE: Internships granted to minority students who are sophomores studying Journalism.
APPLICATION: Write for info. Application deadline is January 31st.
CONTACT: POBOX 300, Princeton, NJ 08543.   609-452-2820

FOUNDATION: Fund for American Studies
REQUISITE: Institutes granted to undergraduate sophomores and juniors studying Journalism.   Internships are in Washington for 6-weeks at Georgetown University worth 6 credits.
APPLICATION: Write for info. Application deadline is March 12th.
CONTACT: 1000 16th Street NW, Suite 401, Washington, DC 20036.
Tel: 202-293-5092

FOUNDATION: Gannett Foundation
REQUISITE: Scholarships granted to undergraduates and graduates in Journalism or to children of Gannett Employees in any field.
APPLICATION: Write for info. Application deadline is January 31st for Journalism majors and January 1st for students of employees.
CONTACT: Lincoln First Tower, 26th Floor, Rochester, NY 14604.
Tel: 716-262-3315

FOUNDATION: International Division Association for Education in Journalism and Mass Communication
REQUISITE: Scholarships granted to undergraduate students with one year of study remaining who are enrolled full-time in an accredited news-

editorial program and have at least a 3.0 GPA.
APPLICATION: Write for info. Application deadline is March 15th.
CONTACT: C/O Communications Arts Department; Spring Hill College, Mobile, AL 36608   205-460-2392

FOUNDATION: International Radio and Television Society
REQUISITE: 9-week during the summer in New York City Fellowships granted to outstanding full-time juniors and seniors with a demonstrated interest in a career in Communications.
APPLICATION: Write for info. Application deadline is November 30th.
CONTACT: 420 Lexington Ave., Rm 531, NY NY 10170   212-867-6650

FOUNDATION: Journalism Foundation of Metropolitan St. Louis
REQUISITE: Scholarships granted to St. Louis Metro residents entering their junior or senior year or graduate school studying Journalism or Communications. Must submit writing samples and have desire to pursue a career in Journalism.
APPLICATION: Write for info. Application deadline is February 28th.
CONTACT: C/O Patricia Rice; 900 N. Tucker Blvd., St. Louis, MO 63101.
Tel: 314-622-7000

FOUNDATION: KNTV Television
REQUISITE: Scholarships granted to minority junior students who are residents of either Santa Clara, Santa Cruz, Monterey or San Benito counties. Must be attending a 4 year accredited institution in California studying Television Broadcasting.
APPLICATION: Write for info. Application deadline is April 30th.
CONTACT: 645 Park Ave., San Jose, CA 95110   408-236-1111

FOUNDATION: Los Angeles Chapter of Society of Professional Journalists - Sigma Delta Chi
REQUISITE: Scholarships granted to students studying Journalism, Writing, Editing or Photography who will be seniors or graduates in the following year and are either LA residents attending school outside of LA or attending school in the LA area but are not LA residents.
APPLICATION: Write for info. Application deadline is February.
CONTACT: 4310 Coronet Dr., Encino, CA 91316   818-345-5044

FOUNDATION: Los Angeles Chapter of Society of Professional Journalists - Sigma Delta Chi
REQUISITE: Scholarships granted to minority students who will be

Communication

juniors, seniors or graduates in the following year. Must be studying Journalism or related Majors and either be a residents of LA attending school in LA or attending school in LA but not a resident.
APPLICATION: Write for info. Application deadline is February.
CONTACT: 4310 Coronet Dr., Encino, CA 91316   818-345-5044

FOUNDATION: Los Angeles Chapter of Society of Professional Journalists - Sigma Delta Chi
REQUISITE: Prize awarded for political or investigative reporting to student, studying Journalism, who is either an LA area resident going to school in LA or a student attending school in LA but is not an area resident.
APPLICATION: Write for info. Application deadline is February.
CONTACT: 4310 Coronet Dr., Encino, CA 91316   818-345-5044

FOUNDATION: Los Angeles Chapter of Society of Professional Journalists - Sigma Delta Chi
REQUISITE: Scholarships granted to female students who will be juniors, seniors or graduates the following year and are either a LA resident attending school in LA or a nonresident attending school in LA and is studying Journalism or related Major.
APPLICATION: Write for info. Application deadline is February.
CONTACT: 4310 Coronet Dr., Encino, CA 91316   818-345-5044

FOUNDATION: Miami International Press Club
REQUISITE: Scholarships granted to Dade county resident undergraduate students attending an accredited institution studying Journalism or Broadcasting. Must be a deserving high school senior.
APPLICATION: Write for info. Application deadline is April 15th.
CONTACT: C/O Omni Hotel, 1601 Biscayne Blvd., Miami, FL 33132.
Tel: 305-376-2783 (Miami Herald)

FOUNDATION: National Association of Hispanic Journalists
REQUISITE: Scholarships granted to juniors, seniors or graduates who are "committed to pursuing a career" in print or broadcast journalism. This does not have to be your college major. Hispanic ancestry is not required.
APPLICATION: Write for info. Application deadline is March 11th.
CONTACT: National Press Building, Suite 634, Washington, DC 20045.
Tel: 202-783-6228

Communication

FOUNDATION: National Association of Real Estate Editors
REQUISITE: Scholarships granted to undergraduate students who are studying to become real estate/business writers/editors or broadcasters at an accredited institution.
APPLICATION: Write for info. Application deadline is May 15th.
CONTACT: POBOX 324, North Olmstead, OH 44070   216-779-1624

FOUNDATION: National Association of Black Journalists
REQUISITE: Scholarships granted to Black undergraduates or graduates who are accepted to or enrolled in an accredited journalism program majoring in Print, Photo, Radio, Television or planning a career in one of those areas.
APPLICATION: Write for info. Application deadline is March 31st.
CONTACT: POBOX 17212, Washington, DC 20041   703-648-1270

FOUNDATION: National Association of Broadcasters
REQUISITE: Scholarships granted to support research on and stimulate interest in the US broadcast industry, especially research on the social, cultural, political and economic features of American broadcasting. Students may be seniors or graduates.
APPLICATION: Write for info. Application deadline is February 1st.
CONTACT: 1771 N. Street NW, Washington, DC 20036   202-429-5380

FOUNDATION: National Federation of Press Women Inc.
REQUISITE: Scholarships granted to women juniors, seniors or graduates majoring in journalism at an accredited institution in the US or Canada.
APPLICATION: Write for info. Application deadline is April 15th.
CONTACT: POBOX 99, 1105 Main Street, Blue Springs, MO 64015.
Tel: 816-229-1666

FOUNDATION: National Federation of Press Women Inc.
REQUISITE: Scholarships granted to women members of NFPW who wish to continue or return to college to study journalism.
APPLICATION: Write for info. Application deadline is April 15th.
CONTACT: POBOX 99, 1105 Main Street, Blue Springs, MO 64015.
Tel: 816-229-1666

FOUNDATION: National FFA Center
REQUISITE: Scholarships granted to FFA member planning to enroll as a freshman in a 4-year undergraduate Agriculture Journalism program at an accredited institution in the US. Must be US citizen or legal resident.

APPLICATION: Write for info. Application deadline is April 1st.
CONTACT: Scholarship Office; POBOX 15160, Alexandria, VA 22309.
Tel: 703-360-3600

FOUNDATION: National Newspaper Foundation
REQUISITE: Scholarships granted to undergraduate juniors and seniors
who are enrolled in an accredited institution studying Print Journalism.
APPLICATION: Write for info. Application deadline is June 15th.
CONTACT: 1627 K Street NW, Suite 400, Washington, DC 20006.
Tel: 202-466-7200

FOUNDATION: National Press Photographers Foundation Inc.
REQUISITE: Scholarships granted to students, at an accredited
institution, who show aptitude and potential in the area of Electronic News
Photojournalism and who intend to pursue a career in the field.
APPLICATION: Write for info. Application deadline is March 31st.
CONTACT: Jim Douglas, C/O WUSA-TV; 441 Boone Ave. N; Minneapolis,
MN 55427   919-383-7246

FOUNDATION: National Press Photographers Foundation Inc.
REQUISITE: Scholarships granted to undergraduates or graduates who
are pursuing a career in newspaper photojournalism.   Special
consideration given to those in or from the state of Florida.
APPLICATION: Write for info. Application deadline is February 1st.
CONTACT: Mary Lou Foy, 11525 NE 9TH Ave., Miami, FL 33161.
Tel: 919-383-7246

FOUNDATION: National Press Photographers Foundation Inc.
REQUISITE: Scholarships granted to the college photographer of the
year who is selected on the basis of a photojournalism portfolio,
scholastic standing; professional aspirations and financial need.
APPLICATION: Write for info. Application deadline is February 15th.
CONTACT: Professor Cliff Edom, POBOX 1105, Forsyth, MO 65653.
Tel: 919-383-7246

FOUNDATION: National Press Photographers Foundation Inc.
REQUISITE: Scholarships granted to undergraduate photographers and
picture editors. Journalism need not be students major, however student
must be planning a career in photojournalism. Portfolio is required. Must
have at least 1/2 year of study remaining in a 4-year accredited program.
APPLICATION: Write for info. Application deadline is March 1st.

CONTACT: Dr. John Ahlhauser, School of Journalism, Indiana University at Bloomington, Bloomington, IN 47405   919-383-7246

FOUNDATION: National Press Photographers Foundation Inc.
REQUISITE: Scholarships granted to undergraduate students at an accredited US institution who shows aptitude and potential in the use of photographs as a communication tool and intends to pursue such a career. APPLICATION: Write for info. Application deadline is February 1. CONTACT: Gary Settle, 4029 NE 204TH St., Seattle, WA 98155.
Tel: 919-383-7246

FOUNDATION: National Press Photographers Foundation Inc.
REQUISITE: Scholarships granted to undergraduates or graduates attending an accredited institution and studying journalism.
APPLICATION: Write for info. Application deadline is December 31st.
CONTACT: Tom Strongman, 5411 W. 79th TER, Prairie Village, KS 66208
Tel: 919-383-7246

FOUNDATION: National Right to Work Committee
REQUISITE: Scholarships granted to undergraduates and graduates attending an accredited institution who exemplify the dedication to principle and high journalistic standards of William B. Ruggles.
APPLICATION: Write for info. Application deadline is 1/1 thru 3/31.
CONTACT: 8001 Braddock Rd, Suite 500, Springfield, VA 22160.
Tel: 703-321-9820

FOUNDATION: Poynter Fund
REQUISITE: Scholarships granted to students who demonstrate outstanding potential for newspaper career through performance or interview. Must be US citizen.
APPLICATION: Write for info. Application deadline is July 1st.
CONTACT: POBOX 1121, 490 First Ave. SO, St. Petersburg, FL 33731.
Tel: 813-893-8526

FOUNDATION: Quill & Scroll Foundation
REQUISITE: Scholarships granted to high school seniors who are winners in the national writing/photo contest and are planning to enroll in an accredited journalism program. Must be US citizen.
APPLICATION: Write for info. Application deadline is May 10th.
CONTACT: University of Iowa School of Journalism and Mass Communication, Iowa City, IA 52242   319-355-5795

FOUNDATION: Radio-Television News Directors Association Foundation
REQUISITE: Scholarships granted to 2nd year+ undergraduates and masters degree candidates whose career objective is broadcast news.
APPLICATION: Write for info. Application deadline is April 15th.
CONTACT: 1717 "K" Street NW, Suite 615, Washington, DC 20006.
Tel: 202-737-8657

FOUNDATION: Ralph McGill Scholarship Fund
REQUISITE: Scholarships granted to juniors and seniors whose roots lie in the 14 southern states and intend to pursue a career in daily or weekly newspaper work. Must have maintained GPA of "B". Must be US citizen.
APPLICATION: Write for info. Application deadline is May 1st.
CONTACT: C/O The Atlanta Constitution, POBOX 4689, Atlanta, GA 30302. Tel: 404-526-5526

FOUNDATION: Scripps Howard Foundation
REQUISITE: Scholarships granted to full time juniors, seniors or graduates or previous recipients who are preparing to work in NY print or broadcast media. Must be US citizen or legal resident.
APPLICATION: Write for info. Application deadline is 12/20 to 2/25.
CONTACT: 1100 Central Trust Tower, POBOX 5380, Cincinnati, OH 45202. Tel: 513-977-3000

FOUNDATION: Society for Technical Communication
REQUISITE: Scholarships granted to full time undergraduate students who have completed at least one year of study and are enrolled in an accredited 2 or 4 year degree program for a career in any area of Technical Communication.
APPLICATION: Write for info. Application deadline is February 15th.
CONTACT: 815 15th St. NW, Washington, DC 20005.   202-737-0035

FOUNDATION: Society of Broadcast Engineers
REQUISITE: Scholarships granted to undergraduate students interested in a career in broadcasting. Must provide two SBE members as references confirming eligibility. Must submit statement of purpose and provide brief biography.
APPLICATION: Write for info. Application deadline is March 1st.
CONTACT: 7002 Graham Rd., #118, Indianapolis, IN 46220.
Tel: 317-842-0836

FOUNDATION: Thoroughbred Racing Associations

REQUISITE: Scholarships granted to high school seniors who wish to become a sports writer attending Vanderbilt University in Tennessee. Must have outstanding potential in the field and be able to meet Vanderbilt's entrance requirements.
APPLICATION: Write for info. Application deadline is March.
CONTACT: 30000 Marcus Ave, Suite 2W4, Lake Success, NY 11042.
Tel: 516-328-2660

FOUNDATION: United Methodist Communications
REQUISITE: Scholarships granted to ethnic minority juniors and seniors who are of the Christian faith and are enrolled in an accredited school of communication or journalism (print, electronic or audiovisual). Must be US citizen or legal resident.
APPLICATION: Write for info. Application deadline is January 16th.
CONTACT: 475 Riverside Drive, Suite 1370, New York, NY 10115.
Tel: 212-663-8900

FOUNDATION: University of Arizona
REQUISITE: Fellowships granted to attend an eight week summer training program at the University of Arizona on editing daily newspaper copy. Open to ethnic minorities with at least one year of experience in the field of journalism or reporting. Must be US citizen.
APPLICATION: Write for info. Application deadline is not specified.
CONTACT: School of Journalism, Franklin Bldg, Room 116, Tucson, AZ 85721. Tel: 602-621-5777

FOUNDATION: William Randolph Hearst Foundation
REQUISITE: Competition for scholarships granted to undergraduate college journalism majors who are currently enrolled in one of the 88 accredited participating institutions.
APPLICATION: Write for info. Application deadline is not specified.
CONTACT: 90 New Montgomery St. #1212, San Francisco, CA 94105.
Tel: 415-543-4057

FOUNDATION: American Society of Newspaper Editors
REQUISITE: Scholarships granted to minority high school seniors attending school to study journalism at any accredited institution in the US. Must be US citizen or legal resident.
APPLICATION: Write for info. Application deadline is November.
CONTACT: POBOX 17004, Minority Affairs Director, Washington, DC 20041 Tel: 703-620-6087

Communication

FOUNDATION: American Society of Newspaper Editors
REQUISITE: Program focus granted to minority freshmen and sophomores attending an accredited institution in the US studying journalism. Must be US citizen or legal resident.
APPLICATION: Write for info. Application deadline is January.
CONTACT: POBOX 17004, Minority Affairs Director, Washington, DC 20041 Tel: 703-620-6087

FOUNDATION: American Women in Radio and Television
REQUISITE: Internships granted to women students who are juniors, seniors or graduates at Greater Houston area institutions. Internship is for an 8 week period at a company chosen to suit the student's interests.
APPLICATION: Write for info. Application deadline is April 10th.
CONTACT: C/O Cathy Coers KLTR-FM, 10333 Richmond #693, Houston, TX 77042.

FOUNDATION: Association for Education in Journalism and Mass Communication
REQUISITE: Scholarships granted to children of print or broadcast journalists who are foreign correspondents for a US media. Must be studying Journalism, Mass Communications, or Liberal Arts as an undergraduate, graduate or post-graduate level at an accredited institution in the US.
APPLICATION: Write for info. Application deadline is April 1st.
CONTACT: C/O College of Journalism; University of South Carolina, Columbus, SC 29208 Tel: 803-777-2005

FOUNDATION: Association for Education in Journalism and Mass Communication
REQUISITE: Internships granted to college students who are completing their junior year and are a member of a minority group. Internship is for a full ten-weeks at a participating company.
APPLICATION: Write for info. Application deadline is not specified.
CONTACT: C/O College of Journalism, University of South Carolina, Columbus, SC 29208 Tel: 803-777-2005

FOUNDATION: Alpha Epsilon Rho
REQUISITE: Scholarships granted to active student members of AER as nominated by local chapters.
APPLICATION: Write for info. Application deadline is March 1st.
CONTACT: Dr. Richard M. Uray, Executive Secretary, USC College of

Journalism, Columbia, SC 29208 Tel: 803-777-6783

FOUNDATION: Young America's Foundation
REQUISITE: Scholarships granted to undergraduate students in Journalism or Communications at an accredited institution in the USA. Must display evidence of an aptitude for leadership.
APPLICATION: Write for info. Application deadline is June 1st.
CONTACT: 11800 Sunrise Valley Drive #808, Reston, VA 22091. Tel: 703-620-5270

EDUCATION

FOUNDATION: Civitan International Foundation
REQUISITE: Scholarships granted to seniors and Master Degree students enrolled in an accredited college or university, planning a career in an educational area and agreeing to uphold ideals of Civitan Creed.
APPLICATION: Write for info. Application deadline is March 1st.
CONTACT: POBOX 2102, Birmingham, AL 35201 (205)591-8910

FOUNDATION: Orton Dyslexia Society; Northern California Branch
REQUISITE: Scholarships granted to students & teachers who are enrolled in accredited courses which provide training in working with children with specific language or learning disabilities. Must be CA resident.
APPLICATION: Write for info. Application deadline is not specified.
CONTACT: 112 Lunado Way, San Francisco, CA 94127. (415)328-7667

FOUNDATION: International Order of the Alhamdra
REQUISITE: Scholarships granted to undergraduate students who will be entering their junior year in an accredited program for teaching the mentally retarded and handicapped.
APPLICATION: Write for info. Deadline is Jan, April, July and Oct.
CONTACT: 4200 Leeds Ave., Baltimore, MD 21229.
(We were not able to verify this listing; it may not be extant.)

FOUNDATION: Roothbert Fund Inc.
REQUISITE: Scholarships granted to students primarily motivated by spiritual values and who are considering teaching as their career. Must have good academic record & appear for interview in NY.
APPLICATION: Write for info. Application deadline is March 1st.
CONTACT: 360 Park Ave. SO 15TH Floor, NY, NY 10010. (212)870-3116

Education

FOUNDATION: United Commercial Travelers of America
REQUISITE: Scholarships granted to juniors, seniors, graduates, teachers and other people interested in vocationally instructing the mentally retarded. Must be US citizen or Canadian citizen.
APPLICATION: Write for info. Application deadline is not specified.
CONTACT: 632 North Park Street, Columbus, OH 43215. (614)228-3276

FOUNDATION: Phi Delta Kappa Inc.
REQUISITE: Scholarships granted to high school seniors in upper 1/3 of their class who plan to pursue career as teacher or educator. Scholarships awarded on scholastic achievement, school-community activities, recommendations and an essay. Must be a US or Canadian citizen or legal resident.
APPLICATION: Write for info. Application deadline is January 31st.
CONTACT: POB 789, 8th & Union Bloomington, IN 47402 (812)339-1156

FOUNDATION: Pilot International Foundation
REQUISITE: Scholarships granted to any undergraduates preparing for a career working directly with persons with disabilities or training those who will. Local pilot club sponsorship in your community required.
APPLICATION: Write for info. Application deadline is April 1st.
CONTACT: POB 5600, 244 College St., Macon, GA 31208 (912)743-7403

FOUNDATION: Pilot International Foundation
REQUISITE: Scholarships granted to any applicant seeking retraining for a 'second-career' in disability training or seeking to improve his or her professional skills in their current occupation in the above areas. Local pilot club sponsorship in your community required.
APPLICATION: Write for info. Application deadline is April 1st.
CONTACT: POB 5600, 244 College St., Macon, GA 31208 (912)743-7403

FOUNDATION: Quota International Fellowship Fund
REQUISITE: Scholarships granted to hearing students of all nationalities preparing to work with the deaf or hearing impaired. Must be attending school full-time, undergraduate or graduate, and study in any country.
APPLICATION: Write for info. Application deadline is May 15.
CONTACT: 1426 21st St NW, Washington, DC 20036 (202)331-9694

ETHNIC

FOUNDATION: American Institute of Polish Culture Inc.
REQUISITE: Scholarships granted to students of Polish descent attending any accredited American college. Scholarships awarded on the basis of achievement, talent & involvement in public life.
APPLICATION: Write for info. Application deadline is September 1st.
CONTACT: Mr. Fred Martin, 1440 79TH Street Causeway, Suite 403, Miami, FL 33141 (305)864-2349

FOUNDATION: Knezevich (Steven) Trust
REQUISITE: Scholarships for those of Serbian descent.
APPLICATION: Application deadline is 9/1. Write for details.
CONTACT: 161 West Wisconsin Avenue, Milwaukee, WI 53203-2644. Stanley F. Hack. TEL: (414)271-6364

FOUNDATION: Sons of Norway Foundation
REQUISITE: Scholarships granted to persons 18 years or older and who demonstrate a keen and sincere interest in the Norwegian heritage and/or American heritage. Must attend an accredited educational institution.
APPLICATION: Write for info. Application deadline is March 1st.
CONTACT: 1455 West Lake St, Minneapolis, MN 55408 (612)827-3611

FOUNDATION: Taiwan Ministry of Education
REQUISITE: Scholarships granted to undergraduate and graduate study for foreign students wishing to study in Taiwan R.O.C. Must be enrolled full-time.
APPLICATION: Write for info. Applction deadline between 2/1 and 4/30.
CONTACT: 5 South Chung-Shan Road, Taipei Taiwan R.O.C.

FOUNDATION: Asian American Journalists Association
REQUISITE: Scholarships granted to Asian undergraduate students attending an accredited institution in the USA studying Broadcasting or Journalism. Must have good academic record, demonstrate journalistic achievement, financial need and a desire to pursue news media career.
APPLICATION: Write for info. Application deadline is April 14th.
CONTACT: 3921 Wilshire Blvd., #315, Los Angeles, CA 90010. Tel: 213-389-8383

FOUNDATION: American Institute of Polish Culture Inc.
REQUISITE: Scholarships granted to encourage young Americans of

General

Polish decent to pursue journalism or public relations as a profession. Must be attending an accredited institution. Scholarships based on achievement, talent and involvement in public life. For full-time undergraduate study only.
APPLICATION: Write for info. Application deadline is September 1st.
CONTACT: Mr. Fred Martin, Chairman Scholarship Committee, 1440 79th St Causeway, Ste 403, Miami, FL 33141   305-864-2349

GENERAL

FOUNDATION: Astraea Foundation
REQUISITE: Scholarships granted to women students whose career path and/or extracurricular activities demonstrate political and/or social commitment analogous to that of Margot Karle (an attorney who actively fought for the civil rights of gays & lesbians.)
APPLICATION: Write for info. Application deadline is 11/30 and 5/31.
CONTACT: 666 Broadway, Room 610, NY, NY 10012   718-857-2849

FOUNDATION: B'Nai B'Rith Youth Organization
REQUISITE: Scholarships granted to Jewish faith, first or second year graduate students attending accredited graduate schools of social work or college seniors planning to attend a graduate school of Social Work. Must be US or Canadian citizen.
APPLICATION: Write for info. Deadline is Spring of Each Year.
CONTACT: 1640 Rhode Island Avenue NW, Washington, DC 20036. Tel: 202-857-6633

FOUNDATION: World Modeling Association
REQUISITE: Scholarships granted to undergraduate applicants who are 16 years old or older and intend to pursue a career in modeling. Must be willing to attend the WMA Showcase Convention in NYC. Must submit a 100-word essay on "Why I Want to Be A Model" with your application.
APPLICATION: Write for info. Application deadline is Sept thru Feb.
CONTACT: POBOX 100, Croton-On-Hudson, NY 10520   914-736-3046

FOUNDATION: Veterans Administration
REQUISITE: Scholarships granted to veterans who have been disabled during active duty and honorably discharged and are in need of rehabilitation services to overcome an employment handicap.
APPLICATION: Write for info. Application deadline is within 12 years from date of notification of entitlement to VA.

CONTACT: Vocational Rehabilitation and Counseling Service, Washington, DC 20420 or your VA Regional Office in your state.

FOUNDATION: Violin Society of America
REQUISITE: Scholarships granted to applicants to study the "Art of Violin Making" at an accredited school in the US. To be considered must have talent and need. Must be US citizen.
APPLICATION: Write for info. Application deadline is not specified.
CONTACT: 85-07 Abingdon Road, Kew Gardens, NY 11415 718-849-1373

FOUNDATION: Vertical Flight Foundation
REQUISITE: Scholarships granted to undergraduate and graduate students in the vocational-technical training who are interested in pursuing a career in some aspect of helicopter or vertical flight at an accredited institution in the US.
APPLICATION: Write for info. Application deadline is February 1st.
CONTACT: 217 N. Washington St Alexandria, VA 22314 703-684-6777

FOUNDATION: Veterans Administration
REQUISITE: Scholarships granted to children (aged 18-26) and spouses/widows of Veterans who are disabled/deceased due to military service/POW or MIA to attend an accredited institution to receive vocational-technical training.
APPLICATION: Write for info. Application deadline is not specified.
CONTACT: Department of Veterans Benefits, Washington, DC 20420, VA Regional Office in Each State

FOUNDATION: Philadelphia College of Textiles and Science
REQUISITE: Scholarships granted to citizens of the US. Must be high school seniors in top 20% of class. Must submit SAT scores, maintain GPA of 3.0 or better to continue scholarship.
APPLICATION: Dorothy Egan, Henry Ave. and Schoolhouse Lane, Philadelphia, PA 19144. Tel: 215-951-2700

FOUNDATION: Soroptimist International of the Americas, Inc.
REQUISITE: Scholarships granted to mature women or heads of households that are not degreed who are interested in vocational-technical training.
APPLICATION: Write for info. Application deadline is December 15th.
CONTACT: 1616 Walnut St Philadelphia, PA 19103 215-732-0512

FOUNDATION: Elks National Foundation
REQUISITE: Scholarships granted to any USA citizen who resides within jurisdiction of a local lodge of the BPO Elks of the US. This is for vocation-technical study for courses leading to a two-year associate degree, certificate or diploma that is less than a bachelor's degree. Membership in BPO Elks is not required.
APPLICATION: Write for info. Application deadline is November 26th.
CONTACT: 2750 Lake View Ave., Chicago, IL 60614 312-929-2100

FOUNDATION: Best Products Foundation
REQUISITE: Scholarships granted to high school graduates who wish to enter vocational-technical programs but not for bachelor-degrees.
APPLICATION: Write for info. Application deadline is March 1st.
CONTACT: 1616 P Street NW #100, Washington, DC 20036.
Tel: 202-328-5188

FOUNDATION: American Board of Funeral Service Education
REQUISITE: Scholarships granted to students who are admitted to or enrolled in a Funeral Service Education Program accredited by the American Board of Funeral Service Education. Must be US citizen.
APPLICATION: Write for info. Application deadline is 3/15 and 10/15.
CONTACT: 14 Crestwood Rd, Cumberland, ME 04021 207-829-5715

FOUNDATION: American Institute of Baking
REQUISITE: Scholarships granted for a 19-week course in Baking Science and Technology at the Institute. Must furnish evidence of experience in baking or an approved alternative is required. Must be US citizen.
APPLICATION: Write for info. Application deadline is 11/1 or 5/1.
CONTACT: 1213 Bakers Way, Manhattan, KS 66502 913-537-4750

FOUNDATION: Aid Association for Lutherans
REQUISITE: Scholarships granted to students who hold an AAL certificate in their name before deadline date and are enrolled or plan to enroll in a course of study leading to vocational-technical diploma or two-year associates degree. Must be US citizen or legal resident.
APPLICATION: Write for info. Application deadline is November 30th.
CONTACT: 4321 North Ballard Rd, Appleton, WI 54919 414-734-5721

FOUNDATION: Delta Sigma Theta Sorority, Inc.
REQUISITE: Scholarships granted to financial members of Delta Sigma

Theta who are studying Social Group Work. Must submit transcripts of all college records. Awards based on meritorious achievement.
APPLICATION: Write for info. Application deadline is March 1st.
CONTACT: 1707 New Hampshire Ave. NW, Washington, DC 20009.
Tel: 202-483-5460

FOUNDATION: Parapsychology Foundation
REQUISITE: Scholarships granted to any undergraduate or graduate student attending an accredited institution in or outside of the USA. This is for study or research in any area of Parapsychology.
APPLICATION: Write for info. Application deadline is July 15th.
CONTACT: 228 East 71st Street, New York, NY 10021. 212-628-1550

FOUNDATION: Fragrance Research Fund
REQUISITE: Scholarships granted to post-graduate students to support research in Olfactory Aroma-Chology. Open to Clinical Psychologists affiliated with recognized accredited programs.
APPLICATION: Write for info. Application deadline is not specified.
CONTACT: 142 East 30th Street, New York, NY 10016. 212-725-2755

FOUNDATION: State Farm Companies Foundation
REQUISITE: Scholarships granted to undergraduate juniors or seniors studying Prelaw. Must be nominated by your Dean or Department Head. Must be US citizen.
APPLICATION: Write for info. Application deadline February 28th.
CONTACT: One State Farm Plaza, Bloomington, IL 61710 309-766-2039

FOUNDATION: International Association of Arson Investigators
REQUISITE: Scholarships granted to IAAI members, their immediate family and non-members who are recommended and sponsored by members in good standing. This is for undergraduate study in Political Science at an accredited institution.
APPLICATION: Write for info. Application deadline is February 15th.
CONTACT: POBOX 91119, Louisville, KY 40291. 502-491-7482

FOUNDATION: Earl Warren Legal Training Program
REQUISITE: Scholarships granted to entering Black law students. Emphasis on applicants who want to enter Law Schools in the South. Must submit proof of acceptance to an accredited Law School. Must be US citizen or legal resident.
APPLICATION: Write for info. Application deadline is March 15th.

General

CONTACT: 99 Hudson St., 16th Floor, NY, NY 10013 212-219-1900

FOUNDATION: Delta Sigma Theta Sorority, Inc.
REQUISITE: Scholarships granted to financial members of Delta Sigma Theta studying Law at an accredited institution. Students must submit all college records. Scholarships are based on meritorious achievement.
APPLICATION: Write for info. Application deadline is March 1st.
CONTACT: 1707 New Hampshire Ave. N.W., Washington, DC 20009.
Tel: 202-483-5460

FOUNDATION: Boy Scouts of America
REQUISITE: Scholarships granted to high school seniors who are registered explorer scouts, active in post specializing in Law Enforcement and have demonstrated interest in pursuing a career in Law Enforcement. This is for undergraduate study only. Must be US citizen.
APPLICATION: Write for info. Application deadline is March 31st.
CONTACT: 1325 W. Walnut Hill Lane, Irving, TX 75105 214-580-2084

FOUNDATION: Alpha Kappa Alpha
REQUISITE: Scholarships granted to women undergraduates sorority members with a "B" average or higher studying Social Science. Must demonstrate leadership ability and excellence in writing an assigned essay.
APPLICATION: Write for info. Application deadline is February.
CONTACT: 5656 SO Stony Island Ave., Chicago, IL 60637 312-684-1282

FOUNDATION: Phi Upsilon Omicron National Office
REQUISITE: Scholarships granted to Phi U members working toward a baccalaureate degree in Home Economics. Scholarships granted based on scholastic record, participation in Phi U collegiate activities and statement of professional goals and personal qualifications.
APPLICATION: Write for info. Application deadline is February 1st.
CONTACT: 252 Mount Hall; 1050 Carmack Road, Columbus, OH 43210.
Tel: 614-421-7860

FOUNDATION: Statler Foundation
REQUISITE: Scholarships granted to undergraduates or graduates who are accepted to or enrolled full-time at a US institution in an accredited program of study in Food, Hotel & Motel Management or Culinary Arts.
APPLICATION: Write for info. Application deadline is April 1st.
CONTACT: Statler Towers, Ste 508, Buffalo, NY 14202 716-852-1104

FOUNDATION: Institute of Food Technologists
REQUISITE: Scholarships to high school graduates planning to enroll in an accredited institution in the US or Canada for Food Service and Technology. For undergraduate also. Must have at least a 2.5 GPA.
APPLICATION: Write for info. Application deadline is 2/1 for juniors/seniors, 2/15 for freshman and 3/1 for sophomores.
CONTACT: 221 N La Salle St #300, Chicago IL 60601 312-782-8424

FOUNDATION: International Food Service Editorial Council
REQUISITE: Scholarships granted to undergraduates or graduates who are enrolled in an accredited Foodservice Communications program at an accredited institution.
APPLICATION: Write for info. Application deadline is May 1st.
CONTACT: 82 Osborne Lane, East Hampton, NY 11937 516-324-2725

FOUNDATION: Educational Foundation of National Restaurant Assoc.
REQUISITE: Scholarships granted to full-time students majoring in food service management who intends to attend school for full academic year beginning with next fall term. Must be US citizen or legal resident.
APPLICATION: Write for info. Application deadline is 12/1 thru 3/1.
CONTACT: 250 S Wacker Dr Ste 1400, Chicago, IL 60606 312-715-1010

FOUNDATION: Educational Foundation of National Restaurant Assoc.
REQUISITE: Scholarships granted to undergraduate students with a GPA of 3.2 or higher who are enrolled full-time in an accredited Food Service/Hospitality program resulting in an associates or bachelor degree.
APPLICATION: Write for info. Application deadline is 12/1 thru 3/1.
CONTACT: 250 S. Wacker Dr Ste 1400, Chicago, IL 60606 312-715-1010

FOUNDATION: Educational Foundation of National Restaurant Assoc.
REQUISITE: Scholarships to Culinary Arts majors in junior community college and food tech majors in senior college. Must be US citizen.
APPLICATION: Write for info. Application deadline is 12/1 thru 3/1.
CONTACT: 250 S Wacker Dr Ste 1400, Chicago, IL 60606 312-715-1010

FOUNDATION: Educational Foundation of National Restaurant Assoc.
REQUISITE: Work-study program for teachers and administrators who wish to update their food service industry knowledge by obtaining 8-weeks of "hands-on" experience in the industry.
APPLICATION: Write for info. Application deadline is December 31st.
CONTACT: 250 S. Wacker Dr Ste 1400, Chicago, IL 60606 312-715-1010

General

FOUNDATION: Frozen Food Association of New England
REQUISITE: Scholarships to permanent residents of any of the 6 New England states who are pursuing an education leading to a career in food industry. For undergraduate study at accredited 2 or 4 year institution.
APPLICATION: Write for info. Application deadline is April 1st.
CONTACT: 77 Great Road, Acton, MA 01720   508-263-1171

FOUNDATION: Sandee Thompson Memorial Foundation
REQUISITE: Scholarships granted to undergraduates who have interest in serving humanity and relieving human suffering. Must attend an accredited institution and maintain an above average academic standing.
APPLICATION: Write for info. Application deadline is March 15th.
CONTACT: 5373 Sky Valley Dr., Hixson, TN 37343   615-877-3920

FOUNDATION: Northeastern Loggers' Association
REQUISITE: Scholarships granted to undergraduate juniors in a four-year programs and 2nd year students in 2-year programs who are enrolled in schools located in the 25 state area that comprises the "Northeastern Region" designated by the US Forest Service.
APPLICATION: Write for info. Application deadline is January 1st.
CONTACT: POBOX 69, Old Forge, NY 13420.
(We were not able to verify this listing; it may not be extant.)

FOUNDATION: Oak Ridge Associated Universities
REQUISITE: Internships at the Dept of Energy Facilities granted to graduate/bachelors and associate degree students. Must be US citizen.
APPLICATION: Write for info. Application deadline varies.
CONTACT: University Programs Division, POBOX 117, Oak Ridge, TN 37831. (615)576-3427

FOUNDATION: Professional Grounds Management Society
REQUISITE: Scholarships granted to undergraduates or graduates who are interested in the greens industry, particularly grounds management. Must be US citizen or legal resident.
APPLICATION: Write for info. Application deadline is May 1st.
CONTACT: 3701 Old Court Rd., Suite 15, Pikesville, MD 21208.
Tel: (410)584-9754

FOUNDATION: Friends of the National Zoo
REQUISITE: Traineeships granted to advanced undergraduates and recent graduates whose interest, scholastic achievement, relevant

experience and letters of reference are good.
APPLICATION: Write for info. Application deadline is February 17th.
CONTACT: Ntnl Zoological Prk, Washington, DC 20008 (202)673-4800

FOUNDATION: Golf Course Superintendents Association of America
REQUISITE: Scholarships granted to applicants who have completed their freshmen year. Must be US citizen or legal resident.
APPLICATION: Write for info. Application deadline is October 1st.
CONTACT: 1617 St. Andrews Drive, Lawrence, KS 66046. (913)841-2240

FOUNDATION: Norwich Jubilee Esperanto Foundation
REQUISITE: Scholarships granted to anyone to travel to the United Kingdom to improve their use of Esperanto. Candidates should be competent in the use of the language.
APPLICATION: Write for info. Application deadline is not specified.
CONTACT: 37 Granville Court, Oxford OX3 OH3 England 0865-245509

FOUNDATION: Sons of the American Revolution
REQUISITE: Contest is open to high school students. Must submit original oration of between 5-6 minutes on a personality. Other types of submission are available.
APPLICATION: Write for info. Application deadline not specified.
CONTACT: 1000 South Fourth St., Louisville, KY 04203 (502)589-1776

FOUNDATION: Ripon College
REQUISITE: Scholarships to students to recognize and encourage academic potential and accomplishments in Music, Debate, and Forensics and intention to pursue this as a career. Must have at least a 2.7 GPA.
APPLICATION: Write for info. Application deadline is March 1st.
CONTACT: POBOX 248, 300 Seward St., Admissions Office, Ripon, WI 54971. (414)748-8102

FOUNDATION: National Junior Classical League
REQUISITE: Scholarships granted to high school seniors who plan to study classics. Preference will be given to a student who plans to pursue teaching as a career in the Classics.
APPLICATION: Write for info. Application deadline is May 1st.
CONTACT: Miami University, Oxford, OH 45056. (513)529-4734

FOUNDATION: George Washington University
REQUISITE: Scholarships granted to needy women continuing or transfer

302

students majoring in English and/or American Literature with a "B" average.
APPLICATION: Write for info. Application deadline is March 1st.
CONTACT: Graduate Studies English Department, Washington, DC 20052. (202)994-6180

FOUNDATION: Eaton Literary Agency
REQUISITE: Scholarships granted for novels, nonfiction books, short stories and articles.
APPLICATION: Write for info. Application deadlines vary.
CONTACT: Richard Lawrence, POBOX 49795, Sarasota, FL 33578.
Tel: (813)366-6589

FOUNDATION: American Legion
REQUISITE: Oratorical competition is open to high school students. Undergraduate students are also eligible to apply.
APPLICATION: Write for info. Application deadline is Sept. thru Oct.
CONTACT: POBOX 1055, Indianapolis, IN 46206. (317)630-1200

FOUNDATION: American Association of Law Libraries
REQUISITE: Scholarships to minority college juniors/seniors or graduate library school student. Student must have definite interest and aptitude in law librarianship and need. Must be Canadian or US citizen.
APPLICATION: Write for info. Application deadline is April 1st.
CONTACT: 53 West Jackson Blvd, Chicago, IL 60604 (312)939-4764

FOUNDATION: Scholastic Inc.
REQUISITE: Scholarships to high school seniors. Students must submit a portfolio and an application. Must be US citizen or legal resident.
APPLICATION: Write for info. Application deadline between 10/1 & 1/1.
CONTACT: 730 Broadway, New York, NY 10003. (212)343-4942

FOUNDATION: Scripps Howard Foundation
REQUISITE: Scholarships granted to juniors, seniors or graduates who are majoring in graphic arts as applied to the newspaper industry and who have potential of becoming an administrator in newspaper production. Must be US citizen or legal resident.
APPLICATION: Write for info. Application deadline is December 25th.
CONTACT: 1100 Central Trust Tower, POBOX 5300, Cincinnati, OH 45202. (513)977-3000

FOUNDATION: American Industrial Arts Student Association
REQUISITE: Scholarships to students members of the American Industrial Arts Association. Students must have need and GPA is not considered. Student must be accepted into an accredited 4-year school.
APPLICATION: Write for info. Application deadline is April 15th.
CONTACT: 1908 Association Dr., Reston, VA 22091.
(We were not able to verify this listing; it may not be extant.)

FOUNDATION: Graphic Arts Technical Foundation
REQUISITE: Scholarships granted to undergraduates attending an accredited 2-or 4-year institution in the US. Must be full-time student studying the field of Graphic Arts, Printing or Printmaking & US citizen.
APPLICATION: Write for info. Application deadline is 1/15 and 3/15.
CONTACT: 4615 Forbes Ave., Pittsburgh, PA 15213. (412)621-6941

FOUNDATION: American Sheep Industry Women
REQUISITE: Competition granted to undergraduate students who sew and model an original wool garment of their own design.
APPLICATION: Write for info. Deadline is not specified.
CONTACT: RTE 3, Box 145, Ranger, TX 76470.
(We were not able to verify this listing; it may not be extant.)

FOUNDATION: American Society of Interior Designers Edctnl Fndtn
REQUISITE: Scholarships granted to senior interior design students. Competition is based on portfolios submitted presenting representative work on a professional level.
APPLICATION: Write for info. Application deadline is 12/1.
CONTACT: 1430 Broadway, New York, NY 10018.
(We were not able to verify this listing; it may not be extant.)

FOUNDATION: Smithsonian Institution
REQUISITE: Internships to juniors, seniors and graduate students. Interns work in one of several museum offices for 10 weeks.
APPLICATION: Write for info. Application deadline is 12/15 and 4/1.
CONTACT: 950 Independence Ave. SW, Washington, DC 20560.
Tel: (202)357-1300

FOUNDATION: Pen American Center
REQUISITE: Scholarships to young or developing translator with a book length translation in progress of a work of Italian literature. Applicants who plan a research trip to Italy are favored. Must be US citizen.

APPLICATION: Write for info. Application deadline is February 1st.
CONTACT: 568 Broadway, Suite 401, NY, NY 10012 (212)334-1660

FOUNDATION: AYN RAND Institute
REQUISITE: Essay Competition open to high school juniors and seniors interested in the fields of Literature, Psychology, English, or Philosophy. Essay must be written on the subject of "The Fountainhead" a novel written by Ayn Rand. Must be for study at a USA or Canadian college.
APPLICATION: Write for info. Application deadline is April 15th.
CONTACT: 30 Washington St., Suite 509, Marina Del Rey, CA 90292.
Tel: (310)306-9232

FOUNDATION: Chautauqua Institution
REQUISITE: Scholarships granted for summer school only. Awards are based on auditions indicating proficiency and financial need.
APPLICATION: Write for info. Application deadline is April 1st.
CONTACT: Schools Office, Box 1098, Chautauqua, NY 14722.
Tel: (716)357-6257

FOUNDATION: Delta Sigma Theta Sorority
REQUISITE: Scholarships granted to financial members of Delta Sigma Theta. Must submit transcripts of all college records. Awards are based on merit.
APPLICATION: Write for info. Application deadline is March 1st.
CONTACT: 1707 New Hampshire Ave., N.W., Washington, DC 20009.
Tel: (202)547-1160

FOUNDATION: National Endowment for the Humanities
REQUISITE: Scholarships granted to young scholar's for a unique opportunity to perform an independent research and writing project for 9 weeks during the summer under supervision of a Humanities scholar. No academic credit is given for this work. Open to high school students, freshman - junior undergraduates. Must be US citizen or legal resident.
APPLICATION: Write for info. Application deadline is November 1st.
CONTACT: 1100 Pennsylvania Ave., NW #316, Washington, DC 20506.
Tel: (202)606-8438

FOUNDATION: Civil Air Patrol
REQUISITE: Scholarships granted to undergraduates studying Humanities or Science at an accredited institution. Open to CAP members. Must be US citizen or legal resident.

APPLICATION: Write for info. Application deadline is March 15th.
CONTACT: National Headquarters/TT, Maxwell AFB, AL 36112.
Tel: (205)953-1110

FOUNDATION: Phi Sigma Iota-Office of the Executive Secretary
REQUISITE: Scholarships granted to active members of Phi Sigma Iota who meet standards of excellence in scholarship in any of the foreign languages. Must maintain a "B" average or better.
APPLICATION: Write for info. Application deadline is March 1st.
CONTACT: C/O Modern Language Department/Southern, Texas State University, San Marcus, TX 78666. (512)245-2360

FOUNDATION: American Association of Teachers of German
REQUISITE: Awards given to high school students studying German. Students scoring in the 90th percentile or above are eligible for an all-expense paid trip to West Germany. Must be US citizen.
APPLICATION: Write for info. Application deadline is November.
CONTACT: 112 Haddontowne Ct #104, Cherry Hill NJ 08034.
Tel: (609)795-5553

FOUNDATION: American Association of Teachers of Italian
REQUISITE: Contest open to undergraduate and graduate students at an accredited institution in North America. Topic must pertain to Literature or Literary figures. North American citizen.
APPLICATION: Write for info. Application deadline is June 30th.
CONTACT: C/O Indiana University, Languages Department, Bloomington, In 47401. (812)855-4848

FOUNDATION: American Institute of Indian Studies
REQUISITE: Fellowships granted in India to students who have a minimum of 2 years or 240 hours of classroom instruction in a language of India. Must be US citizen.
APPLICATION: Write for info. Application deadline is January.
CONTACT: C/O University of Chicago, 1130 E. 59th St, Foster Hall #212, Chicago, IL 60637. (312)702-8638

FOUNDATION: American Association of Teachers of French
REQUISITE: Contest is open to primary and secondary school French students. Exams are administered in Spring. Association determines winners according to exam result.
APPLICATION: Write for info. Application deadline is February 1st.

CONTACT: POBOX 86, Plainview, NY 11803.
(We were not able to verify this listing; it may not be extant.)

FOUNDATION: American Association of Teachers of Italian
REQUISITE: Contest is open to undergraduates and graduate students at an accredited institution in North America. Topic must pertain to literature or literary figures. North American citizen.
APPLICATION: Write for info. Application deadline is June 30th.
CONTACT: C/O Indiana University, Languages Department, Bloomington, IN 47401. (812)337-6251

FOUNDATION: National Association of American Business Clubs
REQUISITE: Scholarships granted to undergraduate juniors, seniors and graduates who have good academic standing and plan to enter practice in his or her field in the US. Must be US citizen.
APPLICATION: Write for info. Application deadline is May 1st.
CONTACT: POBOX 5127, High Point, NC 27262. Tel: (910)869-2166

FOUNDATION: Education Writers Association
REQUISITE: Scholarships granted to the best education reporting in the print and broadcast media during the previous calendar year. Applicants must be working reporters and winning may be used as you see fit.
APPLICATION: Write for info. Application deadline is January 29th.
CONTACT: 1001 Connecticut Ave. NW, Suite 310, Washington, D.C. 20036. (202)429-9680

FOUNDATION: Daughter's of the American Revolution
REQUISITE: Scholarships granted to undergraduate juniors & seniors attending an accredited college or university in the USA. Must be US citizen. No affiliation with DAR needed.
APPLICATION: Write for info. Application deadline is February 20th.
CONTACT: 1776 D. St NW, Washington, DC 20006. (202)628-1776

FOUNDATION: Fund for American Studies
REQUISITE: Scholarships granted to sophomore & junior level students interested in 6-week summer institute held at Georgetown University, Washington internships, policy lectures, media dialogue series, site briefings & career days.
APPLICATION: Write for info. Application deadline is March 12th.
CONTACT: 1000 16TH Street NW, Suite 401, Washington, DC 20036. (202)986-0384

FOUNDATION: Y's Men International
REQUISITE: Scholarship granted to undergraduate men. Scholarship-loan repayment is waived if you agree to work for YMCA after graduation for at least 1 year for each year of funding. USA citizen or legal resident.
APPLICATION: Write for info. Application deadline is May 1st.
CONTACT: C/O William D. Ward, 17909 Manhattan Pl., Torrance, CA 90504 (We were not able to verify this listing; it may not be extant.)

HEALTH & BIOLOGICAL SCIENCES

FOUNDATION: U.S. Department of Health and Human Services
REQUISITE: Scholarships to anyone accepted to or enrolled in a full-time bachelor's degree program for Dietetics and Nutrition at an accredited school in US. Choice is Native Americans but not limited to.
APPLICATION: Write for info. Application deadline is May 15th.
CONTACT: 5600 Fishers Lane, Room 6-12, Rockville, MD 20857
Tel: 301-443-6197

FOUNDATION: U.S. Department of Health and Human Services
REQUISITE: Scholarships granted to undergraduates studying environmental health or occupational health in the USA. Preference to Native Americans but not limited to.
APPLICATION: Write for info. Application deadline May 15th.
CONTACT: 5600 Fishers Lane, Room 6-12, Rockville, MD 20857
Tel: (301)496-2351

FOUNDATION: Water Pollution Control Federation
REQUISITE: Scholarships granted to undergraduate juniors, seniors or graduates for the best paper on water pollution control/quality concerns.
APPLICATION: Write for info. Application deadline is January 15th.
CONTACT: 601 Wythe St., Education Manager, Alexandria, VA 22314.
Tel: (703)684-2400

FOUNDATION: National Environmental Health Association
REQUISITE: Scholarships granted to undergraduate students to be used for tuition purposes for study in environmental health.
APPLICATION: Write for info. Application deadline is January 1st.
CONTACT: 720 S. Colorado Blvd., #970, S. Tower, Denver, CO 80222.
Tel: (303)292-2084

FOUNDATION: Diet Center Inc.

REQUISITE: Scholarships granted to undergraduates with a 3.0 GPA for support of their junior or senior year in Nutrition or Dietetics at an accredited institution.
APPLICATION: Write for info. Application deadline is February 15th.
CONTACT: 220 South Second West, Rexburg, ID 83440. 208-356-9381

FOUNDATION: American Dietetic Association Foundation
REQUISITE: Scholarships granted to seniors or graduatess who pursue graduate work related to nutritional research or nutritional education and consumer awareness at recognized institutions in the US. For citizens of USA; Mexico and Canada.
APPLICATION: Write for info. Application deadline is June 1st.
CONTACT: 216 West Jackson, Chicago, IL 60606 312-899-0040

FOUNDATION: American Dietetic Association Foundation
REQUISITE: Scholarships granted to juniors, seniors and graduates who are ADA members or eligible to be members in US, Mexico or Canada.
APPLICATION: Write for info. Application deadline is February 15th.
CONTACT: 216 West Jackson, Chicago, IL 60606 312-899-0040

FOUNDATION: American Association of Cereal Chemists
REQUISITE: Scholarships granted to undergraduate AACC members who will be entering their senior year of study at an accredited institution and intend to pursue a career in cereal chemistry, milling and baking or related area.
APPLICATION: Write for info. Application deadline is April 1st.
CONTACT: 3340 Pilot Knob Rd., St. Paul, MN 55121 612-454-7250

FOUNDATION: Nurses Educational Funds Inc.
REQUISITE: Scholarships granted to RN's who are US citizens or who intend to become citizens and have been accepted into an undergraduate or graduate nursing degree program accredited by the NLN. Must prove membership in American Nurses Association. Must be full-time student.
APPLICATION: Write for info. Application deadline is March 1st.
CONTACT: 555 West 57th Street, New York, NY 10019 212-582-8820

FOUNDATION: U.S. Department of Health and Human Services
REQUISITE: Scholarships granted to anyone accepted to/enrolled in full-time vocational, undergraduate or master's degree program in Nursing at accredited school in US. Preference to Native Americans but not limited.
APPLICATION: Write for info. Application deadline is May 15th.

CONTACT: 5600 Fishers Lane, Room 6-12, Rockville, MD 20857.
Tel: 301-443-6197

FOUNDATION: Oncology Nursing Foundation
REQUISITE: Scholarships granted to registered nurses who are seeking a bachelor's degree or master's degree in an NLN accredited nursing program and has an interest in Oncology nursing.
APPLICATION: Write for info. Application deadline is January 15th.
CONTACT: 1016 Greentree Road, Pittsburgh, PA 15220.

FOUNDATION: Nurses Association of the American College of Obstetricians and Gynecologists
REQUISITE: Scholarships granted to any member or associate member of NAACOG who is pursuing or already has a nursing degree at any level. Students should have two years experience in Nursing; Obstetrics; Gynecology; Neonatology or research.
APPLICATION: Write for info. Application deadline is April 1st.
CONTACT: POB 71437, 600 Maryland Ave SW #200 Wshngtn DC 20024
Attn: Education and Research Dept. 202-863-2434 or 800-533-8822

FOUNDATION: National Association of School Nurses
REQUISITE: Scholarships granted to NASN members who are school nurses, educators of school nurses or studying to be school nursing.
APPLICATION: Write for info. Application deadline is April 15th.
CONTACT: POBOX 1300, Lamplighter Lane, Scarborough, ME 04074
Tel: 207-883-2117

FOUNDATION: National Black Nurses Association Inc.
REQUISITE: Scholarships granted to students recently enrolled in a nursing program in good scholastic standing. Association members are given preference.
APPLICATION: Write for info. Application deadline is April 15th.
CONTACT: POBOX 18358, Boston, MA 02118. Tel: 617-266-9703

FOUNDATION: National Foundation for Long-Term Health Care
REQUISITE: Scholarships granted to qualified persons for LPN training to continue or further their education in nursing. Must be American Health Care Association Employee 24 months prior to date of application.
APPLICATION: Write for info. Application deadline is July 31st.
CONTACT: 1201 L Street, Washington, DC 20005. Tel: 202-842-4444

FOUNDATION: National Student Nurses Association Foundation
REQUISITE: Scholarships granted to Black; Hispanic and Native US citizens enrolled in an accredited nursing program. Must submit academic record, extracurricular activities and reason for need.
APPLICATION: Write for info. Application deadline is February 1st. Send self-addressed stamped legal-size envelope with 55 cents postage.
CONTACT: 555 West 57th Street, New York, NY 10019. 212-581-2215

FOUNDATION: National Student Nurses Association Foundation
REQUISITE: Scholarships granted to LPN-LVN's enrolled in a program leading to licensure as an RN or RN enrolled in a program leading to a bachelor's degree in nursing at an accredited institution in the USA.
APPLICATION: Write for info. Application deadline is February 1st. Send self-addressed stamped legal-size envelope with 55 cents postage.
CONTACT: 555 West 57th Street, New York, NY 10019. 212-581-2215

FOUNDATION: National Student Nurses Association Foundation
REQUISITE: Scholarships granted to students enrolled in an accredited 2 year or 4-year nursing diploma and generic graduate nursing programs in US. Must have good grades, be involved in a student nursing organization(s) and have good community activity and need.
APPLICATION: Write for info. Application deadline is February 1st. Send self-addressed stamped legal-size envelope with 55 cents postage.
CONTACT: 555 West 57th Street, New York, NY 10019. 212-581-2215

FOUNDATION: Maternity Center Association
REQUISITE: Monthly stipend granted to nurse-midwifery students enrolled in an accredited School of Midwifery and who plan to practice nurse-midwifery in the US for at least one year upon certification.
APPLICATION: Write for info. Application deadline is not specified.
CONTACT: 48 East 92nd St., NY, NY 10128 212-369-7300

FOUNDATION: American Legion National 40 & 8
REQUISITE: Scholarships granted to undergraduate nursing students to help them become registered nurses. Also offers a graduate program.
APPLICATION: Write for info. Application deadline is not specified.
CONTACT: 777 N Meridian St, Indianapolis, IN 46204 317-635-6291

FOUNDATION: Association of Operating Room Nurses
REQUISITE: Scholarships granted to active or associate AORN members for at least one consecutive year prior to deadline date. Must be enrolled

311

in an accredited NLN or other acceptable body.
APPLICATION: Write for info. Application deadline is May 1st.
CONTACT: Credentialing Division, 10170 E. Mississippi Ave., Denver CO
80231. Tel: 303-755-6300

FOUNDATION: Auxiliary of the American Association of Osteopathic
Specialists
REQUISITE: Scholarships granted to student enrolled in accredited
nursing programs. Must have 3.0 GPA and have an AAOS Auxiliary
member as a sponsor before asking for information or an application.
APPLICATION: Write for info. Application deadline is May 31st.
CONTACT: 804-10 Main St. #D, Forest Park, GA 30050 404-363-8263

FOUNDATION: American College of Nurse-Midwives Foundation
REQUISITE: Scholarships granted to students enrolled in ACNE
accredited certificate or graduate programs. Student must be member of
ACNE and have completed one clinical module or semester.
APPLICATION: Write for info. Application deadline is April 1st.
CONTACT: 1522 K St NW #1120, Washington, DC 20005 202-347-5445

FOUNDATION: American Association of Critical Care Nurses
REQUISITE: Scholarships granted to current AACN member and a
registered nurse who is currently enrolled in an NLN accredited BSN
program entering their junior or senior rank. RNs must have previous
work with critical care patients for one year out of the last three. Must
maintain a "B" average.
APPLICATION: Write for info. Application deadline is January 15th.
CONTACT: One Civic Plaza, Newport Beach, CA 92660 714-644-9310

FOUNDATION: American Association of Nurse Anesthetists
REQUISITE: Loans granted to AANA members and associate members
enrolled in a School of Anesthesia approved by the Council on
accreditation of nurse anesthesia educational programs.
APPLICATION: Write for info. Application deadline is not specified.
CONTACT: 216 Higgins Rd, Park Ridge, IL 60068 312-692-7050

FOUNDATION: National Athletic Trainers Association
REQUISITE: Scholarships granted to student members of NATA who
have excellent academic record, excelled as student athletic trainer and
completed at least their freshman year of study at an accredited institution
in the US.

APPLICATION: Write for info. Application deadline is February 1st.
CONTACT: 1001 East 4th St, Greenville, NC 27858 919-752-1725

FOUNDATION: National Strength and Conditioning Association
REQUISITE: Scholarships granted to National Strength and Conditioning ASSN members for undergraduate or graduate study in exercise physiology and/or related areas such as strength training and athletic conditioning.
APPLICATION: Write for info. Application deadline is April 20th.
CONTACT: POB 81410, Lincoln, NE 68501 402-472-3000

FOUNDATION: Daughters of the American Revolution
REQUISITE: Scholarships granted to first year undergraduates who are enrolled in an accredited Therapy program in the US. Must have recommendations and need for financial assistance. Must be US citizen.
APPLICATION: Write for info. Application deadline is September 1st.
CONTACT: 1776 D St. NW, Washington, DC 20006 202-628-1776

FOUNDATION: American Occupational Therapy Association Foundation
REQUISITE: Scholarships granted to undergraduates and graduates who attend an accredited institution with an assistant or professional level program for Occupational Therapy.
APPLICATION: Write for info. Application deadline is December 1st.
CONTACT: 1383 Piccard Dr, Ste 203, Rockville, MD 20850 301-948-9626

FOUNDATION: American Physical Therapy Association
REQUISITE: Scholarships granted to outstanding students in physical therapy who are in their final year of study in an APTA accredited program at assistant, undergraduate, certificate or masters level.
APPLICATION: Write for info. Application deadline is December 1st.
CONTACT: 1111 North Fairfax St., Alexandria, VA 22314 703-684-2782

FOUNDATION: American Respiratory Therapy Foundation
REQUISITE: Scholarships granted to AMA-approved respiratory therapy program for undergraduates or graduates. Must have medical or technical director's sponsorship.
APPLICATION: Write for info. Application deadline is June 15th.
CONTACT: 11030 Ables Lane, Dallas, TX 75229 214-243-8892

FOUNDATION: American Society for Medical Technology
REQUISITE: Scholarships granted to undergraduate students who have

completed the first semester of their sophomore year in an accredited institution degree program for medical technology. Must be US citizen.
APPLICATION: Write for info. Application deadline is March 1st.
CONTACT: 2021 L St NW Ste 400 Wshngtn, DC 20036 202-785-3311

FOUNDATION: American Society for Medical Technology
REQUISITE: Scholarships granted to undergraduates or graduates for advanced specialty study. Scholarships also open to clinical laboratory practitioners and educators who have performed clinical laboratory functions for at least one year.
APPLICATION: Write for info. Application deadline is March 1st.
CONTACT: 2021 L St NW Ste 400, Washington, DC 20036 202-785-3311

FOUNDATION: American Fund for Dental Health
REQUISITE: Scholarships granted to high school graduates who are accepted or are enrolling in an accredited dental laboratory technology program. Must have good academic record and financial need. Must be US citizen.
APPLICATION: Write for info. Application deadline is June 1st.
CONTACT: 211 E Chicago Ave., #820, Chicago, IL 60611 312-787-6270

FOUNDATION: American Kinesitherapy Association
REQUISITE: Scholarships granted to students who hold or are in the process of obtaining a degree in Kinesitherapy and plan to make this their career. Must be sponsored by a kinesitherapist.
APPLICATION: Write for info. Application deadline is May 1st.
CONTACT: 15312 SW 142 CT, Miami, FL 33177

FOUNDATION: American Medical Record Association
REQUISITE: Student loans granted to undergraduate students beginning their final year of an accredited medical record administration or medical record technology program. Must be US citizen.
APPLICATION: Write for info. Application deadline is 6/15 and 10/15.
CONTACT: 875 N Michigan Ave Ste 1850, Chicag, IL 60611 312-787-2672

FOUNDATION: American Medical Technologists
REQUISITE: Scholarships granted to high school graduates or seniors planning to enroll in or currently enrolled in an accredited program in Medical Technology or Medical Assistants
APPLICATION: Write for info. Application deadline is April 1st.
CONTACT: 710 Higgins Roads, Park Ridge, IL 60068   312-823-5169

FOUNDATION: National Institute of Neurological and Communicative Disorders and Stroke
REQUISITE: Summer internship programs granted to undergraduate students to acquire valuable hands-on research training and experience in the neurosciences. Must have a 3.0 GPA or better.
APPLICATION: Write for info. Application deadline is March 16th.
CONTACT: Bldg 31, Room 8A-19, Bethesda, MD 20892 301-496-5332

FOUNDATION: American Association of Blood Banks
REQUISITE: Scholarships granted to students at all levels attending an accredited SBB program. Must submit original essays to the AABB for review. Topics are Scientific, Analytical or Educational
APPLICATION: Write for info. Application deadline is April 1st.
CONTACT: 1117 N 19th St, Ste 600, Arlington, VA 22209 703-528-8200

FOUNDATION: American Association of Medical Assistants Endowment
REQUISITE: Scholarships granted to high school graduates entering college who submit a written statement expressing interest in a career as a medical assistant.
APPLICATION: Write for info. Application deadline is February 1st.
CONTACT: 20 N. Wacker Dr., #1575, Chicago, IL 60606 312-899-1500

FOUNDATION: American Congress of Rehabilitation Medicine
REQUISITE: Contest open to undergraduates or graduates for the best essays relating to physical medicine and rehabilitation. Essays must not exceed 3,000 words.
APPLICATION: Write for info. Application deadline is May 1st.
CONTACT: 122 South Michigan Ave., Suite 1300, Chicago, IL 60603.
Tel: 312-922-9368

FOUNDATION: American Dental Assistants Association
CONTACT: Scholarships granted to high school graduates who are enrolled in or accepted to dental assistant teacher education program leading to a bachelors or graduate degree. Must be US citizen.
APPLICATION: Write for info. Application deadline is July 15th.
CONTACT: 919 N. Michigan Ave., Suite 3400, Chicago, IL 60611.
Tel: 312-664-3327

FOUNDATION: American Dental Hygienists Association
REQUISITE: Scholarships granted to students planning to enter their final year in an associates/certificate program or planning to enter a bachelor

program for dental hygiene. Must have at least a 3.0 GPA.
APPLICATION: Write for info. Application deadline is May 1st.
CONTACT: 444 North Michigan Ave., Suite 3400, Chicago, IL 60601.
Tel: 312-440-8900

FOUNDATION: Lupus Foundation of America
REQUISITE: Summer fellowships granted to undergraduates, graduates
and post-graduates studying or who have received degree in Lupus
Erythematosus Research.
APPLICATION: Write for info. Application deadline is March 1st.
CONTACT: 1717 Massachusetts Ave. NW, Suite 203, Washington, DC
20036. Tel: 202-328-4550

FOUNDATION: Muscular Dystrophy Association
REQUISITE: Scholarships granted for the summer to undergraduate pre-
med students and medical students who wish to conduct scientific
research relevant to neuromuscular diseases. Students are responsible
for arranging work environment and project design with an advisor.
APPLICATION: Write for info. Application deadline is March 10th.
CONTACT: 810 Seventh Ave., New York, NY 10019. 212-586-0808

FOUNDATION: American Foundation for Aging Research
REQUISITE: Scholarships granted undergraduate and graduate students
for research in age-related diseases or the biology of aging. Must be
attending an accredited institution and be a US citizen.
APPLICATION: Write for info. Application deadline is not specified.
APPLICATION: C/O NC State University, Biochemistry Dept., 128 Polk
Hall, Raleigh, NC 27695. Tel: 919-737-2581

FOUNDATION: National Institute of Dental Research
REQUISITE: Scholarships granted to students interested in a career in
Biomedical research. Must be US citizen.
APPLICATION: Write for info. Application deadline is not specified.
CONTACT: Westwood Bldg., Rm 510, Bethesda, MD 20205 301-496-6324

FOUNDATION: Kappa Kappa Gamma
REQUISITE: Scholarships granted to women who are undergraduate
juniors/seniors or masters/doctoral students. Must have completed at
least two years of study on campus with a Kappa Kappa Gamma Chapter
or doing graduate work on a campus with this chapter. Must be studying
health related field. Must be US or Canadian citizen.

APPLICATION: Write for info. Application deadline is February 15th.
CONTACT: Mrs. LA Williams, 4720 Pickett Road, Fairfax, VA 22032.

FOUNDATION: Kappa Epsilon Fraternity
REQUISITE: Scholarships granted to fraternity members who have completed the equivalent of six semesters of undergraduate education in an accredited institution for Pharmacy.
APPLICATION: Write for info. Application deadline is November 1st.
CONTACT: C/O Room 162, School of Pharmacy, Purdue University, West Lafayette, IN 47907. Tel: 317-494-9015

FOUNDATION: American Society for Medical Technology
REQUISITE: Scholarships granted to undergraduate students who have completed the first semester of their sophomore year in an accrediting institution for Medical Technology. Must be US citizen.
APPLICATION: Write for info. Application deadline is March 1st.
CONTACT: 2021 L Street NW, Suite 400, Washington, DC 20036.
(We were not able to verify this listing; it may not be extant.)

FOUNDATION: Office of the Assistant Secretary of Defense
REQUISITE: Scholarships granted to US citizen enrolled in an accredited institution for Medicine or Osteopathy in the US or Puerto Rico. Applicant is appointed as commissioned officer in Navy Reserve.
APPLICATION: Write for info. Application deadline is not specified.
CONTACT: Commander/Navy Medical Recruiting Command, 4015 Wilson Blvd., Arlington, Va 22203-1991. (703)545-6700

FOUNDATION: American Osteopathic Association Auxiliary
REQUISITE: Scholarships granted to undergraduate sophomore attending an accredited institution of Osteopathic Medicine. Must be in top 25% of their class or have honors from first year.
APPLICATION: Write for info. Application deadline is June 1st.
CONTACT: 628 N. Ontario, Chicago, IL 60611. (312)280-5819

FOUNDATION: Teratology Society
REQUISITE: Scholarships granted to undergraduates or graduates for attendance at the Teratology Society's Annual meeting & for an abstract presentation. Students must be interested in the advance study of biological abnormalities.
APPLICATION: Write for info. Application deadline is May 1st.
CONTACT: 9650 Rockville Pike, Bethesda, MD 20814. (301)571-1841

FOUNDATION: Wilson Ornithological Society
REQUISITE: Scholarships granted to support Avian research. Open to anyone presenting a suitable research problem in Ornithology.
APPLICATION: Write for info. Application deadline is March 1st.
CONTACT: C/O Museum of Zoology, University of Michigan, Ann Arbor, MI 48109. (313)764-1817

FOUNDATION: Entomological Society of America
REQUISITE: Scholarships granted to undergraduate students studying Entomology; Biology or related science at an accredited institution in the US, Canada, or Mexico. Students must have accumulated at least 30 semester hours at the time award is given.
APPLICATION: Write for info. Application deadline is July 1st.
CONTACT: 4603 Calvert Rd., College Park, MD 20740. (301)731-4535

FOUNDATION: Friends of the National Zoo
REQUISITE: Internships granted to advanced undergraduates and recent graduates studying zoology. Students must submit statement of interest, transcript(s), relevant experience and letters of reference.
APPLICATION: Write for info. Application deadline is February 17th.
CONTACT: National Zoological Park, Wshngtn DC 20008 (202)673-4800

FOUNDATION: Epilepsy Foundation of America
REQUISITE: Fellowships granted to student actively enrolled in school for a three month study/training project related to epilepsy rehabilitation service, training or research.
APPLICATION: Write for info. Application deadline is February 28th.
CONTACT: 4351 Garden City Dr., Suite 406, Landover, MD 20785.
Tel: (301)459-3700

FOUNDATION: School for Field Studies
REQUISITE: Scholarships granted to high school and undergraduate students for scientific research expeditions. Students must want to study problems and issues of environmental concern.
APPLICATION: Write for info. Application deadline is the first and fifteenth of February, March and April and May 1st.
CONTACT: 376 Hale St., Beverly, MA 01915. (508)927-7777

FOUNDATION: Smithsonian Institution
REQUISITE: Work-Study program granted to undergraduate or graduate students for the opportunity to gain exposure to and experience in

environmental study.
APPLICATION: Write for info. Application deadline is 3/1, 7/1, & 11/1.
CONTACT: POBOX 28, Edgewater, MD 21037. (410)798-4424

FOUNDATION: Soil Conservation Society of America
REQUISITE: Scholarships granted to undergraduates who have completed at least 2 years at an accredited institution and who have interest in Conservation, Ecology, Earth Science or related areas.
APPLICATION: Write for info. Application deadline is April 1st.
CONTACT: 7515 NE Ankeny Road, Ankeny, IA 50021. (515)289-2331

FOUNDATION: National FFA Center
REQUISITE: Scholarships granted to FFA members planning to enroll in an accredited four year program to study Fish and Wildlife Management. Must be US citizen or legal resident.
APPLICATION: Write for info. Application deadline is April 1st.
CONTACT: Scholarship Office, POBOX 15160, Alexandria, VA 22309.
Tel: (703)360-3600

FOUNDATION: Garden Club of America
REQUISITE: Scholarships granted to undergraduate or graduate students for a summer course in environmental studies. Must be US citizen or legal resident.
APPLICATION: Write for info. Application deadline is March 15th.
CONTACT: 598 Madison Ave., New York, NY 10022. (212)753-8287

FOUNDATION: Earthwatch Expeditions Inc.
REQUISITE: Scholarships granted to high school students and teachers to give them an opportunity to work in the field for 2 or 3 weeks with a professional scientist on a research expedition.
APPLICATION: Write for info. Application deadline is March 31st.
CONTACT: POBOX 403, 680 Mount Auburn St., Watertown, MA 02172.
Tel: (617)926-8200

FOUNDATION: School for Field Studies
REQUISITE: Scholarships and loans granted to high school and undergraduate students studying various field sciences who wish to study problems/issues of the environment.
APPLICATION: Write for info. Application deadline is the first and fifteenth of February; March; and April and May 1st.
CONTACT: 376 Hale St., Beverly, MA 01915. (508)927-7777

FOUNDATION: National Campers and Hikers Association
REQUISITE: Scholarships granted to undergraduate students majoring in fields related to Conservation, Ecology, or outdoor activities. Students family must hold membership in NCHA and applicants must be in top 40% of class.
APPLICATION: Write for info. Application deadline is March 25th.
CONTACT: 4804 Transit Road, Bldg 2, Depew, NY 14043. (716)668-6242

FOUNDATION: Argonne National Laboratory
REQUISITE: Internships granted to full-time undergraduate juniors, seniors and first year graduate students to provide them with an opportunity to work in various areas of Earth Science in relation to energy development.
APPLICATION: Write for info. Application deadline is February 1st; May 15th; and October 15th.
CONTACT: Division of Educational Programs, 9700 South Cass Ave., Argonne, IL 60439. (708)252-2000

FOUNDATION: Arthur and Doreen Parrett Scholarship
REQUISITE: Scholarships granted to undergraduate students who are planning a career in Engineering; Science; Medicine; or Dentistry. Must be attending an accredited institution and be a US citizen.
APPLICATION: Write for info. Application deadline is July 31st.
CONTACT: C/O U.S. Bank of Washington, POBOX 720, Trust Department, Seatle, WA 98111. (206)344-4517

FOUNDATION: Explorers Club
REQUISITE: Scholarships granted to high school and undergraduate students to help them participate in field research in the natural sciences anywhere in the world. Must be US citizen.
APPLICATION: Write for info. Application deadline is April 15th.
CONTACT: 46 East 70th St., New York, NY 10021. (212)628-8383

HARD SCIENCES & ENGINEERING

FOUNDATION: Society of Physics Students
REQUISITE: Scholarships granted to SPS members for their final year of full-time study leading to a BS degree in Physics. Must meet all qualifications of SPS.
APPLICATION: Write for info. Application deadline is January 31st.
CONTACT: 335 East 45th St., New York, NY 10017. (212)206-8300

FOUNDATION: Society for the Advancement of Material and Process Engineering
REQUISITE: Scholarships granted to undergraduate freshmen, sophomores and juniors who are recommended by their advisor or department head & are planning to study Material Science; Chemistry or Chemical Engineering. Must submit transcript of all college grades and letters of reference.
APPLICATION: Write for info. Application deadline is January 31st.
CONTACT: POBOX 2459, Covina, CA 91722. (213)550-8043

FOUNDATION: Society of Exploration Geophysicists Education Fndtn
REQUISITE: Scholarships granted to undergraduates and graduates who are accepted to or enrolled in an accredited program in the US or its possessions and intend to pursue a career in Geophysics or related areas.
APPLICATION: Write for info. Application deadline is March 1st.
CONTACT: POBOX 702740, Tulsa, OK 74170. (918)493-3516

FOUNDATION: American Meterological Society
REQUISITE: Scholarship granted to undergraduates attending an accredited university & who write an original paper on Meteorology.
APPLICATION: Write for info. Application deadline is June 15th.
CONTACT: 45 Beacon Street, Boston, MA 02108. (617)227-2425

FOUNDATION: American Meteorological Society
REQUISITE: Scholarships granted to undergraduate juniors majoring in Meteorology or some other aspect of atmospheric science.
APPLICATION: Write for info. Application deadline is June 15th.
CONTACT: 45 Beacon Street, Boston, MA 02108. (617)227-2425

FOUNDATION: Thomas Alva Edison Foundation
REQUISITE: Scholarship granted to outstanding high school students. Must submit proposal on a completed experiment or a project idea having "practical application" in field of science and/or engineering. Must not exceed 1000 words. Must include letters of recommendation from teacher/sponsor describing how you exemplify creativity and ingenuity demonstrated by life/work of Thomas Edison and Max McGraw.
APPLICATION: Write for info. Application deadline is December 1st.
CONTACT: Dr. R. A. Dean, Box 2800, La Jolla, CA 92038-2800.
(We were not able to verify this listing; it may not be extant.)

FOUNDATION: Bausch & Lomb Science Award Committee
REQUISITE: Scholarships granted to high school juniors interested in the field of science.
APPLICATION: Write for info. Application deadline is February 15th.
CONTACT: One Lincoln First Sq, Rochester, NY 14604 (716)338-6000

FOUNDATION: Woods Hole Oceanographic Institution
REQUISITE: Fellowships granted to undergraduate juniors and seniors with an interest in Oceanography and a major in any area of science or engineering. Fellowship is to be used at Woods Hole.
APPLICATION: Write for info. Application deadline is March 1st.
CONTACT: Fellowships Coordinator, Woods Hole, MA 02543.
Tel: (508)548-1400 ext. 2219

FOUNDATION: Society of Mining Engineers
REQUISITE: Scholarships granted to SME members. Juniors, seniors or graduates who desire to develop their skills in industrial minerals.
APPLICATION: Write for info. Application deadline is November 30th.
CONTACT: POBOX 625002, 8307 Shaffer Pkwy, Littleton, CO 80162.
Tel: (303)973-9550

FOUNDATION: Society of Photographic Scientists and Engineers-The Society for Imaging Science and Technology
REQUISITE: Scholarships granted to juniors, seniors or graduates for full-time continuing study in Imaging Science or Photogrammetry.
APPLICATION: Write for info. Application deadline is December 15th.
CONTACT: 7003 Kilworth Lane, Springfield, VA 22151. (703)642-9090

FOUNDATION: American Meteorological Society
REQUISITE: Scholarships granted to undergraduate juniors majoring in meteorology or some other aspect of atmospheric science. Award is to used for senior year only.
APPLICATION: Write for info. Application deadline is June 15th.
CONTACT: 45 Beacon Street, Boston, MA 02108. (617)227-2425

FOUNDATION: American Society for Photogrammetry and Remote Sensing
REQUISITE: Scholarships granted to ASPRS and ACSM members who have completed at least one undergraduate course in Photogrammetry or surveying.
APPLICATION: Write for info. Application deadline is January 1st.

CONTACT: 210 Little Falls St., Falls Church, VA 22046.
(We were not able to verify this listing; it may not be extant.)

FOUNDATION: American Geological Institute
REQUISITE: Scholarships granted to undergraduate or graduate students studying Earth Sciences; Space Sciences or Marine Science. These scholarships are open to Black, Hispanic and Native Americans. Must be US citizen.
APPLICATION: Write for info. Application deadline is February 1st.
CONTACT: 4220 King St., Alexandria, VA 22302. (703)379-2480

1FOUNDATION: General Learning Corporation
REQUISITE: Essay competition open to students in grades 7-12 in US or Canada. Student's Science teacher and one parent receive a trip to the Science conference in St. Louis along with winner.
APPLICATION: Write for info. Application deadline is January 15th.
CONTACT: 60 Revere Dr.,, Northbrook, IL 60062. (708)205-3000

FOUNDATION: Air Traffic Control Association Inc.
REQUISITE: Scholarships granted to men & women who are full-time undergraduates or graduates in Aeronautics, Aviation or related areas. Aviation industry career employees are also eligible. Must be US citizen.
APPLICATION: Write for info. Application deadline is August 1st.
CONTACT: 2020 North 14th St., Suite 410, Arlington, VA 22201.
Tel: (703)522-5717

FOUNDATION: American Radio Relay League Foundation
REQUISITE: Scholarships granted to ARRL members who are residents of ARRL Central Division (IL, IN, OH). Must attend a 4-year college in ARRL Central Division and be a licensed radio amateur.
APPLICATION: Write for info. Application deadline is May 1st.
CONTACT: 225 Main St., Newington, CT 06111. (203)666-1541

FOUNDATION: American Radio Relay League Foundation
REQUISITE: Scholarships granted to students who are residents of ARRL Roanoke Division (NC, SC, VA, WV). Must attend a college in the Roanoke Division as an undergraduate or graduate student. Must be at least a general class licensed radio amateur.
APPLICATION: Write for info. Application deadline is May 1st.
CONTACT: 225 Main St., Newington, CT 06111. (203)666-1541

FOUNDATION: American Radio Relay League Foundation
REQUISITE: Scholarships granted to ARRL Midwest Division Residents (IA, KS, MO, NE) who are licensed radio amateurs. Must be enrolled full-time as an undergraduate or graduate student at an accredited institution in the ARRL Midwest Division.
APPLICATION: Write for info. Application deadline is May 1st.
CONTACT: 225 Main St., Newington, CT 06111. (203)666-1541

FOUNDATION: American Radio Relay League Foundation
REQUISITE: Scholarships granted to licensed radio amateurs and enrolled full-time as an undergraduate or graduate student at an accredited institution studying in the field of Communications.
APPLICATION: Write for info. Application deadline is May 1st.
CONTACT: 225 Main St., Newington, CT 06111. (203)666-1541

FOUNDATION: American Consulting Engineers Council
REQUISITE: Scholarships granted to juniors, seniors and 5th year students in a 5-year program who are in the top half of their class and attending an accredited institution in the US. Must be US citizen.
APPLICATION: Write for info. Application deadline is March 18th.
CONTACT: 1015 15th St NW #802 Washington, DC 20005 (202)347-7474

FOUNDATION: Business and Professional Women
REQUISITE: Scholarships for women who are accepted for undergraduate or graduate level study at an accredited school for Engineering and Technology. Must have at least a junior status and be a US citizen.
APPLICATION: Write for info. Application deadline is May 1st.
CONTACT: 2012 Massachusetts Ave. NW, Washington, DC 20036.
Tel: (202)293-1200

FOUNDATION: American Society for Engineering Education
REQUISITE: Scholarships granted to top 3rd year engineering students. This is a 10-week internship in Washington, DC to learn how engineers contribute to public policy decisions on complex technological issues.
APPLICATION: Write for info. Application deadline is December 31st.
CONTACT: 11 Dupont Crcl #200, Washington, DC 20036 (202)331-3500

FOUNDATION: Argonne National Laboratory
REQUISITE: Internships granted to students studying in areas of Energy Development. Students must be full-time juniors, seniors or 1st year grad students. Must be US citizen or legal resident.

Hard Sciences & Engineering

APPLICATION: Write for info. Deadlines 2/1, 5/15 and 10/15.
CONTACT: Division of Educational Programs, 9700 South Cass Ave., Argonne, IL 60439 Tel: (708)252-2000

FOUNDATION: Cooper Union for the Advancement of Science and Art
REQUISITE: Scholarships granted to US high school graduates with excellent SAT scores. CEEB are eligible for full-tuition scholarships at Cooper Union.
APPLICATION: Write for info. Application deadline is February 1st.
CONTACT: 41 Cooper Square, New York, NY 10003. (212)353-4100

FOUNDATION: General Learning Corporation
REQUISITE: Essay, science related, contest open to US & Canadian students. Grades 7-12. Cash award and trip to St. Louis Science Conference.
APPLICATION: Write for info. Application deadline is January 15th.
CONTACT: 60 Revere Drive, Northbrook, IL 60062. (708)205-3000

FOUNDATION: Illuminating Engineering Society of North America
REQUISITE: Scholarships granted to students interested in studying lighting. Juniors & seniors must be attending an accredited institution in Northern California, Oregon, Washington or Northern Nevada.
APPLICATION: Write for info. Application deadline is not specified.
CONTACT: 345 East 47TH Street, New York, NY 10017. (212)248-5000

FOUNDATION: National Society of Professional Engineers Edctnl Fndton
REQUISITE: Scholarships for high school seniors who are in the top 23% of their class and plan to attend an accredited institution. Special grants given to minorities and females.
APPLICATION: Write for info. Application deadline is November 15th.
CONTACT: 1420 King Street, Alexandria, VA 22314. (703)684-2830

FOUNDATION: Science Service
REQUISITE: Scholarships granted to high school seniors who plan to complete college enrollment by October 1st. All applicants must submit a 1000 word report. Must be a US citizen or legal resident.
APPLICATION: Write for info. Application deadline is December 15th.
CONTACT: 1719 N Street NW, Washington, DC 20036. (202)785-2255

FOUNDATION: Society of Women Engineers
REQUISITE: Scholarships granted to women that are US citizens or legal

325

residents. Incoming freshman must be enrolled in an accredited A.B.E.T. Engineering program.
APPLICATION: Write for info. Application deadline is July 1st.
CONTACT: 345 East 47th St Rm 305, NY, NY 10017 (212)509-9577

FOUNDATION: Society of Women Engineers
REQUISITE: Scholarships granted to women majoring in engineering at an accredited institution in the US. Open to juniors and seniors.
APPLICATION: Write for info. Application deadline is February 1st.
CONTACT: 345 East 47th St Rm 305 NY NY 10017 (212)509-9577

FOUNDATION: Society of Women Engineers
REQUISITE: Scholarships granted to women who have not worked as engineers for at least 2 years and wish to return to school for an engineering program. Undergraduate or graduate study in the USA.
APPLICATION: Write for info. Application deadline is July 1st.
CONTACT: 345 East 47TH ST., New York, NY 10017 (212)509-9577

FOUNDATION: Society of Women Engineers
REQUISITE: Scholarships granted to sophomore women majoring in engineering at an accredited college and preparing for a BS degree. S.W.E. award is for student members. Others are open to non-members.
APPLICATION: Write for info. Application deadline is February 1st.
CONTACT: 345 East 47TH ST., New York, NY 10017 (212)509-9577

FOUNDATION: Technical Marketing Society of America
REQUISITE: Scholarships granted to dependent of member or member of the TMSA who is enrolled in an undergraduate degree program in Marketing, Business or Engineering at an accredited institution. Must maintain a 3.0 GPA.
APPLICATION: Write for info. Application deadline is October 31st.
CONTACT: 3711 Long Beach Blvd., Suite 609, Long Beach, CA 90807. (We were not able to verify this listing; it may not be extant.)

FOUNDATION: Thomas Alva Edison Foundation
REQUISITE: Scholarships granted to outstanding high school students. Must submit a proposal on a complete experiment or a project idea which would have "practical application" in the field of science or engineering. Must be no longer than 1000 words. Must include letter of recommendation from a teacher or sponsor which describes how you exemplify creativity and ingenuity demonstrated by life.

APPLICATION: Write for info. Application deadline is December 1st.
CONTACT: Dr. R. A. Dean; POBOX 2800, La Jolla, CA 92038-2800 when mailing entry. For more info about requirements write: 21000 West Ten Mile RD., Southfield, MI 48075.
(We were not able to verify this listing; it may not be extant.)

FOUNDATION: American Gas Assoc
REQUISITE: Scholarships granted to undergraduate juniors and seniors majoring in various sciences. Applicants must have very good academic record and need.
APPLICATION: Write for info. Application deadline is April 1st.
CONTACT: 1515 Wilson Blvd., Educational Programs, Arlington, VA 22209. Tel: (703)841-8400

FOUNDATION: National Space Club
REQUISITE: Scholarships for juniors and seniors who plan to pursue a career in the Aerospace Sciences and Technology. Must be US citizen.
APPLICATION: Write for info. Application deadline is January.
CONTACT: 655 15th St NW #300, Washington, DC 20005 202)639-4210

FOUNDATION: Radio Technical Commission for Aeronautics
REQUISITE: Scholarships granted to undergraduates and graduates studying in the areas of Aviation Electronics, Aviation and Telecommunications. Must submit written report in the form of an essay, thesis or paper which has been completed within the last 3 years.
APPLICATION: Write for info. Application deadline is June 30th.
CONTACT: 1425 "K" ST NW #500, Washington, D.C. 20005.
(We were not able to verify this listing; it may not be extant.)

FOUNDATION: Smithsonian Institution
REQUISITE: Internships granted to undergraduate and graduate students in various fields such as Aviation, Astronomy, Geology, Space Science, Art, and Museum and Library Operations.
APPLICATION: Write for info. Application deadline is not specified.
CONTACT: Attn: NASM Intern Program Director, Room P700, Washington, DC 20560. Tel: (202)357-1300

FOUNDATION: Tailhook Association
REQUISITE: Scholarships granted to members, dependents or individuals sponsored by members who are in an accredited 4 year program in Aerospace Education. Must have good academic record.

APPLICATION: Write for info. Application deadline is July 15th.
CONTACT: POBOX 40, Bonita, CA 92002. Tel: (619)689-9223

FOUNDATION: Vertical Flight Foundation
REQUISITE: Scholarships granted to undergraduates and graduates studying in the areas in Mechanical, Electrical and Aerospace Engineering and who are planning to pursue a career in some aspect of helicopter or vertical flight.
APPLICATION: Write for info. Application deadline is February 1st.
CONTACT: 217 N. Washington St., Alexandria, VA 22314.
(We were not able to verify this listing; it may not be extant.)

FOUNDATION: American Geological Institute
REQUISITE: Scholarships granted to undergraduate or graduate study in the fields of Earth; Math; or Marine Science. Must be US citizen.
APPLICATION: Write for info. Application deadline is February 1st.
CONTACT: 4220 King St., Alexandria, VA 22302 (703)379-2480

FOUNDATION: American Institute of Aeronautics and Astronautics
REQUISITE: Scholarships granted to undergraduate students enrolled at an accredited college or university who have completed at least half of their freshman year and has a "B" overall average. Must be a US citizen or legal resident.
APPLICATION: Write for info. Application deadline is February 1st.
CONTACT: 370 L'Enfant Promenade SW Washington DC 20024 (202)646-7400

FOUNDATION: AOPA Air Safety Foundation
REQUISITE: Scholarships granted to juniors and seniors enrolled in an accredited aviation degree program with 2.5+ GPA. Must be US citizen.
APPLICATION: Write for info. Application deadline is March 31st.
CONTACT: 421 Aviation Way, Frederick, MD 21701. (301)695-2170

FOUNDATION: American Society of Civil Engineers
REQUISITE: Scholarships granted to undergraduate freshmen, sophomores & juniors who are student members of ASCE in good standing. Awards are tenable at ABET accredited institutions only.
APPLICATION: Write for info. Application deadline is February 1st.
CONTACT: 345 East 47TH ST., New York, NY 10017. (212)705-7496

FOUNDATION: American Society of Civil Engineers

REQUISITE: Fellowships granted to students for research in Civil Engineering. Engineers under the age of 45 and who are members of ASCE are welcome to apply.
APPLICATION: Write for info. Application deadline is February 1st.
CONTACT: 345 East 47TH ST., New York, NY 10017. (212)705-7496

FOUNDATION: Associated General Contractors Edctn & Research Fndtn
REQUISITE: Scholarships granted to high school seniors & college sophomores planning to transfer to a four-year program and all levels of undergraduates except seniors. Must study full-time. Must be US citizen or legal resident.
APPLICATION: Write for info. Application deadline is November 1th.
CONTACT: 1957 E St NW, Washington, D.C. 20006. (202)393-2040

FOUNDATION: Associated General Contractors Edctn & Research Fndtn
REQUISITE: Essay contest is open to full-time undergraduate seniors in a 4-year program. Essay should relate to construction and/or general contracting. The essay should be general management related rather than technical. Must be US citizen or legal resident.
APPLICATION: Write for info. Application deadline is December 1st.
CONTACT: 1957 'E' ST NW, Washington, D.C. 20006. (202)393-2040

FOUNDATION: Foundation of the Wall & Ceiling Industry
REQUISITE: Scholarships granted to undergraduate students who are enrolled in a 2-year or 4-year program at an accredited institution in the US studying construction as a possible career.
APPLICATION: Write for info. Application deadline is December 1st.
CONTACT: 1600 Cameron St 2nd Fl Alexandria VA 22314
(We were not able to verify this listing; it may not be extant.)

FOUNDATION: Merit Shop Foundation
REQUISITE: Scholarships granted to undergraduate students who are enrolled in an accredited 4-year program and intend to pursue a career in the construction industry. Must be US citizen.
APPLICATION: Write for info. Application deadline is December 15th.
CONTACT: 729 15TH Street NW., Washington, D.C. 20005.
(We were not able to verify this listing; it may not be extant.)

FOUNDATION: National Association of Plumbing, Heating, Cooling Contractors
REQUISITE: Scholarships granted to high school seniors and incoming

freshmen who are enrolled in BA programs. Students must have a sponsor who is a member in good standings with NAPHCC for at least 1 year. Must be US citizen.
APPLICATION: Write for info. Application deadline is April 1st.
CONTACT: POBOX 6808, Falls Church, VA 22046. (703)237-8100

FOUNDATION: National Association of Women in Construction
REQUISITE: Scholarships granted to women undergraduate sophomores in a 4-year institution in California. Award is for junior year of study only. Must be US citizen.
APPLICATION: Write for info. Application deadline is May 1st.
CONTACT: 550 Sunol Street, San Jose, CA 95126. (408)379-3280

FOUNDATION: U.S. Air Force ROTC
REQUISITE: Scholarships granted to US citizens at least 17 years of age and under 25 years of age majoring in Aeronautics, Aerospace, Science, Math or Physics. Must provide SAT or ACT scores, high school transcripts and record of extracurricular activities. Must pass Air Force Medical Examination.
APPLICATION: Write for info. Application deadline is December 1st.
CONTACT: AFROTC/RRUF, Maxwell, AFB AL 36112. (205)953-1110

FOUNDATION: U.S. Department of Health and Human Services
REQUISITE: Scholarships granted to anyone accepted into an accredited full-time program in the fields of Civil Engineering, Environmental Engineering or Mechanical Engineering.
APPLICATION: Write for info. Application deadline is May 15th.
CONTACT: 5600 Fishers Lane, Room 6-12, Rockville, MD 20857.
Tel: (301)443-6197

FOUNDATION: Argonne National Laboratory
REQUISITE: Internships granted to students studying Physical, Life, Earth, or Computer Science or Mathematics or Engineering. Must be full-time juniors or seniors or 1st year grad students. Must be USA citizen or legal resident.
APPLICATION: Write for info. Deadlines are 2/1, 5/15, 10/5.
CONTACT: Division of Educational Programs, 9700 South Cass Ave., Argonne, IL 60439. Tel: (708)252-2000

FOUNDATION: National Radio Astronomy Observatory
REQUISITE: Assistantships granted to undergraduate juniors/seniors and

first or second year graduate students studying various fields of science. Awards tenable at NRAO sites.
APPLICATION: Write for info. Application deadline is February 1st.
CONTACT: Edgemont Road, Charlottesville, VA 22903. (804)296-0211

FOUNDATION: National Radio Astronomy Observatory
REQUISITE: Fellowships granted for summer research to undergraduate juniors/seniors and first or second year graduates studying in the fields of high-tech sciences. Must be attending a NRAO site.
APPLICATION: Write for info. Application deadline is February 1st.
CONTACT: Edgemont Road, Charlottesville, CA 22903. (804)296-0211

FOUNDATION: Radio Technical Commission For Aeronautics
REQUISITE: Competition open to undergraduate and graduate students in Aviation Electronics, Aviation, Telecommunications. Must submit written report in the form of an essay, thesis, or paper which has been completed within the last 3 years.
APPLICATION: Write for info. Application deadline is June 30th.
CONTACT: 1425 K ST NW #500, Washington, DC 20005.
(We were not able to verify this listing; it may not be extant.)

FOUNDATION: Vertical Flight Foundation
REQUISITE: Scholarships granted to undergraduates and graduates in the field of Engineering who are pursuing a career in some aspect of helicopter or vertical flight at an accredited institution in the USA.
APPLICATION: Write for info. Application deadline is February 1st.
CONTACT: 217 N. Washington St., Alexandria, VA 22314.
(We were not able to verify this listing; it may not be extant.)

FOUNDATION: American Nuclear Society
REQUISITE: Scholarships granted to undergraduate juniors/seniors majoring in Nuclear Engineering. Must have good academic record and be a US citizen.
APPLICATION: Write for info. Application deadline is March 1st.
CONTACT: 555 N. Kensington Ave LaGrange Park IL 60525
(708)352-6611

FOUNDATION: American Society of Heating; Refrigerating & Air Conditioning Engineers
REQUISITE: Scholarships granted to undergraduate students with at least one full year of study to finish. Must have at least a 3.0 GPA and

attending an accredited institution in the US or Canada.
APPLICATION: Write for info. Application deadline is February 15th.
CONTACT: 1791 Tullie Circle NE, Atlanta, GA 30329. (404)636-8400

FOUNDATION: Association of Official Analytical Chemists
REQUISITE: Scholarships granted to undergraduate sophomores with at least a "B" overall average. Juniors and seniors are eligible for various other scholarships.
APPLICATION: Write for info. Application deadline is May 1st.
CONTACT: 2200 Wilson Blvd Ste 400 Arlington VA 22201 (703)522-3032

FOUNDATION: Institute of Industrial Engineers
REQUISITE: Scholarships granted to undergraduate and graduate students who are active IIE members with one year of study remaining at an accredited institution in North America. Must have at least a 3.0 GPA and a need for financial assistance.
APPLICATION: Write for info. Application deadline is November 1st.
CONTACT: 25 Tchnlygy Prk/Atlanta, Norcross, GA 30092 (404)449-0461

FOUNDATION: International Society for Optical Engineering
REQUISITE: Scholarships granted to students based on an assessment of the student's potential contribution to optics or optical engineering.
APPLICATION: Write for info. Application deadline is May 4th.
CONTACT: POBOX 10, Bellingham, WA 98227. (206)676-3290

FOUNDATION: James F. Lincoln ARC Welding Foundation
REQUISITE: Scholarships granted to undergraduate and graduate students who solve design engineering or fabrication problems involving the knowledge or application of ARC welding.
APPLICATION: Write for info. Application deadline is June 15th.
CONTACT: POBOX 17035, Cleveland, OH 44117. (216)932-1118

FOUNDATION: Material Handling Education Foundation
REQUISITE: Scholarships granted to undergraduate juniors/seniors and graduate students attending an accredited institution in the USA.
APPLICATION: Write for info. Application deadline is February 3rd.
CONTACT: 8720 Red Oak Blvd., #201, Charlotte, NC 28210.
(We were not able to verify this listing; it may not be extant.)

FOUNDATION: North American Die Casting Association
REQUISITE: Scholarships granted to students enrolled at an engineering

college affiliated with the Foundry Educational Foundation and is registered with FEF for the current year. Must be US citizen.
APPLICATION: Write for info. Application deadline is April 10th.
CONTACT: 2000 N Fifth Ave River Grove IL 60171 (708)292-3600

FOUNDATION: Society for the Advancement of Material and Process Engineering
REQUISITE: Scholarships granted to all undergraduates levels except the senior level who are recommended by their advisor or department head. Students must submit transcript and letters of reference.
APPLICATION: Write for info. Application deadline is January 31st.
CONTACT: POBOX 2459, Covina, CA 91722.
(We were not able to verify this listing; it may not be extant.)

FOUNDATION: Society of Manufacturing Engineering Education Fndtn
REQUISITE: Scholarships granted to full-time undergraduate students at an accredited school who are pursuing a career in Manufacturing/Industrial Engineering. Students must demonstrate interest through work & productivity. Must have at least a 3.2 GPA and be a US or Canadian Citizen.
APPLICATION: Write for info. Application deadline is February 1st.
CONTACT: 1 Seme Dr, POBOX 930, Dearborn, MI 48121. (313)271-1500

FOUNDATION: American Society for Metals
REQUISITE: Scholarships granted to undergraduate students who have completed at least one year of study. Must be US, Canadian, or Mexican citizen enrolled in accredited US institution.
APPLICATION: Write for info. Application deadline is June 15th.
CONTACT: ASM Scholarship Selection Committee, Metals Park, OH 44073. Tel: (216)338-5151

FOUNDATION: American Society of Mechanical Engineers
REQUISITE: Scholarships for members of ASME who are undergraduates or graduates enrolled in an accredited Mechanical Engineering Curricula. Must have at least a 2.0 GPA and be a US citizen.
APPLICATION: Write for info. Deadlines are 4/1 and 11/1.
CONTACT: 345 East 47TH St., New York, NY 10017. (212)705-7722

FOUNDATION: American Society of Mechanical Engineers Auxiliary Inc.
REQUISITE: Scholarships granted to students enrolled in their junior year in an accredited ME program in the US. Scholarships are granted for

senior year of study only. Must be a ASME member.
APPLICATION: Write for info. Application deadline is February 15th.
CONTACT: 345 East 47TH St., New York, NY 10017. (212)705-7722

FOUNDATION: American Society of Mechanical Engineers Natnl Office
REQUISITE: Scholarships granted to all undergraduate students except
seniors. Must be a member of ASME and attending school on a full-time
basis in a ABET accredited program in the USA. Must have need for
scholarship.
APPLICATION: Write for info. Application deadline is 1/1 thru 4/1.
CONTACT: 345 East 47TH St., New York, NY 10017. (212)705-7722

FOUNDATION: American Society of Naval Engineers
REQUISITE: Scholarships granted to Engineering Students who are
pursuing a career in Naval Engineering and who demonstrate scholastic
aptitude. Awards good for 3rd & 4th year of study. Must be US citizen.
APPLICATION: Write for info. Application deadline is February 15th.
CONTACT: 1452 Duke St., Alexandria, VA 22314. (703)836-6727

FOUNDATION: Society for the Advancement of Material and Process
Engineering
REQUISITE: Scholarships granted to all undergraduate students except
seniors who are recommended by their advisor or department head.
Must submit transcript and letters of reference.
APPLICATION: Write for info. Application deadline is January 31st.
CONTACT: POBOX 2459, Covina, CA 91722.
(We were not able to verify this listing; it may not be extant.)

FOUNDATION: Society of Mining Engineers
REQUISITE: Scholarships granted to SME members who have chosen
as a career the field of Mining Engineering with an emphasis on coal.
Must be attending an accredited ABET institution and must be engaging
in coal-related activities.
APPLICATION: Write for info. Application deadline is not specified.
CONTACT: POBOX 652002, 8307 Shaffer Pkwy., Littleton, CO 80162.
Tel: (303)973-9550

FOUNDATION: Society of Mining Engineers
REQUISITE: Scholarships granted to undergraduate sophomores who
are pursuing a career in Mining Engineering Must be attending an
accredited institution and be a US citizen

APPLICATION: Write for info. Application deadline is November 30th.
CONTACT: POBOX 652002, 8307 Shaffer Pkwy., Littleton, CO 80162.
Tel: (303)973-9550

FOUNDATION: U.S. Air Force ROTC
REQUISITE: Scholarships granted to US citizen between the ages of 17-25. Must be able to furnish SAT/ACT scores, high school transcripts and record of extracurricular activities. Must qualify on Air Force medical examination.
APPLICATION: Write for info. Application deadline is December 1st.
CONTACT: AFROTC/RRUF, Maxwell AFB, AL 36112. (205)262-7233

FOUNDATION: U.S. Department of Health and Human Services
REQUISITE: Scholarships granted to anyone enrolled/accepted into a full-time bachelor's degree program in the field of engineering at an institution in the US. Preference to Native Americans but not limited. Must be willing to accept rules and regulations after award.
APPLICATION: Write for info. Application deadline is May 15th.
CONTACT: 5600 Fishers Lane, Room 6-12, Rockville, MD 20857.
Tel: (301)443-3783

FOUNDATION: Webb Institute of Navel Architecture
REQUISITE: Scholarships for high school students between the ages of 16-24 who are in the top 10% of their class and have at least a 3.2 GPA; SAT scores must be high; students must demonstrate interest in the field of Naval Architecture and appear for interview. Must be US citizen.
APPLICATION: Write for info. Application deadline is February 15th.
CONTACT: Crescent Beach Rd., Glen Cove, NY 11542. (516)671-2213

FOUNDATION: Woman's Auxiliary to the American Institute of Mining, Metallurgical and Petroleum Engineers
REQUISITE: Loans granted to juniors and seniors. Students will be granted a loan that will pay for half or all of their education but will only be responsible for paying 50% of it back with no interest charges.
APPLICATION: Write for info. Application deadline is March 15th.
CONTACT: 345 E.47TH ST., 14th Floor, NY NY 10017 (212)705-7695

FOUNDATION: Civil Air Patrol
REQUISITE: Scholarships granted to undergraduates studying Humanities or Science at an accredited institution. Open to CAP members. Must be US citizen or legal resident.

APPLICATION: Write for info. Application deadline is March 15th.
CONTACT: National Headquarters/TT, Maxwell AFB, AL 36112.
Tel: (205)953-1110

MINORITIES & HANDICAPPED

FOUNDATION: U.S. Department of Interior; Bureau of Indian Affairs
REQUISITE: Scholarships granted to members of Tribes or Bands who reside on or near a reservation under the jurisdiction of BIA. This is for adult vocational training and job placement services for individual indians.
APPLICATION: Write for info. Application deadline is not specified.
CONTACT: 18th and C Street NW, C490/1350N, Washington, DC 20240.
Tel: 202-343-3668

FOUNDATION: American Foundation for the Blind
REQUISITE: Scholarships granted to undergraduate and graduate legally blind students attending an accredited program within the broad areas of rehabilitation and/or education of the blind and visually impaired. Must be US citizen.
APPLICATION: Write for info. Application deadline is June 1st.
CONTACT: 15 West 16th Street, New York, NY 10011. 212-620-2055

FOUNDATION: National Federation of the Blind
REQUISITE: Scholarships granted to legally blind undergraduate or graduate student studying Law at an accredited institution.
APPLICATION: Write for info. Application deadline is March 31st.
CONTACT: 814 4th Ave. #200, Grinnell, IA 50112.
Tel: 515-236-3366

FOUNDATION: U.S. Department of Health and Human Services
REQUISITE: Scholarships granted to Native Americans enrolled in courses that will prepare them for enrollment or re-enrollment into degree programs in Nursing or Pharmacy at an accredited institution in the USA. Must have at least a 2.0 GPA and be a US citizen.
APPLICATION: Write for info. Application deadline is May 15th.
CONTACT: 5600 Fishers Lane, Room 6-12, Rockville, MD 20857.
Tel: 301-443-6197

FOUNDATION: Inter-Tribal Council of the Five Civilized Tribes
REQUISITE: Scholarships granted to undergraduate Native Americans who are members of the Five Civilized Tribes. Must submit a short essay

on your tribal affiliation; goals; need & philosophy on Indian peoples needs and how you might help during your lifetime.
APPLICATION: Write for info. Application deadline is July 1st.
CONTACT: Bacone College, Muskogee, OK 74403. Tel: 918-683-4581

FOUNDATION: National Institutes of Health-Division of Research Resources
REQUISITE: Scholarships granted to minority high school students to provide a meaningful experience in various aspects of health-related research in order to stimulate their interests in Science.
Must be US citizen.
APPLICATION: Write for info. Application deadline is December 1st.
CONTACT: 9000 Rockville Pike, Room 5B-23 Bldg. 31, Bethesda, MD 20892. Tel: 301-496-6743

FOUNDATION: Western States Chiropractic College
REQUISITE: Scholarships granted to Native Americans to attend Western States Chiropractic College. Student must have documentation to prove blood quantum and evidence of compliance with tribal residency requirements and affiliation.
APPLICATION: Write for info. Application deadline is August 15th.
CONTACT: 2900 NE 132nd Ave., Portland, OR 97230 Tel: 503-256-3180

FOUNDATION: U.S. Department of Health and Human Services
REQUISITE: Scholarships granted to Native Americans accepted/enrolled in undergraduate course of study at an accredited institution that will prepare them for acceptance into professional degree programs in Medicine; Osteopathy; or Dentistry. Must have at least a 2.5 GPA and be a US citizen.
APPLICATION: Write for info. Application deadline is May 15th.
CONTACT: 5600 Fishers Lane, Room 6-12, Rockville, MD 20857.
Tel: (301)443-6197

FOUNDATION: National Center for Indian Education
REQUISITE: Scholarships granted to high school seniors with one-fourth degree or more Indian blood. Must reside in Kansas/Oklahoma/Colorado/Arizona/or San Bernadino county CA.
APPLICATION: Write for info. Application deadline is March 15th.
CONTACT: POBOX 18239 Capitol Hill Station, Denver, CO 80218.
(We were not able to verify this listing; it may not be extant.)

FOUNDATION: American Physical Society
REQUISITE: Scholarships granted to minority undergraduate students at US institutions majoring in Physics. Must be US citizen.
APPLICATION: Write for info. Application deadline is March 31st.
CONTACT: 335 East 45th Street, New York, NY 10017.
(We were not able to verify this listing; it may not be extant.)

FOUNDATION: American Foundation for the Blind
REQUISITE: Scholarships granted to legally blind women studying religious or classical music at a recognized institution.
APPLICATION: Write for info. Application deadline is June 1st.
CONTACT: 15 West 16th St., New York, NY 10011. (212)620-2000

FOUNDATION: American Foundation for the Blind
REQUISITE: Scholarships granted to legally blind women who are enrolled in a four year bachelor's degree program in Creative Writing or Music Performance at a recognized institution. Creative writing sample or Music performance tape will be required. Must be US citizen.
APPLICATION: Write for info. Application deadline is June 1st.
CONTACT: 15 West 16th St., New York, NY 10011. (212)620-2000

FOUNDATION: Black Filmmakers Grants Program
REQUISITE: Scholarships granted to finance only one project on 16MM or 3/4 IN. video. Must be US citizen or legal resident.
APPLICATION: Write for info. Application deadline is January 15th.
CONTACT: 3617 Mont Clair St, Los Angeles CA 90018   (310)201-9579

FOUNDATION: AT&T Bell Laboratories
REQUISITE: Scholarships granted to minorities and women studying engineering. Scholarships include summer employment at Bell Labs. Students must maintain a "B" average and have satisfactory work performance. Must be USA citizen or legal resident.
APPLICATION: Write for info. Application deadline is February 1st.
CONTACT: Crawford's Corner Road, Room 1B-208, Holmdel, NJ 07733. Tel: (908)949-3000

FOUNDATION: AT&T Bell Laboratories
REQUISITE: Scholarships granted to minority students and women in technical employment at Bell Labs. Undergraduate seniors studying at an accredited institution only. Must be US citizen or legal resident.
APPLICATION: Write for info. Application deadline is January 15th.

CONTACT: Crawford's Corner Road, Room 1B-208, Holmdel, NJ 07733. Tel: (908)949-3000

FOUNDATION: AT&T Bell Laboratories
REQUISITE: Scholarships granted to undergraduate juniors at an accredited institution. Open to minority students and women for technical employment experience at Bell Laboratories.
APPLICATION: Write for info. Application deadline is January 15th.
CONTACT: Crawford's Corner Road; Room 1B-208, Holmdel, NJ 07733. Tel: (908)949-3000

FOUNDATION: Smithsonian Institution
REQUISITE: Fellowships open to minority students to fund research and study at Smithsonian or their Cooper-Hewitt Museum of Design in NYC
APPLICATION: Write for info. Application deadline is 3/1, 7/1, and 10/15.
CONTACT: Office of Fellowships and Grants, 955 L'Enfant Plaza, Suite 7300, Washington, D.C. 20560. Tel: (212)860-6898

FOUNDATION: National Urban League Inc.
REQUISITE: Scholarships granted to minority undergraduate students attending an accredited institution who are in the top 25% of their class and will be entering their 3rd or junior year when grant is awarded. Must be US citizen or legal resident.
APPLICATION: Write for info. Application deadline is March 28th.
CONTACT: 500 East 62ND ST., 11TH floor, Director of Education, New York, NY 10021. Tel: (212)310-9000

FOUNDATION: National Action Council for Minorities in Engineering-NACME Inc.
REQUISITE: Scholarships granted to American Indian/American Black/Mexican-American or Puerto Rican. Student must have need and must enroll as a full-time student in one of the participating colleges. Must be USA citizen.
APPLICATION: Write for info. Application deadline is not specified.
CONTACT: 3 West 35th ST., New York, NY 10001. (212)279-2626

FOUNDATION: National Center for Indian Education
REQUISITE: Scholarships granted to high school seniors with one-fourth degree or more Indian blood. Must be a resident of Kansas/Oklahoma/Colorado/Arizona/ or San Bernadino County CA. Students must have good academic record and financial need.

APPLICATION: Write for info. Application deadline is March 15th.
CONTACT: POBOX 18239, Capitol Hill Station, Denver, CO 80218.
(We were not able to verify this listing; it may not be extant.)

FOUNDATION: Ntnl Consortium for Graduate Degrees for Minorities Inc.
REQUISITE: Scholarships granted to Native Americans; Black Americans;
Mexican Americans; and Puerto Ricans undergraduate juniors. Grants
include paid summer research work experience. Must be USA citizen.
APPLICATION: Write for info. Application deadline is December 1st.
CONTACT: POBOX 537, Notre Dame, IN 48556. (219)287-1097

FOUNDATION: National Federation of the Blind
REQUISITE: Scholarships granted to undergraduate or graduate study
in various Sciences. Students must be legally blind an enrolled at an
accredited institution.
APPLICATION: Write for info. Application deadline is March 31st.
CONTACT: 814 4TH Ave., #200, Grinnell, IA 50112. (515)274-1341

FOUNDATION: Electronic Industries Foundation
REQUISITE: Scholarships granted to disabled students who are pursuing
careers in high-tech areas through training. Open to undergraduates and
graduates at accredited institutions. Must be US citizen.
APPLICATION: Write for info. Application deadline is February 1st.
CONTACT: 1901 Pennsylvania Ave. NW, Suite 700, Washington, DC
20006. Tel: (202)955-5810

FOUNDATION: Alexander Graham Bell Association for the Deaf
REQUISITE: Scholarships granted to oral deaf students born with
profound hearing impairment or suffer such a loss before acquiring
language. Must be enrolled full-time. North America citizen.
APPLICATION: Write for info. Application deadline is April 15th.
CONTACT: 3417 Volta Place, Washington, D.C. 20007 (202)337-5220

FOUNDATION: American Foundation for the Blind
REQUISITE: Scholarships granted to the legally blind who is an
undergraduate or graduate student accepted to or enrolled in an
accredited curriculum within the areas of rehabilitation and/or education
of the blind and/or visually impaired. Must be USA citizen.
APPLICATION: Write for info. Application deadline is June 1st.
CONTACT: 15 West 16TH ST., New York, NY 10011. (212)620-2055

Minorities & Handicapped

FOUNDATION: National Center for Indian Education
REQUISITE: Scholarships granted to high school seniors with one-fourth or more Indian blood. Must be a resident of Kansas/Oklahoma/Colorado/ Arizona/or San Bernadino Cnty CA. Need good academic performance and high financial need.
APPLICATION: Write for info. Application deadline is March 15th.
CONTACT: POBOX 18239/Capitol Hill Station, Denver, CO 80218.
(We were not able to verify this listing; it may not be extant.)

FOUNDATION: National Urban League Inc.
REQUISITE: Scholarships granted to minority undergraduate students at an accredited institution who are in the top 25% of their class and will be entering their 3rd or junior year at the time the scholarship commences. Must be US citizen or legal resident.
APPLICATION: Write for info. Application deadline is March 28th.
CONTACT: 500 East 62ND St., 11TH Floor, Director of Education, New York, NY 10021. Tel: 212-310-9000

FOUNDATION: Society of Actuaries
REQUISITE: Scholarships granted to minority students enrolled or accepted in a program in actuarial science. Student must be a US citizen or legal resident and must have financial need.
APPLICATION: Write for info. Application deadline is May 1st.
CONTACT: 500 Park Blvd., Itasca, IL 60143. Tel: 312-773-3010

FOUNDATION: U.S. Dept of Education
REQUISITE: Scholarships granted to American Indians or Alaskan natives who are US citizens and seeking undergraduate or graduate degrees in education, psychology, and related areas.
APPLICATION: Write for info. Application deadline varies each year.
CONTACT: 400 Maryland Ave. SW; RM 2177; Mail Stop 6267, Washington, DC 20202. Tel: (202)708-5366

FOUNDATION: U.S. Dept of Education
REQUISITE: Scholarships granted to American Indians or Alaskan Natives who are US citizens seeking undergrad or graduate degrees in the areas of Business Admin., Engineering or Natural Resources at an accredited institution in the USA.
APPLICATION: Write for info. Application deadline is not specified.
CONTACT: 400 Maryland Ave. SW, Rm 2177, Mail Stop 6267, Washington, DC 20202. Tel: (202)708-5366

FOUNDATION: American Geological Institute
REQUISITE: Scholarships granted to undergraduate or graduate students studying in the field of Earth Sciences; Space Sciences; or Marine Sciences. Blacks, Native Americans, Hispanic are encouraged to apply. Must be US citizen.
APPLICATION: Write for info. Application deadline is February 1st.
CONTACT: 4220 King St., Alexandria, VA 22302. (703)379-2480

FOUNDATION: Woman's Auxiliary to the American Institute of Mining; Metallurgical and Petroleum Engineers
REQUISITE: Loans granted to undergraduate juniors and seniors. Students granted loans to pay for half or all of their education but will only be responsible for paying 50% of it back with no interest charges.
APPLICATION: Write for info. Application deadline is March 15th.
CONTACT: 345 E.47TH ST., 14th Flr, NY, NY 10017. (212)705-7695

FOUNDATION: Creole Ethnic Association Inc.
REQUISITE: Scholarships granted to individuals of mixed racial ancestry who are at least 1/32 Black and is a US citizen. Application must accompany a genealogy chart of at least 5 generations. For both graduate and undergraduate students.
APPLICATION: Write for info. Application deadline is June 30th.
CONTACT: POBOX 2666-Church Street Station, New York, NY 10008.

THE PAST

FOUNDATION: U.S. Marine Corps Historical Center
REQUISITE: Scholarships granted to undergraduate students an accredited institution which will grant academic credit for work experience as interns at the Marine Corps in Washington, DC or Quantico, Virginia.
APPLICATION: Write for info. Application deadline is not specified.
CONTACT: Building 58, Washington Navy Yard, Washington, DC 20374. Tel: 202-433-3839

FOUNDATION: U.S. Naval Institute
REQUISITE: Essay contest is open to anyone for the best essay on a topic that relates to objective of the U.S. Naval Institute "The Advancement of Professional Literary and Scientific Knowledge in the Naval and Maritime Services" and "The Advancement of the Knowledge of Sea Power." Essay must not exceed 4,000 words.
APPLICATION: Write for info. Application deadline is December 1st.

CONTACT: Essay Competition, Annapolis, MD 21402. 301- 268-6110

FOUNDATION: American Historical Association
REQUISITE: Scholarships granted to members only.
APPLICATION: Write for info. Application deadline is not specified.
CONTACT: 400 A Street SW, Washington, DC 20003. 202-544-2422

FOUNDATION: American Historical Association
REQUISITE: Fellowships granted to a doctoral and postdoctoral member
APPLICATION: Write for info. Application deadline is not specified.
CONTACT: 400 A Street SE, Washington, DC 20003 202-544-2422

FOUNDATION: Daughters of the American Revolution
REQUISITE: Scholarships granted to graduating high school seniors in the upper one-third of their class. Must be studying American History at an accredited institution in the USA. Must have good academic record, need and citizenship. No DAR affiliation is required. Must be US citizen.
APPLICATION: Write for info. Application deadline is February 1st.
CONTACT: 1776 D. Street NW, Washington, DC 20006. 202-628-1776

FOUNDATION: Daughters of the American Revolution
REQUISITE: Scholarships granted to undergraduate juniors and seniors attending an accredited school in the US studying History, Government, Political Science or Economics. DAR affiliation is not required.
APPLICATION: Write for info. Application deadline is February 20th.
CONTACT: 1776 D. Street NW, Washington, DC 20006. 202-628-1776

FOUNDATION: National Space Club
REQUISITE: Scholarships granted to any US citizen who writes the best essays dealing with any significant aspect of the historical development of rocketry and astronautics. Essays should not exceed 5000 words and should be fully documented.
APPLICATION: Write for info. Application deadline is November 1st.
CONTACT: 655 15th St NW #300, Washington, DC 20005. 202-639-4210

THEOLOGY

FOUNDATION: Fund For Theological Education
REQUISITE: Scholarships granted to outstanding Black North American students who are interested in becoming Protestant Ministers. Must be US citizen or Canadian citizen.

APPLICATION: Write for info. Application deadline is November 20th.
CONTACT: 475 Riverside Dr., #832, NY, NY 10115. (212)870-2058

FOUNDATION: Fund For Theological Education
REQUISITE: Scholarships granted to North American Christian undergraduate seniors or graduate students (ages 21-28) who have been accepted as a candidate for the ministry. US citizen or Canadian citizen.
APPLICATION: Write for info. Application deadline is November 20th.
CONTACT: 475 Riverside Dr., #832, NY, NY 10115. (212)870-2058

FOUNDATION: Fitzgerald Memorial Fund
REQUISITE: Scholarships granted to undergraduate students preparing for priesthood at a Catholic institution.
APPLICATION: Write for info. Application deadline is not specified.
CONTACT: C/O The Commercial Bank-Trust Dept., 301 SW Adams Street, Peoria, IL 61631. (309)647-7717

FOUNDATION: Christian Church
REQUISITE: Scholarships granted to Black or Afro-American members of Christian Church who are planning to prepare for a professional Ministry. Student must have an above average GPA and is enrolled in an accredited institution or seminary.
APPLICATION: Write for info. Application deadline is April 15th.
CONTACT: POBOX 1986, Indianapolis, IN 46206. (317)353-1491

FOUNDATION: Church of the Brethren General Board
REQUISITE: Scholarships granted to undergraduate and graduate students who are members of the Church of the Brethren who are pursuing a course of study leading to the Ministry in the Church of the Brethren.
APPLICATION: Write for info. Application deadline is not specified.
CONTACT: 1451 Dundee Avenue, Elgin, IL 60120. (708)695-0200

FOUNDATION: Fund for Theological Education
REQUISITE: Scholarships granted to outstanding Black North American students who are interested in becoming Protestant Ministers. Must be US citizen.
APPLICATION: Write for info. Application deadline is November 20th.
CONTACT: 475 Riverside Dr., #832, New York, NY 10115.
Tel: (212)870-2058

Theology

FOUNDATION: Fund for Theological Education
REQUISITE: Scholarships granted to North American Christian undergraduate seniors or graduate students who have been accepted as a candidate for the Ministry. Must be US or Canadian citizen.
APPLICATION: Write for info. Application deadline is November 20th.
CONTACT: 475 Riverside Dr., #832, NY, NY 10115. (212)870-2058

FOUNDATION: International Ministers' Wives and Widows Association
REQUISITE: Scholarships granted to undergraduate students who are members of a religious community and who are recommended by the wife of a minister. Student must have good academic record.
APPLICATION: Write for info. Application deadline is not specified.
CONTACT: C/O Dr. Muriel Johnson, 128 Pennsylvania Ave., Roosevelt, NY 11575.
(We were not able to verify this listing; it may not be extant.)

FOUNDATION: Jimmie Ullery Charitable Trust
REQUISITE: Scholarships granted to Presbyterian students in full-time Christian Service and preferably studying at Presbyterian Theological Seminaries but not limited to. Must be US citizen or legal resident.
APPLICATION: Write for info. Application deadline is not specified.
CONTACT: First National Bank and Trust Company of Tulsa, POBOX 1, Trust Department, Tulsa, OK 74193. (918)493-3100

FOUNDATION: Lutheran Church in America
REQUISITE: Scholarships granted to persons preparing to serve or serving in professional leadership in the Lutheran Church of America.
APPLICATION: Write for info. Application deadline is March 15th.
CONTACT: 2900 W. Queen Lane, Philadelphia, PA 19129. (215)848-3418

FOUNDATION: North American Baptist Seminary
REQUISITE: Scholarships granted to students who are enrolled full-time at North American Baptist Seminary.
APPLICATION: Write for info. Application deadline is not specified.
CONTACT: 1321 West 22nd St, Sioux Falls, SD 57105 (605)336-6588

FOUNDATION: United Methodist Church
REQUISITE: Scholarships granted to members of the United Methodist Church that are students preparing for the ministry or other full-time religious vocation. Must be US citizen or legal resident.
APPLICATION: Write for info. Application deadline is June 1st.

CONTACT: POBOX 871, Office of Loans and Scholarships, Nashville, TN 37202. (615)340-7346

FOUNDATION: William H. Nelson Educational Foundation
REQUISITE: Loans granted to needy active members of the protestant church in USA who are preparing for church related work by attending an institution in the USA.
APPLICATION: Write for info. Application deadline is July 15th.
CONTACT: 1601 N. Front St., Harrisburg, PA 17102.
(We were not able to verify this listing; it may not be extant.)

FOUNDATION: Woman's National Auxiliary Convention
REQUISITE: Loans granted to women for students in the second and following years at Free Will Baptist College.
APPLICATION: Write for info. Application deadline is not specified.
CONTACT: POBOX 1088, Nashville, TN 37202.
(We were not able to verify this listing; it may not be extant.)